HIDDEN FALLACIES IN CORPORATE LAW AND FINANCIAL REGULATION

Challenge your understanding of corporate, securities, and financial law and regulation with this ground-breaking book.

Featuring incisive research from preeminent scholars in the field, this seminal work interrogates long-standing assumptions and beliefs that have remained unexamined for decades.

Taking a novel approach, the book serves as both a conceptual 'deconstruction' and a foundation for future research directions. Each chapter delves deep into the often-overlooked origins, mechanics, and implications of outdated or misleading concepts (termed 'fallacies') that form the backbone of contemporary corporate and securities laws, financial regulations, and related domains.

Beyond simply identifying these fallacies, the authors illustrate the profound implications of recalibrating our analytic perspectives. By expanding the spectrum of inquiry and moving along multiple continuums – such as public to private, micro to macro, transactional to structural, individual to systemic, and static to dynamic – this volume underscores the transformative potential of re-envisioning the fundamentals of these fields. An essential read, this book promises to be a catalyst for change and a must-have for anyone committed to staying at the forefront of law and policy.

CONTEMPORARY STUDIES IN CORPORATE LAW

Series editors: Marc Moore, Christopher Bruner

Corporate law scholarship has a relatively recent history despite the fact that corporations have existed and been subject to legal regulation for three centuries. The modern flourishing of corporate law scholarship has been matched by some broadening of the field of study to embrace insolvency, corporate finance, corporate governance and regulation of the financial markets. At the same time the intersection between other branches of law such as, for example, labour, contract, criminal law, competition, and intellectual property law and the introduction of new inter-disciplinary methodologies affords new possibilities for studying the corporation. This series seeks to foster intellectually diverse approaches to thinking about the law and its role, scope and effectiveness in the context of corporate activity. In so doing the series aims to publish works of high intellectual content and theoretical rigour.

Titles in this series

Reconceptualising Corporate Compliance
Anna Donovan

Corporate Opportunities: A Law and Economics Analysis
Marco Claudio Corradi

The Making of the Modern Company
Susan Watson

Court-Supervised Restructuring of Large Distressed Companies in Asia: Law and Policy
Wai Yee Wan

Activist Shareholders in Corporate Governance: The Australian Experience and its Comparative Implications
Tim Bowley

Investment Management, Stewardship and Sustainability: Transformation and Challenges in Law and Regulation
Edited by Iris H–Y Chiu and Hans-Christopher Hirt

Diversity. Merit and Power in the C-Suite
Eleanore Hickman

Shareholders and Stakeholders: The Unrealised Promise of Company Law Reform in Post-War Britain
Joanne F Sonin

The Origins of Company Law: Methods and Approaches
Edited by Victoria Barnes and Jonathan Hardman

Hidden Fallacies in Corporate Law and Financial Regulation

Reframing the Mainstream Narratives

Edited by
Alexandra Andhov
Claire A Hill
and
Saule T Omarova

•HART•
OXFORD • LONDON • NEW YORK • NEW DELHI • SYDNEY

HART PUBLISHING
Bloomsbury Publishing Plc
Kemp House, Chawley Park, Cumnor Hill, Oxford, OX2 9PH, UK
1385 Broadway, New York, NY 10018, USA
29 Earlsfort Terrace, Dublin 2, Ireland

HART PUBLISHING, the Hart/Stag logo, BLOOMSBURY and the Diana logo are trademarks of Bloomsbury Publishing Plc

First published in Great Britain 2025

First published in hardback, 2025

Paperback edition, 2026

A catalogue record for this book is available from the British Library.

A catalogue record for this book is available from the Library of Congress.

Library of Congress Control Number: 2024944210

ISBN: PB: 978-1-50997-149-7
ePDF: 978-1-50997-152-7
ePub: 978-1-50997-150-3

Typeset by Compuscript Ltd, Shannon

Table of Contents

About the Contributors

Alexandra Andhov, Professor, Chair in Law and Technology, and Director of the Centre for Law and Technology at the Faculty of Law and Faculty of Business and Economics, University of Auckland, New Zealand
Professor Andhov is also an Affiliated Associate Professor at the Faculty of Law, University of Copenhagen, Denmark. Her research focuses on questions of corporate law, corporate governance, capital markets, law and technology from an interdisciplinary and comparative perspective. Her main research interest lies in the integration of legal, economic, and technological analysis, with particular emphasis on more sustainable, inclusive, democratic and fair markets. Professor Andhov's academic excellence was acknowledged with Inge Lehmann and Fulbright Scholarships.

Iris H-Y Chiu, Professor of Company Law and Financial Regulation, University College London, United Kingdom
Professor Iris H-Y Chiu is Director of the UCL Centre of Ethics and Law and advances the public and stakeholder engagement of the Centre's agenda in relation to a wide range of issues in relation to law, regulation, governance and ethics in business and finance. She has published extensively in the areas of corporate governance and financial regulation. She has interests in financial regulation and governance, law and technology, corporate law and governance and the law and policy for business and finance generally. She is a Research Fellow of the European Corporate Governance Institute and, most recently, a Senior Scholar at the European Central Bank's Legal Research Programme.

Nakita Q Cuttino, Associate Professor of Law, Georgetown Law, United States
Associate Professor Cuttino's scholarship examines the interplay between financial innovation, private ordering, and regulation to address economic inequality. She teaches first-year contracts and a seminar titled Fintech and Financial Democratization. Prior to joining Georgetown Law, Associate Professor Cuttino was a Visiting Assistant Professor at Duke University School of Law. Previously, she practised as a corporate associate with Simpson, Thatcher & Bartlett LLP. Prior to joining Simpson, she served as a law clerk to Judge Eric L Clay of the US Court of Appeals for the Sixth Circuit.

Anna Gelpern, Scott K Ginsburg Professor of Law and International Finance, Georgetown Law, United States
Professor Gelpern is a Scott K Ginsburg Professor of Law and International Finance at Georgetown Law and a nonresident senior fellow at the Peterson Institute for International Economics. She has published research on government

debt, contracts, and regulation of financial institutions and markets, co-authored a law textbook on International Finance, and contributed to international initiatives on financial reform and government debt. Between 1996 and 2002, Professor Gelpern served in legal and policy positions at the US Treasury Department.

Sarah C Haan, Class of 1958 Uncas and Anne McThenia Professor of Law, Washington and Lee University School of Law, United States
Professor Haan writes at the intersection of corporate law and democracy on subjects such as corporate governance, shareholder voting rights, and disclosure. Professor Haan's scholarship has appeared in the *Stanford Law Review*, the *Yale Law Journal*, the *Northwestern University Law Review*, and other leading journals, and has been featured in the *New York Times*, the Harvard Law School Forum on Corporate Governance, and the CLS Blue Sky Blog. Her article, 'Corporate Governance and the Feminization of Capital', which was published in the *Stanford Law Review*, was chosen as one of the 10 best corporate and securities law review articles of 2022 by peers in the field.

Claire A Hill, Professor, James L Krusemark Chair in Law, University of Minnesota, United States
Professor Hill's research interests include corporate governance, structured finance, rating agencies, contract theory, law and language, and behavioural economics, including on the role of culture, personality and identity in banks and other organizations, all topics on which she has published numerous articles and book chapters in journals and books in the US, Canada, and Europe, and lectured widely. In addition to her chair, Professor Hill founded and directs its Institute for Law and Rationality, co-directs its Institute for Law and Economics, and is affiliated with its Center for Cognitive Sciences and its Center for Political Psychology.

Jennifer G Hill, Professor & Bob Baxt Chair in Corporate and Commercial Law, Monash University, Australia
Professor Jennifer Hill is the inaugural Bob Baxt AO Professor of Corporate and Commercial Law at Monash University Faculty of Law and the Director of the Centre for Commercial Law and Regulatory Studies (CLARS). Jennifer is an internationally recognised legal scholar in the field of comparative corporate law and governance. Her recent scholarship has focused on governance issues, such as corporate accountability and culture, global shareholder stewardship and activism, directors' duties and transnational legal orders, and executive compensation. Jennifer's work is widely cited in academic literature in Australia, the United States, Europe and Asia.

Cherie Metcalf, Associate Professor at Queen's University in the Faculty of Law and the Department of Economics, Canada
Cherie Metcalf's research focuses on environmental and resource law and policy, especially intersections with Indigenous peoples' rights. She often uses empirical methods and interdisciplinary approaches. She has written on the role

of public vs private actors in environmental risk communication, climate law and policy, and implementation of public law norms. Her work has appeared in journals including the *Northwestern University Law Review*, *International Review of Law & Economics*, and *Journal of Empirical Legal Studies*. Together with her co-author, Ian Keay, she was twice awarded the Vanderkamp Prize for best paper in *Canadian Public Policy*.

Saule T Omarova, Beth and Marc Goldberg Professor of Law, Cornell Law School, United States
Saule Omarova specialises in the regulation of financial institutions and banking law. Her scholarship focuses on systemic risk regulation, financial technology, and structural trends in global financial markets. Professor Omarova serves as Director of Cornell's Jack G Clarke Program on the Law and Regulation of Financial Institutions and Markets. Before joining academia, she practised law in the Financial Institutions Group of Davis Polk & Wardwell, a premier New York firm. From 2006 to 2007, Professor Omarova served as Special Advisor on Regulatory Policy to the Under Secretary for Domestic Finance at the US Department of the Treasury.

Ellen Quigley, Postdoctoral Associate, Cambridge University, United Kingdom
Dr Ellen Quigley is a Principal Research Associate, the Co-Director of Finance for Environmental and Social Systemic Change, and the Special Adviser (Responsible Investment) to the Chief Financial Officer, all at the University of Cambridge. Her work centres on the mitigation of climate change and inequality through the investment policies and practices of institutional investors. Dr Quigley's article, 'Universal Ownership in Practice: A Practical Investment Framework for Asset Owners', won the GRASFI Paper Prize for Potential Impact on Sustainable Finance Practices in 2020.

1

Introduction

SAULE T OMAROVA AND ALEXANDRA ANDHOV

HIDDEN FALLACIES IN *Corporate Law and Financial Regulation* is, in many ways, an experimental book. Unlike many academic collections, it does not claim to cover a specific topic (however broadly defined), highlight the applications of a specific methodology, or advocate a specific normative approach. This book is simultaneously more eclectic in its scope and more cohesive in its focus. Its purpose is to identify and interrogate some of the core axioms and underlying beliefs upon which two related but distinct areas of law and policy – corporate law and financial regulation – have been built. As academic disciplines go, both fields have long been viewed as soberly technical, firmly structured around a few dominant (mainly economic) theoretical concepts, and largely impervious to attempts at wholesale critical examination. Established principles and doctrines within these areas are frequently taken at face value, with the underlying assumptions and historical contexts that inform them often overlooked or taken for granted.

The *Fallacies* project is an attempt to unravel, or at least problematise, some of these principles and doctrines. We see this project as a productive intellectual endeavour, as well as a long-overdue stock-taking exercise in corporate law and financial regulation scholarship. Many of the questionable but unquestioned premises and concepts – or fallacies – examined in this volume have been referenced, re-iterated and re-used so often and in so many ways that they became de facto institutionalised articles of faith every scholar had to accept to be accepted. Operating on a subterranean level, these dynamics have essentially institutionalised certain narrowly drawn perspectives, reflecting very particular normative assessments as markers of objective universal knowledge and tools of impartial scientific analysis. The dominance of these axioms, shielded from meaningful challenges within the relevant field, not only marginalises alternative perspectives but also stifles much-needed intellectual curiosity. The result is an effectively monocultural intellectual environment that inhibits theoretical diversity and constrains the evolution of thought within our disciplines.

By contrast, our book encourages, invites and celebrates a deeper inquiry into the core assumptions, perspectives and claims on which so many of these fields are grounded. As the volume editors, we made a conscious decision to eschew a homogenised narrative. From the beginning, we have embraced a pluralistic editorial approach, allowing each author to articulate their insights in a manner that is authentic to them so that the reader hears each author's voice untainted by our own views. In soliciting contributions to the volume, we intentionally sought out scholars writing about various subjects from different disciplinary perspectives, including not only law but also economics and behavioural science. The primary criterion for selecting chapter contributions was the quality of analysis. At the same time, our editorial strategy reflected the commitment to fostering a more inclusive discourse, particularly by amplifying the contributions of women, whose voices have historically been underrepresented in discussions pertaining to business and finance.

While it is ultimately up to the readers to decide how successful our efforts have turned out to be, we couldn't be more pleased with the results. The chapters within this volume do not shy away from challenging systemic, macro-level assumptions that fundamentally shape the corpus of corporate and financial law. Some of these 'founding myths' are easily recognised for what they are and how influential they have been, while others do their work in obscure corners of law and theory occupied by technical experts. By bringing these multiple ideas out of the shadows and putting them under intense and transparent scrutiny, our volume helps to demystify the workings of today's complex financial markets, business organisations and social networks acting within and upon them. Just as importantly, it also aims to contribute to a broader understanding of how the dominance of these various fallacies affects not only academic and policy debates but the society at large – and the real people inhabiting it. In this sense, the contributors to our volume are engaged in an ambitious project of re-grounding the entire body of modern corporate and financial law and scholarship in the evolving – and inevitably complex – realities of our shared and conflict-ridden world.

The aspiration for this volume is to engage in rigorous conceptual deconstruction and agenda-setting for future research. To this end, each individual chapter delves into a specific set of insufficiently examined or mistaken assumptions – *fallacies* – that are often hidden in plain sight but have a profound influence on the legal frameworks or regulatory design in the author's area of research. By shifting the analytic baseline across various dimensions – public and private, 'micro' and 'macro', transactional and structural – the chapters collectively challenge prevailing narratives and illuminate transformative possibilities for legal and regulatory reform.

Thematically, the chapters are organised into two parts: Corporate Law and Financial Regulation. The first part of the volume comprises five chapters examining several misconceptions that permeate the doctrine and practice of modern corporate law. For the purpose of grouping the chapters, the concept of corporate law is deliberately broadly construed, including matters traditionally encountered in broader discussions of capital markets' operation. Just as real-life corporate entities perform multiple economic and social functions beyond governing themselves, the project of deepening our collective understanding of today's corporate world often crosses into adjacent areas, including securities laws, economic theory, finance, risk management, linguistics, and even psychology.

In the opening substantive chapter of our volume, ***Claire A Hill*** questions foundational assumptions underlying decision-making and other behaviour by deal-makers and other market actors. She argues that market actors' behaviour is less atomistic than conventional economic models assume it is but is also more influenced by individual temperaments. In their deal negotiations and other market behaviour, individuals look to the norms of their communities, or tribes, including, as to deal terms and other practices, 'what's market'. How market actors behave also importantly reflects their temperaments – which refers, among other things, to how confident they are (or are not) and whether their love of winning is stronger than their hatred of losing. Moreover, Claire Hill argues that conventional models mistakenly assume that we live in a world of risk rather than a world of uncertainty. The chapter concludes with a plea and agenda as to the need for an expanded concept of rationality, one which takes into consideration tribes, temperament and uncertainty.

Jennifer G Hill's chapter offers a wide-ranging critique of the agency theory of the firm, which views corporations as creatures of purely private bargaining – the 'nexus of contracts' – and defines core issues of corporate law and governance through the lens of a single problem: managerial opportunism and principal-agent conflicts within the corporate entity. Weaving together history, philosophy and legal doctrine, Jennifer Hill's chapter builds a case for a fundamental reconsideration of the key – often erroneous – assumptions underlying the agency theory. It argues that the single-minded focus on the internal conflict between shareholders and managers presumptively narrows the substantive scope and practical efficacy of corporate law and governance as potentially powerful tools for addressing multiple economic and social problems of the modern era. To overcome these conceptual and normative limitations, the chapter calls for a broader conception of the corporation and its role in today's society.

Sarah C Haan takes a more surgical approach by targeting the widely accepted notion that public company shareholders are inherently and rationally passive. Haan's chapter identifies this 'Passivity Thesis', deeply embedded in US corporate law and beyond, as a fallacy that is both descriptively false and normatively harmful. Tracing the historical and doctrinal evolution of this concept from the early twentieth century to the present day, the chapter recasts shareholder passivity not as an individual choice – and a model of 'normal' investor behaviour – but as a product of the nearly century-long struggle for power over corporate decisions. It examines the role of corporate law and practice in containing shareholder activism and suppressing active governance participation on the part of dispersed retail investors, tying this, historically, to the rise of women shareholders. As Haan argues, the current resurgence of shareholder activism, particularly around environmental, social and governance (ESG) matters, provides further evidence against the Passivity Thesis. She concludes her chapter by drawing big-picture implications of shareholder passivity as the categorical opposite of civic engagement and democratic self-rule.

Cherie Metcalf's chapter argues that the traditional economic account of the corporation as a purely private organisation focused solely on shareholder value maximisation is a fallacy. In the traditional account, the corporation does not have any duty to weigh the social impacts of its actions, except insofar as these are also reflected in potential legal and other costs the corporation might face. On the opposite side of the current debate is stakeholder theory, under which the corporation is obligated to serve the wide-ranging and diverse interests of its multiple stakeholders, such as employees, suppliers and customers, as well as the broader society. Metcalf argues instead for a more nuanced understanding of the nature of a modern business corporation as a fundamentally hybrid public-private entity. Examining various aspects of the complex and dynamic relationship between private firms and their regulators, her chapter brings to the fore the inherent hybridity and fluidity of the modern corporate form as not only a private organisation but also as an active participant in the regulatory process and an essential vehicle for transmission of social values.

Ellen Quigley's chapter focuses on the false narrative of 'responsible investment' as it exists today. Quigley scrutinises this increasingly popular label, applied to a wide variety of investor strategies, exposing its fundamental weaknesses and contradictions. She argues that the category of 'responsible investment' encompasses practices that are neither truly socially responsible nor in furtherance of productive investing needed to achieve that goal. Analysing the operation of specific market strategies commonly deployed in this broad area, the chapter demonstrates that most of these strategies cannot directly influence corporate behaviour or channel capital toward more sustainable economic activities. Instead, as the chapter shows, most of today's 'responsible investment' occurs in secondary markets for tradable financial instruments, which refutes the commonly repeated claims of 'additionality' and other public benefits commonly associated with these strategies. To counteract the harmful consequences of the 'responsible investment' fallacy, the chapter advocates for more effective impact-driven tactics that could bring the practice of socially responsible investment in line with its aspirations.

Following chapter 6, the discussion transitions from traditional corporate law to the law and regulation of financial markets and institutions. As an academic field, financial regulation is highly technical, complex, and internally segmented into multiple specialised subject-areas. Some of these specialty areas are defined by reference to specific industries, such as banking or insurance. Others cut across traditional industry lines, focusing instead on specific market infrastructures (such as exchanges, clearing, or payments systems), products and activities (such as derivatives trading or cryptocurrencies) or public policy concerns (such as financial stability or consumer protection). Modern financial markets are governed by specialised statutes and rules enacted by national, subnational and even supranational agencies with different jurisdictional mandates. At the same time, sophisticated financial market actors regularly engage in highly influential forms of private ordering and self-governance, which either get seamlessly integrated into the official regulatory regime or stealthily erode its efficacy. The financial crisis of 2008 exposed the dark side of these public-private dynamics in the increasingly globalised, interconnected and fragile financial system. It laid bare the high societal costs of financial regulators' failure to detect and prevent the build-up of macro-level, systemic risk in financial markets. However, high-profile regulatory reforms enacted in many jurisdictions and meant to correct the pre-2008 policy myopia fell short of their lofty promises. Today, financial regulation remains structurally fragmented, limited in its substantive reach, and intensely politically contested.

The five chapters comprising the second part of this volume address some of the key conceptual and normative conflicts, gaps and misconceptions that underlie these trends and stand in the way of true progress in various areas of financial law and regulation.

Alexandra Andhov's chapter examines the complex dynamics of disclosure obligations in financial markets through the lens of advancing artificial intelligence (AI) technologies. The chapter challenges an increasingly popular idea that the use of AI augments the quality and efficacy of corporate disclosure, thereby improving the operation of modern capital markets. To put this assumption to test, Andhov discusses specific characteristics of AI technologies – including their inherent opacity, lack of objectivity, and potential feedback effects – that are critical from the perspective of the disclosure regime. She argues that incorporating advanced technological methods in developing disclosure documents introduces new, poorly understood complexities into the process. As her chapter posits, embracing AI without understanding these dangers threatens to render corporate disclosures less, rather than more, informative and useful. From this perspective, the rapid adoption of AI technologies may ultimately compromise the fundamental goal of the disclosure-based regulatory regime: the clear conveyance of meaningful information and its dependable assimilation by investors and the market. The chapter calls for more targeted and rigorous research into the operation of AI-based disclosure tools and their impact on the efficiency and integrity of capital markets.

Nakita Q Cuttino's chapter shifts the discussion to the increasingly hot topic of central banking. Her chapter scrutinises the notion of monetary policy as a racially neutral economic instrument, focusing on the Federal Reserve's engagement with racial inequality in economic outcomes. This topic gained prominence with Chairman Jerome Powell's 2020 acknowledgement of racial disparities in unemployment levels. Despite the Federal Reserve's traditional stance as a race-neutral – or 'colour-blind' – institution, its recent policies and public commitments have sparked debate over its role in perpetuating this systemic problem. Through systematic investigation of the Fed's historical record and policy decisions in the context of their impact on black households, Cuttino's chapter debunks the fallacy of a colour-blind Fed and suggests practical ways to make the US central bank both more accountable and more responsive to racial equality concerns.

Iris H-Y Chiu's chapter questions the widespread idea that financial inclusion is an unequivocal social good, particularly in the context of consumer credit regulation in developed economies like the UK, EU and US. Chiu's chapter critically assesses mainstream policies that focus on facilitating consumer access to credit, mainly through greater competition among private lenders, without addressing the dark side of consumer over-indebtedness. The chapter discusses the principal shortcomings of current consumer credit regulations, noting that such regulations are often preoccupied solely with the point-of-sale phase while disregarding the less visible post-sale problems associated with consumer over-indebtedness. Chiu uses as an example specific adversities faced by female consumers and argues that an approach mechanically emphasising 'inclusive' access to credit does not address these adversities. As an alternative, she advocates a more nuanced and socially aware regulatory approach as to consumers' financial welfare, which would more effectively incorporate their social needs.

Saule Omarova continues the theme by taking on the ubiquitous yet poorly understood concept of financial innovation. She identifies certain background assumptions, or hidden fallacies, that quietly derail the much-needed public debate on the purposes, dynamics and systemic effects of financial innovation. In today's technology-driven finance, the label of 'innovation' is inevitably imbued with a strong normative bias, which creates a default presumption that 'innovative' financial products are inherently socially beneficial. Despite the mounting evidence of the systemically destabilising impact of many financial innovations in recent decades, this generalised belief is surprisingly persistent. Omarova's chapter shows that it is fundamentally rooted in specific misconceptions about the transactional context, defining characteristics and principal motivations behind financial innovation. By identifying and analysing these fallacies, the chapter offers a new way of understanding what drives regulatory complacency, deregulation, and misguided regulatory actions in the financial sector. It shows, moreover, how these fallacies obstruct thorough democratic deliberation on key public policy decisions, particularly during periods of significant technological change in financial markets. Given the ongoing digital transformation of finance, the chapter emphasises the urgency of addressing these hidden errors in our collective thinking.

In the last substantive chapter of our volume, ***Anna Gelpern*** takes a deep dive into some of the darkest corners of the modern financial market, where the traditionally drawn boundary between sophisticated private contracting and rigid statutory regimes morphs into a far more complicated public-private co-dependency. The focus of Gelpern's chapter is on regulators' use of standard-form derivative contracts promulgated by the International Swaps and Derivatives Association (ISDA), a global trade association, to effectuate certain critical elements of the regulatory reforms enacted in the wake of the 2008 crisis. On its face, this was a story of successful collaboration between regulatory agencies and the industry, a pragmatic solution to potentially debilitating cross-border coordination problems. Responding to political pressure to provide a workable resolution alternative to big bank bailouts, US policymakers have effectively enlisted the elaborate architecture of ISDA contracts to ensure that derivatives traders around the globe accommodate new post-crisis laws by agreeing to refrain from exercising their creditor rights against systemically important financial firms in bankruptcy. As Gelpern argues, however, hitching a ride on ISDA's boilerplate to get to an otherwise tricky policy result comes with unexpected and under-appreciated costs. It binds the regulators and the industry actors to one another in ways that severely limit their choices – and potentially irreversibly narrows the space for public policy change.

The book concludes with a final chapter 12. Building on the rich substantive material in the preceding chapters, the concluding chapter takes a step back and offers a deeper, more reasoned definition of the term 'fallacy' that unites multiple perspectives reflected in the volume. It explains how the specific fallacies discussed in our book are, in an important sense, collective phenomena. The fallacies ground many laws, regulations, policies, and much public opinion; they also shape and reflect the structural, political, economic and social features of the society. The concluding chapter aims not only to unify some of the themes in the volume's chapters but also to stimulate ongoing dialogue and re-evaluation of the unchallenged and under-challenged axioms that shape the disciplines of corporate and finance law.

As any academic collection of this kind, this book is a product of many people's labour. We are proud to have worked with all of them and owe them all a deep debt of gratitude. Our special thanks go to the great group of colleagues who gathered in New York City in the autumn of 2023 to discuss and comment on our collection of chapter drafts: Dan Awrey (Cornell), Miriam Baer (Brooklyn), June Carbone (University of Minnesota), Peter Conti-Brown (Wharton), Talia Gillis (Columbia), Patricia McCoy (Boston College), Lev Menand (Columbia), Dana Brakman Reiser (Brooklyn), Bob Thompson (Georgetown), Rory Van Loo (Boston University), Yesha Yadav (Vanderbilt), and David Zaring (Wharton). This esteemed panel's generosity of spirit and willingness to engage with and rigorously challenge our hypotheses have been truly invaluable. We hope that the chapters presented here stand as a testament to the dedication and collective effort that have shaped them into the finished works you find before you.

Part I

Corporate Law

2

Tribes and Temperament(s): Two Underappreciated Determinants of Market Actor Behaviour, Motivations and Beliefs

CLAIRE A HILL*

2.1. INTRODUCTION

WHY DO MARKET actors behave as they do? There is a classic law and economics/rational person answer: 'they are rational utility maximisers' with rationality meaning sufficient aptitude (as to decision-making and inputs thereto) and utility typically implicitly referring to certain preferences (money, power and prestige). The classic answer is complemented – or critiqued – by the now-classic behavioural answer, 'but sometimes they make mistakes, such as by being overconfident or otherwise biased.'

This formulation conjures up people who are atomistic and self-directed but, importantly, homogeneous as to what they seek and how they view the world. But people are both less and more individualistic than this formulation suggests: their views and values have an important social component, and they differ as to what they seek and how they view the world. Of course, if we try to fully capture the nuances, we will lose all possibility of a tractable theory. But we can do far better than we do now, by taking into account three things: that we live in a world of uncertainty ('unknown unknowns'), not just risk;[1] that our cognitive

* I would like to acknowledge extremely useful conversations with and comments from Miriam Baer, Margot Bloomfield, June Carbone, Eric Hillemann, Scott Faga, Jim Freund, George Georgiev, Dale Nance, Saule Omarova, Alexandra Andhov, Rory Van Loo, Richard Warner, Andy Winton, and David Zaring, and invaluable and extraordinary research assistance of Scott Dewey.

[1] The original distinction between risk and uncertainty was made by Frank Knight, in FH Knight, *Risk, Uncertainty, and Profit* (New York, Houghton Mifflin, 1921). A recent discussion is in J Kay and M King, *Radical Uncertainty: Decision-Making Beyond the Numbers* (New York, WW Norton & Company, 2021). (The phrase 'unknown unknowns' was famously used by Donald Rumsfeld.)

capacity is limited;[2] and that how people react to uncertainty and cognitive limitations turns on who they are and how they view themselves.

To that end, this chapter argues that we can and should take into account two underappreciated determinants of behaviour, motivations and beliefs: one social (tribes) and one individual (temperaments). What I mean by tribe is a community, with its own norms, rituals and institutions.[3] Consider in this regard the market community that does big deals. The existence of the term and concept, and at least one major database – 'what's market'[4] – attests to a consensus among the group on the deal terms that are considered standard and acceptable. As evidenced by this example, tribes are often not 'tribal' in the oppositional sense of that term. I use temperament in its colloquial sense. I make my case in significant part with real-world examples that tap into broadly held intuitions, showing how taking tribes and temperament into account injects necessary, useful and tractable realism into accounts of market behaviour.

I, a 'sophisticated' institutional investor, will buy security x – it was rated investment grade by Moody's and Standard and Poor's (who have screwed up before but are still 'listened to'), and all those scary-sounding risk factors are lawyer and company executive CYA (that is, self-protection), which, in any event, are not appreciably scarier than risk factors for the other securities I might buy. Besides, the security has been anointed as the 'hot new issue'. This isn't just herding – it is a whole herding kit, one that includes the creation, dissemination, and easy-enough identification, of norms and rituals. So much for the fallacy of atomistic decision-making by an appropriately motivated buyer based on what is (and what they consider to be) sufficient information. And indeed, more broadly, as I will argue, so much for the idea that market-relevant (and indeed, other) beliefs are importantly developed and maintained individually, based on, and subject to disconfirmation by, current data.

The herd-member buyer described above is what I have elsewhere called a 'sheep'.[5] The sheep loves direction, and takes it eagerly, following along with all the other sheep. (Here, I will characterise this person as 'less confident'.) But, of course, not everyone is a sheep. Other personas I have written about in other work include those who are more confident, of whom contrarians are a subset.[6]

[2] There are various terms used to summon up a variety of related concepts: people have bounded rationality, they are cognitive misers, they have cognitive limits, etc. My exposition here is largely based on one term in this family, Herbert Simon's concept of satisficing, discussed in nn 20–22 below and accompanying text.

[3] See K Ho, *Liquidated: An Ethnography of Wall Street* (Durham, Duke University Press, 2009).

[4] A search on Google (7 February 2024) for 'what's market' yields a significant number of apt hits, including a database on Westlaw's Practical Law, http://content.next.westlaw.com/practical-law/whats-market?transitionType=Default&contextData=(sc.Default). The database lists Corporate and M&A as one area, as well as other types of agreements. The database also contains 'Practice Analysis' of the market terms.

[5] CA Hill, 'A Personality Theory of Sophisticated Investor Decision-Making (In the 2008 Financial Crisis), with Some Policy Implications' (2017) 2 *Revue Internationale Des Services Financiers/International Journal for Financial Services* 1, 7.

[6] ibid.

(Two business strategies considered in standard theory – arbitrage and short selling – can be good fits for contrarians, although there are also 'herds' who get involved in them after the territory has been staked out.)

There are a multitude of other relevant personas. But attempts to be comprehensive quickly become more unwieldy than useful. I will therefore suggest just one other temperament, motivated by Tory Higgins' work on regulatory focus and fit.[7] According to regulatory focus theory, some people are more prevention-focused and inclined towards vigilance; some are more promotion-focused and are more eager than vigilant. The former hate to lose and seek to minimise their downside; the latter love to win and seek to maximise their upside.[8] The less confident seek to minimise their downside; the contrarians seek to maximise their upside; confident people who are not contrarians could have either aim.

The prevention-focused might be in the business of making well-collateralised loans (or writing the risk factor disclosure); the promotion-focused might be traders (or 'bid em up Bruce' Wasserstein[9] types, a reference that should summon up the temperament at issue even among those who don't remember BW).

A person's temperament will clearly affect how they react to law, workplace incentives (and disincentives), culture, and many other things exceedingly relevant to law and policymakers. So much for the outsized and myopic role of canonical forms of incentive alignment (money and professional recognition and advancement, or their opposites) in motivating behaviour. This is not to say that canonical incentive alignment does not work 'at the margin'. Rather, it is to say that there may be many fewer marginal cases than might be imagined once temperament is taken into account. Imagine how much (especially variable) compensation a less confident, prevention-focused person would require in order to be a trader. Of course, people are not necessarily the same in all aspects of their life: for instance, someone could be a sheep at work but far more confident in some other sphere. Similarly, a person's tribe for one purpose is not necessarily their tribe for all purposes. A person might be in one 'tribe' for professional purposes ('Wall Street lawyer') but quite different ones in their personal life.

[7] See generally ET Higgins, *Beyond Pleasure and Pain: How Motivation Works* (Oxford, Oxford University Press, 2012). See also CA Hill and RW Painter, *Better Bankers, Better Banks: Promoting Good Business Through Contractual Commitment* (Chicago, University of Chicago Press, 2015) 117, 122, 123, and 223 fn 26 and 225 fn 45. Both these sources, especially Higgins, have considerable nuance as to temperament; in the interests of parsimony, I use very rough and simplified versions of the concepts here.

[8] ibid 251; Higgins describes the promotion-focused as concerned with 'approaching gains and avoiding non-gains'; the prevention-focused person's concern is with 'approaching non-losses and avoiding losses'. See also N Dunbar, *The Devil's Derivatives: The Untold Story of the Slick Traders and Hapless Regulators who Almost Blew Up Wall Street … and are Ready to Do it Again* (Cambridge, Massachusetts, Harvard Business Press, 2011) xii.

[9] See www.forbes.com/2009/10/14/bruce-wasserstein-dies-business-wall-street-lazard.html?sh=5db46740592e.

A unifying intuition is this: people's market behaviour reflects their assessment of costs and benefits of the behaviour, but their assessment reflects what they think is true about the world and themselves.[10] As I will explain, the fallacy comes in when 'what people think is true about the world' is transmuted, as it generally is in analyses of the behaviour of market participants, into 'what is true about the world', and 'what people think about themselves' is ignored altogether. While the broader implications are beyond the scope of this chapter, an exploration of the role of tribes and temperaments in understanding how market actors compute their costs and benefits is an important first step.

My arguments succeed, or not, by persuasion rather than 'proof' – it's not clear what proof would look like in any event. Certainly, the personality types I describe are well-known in the literature and in real life, as are, at some level of generality, the social dynamics I describe such as herding, and the existence of market communities, broadly construed, that have norms, rituals and institutions.[11] My burden is to show that taking tribes and temperament into account in analyses of market behaviour is feasible and desirable, and that *not* doing so unnecessarily sacrifices realism. To paraphrase Herbert Simon's Nobel Prize lecture, we can choose between 'optimum solutions for a simplified world' and 'satisfactory solutions for a more realistic world'.[12]

'Feasible' for this purpose does not mean that it translates readily into particular policy prescriptions, or specific recommendations as to what judges should do in contexts such as contract interpretation. It does, however, yield suggestions as to areas in which we can expect standard tools to sometimes be ineffectual or even counterproductive. It suggests that disclosure may not be nearly as effective as might be hoped, given how even 'sophisticated' market actors take in information.[13] It suggests greater vigilance for the kinds of dynamics that yield herding and conformity in many different market contexts, including sales and purchases of financial instruments as well as behaviour on corporate boards.[14] Indeed, it suggests greater attention to group dynamics in many market contexts. It also suggests the existence and importance of perverse incentives in siloed

[10] See Hill and Painter (n 7) 123.

[11] See generally JC Freund, *Anatomy of a Merger: Strategies and Techniques for Negotiating Corporate Acquisitions* (New York, Law Journal Press, 1976) 479–540. For a specific illustration of norms and rituals in contracting, see below (n 42) and accompanying text. Freund wrote the playlet to illustrate the contract provisions discussed in the remainder of his book, and the rationales therefor and associated negotiation dynamics.

[12] HA Simon, 'Rational Decision Making in Business Organizations' (1979) 69 *The American Economic Review* 493, 498. (Note that Simon said expressly that realism was not always preferable, '[D]ecision makers can satisfice either by finding optimum solutions for a simplified world, or by finding satisfactory solutions for a more realistic world. Neither approach, in general, dominates the other …'.)

[13] See SM Davidoff Solomon and CA Hill, 'Limits of Disclosure' (2013) 36 *Seattle University Law Review* 599.

[14] See CA Hill, 'Justification Norms Under Uncertainty: A Preliminary Inquiry' (2010) *17 Connecticut Insurance Law Journal* 27.

contexts – to game laws and engage in sharp dealing – including in contexts potentially yielding significant negative externalities.[15]

My ultimate bottom line is both ambitious and optimistic. The standard *modus operandi* of economic analyses can accommodate tribes, temperaments, and much else, within the rationality paradigm. Since around the mid-1990s, there has been a push to make economics, and law and economics, more realistic. Exploring the neglect of tribes and temperament and how this could be remedied can be an effective means of doing so: rather than characterising ways in which people are less rational than law and economics assumes them to be, law and economics can instead reconceive what rationality requires.[16]

The reconception of rationality should, in my view, be radical as to economics' ontology but not as to its conceptual toolbox. Underlying the standard economics worldview is a metaphorical or perhaps literal acceptance of the credo 'survival of the fittest'. But an alternative view, advanced by philosopher Daniel Milo, 'survival of the good enough', seems far more plausible:

> It is a jungle out there, but unlike deserts, jungles are not very competitive places. They are full of resources and opportunities and thus are hotbeds of life. It is true that every species in the jungle – and everywhere else – has traits that are the products of selection, but each also possesses traits that are merely tolerated.[17]

What follows? I think that Nobel Prize-winning economist Herbert Simon and, more recently, John Kay and (Lord) Mervyn King, prominent British economists (the latter having served as the Governor of the Bank of England), have it right. We live in a world of uncertainty in which 'probabilities cannot meaningfully be attached to alternative futures'.[18] Much is unknowable, and we often cannot appraise with much precision the relationship between our present knowledge and what 'complete knowledge' would look like, much less how to acquire such knowledge. In any event, our cognitive resources are limited: imagine, for instance, having to revisit our prior beliefs continually. Indeed, it's not clear we would be better off using more of our cognitive resources to the point of exhaustion.[19] Thus, we 'satisfice', a term coined by Simon that is

[15] Hill and Painter (n 7).

[16] In this regard, see Simon (n 12) 497 fn 2, where Simon notes that Becker considers what Simon calls 'bounded rationality' to be irrationality.

[17] DS Milo, *Good Enough: The Tolerance for Mediocrity in Nature And Society* (Cambridge, Harvard University Press, 2019) 20.

[18] See Kay and King (n 1) xvi.

[19] See also Gerd Gigerenzer's concepts of 'fast and frugal' heuristics and the 'adaptive toolbox'. Putting aside the merits of specific examples, the general approach is one that sees people as proceeding rationally given certain background conditions, notably uncertainty. See generally DG Goldstein and G Gigerenzer, 'Models of ecological rationality: the recognition heuristic' (2002) 109 *Psychological Review* 75 and Gigerenzer, 'The Adaptive Toolbox', ch 3, in G Gigerenzer and R Selten (ed), *Bounded Rationality: The Adaptive Toolbox* (Cambridge, MIT Press, 2001).

an amalgam between sufficing and satisfying.[20] This chapter identifies ways market actors satisfice.

A debate between this worldview and the neoclassical one has been raging and shows no sign of nearing a conclusion, although intuition would seem very much to favour what I will call Simon's view.[21] The neoclassical response might be to argue that the increments of realism the Simon view offers don't offer enough bang for the buck to justify the additional complexity.[22] This chapter is my argument to the contrary.

2.2. THE FALLACY AND WHY IT'S A FALLACY

2.2.1. Setting the Stage

Let us consider the task of the market actor trying to determine how to proceed. For expository ease, I will generally use examples such as whether and on what terms to buy a company or a security; where appropriate, I characterise what is going on as a 'decision' and the actor as a 'decision-maker'.

First, what do they look for in deciding whether or how to proceed? Second, how, from whom or from what source? Third, to what end? In what I will call the standard story, the answers would be 'what should be looked for, the "best" method, from authoritative and credible sources, in order to make the best possible decision (which is then made when the costs of obtaining additional information exceed the benefits)'.[23] The examples I present below suggest that this story is incomplete and sometimes mistaken, ignoring both social and individual aspects of judgement and decision-making. To explain what is missed, I use a few stylised types and descriptions, taken from others' work and my own;[24] I argue that the story I present better and far more intuitively explains what we observe than does the standard story.

[20] HA Simon, 'Rational Choice and the Structure of the Environment' (1956) 63 *Psychological Review* 129.

[21] See Kay and King (n 1) 147–48.

[22] I discuss this issue in the specific context of unstable preferences in CA Hill, 'The Rationality of Preference Construction (and the Irrationality of Rational Choice)' (2008) 9 *Minnesota Journal of Law, Science and Technology* 689, 702–11, and fns 42 and 52.

[23] What I am calling the standard story differs from my story in assuming more of a consensus as to objective reality than I do, something I have called 'the assumption of perfect consensus', assuming away the extent of uncertainty, and assuming away the importance of temperament. Among the relevant work is the seminal piece by RJ Gilson, 'Value Creation by Business Lawyers: Legal Skills and Asset Pricing' (1984) 94 *Yale Law Journal* 239, and other articles, including L Bernstein, 'Opting Out of the Legal System: Extralegal Contractual Relations in the Diamond Industry' (1992) 21 *The Journal of Legal Studies* 115; M Gulati and RE Scott, *The Three and a Half Minute Transaction: Boilerplate and the Limits of Contract Design* (Chicago, University of Chicago Press, 2012); R Anderson IV and J Manns, 'The Inefficient Evolution of Merger Agreements' (2017) 85 *George Washington Law Review* 57; C Hwang and M Jennejohn, 'Deal Structure' (2018) 113 *Northwestern University Law Review* 279.

[24] As to the standard story, see ibid. As to the story presented here, see CA Hill, 'Repetition, Ritual, and Reputation: How Do Market Participants Deal with (Some Types of) Incomplete

Let us begin with the social aspects of judgement and decision-making. No one doubts that there is a deal-making community (tribe) with its own norms, rituals and institutions. The community, of course, has some penumbras as to both who and what the community consists of. The community can efficiently accumulate the wisdom of its members; it can also sort by reputation and mete out rewards and punishments.[25]

Using the example of M&A and like transactions, at the centre are transactional lawyers in big firms, using 'form' contracts in a ritualised negotiating process that involves relying on particular institutions and methodologies anointed as acceptable, and other parties routinely involved in such deals, including firms buying and selling other firms, bankers, institutional investors, and so on, using their accepted forms, methods and institutions. What market actors look for, how, from whom or from what source, and to what end, is influenced by the community. To the extent that this is simply an efficient way of combining and cumulating experience and knowledge, standardising information production and presentation and other necessary tasks and enabling an extra-legal system of norms and punishments that is better executed within a community than in a formal legal system, there is no 'fallacy' involved. But, as the examples below demonstrate, there is more going on.

Individual attributes matter as well. A market actor may be more or less confident as to their own judgements: their own confidence will influence the extent to which they accept the 'received wisdom'. I will focus on three stylised types: the less confident, the confident, and the confident contrarian. The less confident have a strong default acceptance of received wisdom. (They may – or may not – later become more confident.) The confident may have a rebuttable presumption or be agnostic as to the received wisdom. The confident contrarian seeks out opportunities where their strong presumption is that the received wisdom is wrong.

The first two types are well illustrated by examples from The Software Caper, a 'playlet' at the end of the book, *Anatomy of a Merger*, by M&A lawyer James Freund describing an acquisition of Suggestive by Proliferating.[26] The cast of characters includes Preppie, the junior (outside) lawyer for the purchaser, and Somnolent, the aptly named in-house lawyer for the seller; both lack confidence. The confident ones are the senior (outside) lawyer who berates Preppie, Prudent; Prudent's counterpart, Sagacity, the outside lawyer for the seller; and Stratosphere, the president of the seller. One interaction between Preppie and Prudent demonstrates these two temperaments. Prudent has assigned Preppie

Information?' (2020) *Wisconsin Law Review* 515; CA Hill, 'Why Contracts Are Written In Legalese' (2001) 77 *Chicago-Kent Law Review* 59; CA Hill, 'Bargaining in the Shadow of the Lawsuit', A Social Norms Theory of Incomplete Contracts' (2009) 34 *Delaware Journal of Corporate Law* 191; CA Hill, 'Justification Norms Under Uncertainty' (n 14) above; Hill (n 5).

[25] See Bernstein (n 23).

[26] Freund (n 11) 479–540.

to do the first draft of the acquisition agreement, giving him one week – from 20 December to 27 December. Not surprisingly, Prudent finds much to critique about Preppie's work product, including this:

> **PRUDENT:** Merry Christmas, Pete. Now look, fella, you'll just have to forgive my candour, but time's short, and this draft of the Proliferating-Suggestive agreement is an *inferior* job. The problem is that you *just didn't think!* You walked out of here, you [used an agreement one of our clients had entered into, Screwloose, and] marked it up for purposes of this draft. Don't you realize that the *final* Screwloose agreement represented the culmination of three weeks of intensive negotiation on the part of a pretty smart seller's attorney? You've got to start with the *first draft* of the Screwloose contract! … You have to *think*, boy. And then, in the one place you *did* a little thinking, Pete, it seems to me you went too far. I know it's *possible* that they'll repeal the Copyright Act some day, but it doesn't really rise to a level of probability sufficient to warrant three pages of provisions conditional upon that event.[27]

Preppie presumably mostly just copied what had been done before – he did not think he was in any position to second-guess a completed deal. But, being industrious and wanting to impress, he thought he'd add just a little something extra, a reference to another law, in a section addressing contingencies. We will return to this example later, but for present purposes, note Preppie and Prudent's relative levels of confidence. Now, of course, Preppie is inexperienced, and Prudent is experienced, but my strong suspicion is that Preppie will never be as confident as Prudent, and Prudent never lacked confidence to nearly the extent Preppie does.

The third type, the confident contrarian, is wonderfully instantiated in the person of Michael Burry, who made bets that real estate would fall in value in the years leading up to the 2008 financial crisis. Burry was a leading character in Michael Lewis's book, *The Big Short*. In the movie made from the book, Goldman Sachs bankers are meeting with Burry about his request that they sell him financial instruments that would enable him to short the housing market:

> *Goldman Sachs to Burry*: 'You want to bet against the housing market. Why? These bonds only fail if millions of Americans don't pay their mortgages. That's never happened in history. If you'll excuse me, Dr. Burry, that seems like a foolish investment.'
>
> *Burry to Goldman Sachs*: 'Based on prevailing sentiment of the market and banks and popular culture, yes, it's a foolish investment – but everyone's wrong.'[28]

As it happens, in this situation, Burry was right, but, importantly, contrarians are not always right.

In addition to their level of confidence, market actors also differ on other important dimensions. The other dimension I will discuss here, not completely

[27] ibid 500–01.

[28] M Lewis, *The Big Short: Inside The Doomsday Machine* (New York, W W Norton & Company, 2010). The movie clip I quoted from the 2015 movie is at www.youtube.com/watch?v=dqDu1sHoIAw. See also A von Tunzelmann, 'How Historically Accurate is The Big Short?', *The Guardian* (London, 27 January 2016).

unrelated to levels of confidence, is a promotion vs prevention focus. Very roughly speaking, the former is an inclination to maximise the upside, while the latter is an inclination to minimise the downside.[29] Confident contrarians will generally be promotion-focused, while less confident people are generally prevention-focused.

If a market actor is an agent, the upside and downside at issue may be that of their principal, or of their own upside or downside. An important dynamic involving a less confident market actor who is an agent is this: the less confident person, wanting to minimise their downside, may seek safety in numbers, knowing they will be judged relative to their peers or for deviations from norms. Justification will be prominently on their mind as they make decisions; what is justified is what others would do and, in fact, did. The other 'numbers' are doing the same, creating a demand for institutions that can anoint particular actions (buying the AAA-rated security) as justified. The dynamic will have particular resonance in the face of uncertainty.[30]

Contrast all this with a standard story about, for example, buying a company. What does the buyer want to know about the seller, and how does the seller communicate the information? A critical part of the story concerns misaligned incentives and how they are addressed. The seller wants to depict their business as being of high quality, the buyer is sceptical and unwilling to pay a price acceptable to the seller, and some means of providing credible information is arrived at.[31] Or, the buyer is concerned that the seller will take a short-term perspective on the business before it's about to be sold, and the seller assuages the concern by promising not to do so. Other aspects of deal-making are characterised generically with reference to cost-minimisation: information is supplied by, or tasks are done by, the best-situated party. More detail is beyond the scope of this chapter, but what is important is that while the players differ in their access to information and in their incentives, they are homogeneous in their worldview, something I have elsewhere called an 'assumption of perfect and complete consensus',[32] and in their temperaments. The seller's incentive to puff, the buyer's understanding of the seller's incentive, and what makes information credible and why (usually, the party providing the information agrees to pay a penalty if the information is not true), are all viewed and understood the same way by all parties.[33] Credibility and logistical hurdles are the obstacles to acquiring the needed information – what counts as the needed information is, again,

[29] See n 7 and n 8 and accompanying text.

[30] On this dynamic, see Hill (n 14) and CA Hill and AM Pacces, 'The Neglected Role of Justification under Uncertainty in Corporate Governance and Finance' (2018) 3 *Annals of Corporate Governance* 276.

[31] The seminal exposition of the problem is George Akerlof, 'The Market For Lemons: Quality Uncertainty and the Market Mechanism' (1970) 84 *Quarterly Journal of Economics* 488.

[32] CA Hill, 'Beyond Mistakes: The Next Wave of Behavioural Law and Economics' (2004) 29 *Queens Law Journal* 563.

[33] ibid.

a matter of perfect and complete consensus. The other seemingly important hurdle – who (beyond the principals) is authoritative – is also a matter of consensus and, indeed, assumed away insofar as the authority's reputational stake gives the authority an incentive to give accurate information. Given this worldview, beyond what's efficient regarding, for instance, standardisation and cumulation of information, there is no place for tribes, with their ability to delineate what 'should' be asked about and from whom, and when a person knows enough to act, nor is there a place for differences among individuals beyond their respective knowledge and (canonical) incentives.

It is easy enough to complicate this story. As noted above, there is enormous guidance as to what information is routinely sought and obtained, including from obvious but credibility-impaired parties, and from other sources. But quickly, we start to see that the inquiry as to what information is sought and when 'enough' information has been obtained is less mechanical than it might seem to be. For instance, while finding out whether a corporation is 'duly incorporated in jurisdiction x' is mechanical, something that sounds like it – 'qualified to do business in other jurisdictions in which it does business' – is not. What jurisdictions a company should be qualified to do business in is sometimes a difficult question that reasonable people can and do disagree about, such that an approach based on a norm as to where and how hard to look – 'what is usually done' – may be the best one can do.

While ample, the guidance as to what to look for cannot be comprehensive, based as it is on the past and people's imaginations as to what might matter. In general, what we know to look for is 'good enough', but not always. Consider in this regard the phrase 'hindsight is 20/20' – we may not know until afterwards what we would have wanted to know beforehand.

2.2.2. Some Examples on Information Acquisition

Two disparate examples discuss some complexities involved in the pursuit of information.

One is the inclusion in the Integrated Financial Reporting Standard's Sustainability Accounting Standard for the casino industry of the following two items: 'Percentage of gaming floor where smoking is allowed'; and 'Percentage of gaming staff who work in areas where smoking is allowed'.[34] Is this important

[34] See Casinos & Gaming, Sustainability Accounting Standard 5–6, https://d3flraxduht3gu.cloudfront.net/latest_standards/casinos-and-gaming-standard_en-gb.pdf. 'SASB Standards are intended to aid entities in disclosing information about sustainability-related risks and opportunities that could reasonably be expected to affect the entity's cash flows, its access to finance or cost of capital over the short, medium or long term.' This articulation is investor focused. For an argument that disclosure should not just be for investors, see AM Lipton, 'Not Everything Is About Investors: The Case for Mandatory Stakeholder Disclosure' (2020) 37 *Yale Journal on Regulation* 499, arguing that 'securities disclosures do not provide the comprehensive picture necessary to maintain social

disclosure? If so, to whom? And what information is conveyed?[35] In disclosure and acquisition documents for casinos, it has not been mentioned; disclosure on smoking is in generic references to regulation of smoking and the extent to which changes in regulation could adversely affect the casino's business and reputation.[36] Is the specificity important, and if so, why? Can one draw broader inferences, including whether the percentage correlated with other ways the business viewed itself and other actions it was taking? Should this information have been sought before it was?

My next example involves a potential real estate acquisition. Assume the acquisition is by an investor.

Figure 2.1 shows a photo of an actual for sale sign stating that a house is not haunted.[37]

Whether a house is haunted has sometimes been considered relevant in this context. There are court cases and statutes dealing with sales of haunted houses (and related matters, such as whether a violent crime took place in a house); in some regions of the US, contracts generally have provisions addressing these sorts of matters.[38] A rational buyer might have ample reason to care.[39]

control over corporate behaviour', recommending an explicit acknowledgement of 'the importance of disclosure for non-investor audiences' and that 'the feasibility of designing a disclosure system geared to their interests' be considered.

[35] In this regard, consider work on whether use of aggressive tax minimisation techniques is seen by a company's investors as a good thing, indicating the company's attentiveness to cost reduction, or a bad thing, indicating a willingness to push the envelope regarding other regulatory requirements or shaft investors. See MA Desai, A Dyck and L Zingales, 'Theft And Taxes' (2007) 84 *Journal of Financial Economics* 591.

[36] See, eg, Caesars Entertainment, Inc, Form 10-K, 2020, www.sec.gov/Archives/edgar/data/0001590895/000159089521000085/czr-20201231.htm (discussing a new CSR policy initiative and warning of potential adverse impacts from 'legislation in various forms to ban indoor tobacco smoking'); Eldorado Resorts, Inc, Form 10-K, 2019, www.sec.gov/ix?doc=/Archives/edgar/data/0001590895/000156459020007599/eri-10k_20191231.htm (including brief language regarding smoking and almost nothing on CSR); and MGM Resorts International, Form 10-K, 2019, www.sec.gov/Archives/edgar/data/0000789570/000156459020007393/mgm-10k_20191231.htm (noting emergence of smoking restrictions and possible negative impacts thereof, and noting CSR risks and the company's approach to CSR).

[37] This image is used by permission of the person who took the picture, Margot Bloomstein, author of *Trustworthy* (Page Two, 2021).

[38] R Alberts, 'Blame it on Stambovsky: Stigmatized Houses Are Now Online So What's a Buyer or Broker to Do?' (2014) 42 *Real Estate Law Journal* 431; HM Goldberg, 'Disclosing the Inevitable: Reconciling the Varied Requirements for the Disclosure of Death on Real Property' (2018) 32 *Notre Dame Journal of Law, Ethics and Public Policy* 183; www.economist.com/graphic-detail/2019/10/31/haunted-houses-have-a-chilling-effect-on-the-property-market; www.businessinsider.com/scary-stories-expensive-haunted-houses#the-sallie-house-in-atchison-kansas-has-been-investigated-by-multiple-ghost-hunters-6. See also Massachusetts General Laws C 93, Section 114, which provides, in relevant part, that '[n]o cause of action shall arise or be maintained against a seller or lessor of real property or a real estate broker or salesman, by statute or at common law, for failure to disclose to a buyer or tenant that the real property is or was psychologically impacted'.

[39] I use the investment context since this paper is about market fallacies. The issue is also presented by a homebuyer purchase whether or not the buyer is thinking of resale. See www.slate.com/human-interest/2013/08/dear-prudence-we-want-to-buy-a-murder-house.html.

Figure 2.1 For Sale sign

They might reasonably think resale will be harder or the resale price will be lower. Other possible negative financial effects an investor might take into account are that tenants might be more inclined to break their lease, either pretextually or 'honestly'. It is possible, too, that notoriety might have its benefits – one can envision an Airbnb listing for such a house commanding attention and a premium, perhaps, but thus far the evidence seems more consistent with diminution of value rather than enhancement.[40]

Is data about whether a house for sale is haunted 'information' that would, or should, be sought by a buyer? Is such data always important, or even relevant? Not necessarily ex ante, and even ex post. By contrast, all buyers would presumably find inquiries about the seller's title or the house's infestation with termites important. How would the manner in which the information is presented affect its importance or credibility? Again, it's not clear. (As it happens, the seller of

[40] See Goldberg (n 38).

the house pictured above was not responsible for the sign and does not know who is.)[41]

The haunted house example shows that appropriate subjects of inquiry aren't necessarily obvious and depend on many factors. The region at issue is one such factor: the sign was in Massachusetts, which of course has historical associations with witchcraft. The contractual norms, as to whether, and how, this type of issue will be addressed in the purchase contract, tend to be local as well. Thanks to the internet, the example is less good at showing the difficulties of obtaining information once the issue has been raised – a house's reputation as haunted (and the reasons for the reputation) would presumably be easy to determine – although how much weight the information should be given is another matter.

What are these examples examples of? That characterising this aspect of contracting as 'getting information until the cost of getting more information exceeds the benefits' assumes various things that are not so, including that it's clear what counts as information and that the costs and benefits of the 'information' are determinate and determinable. There are many theoretical implications, but what about practical ones? Certainly, there are pedagogical/descriptive payoffs in explaining the process of negotiation in many market contexts. Going further, there are also insights as to why reliance on disclosure may seem more helpful than it turns out to be.

2.2.3. More Examples, on Contract Drafting and Negotiations

Above, I discussed The Software Caper, a 'playlet' about an acquisition negotiation and consummation, introduced the major characters, and discussed one example. Below, I revisit that example and discuss several more from the same source.

In the example discussed above, I quoted one portion of senior lawyer Prudent's critique of junior lawyer Preppie's first draft of the acquisition agreement: 'I know it's possible that they'll repeal the Copyright Act someday, but it doesn't really rise to a level of probability sufficient to warrant three pages of provisions conditional upon that event.'[42]

What makes Prudent able to assess this likelihood? Presumably, many years of experience. Prudent is set up as an arbiter of 'what's reasonable to anticipate' in this saga – he and his peers thinking it is so makes it so. But maybe he is wrong. Maybe another 'Preppie' could come up with something that might seem unlikely at the time but, with hindsight, would prove to be prescient. It's

[41] Ms Bloomstein, who took the picture, made inquiries and determined that the 'not haunted' part of the sign was not placed there by the people who created and placed the rest of the sign.

[42] Freund (n 11) 500.

not as though there aren't major changes in 'what's market'. Certainly, the transactional world has seen interesting shifts over time, prompted by the world changing in ways that had not been sufficiently well anticipated, notably the advent of hostile deals, the eagerness of buyers to walk away from deals during (and sometimes since) the 2008 financial crisis, and, most recently, Covid-19. Indeed, it is not as though the contingencies provisions in acquisition agreements are regularly 'pruned' – in general, the dynamic is to retain what is there (that is, what was used in the previous deal being used as a form, which itself is the product of a previous deal in which it was used as a form, and so on) absent an extremely good reason to remove it. The result is a community norm as to the standard contents of such portions of the agreement, with no affirmative justification needed, whereas deviations or new provisions need justification – by, generally, a confident person within the community, like Prudent. (A real-life 'confident' practitioner is Marty Lipton, the inventor of the poison pill.)[43]

The next example, also from The Software Caper, recounts the seller's reaction and that of its inside and outside counsel upon receiving the first draft of the acquisition agreement prepared by the purchaser. Recall that Stratosphere is the President of the seller, Somnolent is the in-house counsel, and Sagacity is Prudent's counterpart, the seller's outside counsel:

> **STRATOSPHERE:** I've read this wretched agreement. It's awful. I don't have the slightest intention of warranting all those things about my company; I don't know if they're true or not. And it's so one-sided. … How can we ever get up that disclosure schedule? It'll be next Thanksgiving before we finish up. … And that employment contract! It's like signing your life away … I feel like walking out on the whole deal. Who needs it? I'd just as soon run my own business.
>
> **SOMNOLENT:** Stan, I've never seen anything like it in my thirty years of lawyering. You've got every justification to be irate.
>
> **SAGACITY:** Now, wait a minute, gentlemen; let's just calm down. This is a perfectly normal first draft of an acquisition agreement. I've seen – and drafted – hundreds of them. Prudent [outside counsel for the purchaser] is simply attempting to obtain whatever protections he can for his client, who otherwise would be buying a pig in a poke. It's the opposite of *caveat emptor*; you don't buy a business like a used car. Perry [Prudent]'s job is to represent the purchaser. Sy [Somnolent]and I are representing the seller, and we're the ones who have to dream up revisions and deletions and supplements that protect you; we shouldn't expect Perry Prudent to do that. And, by the way, just so it won't come as too much of a shock as we go through this document, most of the things Prudent is asking for, he's absolutely entitled to get.[44]

In this example, Prudent and Sagacity know and act in accordance with the norms and rituals of 'the game' (and the tribe) and expect the same of each other. Somnolent does not, and not just because he is, well, somnolent. He is an

[43] In this regard, consider the role of Marty Lipton in creating the poison pill. See M Lipton, 'Takeover Bids in the Target's Boardroom' (1979) 35 *Business Lawyer* 101.

[44] Freund (n 11) 501–02.

old-time lawyer, not part of the transactional community. He is willing to accept the outside counsels' say-so – and his own irrelevance. Prudent and Sagacity are presented as being evenly matched not only in their aptitudes but also in their standards as to how to comport themselves; the play has a variety of references to what each thinks the other is, and is not, capable of doing. Implicit in this discussion, and, I think, uncontroversially (and based on my own practice experience), there is some heterogeneity in the relevant community on this dimension. There is a range of behaviour that is countenanced within and by the tribe; there is some behaviour that is not. Consider the reputations some lawyers in the community might have for being 'aggressive' and more willing to 'push the envelope'.[45] Market actors who go beyond what's accepted within the community may be effectively excluded, or only allowed to engage within the community using strong assurance mechanisms, particularly those that rely on trusted third parties.[46] That being said, community norms may change to make acceptable that which was previously not accepted. Hostile acquirers offer a notable example. What counts as aggressive is clearly determined by reference to community standards. When the world was less globalised, US-style dealmakers were, it seems fair to say, generally considered aggressive by the standards of the local deal-making communities, whose negotiations stopped considerably sooner in the process of coming to an agreement.[47]

Here is another example, courtesy of a senior capital markets lawyer:

> Swap documentation is generally documented using a master agreement, supplemented by a schedule with certain specific toggles and a section for free hand revision, as it were, and a confirmation that includes the specific economic terms of a given trade. The terms of the master agreement do not change – this is an invariant norm in the community. In one transaction I worked on, lawyers on the other side made up their own master where they changed some of the neutral terms to be slanted, while retaining the exact structure of the master, using the same words at the beginning and end of each page. They didn't expressly say the master was unmodified, but all that was missing from the format of the form was the 'copyrighted by ISDA' footer that appears, but very unobtrusively, on the typical master agreement.

[45] On tax lawyers in this context, see CA Hill, 'Tax Lawyers are People Too: Commentary on Victor Fleischer's Options Backdating, Tax Shelters And Corporate Culture' (2007) 26 *Virginia Tax Review* 1065. See generally FC Zacharias, 'Effects of Reputation on the Legal Profession' (2008) 65 *Washington and Lee Law Review* 173.

[46] Also see CA Hill, 'A Comment on Language and Norms in Complex Business Contracting' (2002) 77 *Chicago-Kent Law Review* 29, 52, which discusses the range of reputations that market communities can and do accommodate.

[47] I compared US and German contracting in CA Hill and C King, 'How Do German Contracts Do As Much With Fewer Words' (2004) 79 *Chicago-Kent Law Review* 889. Germany at the time used much shorter and far less extensively negotiated contracts, as did other civil law countries. There were 'substantive' reasons for the difference, but norms were also part of the story, such that a US-style lawyer negotiating on every contingency would have been thought overly aggressive had they proceeded in the style to which they were accustomed. See generally CA Hill, 'The Trajectory of Complex Business Contracting in Latin America' (2008) 83 *Chicago-Kent Law Review* 179 and CA Hill, 'Why Are Non-US Contracts Written in US Legalese?' in M Freeman and F Smith (eds), *Law and Language: Current Legal Issues*, vol 16 (Oxford, Oxford University Press, 2013).

> That this party made this modification did not cause me to change how I approach my review of the documentation in these transactions. I continued to assume that the probability that another party would do what this party did was low enough that checking to make sure a party hadn't done it wasn't worthwhile. My bottom line was that checking would cost a huge amount given the high volume of transactions; that the reputational cost in an extremely repeat market made it exceedingly unlikely that anybody else would do this; and that the party seeking enforcement of the covertly changed provisions would incur considerable expense for an uncertain prospect of success.[48]

In this example, the (confident) lawyer concluded that something that happened once was not worth checking for in the future. Note that his conclusion was based on his assessment of costs and benefits to him, his firm, his client, and their counterparts. This incident occurred many years ago, and, thus far, he has had no reason to doubt that he made the right call. But note the trajectory from 'this happened' to 'it is safe to assume that it won't happen again' is based on an intricate set of inferences. Could someone else have come to another conclusion? Would they have been wrong to do so?

What follows? One insight is the extent to which social norms are embedded in and dictate how contracting parties interact and what their 'deals' with one another turn out to be. This suggests, too, a certain advantage to insiders to a system or tribe – to those who know the shorthand. Again, there are obvious pedagogical and descriptive payoffs. One practical payoff may be the importance to an organisation of having the right balance of promotion and prevention-focused employees. The form-altering lawyer discussed above seems likely to have been promotion-focused, and have colleagues who did not have sufficient interest in reining in such a focus. Firms as a whole might be well-advised to attend to this issue. Yet another practical payoff may relate to the transition to a more mechanised and globalised community. The dynamics I describe here are intricately 'human' – how do they map onto transacting and investing in a world of even more globalisation and a great deal of non-human 'conduct'? The inferences discussed above reflect views about how people reason – how will we proceed when much more of what's being done involves AI rather than humans?

2.2.4. Examples, on Expertise

Thus far, my examples have concerned what market actors do as they seek to make deals, and how they interpret what other market actors involved do, given the community's norms, rituals and institutions.

[48] Interview with senior capital markets lawyer from major law firm, on file with author. I discussed this example, albeit in less detail, in an online symposium on behavioural law and economics, www.laweconcenter.org/resource/claire-hill-on-the-promise-of-behavioral-law-and-economics/.

My next example concerns expertise. The broader topic is still the characterisation of deal-making as importantly including the search for credible information. Experts play an important role in the standard account. Because they have a reputational stake in their status as experts, their information is credible. But the expert's incentive to get or to keep a good reputation is not sufficient to assure that they are credible; an expert's competence is at issue too, as is whether there is a consensus as to the matter at issue. The expert might have a genuine belief on which they are willing to stake their reputation. They might be wrong, or the matter might admit of reasonable disagreement such that it's not clear whether they are wrong.

Some types of expertise are demonstrable matters of consensus – for instance, expertise requiring knowledge that can be tested or yields measurable or evident results. The standard story's prototype involves expertise of this type: the seminal exposition of the 'lemons problem', in which the buyer and seller cannot make a deal because the buyer assumes the seller is self-servingly and falsely depicting the car as high quality when it might be a 'lemon'. The mechanic-as-solution-to-the-lemons-problem in that context involves expertise as to a matter commanding significant consensus: whether the mechanic is an expert at fixing cars. The mechanic has a stake in having and keeping a good reputation. But the reputation is for competence and is assessed by reference to an underlying consensus as to what constitutes an expert mechanic. (Note that this solution assumes away the real-world complication that, at least historically, people have not been able to assess a mechanic's reputation and hence have not infrequently employed incompetent mechanics.)

By contrast with that sort of technical and demonstrable expertise, there are many middle-ground cases, including some where there is significant room for disagreement, either because of the present state of knowledge or because of the subject matter at issue. The first category would include cyber risk; the latter would include art expertise, as to quality and value.

Failing a fool-proof consensus test, what do we do to figure out whether somebody knows something we would like to know but don't? By definition, if one requires an expert, one won't know whether the expert is correct except by reference to some sort of proxy, such as credentials, track record or experience. As noted above, the standard analyses focus on stake – we can trust the expert because he's built up his reputation, and won't want to lose it, and hence has credibility. But stake speaks to the 'will' – the incentive. What about the 'way' – the ability?[49] In that regard, consider the following, from a recent article in the *Economist* on troubles at McKinsey:

> One of the best explanations for the triumph of a 'solution shop' like McKinsey was co-written by the late Clayton Christensen of Harvard Business School in 2013. When hiring a management-consulting firm, he said, clients do not know what they

[49] See Hill, 'Repetition' (n 24).

> are getting in advance, because they are looking for knowledge that they themselves lack. They cannot measure the results, either, because outside factors, such as the quality of execution, influence the outcome of the consultant's recommendations. So, they rely on reputation and other squishy factors – the consultants' 'educational pedigrees, eloquence, and demeanour' – as substitutes for tangible results.[50]

What would make these factors appropriate indicia of expertise? I would argue that 'appropriate' for this purpose often includes a community (tribe) assessment – is the person generally regarded as an expert? History suggests that the community assessment is not just about the collective 'best guess' from a purely substantive perspective. People need to know who it's considered acceptable to rely on; certain observable markers are helpful.

A final observation: there is a considerable irony in assuming away the issue of whether an expert is authoritative. Evidence that expertise is contestable and not a matter of consensus is pervasive. Battles of the experts are a common feature of litigation. In business law in particular, valuation and appraisal are often hotly contested, with highly-credentialed experts taking vastly different positions (and the judge not infrequently staking out yet another position).[51] Finally, most (US) lawyers have at least heard of *Daubert*, the standard by which a court decides whether to admit expert evidence.[52]

What follows from this observation – that 'obtaining information until the costs of additional information exceed the benefits' is not an apt description of the process by which 'information' is actually obtained? Again, the theoretical payoffs are the most obvious. The role expertise plays in solving the lemons problem is overstated, and, again, social dynamics are at play in who is anointed as an expert. We don't have a substantive test, so we use community acceptance or something else that 'looks' authoritative as a proxy. Doing so leads, though, to an important practical implication, which is that anointed experts can retain their status notwithstanding apparent showings that they are importantly or often wrong, a dynamic I have discussed at length in the context of credit rating agencies and discuss at 2.3 below.

2.2.5. Examples, on when Enough is Enough

My last set of examples concerns when 'enough is enough': when a market actor feels they know enough to proceed – to buy the company, to conclude the negotiation, to buy the security? The standard story does not offer much guidance, assuming that the decision is made based on the decision-maker's best

[50] See www.economist.com/business/2021/03/03/mckinseys-partners-suffer-from-collective-self-delusion.

[51] See CA Hill, BJM Quinn and SD Solomon, *Mergers and Acquisitions: Law, Theory, and Practice*, 3rd edn (Minnesota, West Academic Publishing, 2023) 79–98 and 249–59.

[52] See generally www.law.cornell.edu/wex/daubert_standard.

assessment that they know enough, and that additional information would not be worth the cost.

Let us return to The Software Caper:

> **SERPENTINE:** You won't believe this, but Stan and Paul want to sign up by this Friday! How will we ever get the disclosure schedule finished in time?
>
> **SAGACITY:** That's standard operating procedure, Sid. Everyone's afraid that if there's any delay, *someone else* might change his mind. I'll send over one of our associates to help you out …[53]

In my article, *Bargaining in the Shadow of the Lawsuit*,[54] I note that parties to complex business contracts:

> do less than they might to 'complete' their contracts. All immediate issues are addressed, as are parties' (or their lawyers') 'hot button' issues and other issues that become salient to one or both parties. But the documents used as forms for the transaction are not kept up to date, nor is the final product in a particular transaction cleaned up to eliminate confusing cross-references and possible ambiguities before the parties bind themselves to it (or afterwards, for that matter). While parties do ask themselves throughout the contracting process what they might have missed, the inquiry isn't nearly as systematic as it might be.[55]
>
> The stereotype of bleary-eyed corporate lawyers negotiating late into the night is indeed true. Lawyers don't take a dispassionate day or two after the dust clears to afford their more rested selves a chance to review and correct if necessary what their very tired selves wrote. And they have ample reason to fear that their more rested selves might catch something their tired selves did not.[56]

I argue that:

> [i]f parties seek to capture the last, costliest attempts at precision, they probably won't commensurately reduce their end-game costs. Indeed, they may increase such costs. Bargaining more than is the community norm may shrink the reputational penumbra otherwise created by the contract, encouraging an ethos in which whatever isn't prohibited is permitted. Accommodation that might help relationship preservation may thereby be crowded out, replaced by a more literalistic and opportunistic mindset on the part of both parties.[57]

On this view, the point at which the deal is signed up is *not* when the parties have learned and agreed on enough. At what point is the deal signed up? When the parties know 'enough' and the applicable norms and rituals have been abided by and performed.

My final example – that market actors do not in some simple determinate sense seek information until the cost of doing so is greater than the associated

[53] Freund (n 11) 529.
[54] Hill, 'Bargaining' (n 24).
[55] ibid 192–93.
[56] ibid 195.
[57] ibid 193.

benefit and make their decisions at that point – is of the eagerness that even some sophisticated money managers have had to purchase 'hot new issues'. In cases I was told about, some big money managers' most pressing concern was how much of a forthcoming new issue they could purchase, even though they had not seen the offering documents.[58] Making the same point, a credit officer from a German bank characterised the pressure from higher-ups to buy CDOs from Wall Street as intense, stating that if he 'delayed things more than 24 hours, someone else would have bought the deal'.[59] Whatever else is occurring, the decision-maker is not obtaining and appraising information and making a decision based thereon in the way the standard theory contemplates.

Again, beyond the theoretical payoffs, practical payoffs here include regulators' greater understanding as to how disclosure might or might not function to inform market decisions – and in particular, that giving market actors, even sophisticated ones, 'accurate and complete' information may not do as much for decision-making as it is thought to do.

2.2.6. On Temperament (and Culture)

The foregoing examples are largely focused on how tribes influence and determine norms, rituals and institutions. There was some discussion of the respective roles of less and more confident people. For instance, confident people would be more apt to innovate; less confident people would be more apt to cling to 'how things are done' (or what they expect others to do, aka herding). But tribes also enormously influence even confident market actors, as the examples above demonstrate. In The Software Caper, the playlet I discussed earlier, the purchaser is eager to get the seller to proceed with a merger transaction after some early discussions, and its lawyer, Prudent, uses this argument with the seller to suggest that a preliminary letter of intent be signed very quickly:

> **PRUDENT:** … You see, Stan [president of the seller], when the parties' minds have met, we are obligated to make an immediate public announcement. Before we do that, it makes sense to have a document evidencing our mutual intent, to serve as a back-up for the announcement. And we might as well get it done while everyone is here and available.
>
> *[There is, of course, some truth to this; but if you ask me, the Proliferating people are worried that Serpentine [VP of the seller] will convince Stratosphere how naïve he was to agree so quickly, or that someone else will find out SSL is for sale and get to them with a better offer. Once Stratosphere signs a document, he is much less likely to renegotiate the price, and he will probably feel a moral obligation not to talk to any other prospective purchasers.]*

[58] Interview with a lawyer who had a major Mortgage-Backed Securities practice at the time of the 2008 financial crisis.

[59] W Cohan, *Money and Power: How Goldman Sachs Came to Rule the World* (New York, Doubleday, 2011) 15. See also Davidoff Solomon and Hill (n 13).

This obligation is clearly grounded on 'tribal norms'. Reports of what went wrong in major business scandals in industrial and financial companies also offer examples. There are many richly detailed such reports, which discuss how particular individuals' behaviour contributed to financial losses, bad culture, and illegality.[60] One important story as to financial institutions is the extent to which those with a promotion focus became more influential and those with a prevention focus became less so.[61]

The standard story focuses importantly on incentives as they operate on people generally – the more particular conduct offers benefits in excess of costs, the more such conduct can be expected. While that is surely right at the margin, there are clearly enormous differences as to which benefits and costs count for different people, importantly reflecting their regulatory focus. Beyond that, differences in temperament very much affect how a person would do a cost/benefit analysis, with potential benefits and costs not just being the canonical ones (to simplify, money vs probability of jail for x years). For instance, some market actors are in the business of being, as Andrew Fastow, formerly of Enron put it, rule 'users' or rule 'exploiters'.[62] For such people, who are often promotion-focused, there may be a significant benefit from a particularly ingenious way to honour the letter of a rule while violating its spirit; others may not experience a benefit from such a thing, and others, often prevention-focused, might experience a cost. I don't mean to argue that 'pushing the envelope' should always be considered bad – some rules arguably overreach, or there may be a sympathetic reason why an end-run is warranted in a particular case. New York City, faced with a need for revenue, but also a borrowing limit and no time (and perhaps no ability) to get it lifted, sold, in exchange for an upfront payment, the right to collect a certain amount from its delinquent tax receivables, something that was borrowing in spirit, albeit not in fact as borrowing was defined.[63]

[60] See, eg, A Salz and R Collins, 'Salz Review: An Independent Review of Barclays' Business Practices' (*Barclays PLC*, 2013), www.online.wsj.com/public/resources/documents/SalzReview04032013.pdf; AR Valukas, 'Report to Board of Directors of General Motors Company Regarding Ignition Switch Recalls' (*Jenne & Block*, 2014), www.aieg.com/wp-content/uploads/2014/08/Valukas-report-on-gm-redacted2.pdf; and Reports on the Boeing Max 737 Investigation, https://democrats-transportation.house.gov/committee-activity/boeing-737-max-investigation. See also Fin Crisis Inquiry Bd, Financial Crisis Inquiry Report: Final Report of the National Commission on the Causes of the Financial and Economic Crisis in the United States (2011), www.govinfo.gov/content/pkg/GPO-FCIC/pdf/GPO-FCIC.pdf. See in particular the testimony of Mark Froeba, formerly of Moody's, available at www.fcic-static.law.stanford.edu/cdn_media/fcic-testimony/2010-0602-Froeba.pdf.

[61] Salz Review, ibid 82–83.

[62] See, Russ Banham, 'First Person: Andy Fastow and Me', *CFO.com*, April 24, 2019, www.cfo.com/news/first-person-andy-fastow-and-me/657922/. See also Hill (n 45) and Hill and Painter (n 7) 112–13.

[63] 'Once sold, the collections of prior year levies were turned over to the purchaser until the purchase price (interest and expenses) was satisfied.' *Tax Revenue Forecasting Documentation, Financial Plan, Fiscal Years 2004–2008*, www.nyc.gov/html/records/pdf/govpub/1677trfd6_04.pdf, 6, at note 3.

But there are clearly important differences among people as to the extent to which an applicable rule is presumptively to be followed.

2.3. WHERE DOES THIS LEAVE US?

What follows? (Or, as is often the first question at many faculty talks, 'So what'?)

First, that the standard story is incomplete and sometimes wrong is itself worthy of note. For those conducting scholarship, pedagogy, policy, and practice in business law and in business, understanding what's going on and why is important.

Second, I discussed above some specific lessons suggested by a greater focus on tribes and temperaments. Some general themes emerge. I use the term 'costs' because of its familiarity, but the word 'effects' would be more apt. First, there may be offsetting 'benefits'. Moreover, what counts as a 'cost' from, for instance, a principal's perspective may count as a benefit from a societal perspective. Sometimes, and in particular, as to herding and as to cultures in which a promotion focus yields a problematic corporate culture, we can and should do better. But in many of these cases, the costs are simply necessary features of the world as it is, and characterising them as costs, frictions, or undesirable misses the point – that they just 'are'.

The themes relate to some familiar costs and some costs that are less familiar. More familiar costs are stickiness and barriers to entry. Less familiar costs are ones I call justification costs, internal costs, costs of rituals, and satisficing costs.

Starting with stickiness and barriers to entry, in theory, a 'better' alternative as to how something is done or who is offering services should win out. But, in addition to generic switching costs, once a particular practice or service provider becomes established, there are additional costs that discourage a switch: a tribe member thereby demonstrates that they do not know the tribal norm or do not care. If the 'better' alternative were clearly and quickly demonstrable as such, there would be no issue. But these conditions may not be met. Maybe the 'better' alternative will take time to reveal itself as better, or maybe there will be enough noise that its superiority won't be clear. (Or maybe there is simply no 'fact of the matter' – there is no one right answer.)

One example I have given is the persistence of the major rating agencies' market shares notwithstanding well-publicised debacles.[64] Money-manager

[64] Office of Credit Ratings, Annual Report on Nationally Recognized Statistical Rating Organizations, February 2024, www.sec.gov/files/feb-2024-ocr-staff-report.pdf. The three main agencies, Moody's, Standard and Poor's, and Fitch, still command the bulk of the marketplace, notwithstanding the strong critiques they have received over the years. See CA Hill, 'Why Did Anyone Listen to the Rating Agencies After Enron?' (2009) 4 *Maryland Journal of Business and Technology Law* 283 and CA Hill, 'Limits of Dodd-Frank's Rating Agency Reform' (2011) 15 *Chapman Law Review* 133.

members of the tribe, especially less confident ones, know that others will also buy highly-rated securities; they can therefore minimise their downside costs by assuring they will do no worse than their peers. It apparently takes more than debacles – even multiple, large, debacles, over many years – to change people's practices. And once the practices are entrenched, forces combine to solidify the entrenchment. If issuers are generally getting 2 or 3 ratings from the leading agencies for their issuance of bonds, there is a negative inference for the issuer who does not do so – rebuttable, to be sure, but only at a cost. It seems that the agencies were able to exploit this situation to get above-market prices and limit other entrants into the market.[65] The stage was also set for new entrants to attempt to compete on laxity, since they were being hired by issuers: 'hire our agency, and we will find a way to rate you more highly.'[66] Interestingly, though, this entrenchment was not wholly negative. When there was a 'partner monopoly' between Moody's and Standard and Poor's, where all issuers effectively had to get both agencies' ratings, a system in which the issuers paid for their ratings could nonetheless work precisely because the market norm gave the agencies leverage to resist any issuer pressure to give higher ratings than were warranted. With credible new entrants and, as importantly, a small set of issuers each commanding a huge share of the market, as was the case for subprime securities, the competition for market share, achievable only through laxity, led to ratings that were much too high – and the 2008 financial crisis.[67]

Another example I have given is 'duelling notwithstandings', contract provisions that purport to override everything else in a contract, where several such provisions may occur in the same contract. The contracting process apparently works well enough within the community that it's not worthwhile to fix this (or other similar pathologies): heavily and expensively negotiated contracts continue to have these provisions.[68]

Related to stickiness are barriers to entry for various sorts of services, including expertise in various fields. Besides the rating agency example, recall the McKinsey example above. Their results are hard to measure definitively and objectively, so, once they get a certain status, they can keep it insofar as they are assessed via 'squishy factors' such as the consultants' 'educational pedigrees, eloquence, and demeanour'.[69]

Given that there is no objective test, who would not want to use someone 'accepted' rather than justify why one was not doing so? Again, knowing who is accepted and being willing to use them serves as a signal of one's willingness – and ability – to be a member of the tribe.

[65] CA Hill, 'Regulating The Rating Agencies' (2004) 82 *Washington University Law Quarterly* 43.

[66] ibid 62–64.

[67] CA Hill, 'Why Did Rating Agencies Do Such A Bad Job Rating Subprime Securities?' (2010) 71 *University of Pittsburgh Law Review* 585.

[68] See Hill, 'Bargaining' (n 24).

[69] See n 50 above and accompanying text.

Yet another type of cost is the cost of justification: the incremental cost of doing something with a view to justification where what is justifiable may diverge from what (the person, or a reasonable person, would conclude) is best, all things considered. Justification costs may be agency costs too, if the person who wants to justify their action is an agent (a money manager or a corporate fiduciary, for instance) acting on someone else's behalf. As I discussed above, the agent buying 'the hot new issue' as part of an unthinking herd may serve themselves best by knowing they won't do worse than their peers even though their principal would do better if they took more risk. The standard story usually assumes this difference away because the conditions that give rise to the divergence between a justifiable decision and the 'best' decision, principally uncertainty, are assumed away.[70] A person making a comparable decision as a principal themselves would presumably be considered irrational.

There are also costs associated with various rituals, notably the rituals of contracting, as described above in the examples from The Software Caper, and in more detail in the remainder of The Software Caper and in articles bemoaning the inartful language and length of acquisition and other similar corporate agreements,[71] and the excruciating and detailed negotiating process, haggling over the proverbial semicolon.[72] There are always attempts to streamline the process and rationalise the documents; somehow, these never succeed.

Another type of cost is internal costs. The (less confident) buyer tempted to herd would presumably bear significant internal costs if they had to rely on their own judgement. A promotion-focused person might design a company strategy involving risky high-priced acquisitions; a prevention-focused person might focus more on preserving the company's existing market share. Compensation that attempted to encourage either person to act in accordance with a focus not their own might have limited effect.

The final type of cost is the increment between what market agents do – make 'good enough' decisions – and the maximising decisions they could make.

On balance, it is hard to assess the net costs and benefits. Insofar as herding can be attributed in part to these sorts of dynamics, there would seem to be some societal costs, especially when herd-inflated bubbles burst. I have argued elsewhere, too, that the will to herd can be strong enough to make efforts to legislate disclosure requirements and craft disclosures far less productive than they might seem – disclosures can be dismissed as boilerplate, offering, ultimately, far less information than the popularity a security is getting among investors.[73] Stickiness and barriers to entry of the sort I describe above, and the motivation, especially of less confident and prevention-focused people, to proceed in ways they can justify, limits innovation and the prospects of third

[70] See Hill and Pacces (n 30).
[71] Freund (n 11) 233, referring to 'three-pound acquisition agreements'.
[72] See generally Freund (n 11); Hill, 'Bargaining'(n 24); Hill, 'Legalese'(n 24).
[73] See Davidoff Solomon and Hill (n 13).

parties. But they do economise on certain sorts of costs and give tribe members a way to signal their ability and willingness to be in the tribe. Dynamics of tribes that allow for 'moral obligations' for things that would be difficult to enforce in courts and allow for fine-grained reputational distinctions seem mostly like benefits, albeit, again, serving to some extent as a barrier to entry to those who don't know the tribal intricacies. What about internal costs? One possible lesson is that supercharging incentives for 'pushing the envelope' may yield real social costs unless the firm is vigilant in limiting the influence of promotion-focused people. The firm may suffer moderate-term costs as well. The many studies of business culture, and how it went wrong in the 2008 financial crisis and in other debacles, provide suggestive evidence to this effect.[74]

My claims are far more descriptive than normative; I mostly don't seek to appraise the dynamics I describe, focusing instead on making the case that we can do better than we presently do in understanding market behaviour. I do, however, have one more aim: to make the case for a new conception of rationality, a subject to which I now turn.

2.4. WHERE DOES THIS LEAVE US, MORE BROADLY?

A sensible view of people, held both in economics and in psychology, was summarised by Herbert Simon as follows: 'Everyone agrees that people have reasons for what they do. They have motivations, and they use reason (well or badly) to respond to these motivations and reach their goals.' He continued, articulating a not-so-sensible view that economics then generally held: 'The rational person of neoclassical economics always reaches the decision that is objectively, or substantively, best in terms of the given utility function.' This is possible because there exists 'an objective description of the world as it really is' such that we don't need to 'distinguish between the real world and the market actor's maker perception of it: he or she perceives the world as it really is.' Economics has moved away from some of this, particularly that people 'reach the best decision' and 'perceive the world as it really is', in behavioural law and economics' acceptance of the 'mistakes' people make (that presumably don't lead to the best decisions), but not as to what is important for my purposes, the existence of 'an objective description of the world'.

If an 'objective description of the world' existed in some straightforward sense (and, presumably, was recognisable as such), we would expect market actors simply to try to acquire as much information – known, somehow, to be such – as possible. When would they stop? The stopping point would be 'when the costs of acquiring more information exceed the benefits', at which point the market actor will make the decision the information obtained indicates is

[74] See n 60.

best. Accounts of the workings of the securities laws (in particular, the emphasis on disclosure), of deal-making and, indeed, of the behaviour of market actors generally, including the efficient capital markets hypothesis, all embed this characterisation.

I have argued that this characterisation, while not wrong, is incomplete. A recent book by John Kay and Meryn King argues that:

> [E]conomists have relied on the claim that if people observed certain axioms which constituted 'rationality,' they would unconsciously be optimising ... But ... the axiomatic approach to the definition of rationality comprehensively fails when applied to decisions made by businesses, governments or households about an uncertain future .... [T]his failure is not because these economic actors are irrational, but because they are rational and – mostly – do not pretend to knowledge they do not and could not have. Frequently, they do not know what is going to happen and cannot successfully describe the range of things that might happen, far less know the relative likelihood of a variety of different possible events.[75]

We live, according to the authors, in a world of 'uncertainty', some of which is resolvable by 'looking something up' (resolvable uncertainty) and some of which is not. This latter type of uncertainty, 'radical uncertainty', 'has many dimensions: obscurity; ignorance; vagueness; ambiguity; ill-defined problems; and a lack of information that in some cases but not all we might hope to rectify at a future date'.[76] Thus, '[d]ifferent individuals and groups will make different assessments and arrive at different decisions, and often there will be no objectively right answer, either before or after the event'.[77]

This would be untenable and, indeed, unlikely if, in our world, only the fittest survived, as is implicitly or explicitly hypothesised in the underlying theory. Those who don't 'get it right' go extinct – almost tautologically, it might seem. A recent critique by philosopher Daniel Milo makes a full-frontal attack on this perspective. Milo argues that the force and effect of natural selection has been exaggerated, as though it were far more purposive to a competitive end, and less tolerant of 'losers' in the competition. 'Human society is not ruthlessly competitive, and neither is nature. Both are tolerant of excess, inertia, error, mediocrity and failed experiments. Where great successes occur in society and in nature, luck can be far more important than talent.'[78] Indeed, while 'behavioural law and economics', which purports to make law and economics more realistic, has come to generally be associated with 'mistakes', there has long been a competing view that, together with Milo's critique, yields the view this chapter ultimately espouses: that what is rational in a world of uncertainty and

[75] Kay and King (n 1) xv.
[76] ibid 14.
[77] ibid 16.
[78] Milo (n 17) 6.

limited cognitive resources is doing the best one can, which Nobel Prize-winning economist Herbert Simon calls 'satisficing'.[79]

2.5. CONCLUSION

The examples discussed above demonstrate various respects in which the standard story of rational market actors is incomplete and sometimes wrong. There is, of course, much more to be explored – many more aspects of tribes than those I have discussed, and many other types of temperament beyond levels of confidence and regulatory focus that matter. My hope is that my discussion here will spur more exploration. Doing so has many payoffs – not just in the academic and policy spheres, but also, importantly for a law professor, in the pedagogical sphere as well. It should also have use and resonance for practitioners. That tribes and temperament matter is clear. What's needed is a way to understand *how*, in a manner that, as Albert Einstein may have said, is as simple as possible – but no simpler.[80]

[79] See also Kay and King (n 1) 16–17.
[80] See www.quoteinvestigator.com/2011/05/13/einstein-simple/.

3

Hidden Fallacies in the Agency Theory of the Corporation

JENNIFER G HILL

3.1. INTRODUCTION

'Logic is not concerned with the false opinions which people happen to entertain, but with the manner in which they come to entertain them.'

John Stuart Mill[1]

SINCE ARISTOTLE IDENTIFIED his 13 fallacies in *Sophistical Refutations*,[2] the study of logical fallacies has ebbed and flowed across time and jurisdictions.[3] So, too, has the number of possible logical fallacies in existence – it has been reported, for example, that one seventh-century Indian logician succeeded in identifying 2,032 types of fallacy.[4] Logical fallacies have particular resonance in the areas of law and politics, given Jeremy Bentham's seminal 1809 work, *The Book of Fallacies*,[5] that sought to expose fallacious political arguments used to frustrate legal reform.[6]

Although there is disagreement as to the precise meaning of the term 'fallacy',[7] it is generally accepted that the concept involves flawed or erroneous reasoning.[8] From this perspective, a fallacious argument is said to be one that '*seems* to be valid but is not'.[9]

The purpose of this chapter is to explore some aspects of the reasoning that underpins the agency theory of the firm (otherwise known as the 'contractual'

[1] JS Mill, *A System of Logic, Ratiocinative and Inductive*, 8th edn (Franklin Square, Harper & Brothers, 1882), Book 5, ch 2, para 1.

[2] See Aristotle, *Sophistical Refutations* (Hawthorne, Aeterna Press, 2015).

[3] See generally CL Hamblin, *Fallacies* (London, Methuen & Co Ltd, 1970).

[4] ibid ch 5.

[5] P Schofield (ed), *The Book of Fallacies* (Oxford, OUP, 2015).

[6] P Singer, *Ethics in the Real World* (Princeton, Princeton University Press, 2016) 211.

[7] See MA Finocchiaro, 'Fallacies and the Evaluation of Reasoning' (1981) 18 *American Philosophical Quarterly* 13, 13.

[8] ibid 14–15.

[9] Hamblin (n 3) 194.

or 'nexus of contracts' model). The classical agency theory of the firm treats the corporation as a fictitious – and purely financial – vehicle, devoid of social connection or responsibilities. The theory applies a single-minded focus on one particular agency problem, namely, that which exists between shareholders and managers.[10]

This chapter argues that, by amplifying a single agency problem, namely that of managerial opportunism, the agency theory of the firm potentially blinds us to several different problems, including the economic power of some corporations[11] and harm caused by negative externalities.[12] And, by elevating the role of private ordering between firm participants, the agency theory discounts the importance of corporate regulation as an accountability mechanism.

The chapter suggests that some of the assumptions underpinning the agency theory of the firm are now outdated and sit uncomfortably with contemporary 'on the ground' corporate law and governance developments. This dissonance between the dominant theory of modern corporate law and the real world suggests that the time may have come to re-evaluate the assumptions that support the use of agency theory as the only comprehensive analytical tool for understanding the corporation[13] and to introduce a broader conception of the public corporation and its role in modern society.

3.2. THE RISE TO DOMINANCE OF THE AGENCY THEORY OF THE CORPORATION AND SOME OF THE ASSUMPTIONS EMBEDDED IN IT

> 'The publicly held business corporation is an awesome social invention.'
>
> Michael C Jensen and William H Meckling[14]

The agency theory of the corporation has now been the dominant paradigm for over four decades.[15] Its emergence in the 1970s–1980s broke new ground in a variety of ways, not least of which was its resurrection of theoretical debate about the nature of the corporation – a debate that had undergone a long

[10] DC Langevoort, 'The Effects of Shareholder Primacy, Publicness, and "Privateness" on Corporate Cultures' (2020) 43 *Seattle University Law Review* 377, 378.

[11] See, eg, M Babic, E Heemskerk and J Fichtner, 'Who is More Powerful – States or Corporations?, *The Conversation*, 10 July 2018.

[12] See, eg, C Hill and Y Nili, 'Independence Reconceived' [2023] *Columbia Business Law Review* 589; RM Buxbaum, 'Corporate Legitimacy, Economic Theory, and Legal Doctrine' (1984) 45 *Ohio State Law Journal* 515, 517–20.

[13] See generally E Micheler, *Company Law: A Real Entity Theory* (Oxford, OUP, 2021) ch 1; EL Rubin, 'Images of Organizations and Consequences of Regulation' (2005) *Theoretical Inquiries in Law* 347.

[14] MC Jensen and WH Meckling, 'Theory of the Firm: Managerial Behavior, Agency Costs and Ownership Structure' (1976) 3 *Journal of Financial Economics* 305, 357.

[15] See, eg, M Klausner, 'Fact and Fiction in Corporate Law and Governance' (2013) 65 *Stanford Law Review* 1325, 1326–29.

hiatus in US corporate law.[16] By reviving legal theory, contractarian scholars succeeded in redirecting public discourse about corporations, including the relationship of corporations with society and how corporations should be regulated.

The rise of the agency theory of the corporation represented a 'radical rejection'[17] of the earlier managerialist image of the corporation, which focused on questions relating to the hierarchical power of corporate management and whether or not such power was legitimate.[18] Pro-managerialists had previously viewed the corporation as a 'social institution',[19] where managers act as 'corporate statesmen'[20] with broad discretionary powers enabling them to perform a public role, and to 'consciously direct economic forces for the common good'.[21] Anti-managerialist scholars, on the other hand, had argued that corporate managers held power without accountability, leaving shareholders vulnerable and unprotected. These scholars regarded Delaware as the prime villain in this narrative, arguing that the State had 'watered the rights of shareholders vis-à-vis management down to a thin gruel'.[22]

The subsequent emergence of the agency theory of the corporation subverted both sides of this earlier debate. Contractarian scholars rejected the managerialist perception of the corporation as a social institution, while at the same time criticising the anti-managerialist assumption that shareholders were defenceless and unprotected by US corporate law. Rather, contractarians considered that shareholders were adequately protected by the market and that their alleged abuse was therefore 'largely mythical'.[23]

The genesis of the agency theory of the corporation in Jensen and Meckling's classic 1976 article reframed corporate law in terms of agency relationships.[24]

[16] The decline of theoretical debate in the 1920s is often attributed to an influential article by John Dewey: J Dewey, 'The Historic Background of Corporate Legal Personality' (1926) 35 *Yale Law Journal* 655, 666–68. Prior to that, the theoretical nature of the corporation had been a 'virtual obsession' in the US for several decades: MJ Horwitz, *The Transformation of American Law, 1870–1960: The Crisis of Legal Orthodoxy* (Oxford, OUP, 1992) 101.

[17] WW Bratton, 'The New Economic Theory of the Firm: Critical Perspectives from History' (1989) 41 *Stanford Law Review* 1471, 1477.

[18] ibid 1475–76.

[19] H Wells, '"Corporation Law is Dead": Heroic Managerialism, Legal Change, and the Puzzle of Corporation Law at the Height of the American Century' (2013) 15 *University of Pennsylvania Journal of Business Law* 305, 331.

[20] ibid 353.

[21] FX Sutton et al, *The American Business Creed* (Cambridge, Mass, Harvard University Press, 1956) 34.

[22] WL Cary, 'Federalism and Corporate Law: Reflections upon Delaware' (1974) 83 *Yale Law Journal* 663, 666.

[23] GA Mark, 'Some Observations on Writing the Legal History of the Corporation in the Age of Theory' in LE Mitchell (ed), *Progressive Corporate Law* (Oxfordshire and New York, Taylor & Francis, 2020) 71.

[24] See Jensen and Meckling (n 14). Earlier work in this area represented important antecedents: see, eg, MA Eisenberg, 'The Conception That the Corporation Is a Nexus of Contracts, and the Dual Nature of the Firm' (1999) 24 *The Journal of Corporation Law* 819, 820–22, discussing the intellectual transition from RH Coase, 'The Nature of the Firm' (1937) 4 *Economica* 386, to Jensen and Meckling.

The theory is undeniably elegant. It encompasses a 'single, universal, organising principle',[25] which treats a particular agency problem – namely, the misalignment of interests between corporate managers and providers of capital – as the key problem of corporate law.[26]

A central aspect of Jensen and Meckling's agency theory of the firm was that most organisations, including corporations, are 'simply *legal fictions*' (emphasis in original).[27] In reaching this conclusion, Jensen and Meckling adopted an aggregate theory of the corporation, deconstructing it into a 'nexus of contracting relationships'[28] (a phrase that later morphed into the more familiar term, 'nexus of contracts').[29] They interpreted 'legal fiction' to mean 'the artificial construct under the law which allows certain organizations to be treated as individuals'.[30]

The idea that a corporation is a legal fiction (or a '*persona ficta*') accords with legal history. However, the fact that Jensen and Meckling added the word 'simply' before the reference to 'legal fiction' is revealing. It demoted the concept of legal personality,[31] and indeed, in later interpretations of agency theory, there is a transformation from understanding the corporation as a 'legal fiction' (ie artificial, but real)[32] to viewing it as 'fictitious' (ie non-existent).[33] These later interpretations of Jensen and Meckling's agency paradigm dissolved the corporation into nothing more than a 'complex set of explicit and implicit contracts'[34] between various self-interested resource holders.[35] The corporation effectively became 'a matter of convenience rather than reality'.[36]

[25] I Berlin, *The Hedgehog and the Fox: An Essay on Tolstoy's View of History*, 2nd edn (Henry Hardy (ed), Princeton University Press, 2013) 2.

[26] This misalignment in interests is sometimes viewed more broadly as applying, not merely to shareholders, but to 'suppliers of finance', which also includes creditors: see A Shleifer and RW Vishny, 'A Survey of Corporate Governance' (1997) 52 *The Journal of Finance* 737, 737–38.

[27] Jensen and Meckling (n 14) 310.

[28] ibid 311.

[29] See MT Moore, *Corporate Governance in the Shadow of the State* (Oxford, Hart Publishing, 2013) 72 fn 50, attributing the first use of the phrase 'nexus of contracts' to E Fama, 'Agency Problems and the Theory of the Firm' (1980) 88 *Journal of Political Economy* 288, 290.

[30] Jensen and Meckling (n 14) 310 fn 12. They also considered that this legal fiction was itself a party to the nexus of contracts: at 311.

[31] See J Hardman, 'Fixing the Misalignment of the Concession of Corporate Legal Personality' (2023) *Legal Studies* 1, 2, describing transaction cost economics as reducing the role of separate legal personality by rendering it 'merely a cheaper mechanism to achieve private ordering'.

[32] ibid 5, where Hardman argues that separate legal personality 'is a state concession to a real entity'. See also N Naffine, 'Who Are Law's Persons? From Cheshire Cats to Responsible Subjects' (2003) 66 *Modern Law Review* 346, 347, stating that '[p]erhaps the greatest political act of law is the making of a legal person'.

[33] See AW Machen, 'Corporate Personality' (1911) 24 *Harvard Law Review* 253, 257, in relation to this distinction. See also See Hardman (n 31) 6–7.

[34] FH Easterbrook and DR Fischel, 'The Corporate Contract' (1989) 89 *Columbia Law Review* 1416, 1418.

[35] See Fama (n 29) 289.

[36] FH Easterbrook and DR Fischel, *The Economic Structure of Corporate Law* (Harvard University Press, 1991) 12.

This shift in the depiction of the corporation had important implications, generating a range of assumptions that subsequently became bedrock principles of modern US corporate law. First, the methodological individualism of this approach offered little scope for recognition of the corporation as an autonomous actor,[37] or for intrinsically organisational accountability.[38]

Second, the agency theory's emphasis on free contractual choice resulted in an assumption that the various contractual exchanges between stakeholders were voluntary. This focus on contract relied on a sharp divide between the public and private spheres,[39] while at the same time placing the corporation firmly within the latter realm.[40]

Third, the theory interpreted the relationship between shareholders and corporate managers as one of 'pure agency'.[41] Jensen and Meckling treated outside equity and debt holders as 'principals' in this relationship, with corporate managers acting as their agents.[42] Their analysis interpreted agency as a very narrow economic concept, thereby creating a limited viewpoint, which focused on a single relationship and did not purport to comprehend the larger picture.

Fourth, by interpreting contracts as the 'essence' of the firm,[43] the paradigm enhanced the significance of private ordering over mandatory rules and emphasised the 'enabling structure of US corporate law'.[44] This suggested that corporate law's role as a regulatory mechanism is extremely limited, effectively restricted to providing malleable default rules,[45] and enforcing the voluntary bargains created under the nexus of contracts.[46] Under the agency theory of the corporation, mandatory legal rules and doctrines, such as fiduciary duties, designed to control managerial conduct, were largely unnecessary. Instead, the theory optimistically assumed that market forces[47] would do the heavy

[37] See, eg, PE Wilson, 'Barring Corporations from the Moral Community: The Concept and the Cost' (1992) 23 *Journal of Social Philosophy* 74; Richard B Stewart, 'Book Review: Organizational Jurisprudence' (1987) 101 *Harvard Law Review* 371.

[38] *cf* Bratton (n 17) 1480, discussing the institutional version of the agency model of the corporation.

[39] R Claassen, 'Political Theories of the Business Corporation' (2023) 18 *Philosophy Compass* 1, 5.

[40] See, eg Moore (n 29) 71.

[41] Jensen and Meckling (n 14) 309.

[42] ibid 310.

[43] Jensen and Meckling (n 14) 310, stating that '[c]ontractual relations are the essence of the firm, not only with employees but with suppliers, customers, creditors, etc'.

[44] M Barzuza, 'Inefficient Tailoring: The Private Ordering Paradox in Corporate Law' (2018) 8 *Harvard Business Law Review* 131, 133.

[45] Easterbrook and Fischel (n 36) 34.

[46] Jensen and Meckling (n 14) 311 fn 14, stating that '[t]he police powers of the state are available and used to enforce performance of contracts or to enforce the collection of damages for non-performance'.

[47] Eisenberg (n 24) 823; D Campbell, 'The Role of Monitoring and Morality in Company Law: A Criticism of the Direction of Present Regulation' (1997) 7 *Australian Journal of Corporate Law* 343, 361.

regulatory lifting as an economic constraint which forced managers to promote shareholder interests.[48]

Fifth, the paradigm dissolved any presumed boundaries around the firm.[49] Jensen and Meckling perceived themselves as cracking open the prior economic 'black box' of the firm and peering inside it to discern the conflicting objectives of its various stakeholders.[50] They treated the earlier 'black box' approach to the corporation as not a theory of the firm at all, but 'actually a theory of markets in which firms are important actors'. Under Jensen and Meckling's paradigm, however, the image of public corporations as important actors (either in markets or society as a whole) disintegrated. Indeed, the paradigm's deconstruction of the corporation into a network of contracts rendered meaningless any attempt to define what lay inside or outside the firm.[51]

Sixth, the agency theory became commingled with the shareholder primacy movement.[52] Jensen and Meckling's multi-stakeholder contractual approach did not necessarily compel a shareholder-centred view of the corporation.[53] In fact, Blair and Stout would subsequently employ a similar aggregate economic theory of the firm to argue against the pre-eminence of shareholder interests.[54] Nonetheless, there is little doubt that Jensen and Meckling's article provided the springboard for the shareholder primacy movement.[55] This is not on the basis that shareholders are 'owners' of the firm (ownership essentially being an 'irrelevant concept' under the agency theory of the firm),[56] but rather on the basis that shareholders are 'residual' claimants,[57] who, unlike other stakeholders, cannot sufficiently limit their risk by contract.[58]

Finally, the agency theory's relentless private law focus and reliance on stakeholder contracts explicitly banished corporate social responsibility (CSR) from the realm of corporate law. After all, why would CSR be required vis-à-vis employees, if employees could be 'guardians of their own interests'

[48] Klausner (n 15) 1327.

[49] Hardman (n 31) 9–12 (on the meaning of 'the firm').

[50] Jensen and Meckling (n 14) 306–07.

[51] ibid 311; Rubin (n 13) 351. *cf* Fama (n 29) 289, stating that corporate managers are subject to discipline 'by the markets for their services, *both within and outside of the firm*' (emphasis added).

[52] Claassen (n 39) 4–5.

[53] See, eg, Eisenberg (n 24) 833, stating '[i]t is commonly thought that the nexus-of-contracts conception is connected in some fundamental way to the concept of shareholder primacy. It isn't.'

[54] MM Blair and LA Stout, 'A Team Production Theory of Corporate Law' (1999) 85 *Virginia Law Review* 247, 253–54.

[55] See BR Cheffins, 'What Jensen and Meckling Really Said about the Public Company' in E Pollman and RB Thompson (eds), *Research Handbook on Corporate Purpose and Personhood* (Cheltenham, Edward Elgar Publishing, 2021) 12–13, 16–17.

[56] Fama (n 29) 290.

[57] Moore (n 29) 76. See also at 74–78, where Moore discusses the link between the contractual theory of the firm and 'shareholder exclusivity in corporate governance law': at 78.

[58] See generally BR Cheffins, 'The Team Production Model as a Paradigm' (2015) 38 *Seattle University Law Review* 397, 408–09.

and self-protect via their contracts with the company?[59] According to Jensen and Meckling, questions such as 'what should be the objective function of the firm' or 'does the firm have a social responsibility' were logically inconsistent with their agency theory of the firm as a fiction.[60] As they stated, '*[t]he firm is not an individual*' (emphasis in original).[61]

The narrowness and descriptive inadequacies of this approach morphed into normative inadequacies. Milton Friedman's famous 1970 pronouncement that '[t]he social responsibility of business is to increase its profits' is emblematic of this deficiency.[62] The so-called Friedman doctrine encompassed all the assumptions that Jensen and Meckling would subsequently weave into scholarly economic arguments in their 1976 article. Friedman held very clear views on corporate managers who take seriously CSR/Environment, Social and Governance (ESG) issues, such as employment, anti-discrimination and environmental protection;[63] he accused them of 'preaching pure and unadulterated socialism'.[64] Friedman also stated that '[o]nly people can have responsibilities' and that the responsibility of corporate managers, as agents of the shareholders, is to comply with their principals' desires, 'which generally will be to make as much money as possible'.[65] Under this approach, shareholders and their desires are viewed as relatively homogeneous, with monetary gain[66] or 'shareholder value maximisation' becoming the corporate lodestar.[67]

Of course, it might be argued that my description of early agency theory constitutes a fallacy in its own right, namely, the fallacy of inaccurate or uncharitable reconstruction, by failing to take sufficient account of the theory's subsequent evolution.[68] It is certainly true that the agency theory has not remained static, with some legal scholars pushing back against a purely contractual portrayal of the corporation to include property elements.[69] Nonetheless, it is fair to say that, despite attempted fine-tuning, the central tenets of

[59] See *BTI 2014 LLC v Sequana SA & Ors* [2022] UKSC 25, [2023] 2 All ER 303, 315–16, [27]–[28] (Lord Reed P). See also at 322–23, [52]–[54] (Lord Reed P), noting that this was the traditional approach in relation to corporate creditors.

[60] Jensen and Meckling (n 14) 311.

[61] ibid.

[62] M Friedman, 'A Friedman Doctrine – The Social Responsibility of Business Is to Increase Its Profits' *The New York Times* (New York, 13 September 1970).

[63] ibid.

[64] ibid 32. Friedman also accused such business leaders as being 'unwitting puppets of the intellectual forces that have been undermining the basis of a free society these past decades'.

[65] ibid. Friedman's famous quote continued with the following qualification: 'while conforming to the basic rules of the society, both those embodied in law and those embodied in ethical custom'.

[66] ibid.

[67] See generally O Hart and L Zingales, 'The New Corporate Governance' (2022) 1 *The University of Chicago Business Law Review* 195, 196.

[68] Finocchiaro (n 7) 18, 22.

[69] See, eg, H Hansmann and R Kraakman, 'The Essential Role of Organizational Law' (2000) 110 *Yale Law Journal* 387, 406.

original agency theory (including assumptions about the fictitious nature of the corporation, the hegemony of contract law[70] and the centrality of the shareholder value maximisation norm) have proven to be remarkably resilient and continue to hold a powerful sway today in both law[71] and finance.[72]

3.3. QUESTIONABLE ASSUMPTIONS UNDERPINNING THE AGENCY THEORY OF THE CORPORATION

> 'I had fallen victim to the fallacy of the "growing edge"; the belief that only the very frontier of scientific advance counted; that everything that had been left behind by that advance was faded and dead.'
>
> Isaac Asimov[73]

The agency theory of the corporation contains several assumptions that are questionable from a historical and legal perspective. For example, although many commentators assumed that the agency theory of the corporation amounted to a 'revolution',[74] from a historical perspective, the theory was, in fact, less radical than it first appeared. Similar aggregate/contractual theories of the corporation flourished in the US during the nineteenth century[75] (albeit in competition with entity theories of the corporation),[76] before waning at the turn of the twentieth century.[77] Writing in the late 1980s, Bratton described the supposedly new agency theory of the firm as 'merely the latest in a long series of attempts to describe and justify the phenomenon of collective production in individualist terms'.[78] The theory has also been labelled 'contractualism with economic foundations'.[79]

Nor was the use of contractual language new. The famous 1819 US Supreme Court decision, *Trustees of Dartmouth College v Woodward*,[80] interpreted a

[70] Eisenberg (n 24) 836.

[71] See generally DS Lund and E Pollman, 'The Corporate Governance Machine' (2021) 121 *Columbia Law Review* 2563.

[72] See Hart and Zingales (n 67) 204–07, discussing why shareholder value maximisation became, and stayed, the business norm.

[73] I Asimov, *Adding a Dimension: Seventeen Essays on the History of Science* (Garden City, Doubleday, 1964).

[74] See, eg, R Romano, 'After the Revolution in Corporate Law' (2005) 55 *Journal of Legal Education* 342, 342; MC Jensen, 'Organization Theory and Methodology' (1983) 58 *The Accounting Review* 319, 324.

[75] See MJ Horwitz, '*Santa Clara* Revisited: The Development of Corporate Law Theory' (1985) 88 *West Virginia Law Review* 173, 182, noting that 'through the 1880s, there was a strong tendency to analyse corporation law not very differently from the law of partnership'.

[76] See Bratton (n 17) 1490–91; Horwitz (n 75) 176, arguing that the '"natural entity"' theory of the corporation was instrumental in 'legitimating big business'.

[77] See Bratton (n 17) 1490.

[78] ibid 1472–73.

[79] Claassen (n 39) 4.

[80] *Trustees of Dartmouth College v Woodward*, 17 US 518 (1819).

corporation's charter as a contract between its original parties, namely 'the donors, the trustees, and the crown'.[81] This approach became legal orthodoxy in the US, with an 1865 US federal court case brief stating that:

> [a] charter of a corporation is a contract of a two-fold character; it is, 1st, a contract between the State and the corporation; and 2dly, between the corporation and the stockholders.[82]

By the late nineteenth century, however, the first of these two types of contracts (which would certainly attract the censure of agency theorists) was headed for extinction in the US. In the era of competition for corporate charters, the state receded, in favour of the corporation itself, as the primary 'law-maker'.[83]

In the UK, nineteenth- and early-twentieth-century case law also used the terminology of 'contract' to describe the effect of the constitutional document, the articles of association.[84] These cases treated the articles of association as a 'contract' between the shareholders *inter se*,[85] but it was also accepted that a binding contract existed between the shareholders and the company itself.[86] The state was not considered to be a contracting party under early UK company law.[87]

Even though the language of contract was historically a significant and familiar aspect of UK company law, contract was certainly not all that mattered. Trust law was just as important for developing unincorporated joint stock ('deed of settlement') companies,[88] which ultimately provided the blueprint for modern UK company law.[89] These companies, which have been described as 'an inferior substitute' for chartered corporations,[90] nonetheless

[81] ibid 643.

[82] E Anthony, *A Treatise on the Law of Consolidation of Railroad Companies* (Brach & Barnard, 1865) v.

[83] J Seligman, 'A Brief History of Delaware's General Corporation Law of 1899' (1976) 1 *Delaware Journal of Corporate Law* 249, 273. See generally CM Yablon, 'The Historical Race Competition for Corporate Charters and the Rise and Decline of New Jersey: 1880–1910' (2007) 32 *The Journal of Corporation Law* 323.

[84] See, eg, *Pritchard's Case* (1873) 8 Ch App 956, 960 (Mellish LJ), 961 (James LJ); *Eley v Positive Government Security Life Assurance Co Ltd* (1875) 1 Ex D 20, 26 (Amphlett B).

[85] *Pritchard's Case* (n 84) 960 (Mellish LJ, James LJ agreeing at 961); *Eley* (n 84) 26 (Amphlett B, Cleasby B agreeing at 29–30).

[86] See *Hickman v Kent or Romney Marsh Sheepbreeders' Association* [1915] 1 Ch 881, [1914–15] All ER Rep 900 (Astbury J).

[87] This was due to the different organisational origins of UK and US corporate law: see JG Hill, 'The Trajectory of American Corporate Governance: Shareholder Empowerment and Private Ordering Combat' [2019] *University of Illinois Law Review* 507, 540–47.

[88] ibid 544–47.

[89] A legislative attempt to outlaw deed of settlement companies via the famous UK Bubble Act of 1720 was a regulatory failure: see LCB Gower, 'Some Contrasts between British and American Corporation Law' (1956) 69 *Harvard Law Review* 1369, 1370. US corporate law, by way of contrast, derived from royal chartered corporations: see Hill (n 87) 541–44.

[90] See TW Guinnane, R Harris and NR Lamoreaux, 'Contractual Freedom and Corporate Governance in Britain in the Late Nineteenth and Early Twentieth Centuries' (2017) 91 *Business History Review* 227, 231.

made the best of the legal tools at hand. They used contract law to operate as large partnerships, but they also employed the trust concept as a means of holding property.[91] In both the US and the UK, directors and officers were regarded as fiduciaries and their corresponding duties provided a constraint on managerial discretion.[92]

Since Jensen and Meckling's agency theory of the corporation rose to prominence, some US scholars have also sought to deconstruct trusts[93] and fiduciary duties[94] into mere contracts. However, these reductionist attempts mischaracterise aspects of both trust law and fiduciary duties, undermining their rich and complex historical foundations.[95] The conflation of contract and fiduciary duties, for example, overlooks their 'profound dissimilarity' in terms of origin and scope.[96] Whereas contract law is a common law doctrine, fiduciary duties and trust law originated in equity.[97] Whereas contract law is firmly based on the parties' intention, fiduciary obligation often subverts the parties' intention.[98] Furthermore, some aspects of trust law, such as a prohibition on exculpatory provisions in trust instruments, are incompatible with contractual principles.[99]

Agency theory places the corporation firmly in the private realm, yet it is by no means obvious that it belongs there for all purposes and at all times. Berle and Means in their seminal 1932 text, *The Modern Corporation and Private Property*, viewed the public corporation as a deeply ambiguous entity, straddling both public and private law.[100]

This public-private divide created ongoing tension in corporate law history and practice,[101] as conceptions of the corporation shifted between these

[91] See LCB Gower, 'The English Private Company' (1953) 18 *Law and Contemporary Problems* 535, 535. On the importance of the trust concept for deed of settlement companies, see J Morley, 'The Common Law Corporation: The Power of the Trust in Anglo-American Business History' (2016) 116 *Columbia Law Review* 2145, 2157–59, 2161.

[92] Gower (n 89) 1383.

[93] See, eg, JH Langbein, 'The Contractarian Basis of the Law of Trusts' (1995) 105 *Yale Law Journal* 625. Although Langbein states that it is 'not my wish to fold the law of trusts into the law of contracts' at 671, his claim that '[t]rusts are contracts' at 627 arguably does precisely that. It has, therefore, been said that Langbein 'kick-started the obligational approach to trusts': MW Lau, *The Economic Structure of Trusts: Towards a Property-based Approach* (OUP, 2011) 21 fn 1.

[94] See FH Easterbrook and DR Fischel, 'Corporate Control Transactions' (1982) 91 *Yale Law Journal* 698, 702; FH Easterbrook and DR Fischel, 'Contract and Fiduciary Duty' (1993) 36 *The Journal of Law and Economics* 425.

[95] See, eg, DA DeMott, 'Beyond Metaphor: An Analysis of Fiduciary Obligation' (1988) *Duke Law Journal* 879, 923–24. See also at 889 fn 45.

[96] ibid 888.

[97] ibid 881–82 fn 10, stating that '[f]ew areas of the law are as distinctively equitable in character as fiduciary obligation'.

[98] ibid 887.

[99] ibid 923.

[100] See AA Berle and GC Means, *The Modern Corporation & Private Property*, 2nd edn (Routledge, 2017).

[101] See generally WT Allen, 'Our Schizophrenic Conception of the Business Corporation' (1992) 14 *Cardozo Law Review* 261.

'different visions of corporatism'.[102] Yet, various other theories have viewed the corporation through a more public lens. According to some of these theories, the corporation is an entity, akin to a political body.[103] Other contemporary theories of the firm have criticised the common use of human metaphors and personification to describe the corporation, while stressing its unity and autonomy as a distinctive legal person.[104]

Corporate history highlights this public-private duality. The early period of special charters, for example, combined public and private goals.[105] Yet, over time, a schism developed between some corporations, such as municipal corporations, which were treated as public bodies, in contrast to business corporations, which tended to be classified as private entities. Nonetheless, Berle and Means were arguably correct in their view that public corporations encompass elements of both. Eisenberg captures this duality in his statement that '[c]orporation law is private law, but the public has an interest in it'.[106] This duality is also evident in the current academic debate about corporate purpose, which, it has been argued, can include both the idea of private ordering in an individual corporation and a broader notion about the role of public corporations generally vis-à-vis society.[107]

In the quest to position the corporation in the purely private realm, Jensen and Meckling's view of agency ignored, and failed to correspond with, legal theory. Specifically, Jensen and Meckling interpreted agency as a purely economic concept and thereby jettisoned fiduciary law from its ambit. Furthermore, their treatment of corporate managers and directors as agents *of the shareholders* does not accord with modern legal theory or practice in common law jurisdictions. A central feature of the law of agency is that the agent is subject to the ongoing control of the principal,[108] and this concept of agency accords with Friedman's view that corporate managers, as agents, must comply with the shareholders' wishes. Yet, this approach is not consistent with modern UK or US corporate law. Although during the nineteenth century, UK courts accepted that shareholders had ultimate control and could therefore override decisions of the board of directors,[109]

[102] WW Bratton and ML Wachter, 'Shareholder Primacy's Corporatist Origins: Adolf Berle and *The Modern Corporation*' (2008) 34 *The Journal of Corporation Law* 99, 124.

[103] See generally J Hill, 'Visions and Revisions of the Shareholder' (2000) 48 *The American Journal of Comparative Law* 39, 51–57.

[104] See, eg, M Dan-Cohen, *Rights, Persons, and Organizations: A Legal Theory for Bureaucratic Society*, 2nd edn (New Orleans, Quid Pro, LLC, 2016); Stewart (n 37).

[105] Mark (n 23) 68–69; Hill (n 103) 51–52.

[106] MA Eisenberg, 'New Modes of Discourse in the Corporate Law Literature' (1984) 52 *George Washington Law Review* 582, 588.

[107] See, eg, DS Lund and E Pollman, 'Corporate Purpose' in JN Gordon and WG Ringe (eds), *The Oxford Handbook of Corporate Law and Governance*, 2nd edn (OUP, forthcoming); C Mayer, 'What is Wrong with Corporate Law? The Purpose of Law and the Law of Purpose' (2022) *Annual Review of Law and Science* 283.

[108] See, eg, American Law Institute, *Restatement (Third) of Agency* (2006) § 1.01.

[109] See, eg, *Isle of Wight Railway Co v Tahourdin* (1883) 25 Ch D 320.

by the early twentieth century, this approach was decisively rejected by the judiciary.[110] The modern UK approach is that a company's directors are not the agents of the shareholders, and that the latter have no legal right to give directions or override board decisions, absent an explicit provision in the company's constitution.[111] In the US context, the formidable protection given to board decisions by the business judgement rule, combined with the precatory nature of many shareholder resolutions, provides further evidence that the relationship between shareholders and directors does not satisfy the legal test for agency. US rules relating to charter alteration and shareholder voting suggest that the relationship between directors and shareholders under traditional US corporate law is not a principal-agent relationship – rather, directors act as 'gatekeepers',[112] and shareholders occupy the role of 'supplicants'.[113]

One problem with agency theory's contractual rhetoric and image of directors as agents of the shareholders is that it conceals both corporate power and managerial power. The private focus of agency theory, for example, masks the fact that many multinational corporations now rival nation states in terms of revenue and influence.[114] Also, by employing the concept of contract as a 'vehicle for voluntary exchange',[115] agency theory introduced an assumption of equality of bargaining power between various stakeholders. No legal doctrine captures the ideal of decisional autonomy and entrepreneurial freedom as effectively as contract law.[116] This theoretical lens, together with the concept of private ordering, minimised the perception of managerial power and disguised management's positional conflict of interest (even as the theory presented itself as an antidote to rampant managerial conflicts of interest).[117] These features of agency theory also had a legitimising effect, suggesting that shareholders,

[110] *Automatic Self Cleansing Filter Syndicate Co Ltd v Cuninghame* [1906] 2 Ch 34, 45–46 (Cozens-Hardy LJ); Hill (n 103) 42–44, 48.

[111] It appears, however, that this was commonly the case in the UK: see PL Davies and S Worthington, *Gower: Principles of Modern Company Law*, 11th edn (Sweet and Maxwell, 2021) 360 [14-7]–[14-8]. Shareholders also had ultimate control over the allocation of power in UK companies through their ability to alter the companies' articles of association: at [3-31]–[3-32].

[112] See SM Bainbridge, '*UNOCAL* at 20: Director Primacy in Corporate Takeovers' (2006) 31 *Delaware Journal of Corporate Law* 769, 771.

[113] See, eg, *Continental Securities Co v Belmont* 99 NE 138 (1912) 141, stating that any action by shareholders is 'necessarily in the form of an assent, request, or recommendation'.

[114] See Babic, Heemskerk and Fichtner (n 11).

[115] Jensen and Meckling (n 14) 310, citing AA Alchian and H Demsetz, 'Production, Information Costs, and Economic Organization' (1972) 62 *The American Economic Review* 777 for this point.

[116] See EB Rock and Michael L Wachter, 'Islands of Conscious Power: Law, Norms, and the Self-Governing Corporation' (2001) 149 *University of Pennsylvania Law Review* 1619, 1628, describing the nexus of contracts as a 'powerful metaphor' in this regard.

[117] See MA Eisenberg, 'The Structure of Corporation Law' (1989) 89 *Columbia Law Review* 1461, 1471–72; Rubin (n 13) 350–51.

and private ordering by shareholders, could provide an effective constraint on corporate managers.[118]

Jensen and Meckling's agency theory placed considerable faith in the ability of the market to operate as a regulatory substitute.[119] Yet, doubts have also grown over time about the effectiveness of the market as a managerial constraint.[120] In the aftermath of the global financial crisis, the UK Turner Review stated that the crisis challenged a central assumption concerning the market's efficiency, rationality and ability to self-regulate that had previously underpinned financial law.[121] If the agency theory of the firm encompasses an assumption that there are clear costs to over-regulation, the global financial crisis showed that the opposite is also true and there are also serious 'costs to under-regulation'.[122]

3.4. GROWING DISSONANCE BETWEEN THE CONTRACTUAL THEORY OF THE FIRM AND CONTEMPORARY CORPORATE GOVERNANCE DEVELOPMENTS

> '**Geronte**: It seems to me you are locating them wrongly: the heart is on the left and the liver is on the right.
>
> **Sganarelle**: Yes, in the old days that was so, but we have changed all that, and we now practise medicine by a completely new method.'
>
> Molière[123]

In his 1937 article on 'The Nature of the Firm',[124] Ronald Coase accepted that one of the key questions to be asked in relation to economic assumptions is '[d]o they correspond with the real world?'.[125] Over the last few decades, many of the assumptions underpinning the agency theory of the corporation have acquired

[118] GE Frug, 'The Ideology of Bureaucracy in American Law' (1984) 97 *Harvard Law Review* 1276, 1305. *cf* political theories of the corporation that treat the corporate power as legitimate only to the extent that it aligns with purposes that society accepts as legitimate: see Claassen (n 39) 2–3.

[119] See Buxbaum (n 12) 516, arguing that agency theory focuses too much on the effect of markets on firms and insufficiently on the effect of large enterprises on social institutions, including markets.

[120] See, eg, WW Bratton and SM Sepe, 'Corporate Law and the Myth of Efficient Market Control' (2020) 105 *Cornell Law Review* 675; Barzuza (n 44) 134.

[121] Financial Services Authority, *The Turner Review: A Regulatory Response to the Global Banking Crisis* (March 2009) 39 ff.

[122] JC Coffee, 'Financial Crises 101: What Can We Learn from Scandals and Meltdowns – from Enron to Subprime?' in RP Austin (ed), *The Credit Crunch and the Law* (Sydney, The Ron Parsons Centre of Commercial, Corporate and Taxation Law, 2008) 37.

[123] Molière, *Le Médecin Malgré Lui*, Act II.

[124] See Coase (n 24).

[125] ibid 386, quoting J Robinson, *Economics is a Serious Subject: The Apologia of an Economist to the Mathematician, the Scientist and the Plain Man* (Heffer & Sons, 1932) 12.

the status of axiomatic and unassailable truths, yet they fit uncomfortably with a variety of recent corporate governance developments.[126]

These developments suggest that there is now far greater attention paid to the role of the corporation in society and to issues of corporate accountability. The next section considers developments in the following areas – the relationship between corporate managers and shareholders and private ordering; shareholder activism and ESG; executive compensation; and corporate criminal liability.

3.4.1. Contemporary Developments Concerning the Relationship between Corporate Managers and Shareholders and Private Ordering

Contemporary developments concerning the relationship between corporate managers and shareholders provide an uneasy fit with Jensen and Meckling's paradigmatic agency relationship, which assumes that corporate managers must comply with the shareholders' wishes. As noted previously, this presumed relationship does not satisfy the legal test for agency. Nonetheless, even if it did, governance patterns in some contemporary corporations, such as start-ups, deviate substantially from this blueprint.

Jensen and Meckling's theory envisaged a corporate world in which outside shareholders have only a vertical agency relationship with corporate managers.[127] Yet, as Pollman has demonstrated, the governance structure of start-ups is typically at odds with this paradigm. Start-ups include not only vertical tensions between shareholders and managers, but also major horizontal conflicts between investors with divergent interests.[128] Also, whereas Jensen and Meckling's paradigm is relatively static, start-up governance structures are dynamic; they evolve over time and encompass overlapping and shifting roles for participants.[129] Furthermore, although fissures can undoubtedly develop, the relationship between various start-up participants is often highly collaborative. Rather than conforming to a fixed vertical relationship, the interactions between venture capitalists and start-up entrepreneurs are more complex, exhibiting partnership-like qualities of 'give-and-take'[130] and 'shared decision-making power'.[131]

[126] See DN McCloskey, *The Rhetoric of Economics*, 2nd edn (University of Wisconsin Press, 1998) 23–28, discussing how some economic 'truths', such as the law of demand, rest on rhetorical, rather than purely scientific, foundations.

[127] E Pollman, 'Startup Governance' (2019) 168 *University of Pennsylvania Law Review* 155, 177.

[128] ibid 178; RP Bartlett, 'Venture Capital, Agency Costs, and the False Dichotomy of the Corporation' (2006) 54 *University of California Law Review* 37, 61–64.

[129] Pollman (n 127) 160.

[130] DG Smith, 'Venture Capital Contracting in the Information Age' (1998) 2 *Journal of Small and Emerging Business Law* 133, 139.

[131] JE Fisch and SM Sepe, 'Shareholder Collaboration' (2020) 98 *Texas Law Review* 863, 874.

Nor is this pattern necessarily restricted to start-ups. As Fisch and Sepe show, such collaboration is also increasingly evident in modern public companies with high levels of institutional investor shareholding.[132] Two other assumptions in Jensen and Meckling's agency paradigm fail to reflect contemporary corporate governance developments. The first is that shareholders have homogenous interests.[133] The second is that directors and executives constitute a unified managerial group,[134] an assumption that no longer holds true since the rise of independent directors[135] as a check on managerial shortcomings or overconfidence.[136]

As noted previously, agency theory also suggests that private ordering by shareholders is an effective constraint on corporate managers and therefore has a legitimising impact.[137] Yet the concept of private ordering, which is so deeply embedded in US corporate law, itself contains some potentially flawed assumptions that fail to correspond with the real world. For example, the widely accepted view that private ordering is an efficient corporate governance tailoring mechanism (and that the market provides incentives for corporations voluntarily to adopt pro-shareholder governance provisions) has been challenged in recent times.[138] Another matter of concern is that some organisations, such as VC-funded start-ups, commonly effect private ordering not via changes to the charter or bylaws, but rather by means of opaque shareholder agreements[139] – a development that has been described as 'stealth governance'.[140] Even in the context of alternative entities, such as LLCs, commentators have suggested that the goal of private ordering is often not to promote economic efficiency but instead as a means of legitimising opportunism.[141]

In a recent Delaware Court of Chancery decision, *New Enterprise Associates 14 v Rich*,[142] Vice-Chancellor Laster rejected an assumption,

[132] ibid.

[133] Pollman (n 127) 177.

[134] ibid.

[135] See JN Gordon, 'The Rise of Independent Directors in the United States, 1950–2005: Of Shareholder Value and Stock Market Prices' (2007) 59 *Stanford Law Review* 1465.

[136] See Hill and Nili (n 12).

[137] Frug (n 118) 1305. *cf* political theories of the corporation that treat the corporate power as legitimate only to the extent that it aligns with purposes that society accepts as legitimate. See Claassen (n 39) 2, 3.

[138] Barzuza, 'Inefficient Tailoring' (n 44) 132–34; JE Fisch, 'Stealth Governance: Shareholder Agreements and Private Ordering' (2021) 99 *Washington University Law Review* 913.

[139] See Fisch (n 138).

[140] ibid.

[141] P Molk, 'How Do LLC Owners Contract Around Default Statutory Protections' (2017) 42 *The Journal of Corporation Law* 503; LE Strine, Jr and JT Laster, 'The Siren Song of Unlimited Contractual Freedom' in RW Hillman and MJ Loewenstein (eds), *Research Handbook on Partnerships, LLCs and Alternative Forms of Business Organizations* (Cheltenham, Edward Elgar Publishing, 2015) 11.

[142] See *New Enterprise Associates 14 v Rich* CA No 2022-0406-JTL (Del Ch 2 May 2023).

accepted in many prior Delaware cases,[143] that corporations and LLCs are purely 'creatures of contract'.[144] Although acknowledging that contract law has an important role to play, he stated that:

> [j]ural entities are thus never wholly creatures of contract. Nor are they a nexus of contracts. However attractive that metaphor might be for economic modelling, entities are reified constructs.[145]

The approach adopted in *New Enterprise Associates 14 v Rich* introduces the state, together with a public policy vision, into the corporate law arena.[146] It also provides limits on the scope of private ordering and reasserts the significance of fiduciary duty law in relation to corporations and even LLCs, which have often been regarded as quintessentially contractual.[147]

Traditional assumptions concerning the power of private ordering are also associated with the idea that US corporate law is highly protective of shareholder rights, a narrative embedded in La Porta et al's famous 'law matters' hypothesis.[148] In fact, however, US shareholders possess far fewer corporate governance rights than shareholders in other common law jurisdictions, where such rights are often guaranteed by mandatory laws.[149] The 2006 Paulson Committee noted that '[o]verall, shareholders of US companies have fewer rights … than do their foreign competitors'.[150]

An important aspect of private ordering is 'who is doing the ordering?' and this can differ across time and jurisdictions. In contrast to the United Kingdom, where the 'free contracting' aspect of the articles of association was viewed as one of the cornerstones of shareholder rights,[151] private ordering in the US was traditionally the domain of the board of directors. Nonetheless, in recent times, this has shifted, with institutional investors using private ordering to adopt bylaw amendments on a company-by-company basis. These bylaw amendments have resulted in the transplantation in some US corporations

[143] M Manesh, 'Creatures of Contract: A Half-Truth About LLCs' (2018) 42 *Delaware Journal of Corporate Law* 391, 458–66.

[144] *New Enterprise* (n 142) fn 159.

[145] ibid.

[146] ibid. See also Vice Chancellor Laster's decision in *Obeid v Hogan*, 2016 WL3356851 (Del Ch 2016), fn 2, where he states that 'an LLC agreement is not an exclusively private contract among its members precisely because the LLC has powers that only the State of Delaware can confer'.

[147] ibid.

[148] R La Porta, F Lopez-de-Silanes, A Shleifer and RW Vishny, 'Law and Finance' (1998) 106 *Journal of Political Economy* 1113; R La Porta, F Lopez-de-Silanes and A Shleifer, 'Corporate Ownership around the World' (1999) 54 *The Journal of Finance* 471.

[149] See generally JG Hill, 'Subverting Shareholder Rights: Lessons from News Corp's Migration to Delaware' (2010) 63 *Vanderbilt Law Review* 1.

[150] Committee on Capital Markets Regulation, *Interim Report* (30 November 2006) 16.

[151] RC Nolan, 'Shareholder Rights in Britain' (2006) 7 *European Business Organization Law Review* 549, 554–56.

of certain pro-shareholder protections that are mandatory in other common law jurisdictions.[152] Whereas the United States was traditionally viewed as the dominant exporter of corporate law,[153] this development has rendered it a corporate importer. The development also challenges the assumption that global corporate law transmission is in one direction only.[154] Rather than driving global convergence, as predicted by La Porta et al and others,[155] Cabrelli and Siems have argued that the US is increasingly an 'outlier' in international corporate governance.[156]

Although agency theory assumes that the board's role is to carry out the wishes of shareholders, the recent appropriation of private ordering by shareholders has led many US boards of directors to engage in a form of 'private ordering combat',[157] where their aim is to subvert, rather than implement, investors' wishes. Boards have, for example, used their own bylaw amendment powers to reduce the efficacy of shareholder proposals, and to exert control over the forums in which investors can bring litigation.[158] These developments rest heavily on the assumption that bylaw provisions are contractually binding on shareholders, even though the provisions were drafted and adopted by the board of directors,[159] leading one scholar to ask 'whose law is it?'.[160]

3.4.2. Shareholder Activism and ESG

Problem-framing is all-important in corporate law and theory.[161] Corporate financial performance, which takes centre stage as the key problem to be solved under the agency theory of the firm, is undoubtedly a legitimate concern. It was viewed as such in the 1970s when financial economists sought an antidote to

[152] JG Hill, 'Transnational Migration of Laws and Norms in Corporate Governance: Fiduciary Duties and Corporate Codes' in S Davis, T Kuntz and G Shaffer (eds), *Transnational Fiduciary Law* (Cambridge, Cambridge University Press, 2023) 227.

[153] D Cabrelli and M Siems, 'Convergence, Legal Origins, and Transplants in Comparative Corporate Law: A Case-Based and Quantitative Analysis' (2015) 63 *The American Journal of Comparative Law* 109, 127.

[154] Hill (n 152) 227.

[155] See H Hansmann and R Kraakman, 'The End of History for Corporate Law' (2001) 89 *Georgetown Law Journal* 439, 468.

[156] Cabrelli and Siems (n 153) 152.

[157] See Hill (n 87).

[158] See, eg, *Boilermakers Local 154 Retirement Fund v Chevron Co* 73 A 3d 934 (2013). See also *Salzberg v Sciabacucchi* 227 A 3d 102 (Del 2020); A Frankel, 'Dela. Supreme Court: Companies Can Pick Forum for Shareholders' Section 11 Claims', *Reuters* (London, 18 March 2020).

[159] Fisch (n 138) 921–23.

[160] See JD Cox, 'Whose Law Is It? Battling over Turf in Shareholder Litigation' in JG Hill and RS Thomas (eds), *Research Handbook on Shareholder Power* (Cheltenham, Edward Elgar Publishing, 2015).

[161] See generally T Bowley and JG Hill, 'Stewardship Codes, ESG Activism and Transnational Ordering' in T Kuntz (ed), *Research Handbook on Environmental, Social, and Corporate Governance* (Cheltenham, Edward Elgar Publishing, 2024).

the problem of managerial opportunism, entrenchment and empire-building.[162] Shareholding was traditionally assumed to be a voluntary act, according with Stout's claim that 'investors are not forced to purchase shares in public corporations at gunpoint'.[163] Today, however, members of the public in many jurisdictions are, in fact, involuntary investors via mandatory retirement saving schemes.[164] In an environment of 'forced capitalism',[165] corporate financial performance matters more than ever.

However, the manager-shareholder agency problem is not the only problem to which corporate law needs to respond. In many jurisdictions, the parties to agency problems concerning financial performance will be different. In parts of Asia and Europe, for example, where concentrated ownership structures are the norm,[166] and institutional investment is minimal, the key agency problem will be between controlling and minority shareholders (or 'principal-principal' agency problems).[167] Historically, similar problems existed in US public corporations between wealthy elites with large shareholdings on the one hand, and small shareholders and corporate managers, on the other.[168]

In recent years, financial scandals, such as the Wells Fargo fraudulent accounts scandal, emphasised that there are multiple substantive problems in corporate law.[169] These include the danger of defective corporate cultures[170] that can result in negative externalities.[171] The scandals also demonstrated that classic alignment of interest techniques under agency theory, such as performance-based pay, can exacerbate negative externalities, by creating perverse incentives for corporate misconduct that can harm various stakeholders (including shareholders) and society as a whole.[172] These developments show

[162] See MC Jensen, 'Agency Costs of Free Cash Flow, Corporate Finance, and Takeovers' (1986) 76 *The American Economic Review* 323, 323.

[163] LA Stout, 'The Mythical Benefits of Shareholder Control' (2007) 93 *Virginia Law Review* 789, 801.

[164] See LE Strine, 'Toward Common Sense and Common Ground? Reflections on the Shared Interests of Managers and Labor in a More Rational System of Corporate Governance' (2007) 33 *The Journal of Corporation Law* 1, 4.

[165] ibid.

[166] OECD, *OECD Corporate Governance Factbook 2023* (2023) 17 ff.

[167] See G Sánchez-Marin et al, 'Excess Executive Compensation and Corporate Governance in the United Kingdom and Spain: A Comparative Analysis' (2022) 43 *Managerial and Decision Economics* 2817, 2818.

[168] At least before corporate managers became powerful and prosperous. See generally SC Haan, 'The Pathology of Passivity: Shareholder Passivity as a False Narrative in Law' in S Omarova, A Andhov and C Hill (eds), *Hidden Fallacies in Corporate and Financial Regulation: Reframing the Mainstream Narratives* (Oxford, Hart Publishing, forthcoming).

[169] JG Hill, 'Corporations, Directors' Duties, and the Public/Private Divide' in AB Laby and JH Russell (eds), *Fiduciary Obligations in Business* (Cambridge, Cambridge University Press, 2021).

[170] ibid 292–93.

[171] Buxbaum (n 12) 517–18.

[172] See generally JG Hill, 'Deconstructing Sunbeam – Contemporary Issues in Corporate Governance' (1999) 67 *University of Cincinnati Law Review* 1099, 1120–25.

that an undiluted version of the nexus of contracts model of the corporation can be normatively unappealing.

There is also increasing recognition of a new, and unprecedented set of risks concerning the environment, particularly in relation to climate change, which have helped ESG go 'mainstream'.[173] These risks are now treated as key financial risks for corporations; BlackRock, for instance, has estimated that climate change poses a US $8.2 billion risk to its portfolio.[174]

Issues involving negative externalities, including environmental harm, go to the heart of corporate legitimacy.[175] Growing concern about these issues has led to greater regulatory focus on issues of corporate culture,[176] negative externalities and misconduct risk, in addition to a more public conception of the corporation. These developments are manifested at an aspirational level and in 'on the ground' ESG shareholder activism. At the aspirational level, shareholder stewardship codes, which have proliferated around the world since their introduction in the UK in 2010 following the global financial crisis,[177] now pay greater attention to sustainability and ESG issues.[178] The 2020 version of the UK Stewardship Code exemplifies this trend, leading one commentator to ask whether, in the space of a decade, the UK Stewardship Code has gone from 'saving the company to saving the planet'.[179]

Activist campaigns, such as that at ExxonMobil in 2020, reflect a dramatic increase in 'on the ground' activism by institutional investors[180] in areas like climate change risk, board and workforce diversity, and human capital management.[181] There has been escalating institutional support for shareholder resolutions involving social and environmental issues.[182] For example, annual 'say on climate' votes have now become a global phenomenon. ESG pressures are, moreover, being generated at an international level,[183] rather

[173] See A Edmans, 'The End of ESG' (2023) 52 *Financial Management* 3, 4, describing 'ESG's evolution from a niche subfield into a mainstream practice'.

[174] See F Jaeger, 'Say No to Climate Change, Say Yes to "Say on Climate"' (Oxford Business Law Blog, 13 July 2021).

[175] See, eg, Langevoort (n 10).

[176] ibid.

[177] Financial Reporting Council, *The UK Stewardship Code* (July 2010).

[178] See D Katelouzou and A Klettner, 'Sustainable Finance and Stewardship: Unlocking Stewardship's Sustainability Potential' in D Katelouzou and DW Puchniak (eds), *Global Shareholder Stewardship* (Cambridge, Cambridge University Press, 2022).

[179] P Davies, 'The UK Stewardship Code 2010–2020: From Saving the Company to Saving the Planet?' in D Katelouzou and DW Puchniak (eds), *Global Shareholder Stewardship* (Cambridge, Cambridge University Press, 2022).

[180] See generally Bowley and Hill (n 161).

[181] DM Silk, SV Niles and CXW Lu, 'ESG and Sustainability: Key Considerations for 2021' (Harvard Law School Forum on Corporate Governance, 30 January 2021).

[182] ibid.

[183] T Bowley and JG Hill, 'The Global ESG Stewardship Ecosystem' (2024) 25 *European Business Organization Law Review* 229; M Pargendler, 'The Rise of International Corporate Law' (2021) 98 *Washington University Law Review* 1765.

than through horizontal adoption of national laws, which La Porta et al assumed would constitute the main method of legal transplantation.[184]

Reductionist theories that portray the corporation as fictitious have led to a vigorous debate between shareholder-centred and stakeholder-centred theories.[185] There is no doubt that 'stakeholderism' is on the rise. For example, in his 2018 Annual Letter to CEOs, Larry Fink of BlackRock stated that companies 'must benefit all of their stakeholders, including shareholders, employees, customers, and the communities in which they operate',[186] and his 2022 letter continued to extol the benefits of 'stakeholder capitalism'.[187] In 2019, the US Business Roundtable announced that it, too, would embrace stakeholderism.[188] However, the binary approach, in which the interests of shareholders and stakeholders is treated as irreconcilable, is ultimately unhelpful and disguises the fact that such opposition can disappear when a longer term view of the corporation and corporate performance is taken.[189]

The British Academy's *Future of the Corporation* project and the concept of corporate purpose are premised on a more holistic depiction of the corporation than stakeholderism. They also envisage a distinctly public role for the corporation, together with a concern about negative externalities. For example, the mantra of the *Future of the Corporation* project is that 'the purpose of business is creating profitable solutions for problems of people and planet, and not profiting from creating problems'.[190] Consistent with this approach, the 2018 UK Corporate Governance Code now includes references to corporate culture and the responsibility of public companies, not only to create value for shareholders, but also to contribute to 'wider society'.[191]

None of these developments sits comfortably with traditional assumptions that underpin the agency theory of the firm. This is indicated by the recent attempt by Hart and Zingales to argue that these developments reflect a paradigm shift from a shareholder value maximisation norm to one of shareholder welfare maximisation.[192] In their reinterpretation of agency theory, Hart and Zingales have, to be sure, tweaked the agency theory, but they have tweaked it only in terms of shareholder preferences, not in terms of the corporation as a social actor.

[184] La Porta, Lopez-de-Silanes and Shleifer (n 148).

[185] KJ Hopt, 'Corporate Purpose and Stakeholder Value – Historical, Economic and Comparative Law Remarks on the Current Debate, Legislative Options and Enforcement Problems', European Corporate Governance Institute – Law Working Paper No 690, 2023 (16 March 2023).

[186] Letter from Larry Fink to CEOs (January 2018).

[187] Letter from Larry Fink to CEOs (January 2022).

[188] Business Roundtable, 'Business Roundtable Redefines the Purpose of a Corporation to Promote "An Economy That Serves All Americans"' (19 August 2019).

[189] Hill (n 69) 289, 292.

[190] The British Academy, *Policy & Practice for Purposeful Business* (September 2021) 6.

[191] Financial Reporting Council, *The UK Corporate Governance Code* (July 2018) 4.

[192] Hart and Zingales (n 67).

3.4.3. Executive Compensation

Jensen and Meckling's 1976 article did not discuss the full implications of theory for specific areas of corporation governance, including executive compensation.[193] Yet the article provided the basis for such later elaboration of the original thesis. This elaboration would have significant implications for the development of executive pay.

In 1990, Jensen and Murphy adopted an agency theory of the firm to transform executive pay in their famous article, 'CEO Incentives – It's Not How Much You Pay, But How'.[194] The article re-examined executive pay, which had traditionally been treated as a fiduciary duty issue,[195] exclusively through the lens of misaligned interests between managers and shareholders. They presented the use of incentives in executive compensation contracts as a corporate governance solution to the agency problem of corporate underperformance and paved the way for the era of performance-based pay.[196]

Performance-based pay functioned as a self-regulatory device to deal with the problem of corporate underperformance, offering the promise of higher compensation for superior corporate performance and reduced pay for sub-standard performance.[197] Within this economic framework, quantum of pay was rendered irrelevant, provided that the compensated performance increased shareholder wealth.[198]

The 1990s was a decade of spiralling executive pay,[199] fuelled by the widespread adoption of performance-based pay in combination with huge stock option awards.[200] It is worth noting that, although stock option awards declined over the subsequent decade,[201] they are by no means a thing of the past. In 2018, for example, Tesla CEO, Elon Musk, received a performance-based stock option

[193] See generally Cheffins (n 55), arguing that there is a wide gap between what Jensen and Meckling actually said and what they were perceived to have said in their 1976 article.

[194] MC Jensen and KJ Murphy, 'CEO Incentives – It's Not How Much You Pay, But How' (1990) 68 *Harvard Business Review* 138.

[195] CM Yablon, 'Bonus Questions – Executive Compensation in the Era of Pay for Performance' (1999) 75 *Notre Dame Law Review* 271, 279–80.

[196] ibid. See also F Dobbin and D Zorn, 'Corporate Malfeasance and the Myth of Shareholder Value' in Diane E Davis (ed), *Political Power and Social Theory*, vol 17 (Leeds, Emerald Group Publishing Ltd, 2005).

[197] See Jensen and Murphy (n 194); C Frydman and RE Saks, 'Executive Compensation: A New View from a Long-Term Perspective, 1936–2005' (2010) 23 *The Review of Financial Studies* 2099.

[198] See MJ Loewenstein, 'Reflections on Executive Compensation and a Modest Proposal for (Further) Reform' (1996) 50 *SMU Law Review* 201, 206–07.

[199] See, eg, A Edmans, X Gabaix and D Jenter, 'Executive Compensation: A Survey of Theory and Evidence' in BE Hermalin and MS Weisbach (eds), *The Economics of Corporate Governance* (Amsterdam, North-Holland, 2017), vol I, 388–95.

[200] See generally ibid 398–404.

[201] ibid.

grant that was potentially worth US $55 billion, the largest executive compensation deal in US history.[202]

The rapid escalation of executive pay led to an academic debate between two different schools of thought: optimal contracting and managerial power theory.[203] Optimal contracting scholars, relying on the agency theory of the firm, argued that executive compensation contracts operated as an efficient means of maximising net shareholder value of contracting costs and transactions costs, thereby aligning the interests of shareholders and managers. Managerial power scholars, on the other hand, claimed that this analysis was defective in disguising and failing to recognise a power imbalance that effectively allowed US executives to set their own pay.[204]

Further concerns about design and operation of executive pay contracts emerged following the Enron and WorldCom scandals at the turn of the century and the 2007–09 global financial crisis. The dual collapses of Enron and WorldCom (and several other companies around the world) showed that attempting to solve the problem of misaligned incentives between managers and shareholders could, when taken to extremes, create a different set of problems. Specifically, the scandals showed that high-powered incentive pay contracts could create perverse incentives to engage in misconduct, including earnings management, in order to meet profit targets.[205]

The global financial crisis brought a new set of problems into the mix, namely the danger that flawed executive compensation structures could create perverse incentives that encouraged short-termism, over-leveraging and excessive risk-taking.[206] The crisis also led to recognition that misalignment of interests between management and shareholders was not the only problem that the executive pay design needed to address. Equally important was the need to align the interests of management with the interests of society as a whole.[207]

Enron, WorldCom and the global financial crisis demonstrated that, although corporate financial success matters, an exclusive focus on wealth maximisation can create perverse incentives for corporate misconduct and negative

[202] J Feeley and S Carpenter, 'How Elon Musk Scored a $55 Billion Pay Package That's Now Under Fire' (*Bloomberg*, New York, 14 November 2022).

[203] JG Hill and RS Thomas, 'Introduction' in RS Thomas and JG Hill (eds), *Research Handbook on Executive Pay* (Cheltenham, Edward Elgar Publishing, 2012) 1–2.

[204] ibid.

[205] See generally R Barontini and JG Hill, 'Sustainability and Executive Compensation' in M Siri, K Alexander and M Gargantini (eds), *Handbook of EU Sustainable Finance: Regulation, Supervision and Governance* (Cambridge University Press, forthcoming); Dobbin and Zorn, 'Corporate Malfeasance' (n 196).

[206] See LA Bebchuk and H Spamann, 'Regulating Bankers' Pay' (2010) 98 *Georgetown Law Journal* 247, 255–68.

[207] See JG Hill, 'Regulating Executive Remuneration After the Global Financial Crisis: Common Law Perspectives' in RS Thomas and JG Hill (eds), *Research Handbook on Executive Pay* (Cheltenham, Edward Elgar Publishing, 2012) 233–34.

externalities and has sometimes 'dulled the senses' of institutions, boards of directors and managers to other kinds of risk.[208]

A burgeoning development in executive pay relates to a new set of risks, particularly those involving the environment and climate change. As noted previously, these risks constitute negative externalities that are now treated by investors and regulators as key long-term financial risks,[209] and, as a result, a growing number of listed firms include drivers related to sustainable performance in their executive remuneration packages.[210] However, at this point in time, ESG-linked pay tends to represent only a relatively small proportion of total executive pay packages,[211] and it is not surprising that there are conflicting studies as to its effectiveness as an antidote to short-term shareholder profit maximisation.[212]

3.4.4. Corporate Criminal Liability

> 'Corporations don't commit offences; people do.'
>
> E Bodenheimer[213]

Nowhere is the 'schizophrenic'[214] nature of the corporation in legal theory more evident than in the context of corporate crime. Modern developments in corporate criminal liability also sit uncomfortably with the individualism that underpins the agency theory of the firm.

The historical notion of the corporation as a *persona ficta* recognised the corporation as an artificial legal person, but one that was not identical to a human being.[215] As Watson notes, this reasoning provided certain benefits to early ecclesiastical bodies or '*universitas*'.[216] Although these bodies were regarded as separate legal entities for certain purposes, such as holding property, they were also protected from excommunication and liability for some

[208] Australian Prudential Regulation Authority, *Prudential Inquiry into the Commonwealth Bank of Australia* (April 2018) 3.

[209] See Jaeger (n 174).

[210] See, eg, S Gadinis and A Miazad, 'Corporate Law and Social Risk' (2020) 73 *Vanderbilt Law Review* 1401, 1407, 1419, and the examples cited therein.

[211] See C Flammer, B Hong and D Minor, 'Corporate Governance and the Rise of Integrating Corporate Social Responsibility Criteria in Executive Compensation: Effectiveness and Implications for Firm Outcomes' (2019) 40 *Strategic Management Journal* 1097, 1101.

[212] ibid. *cf* K Maas, 'Do Corporate Social Performance Targets in Executive Compensation Contribute to Corporate Social Performance?' (2018) 148 *Journal of Business Ethics* 573.

[213] E Bodenheimer, *Philosophy of Responsibility* (Littleton, Colorado, FB Rothman, 1980) 117.

[214] See Allen (n 101).

[215] See N Lacey, 'Philosophical Foundations of the Common Law: Social Not Metaphysical' in J Horder (ed), *Oxford Essays in Jurisprudence: Fourth Series* (Oxford, Oxford University Press, 2000) 25, noting that the history of debate about corporate liability has been riddled with 'analogies and disanalogies' between corporate persons and human beings.

[216] S Watson, *The Making of the Modern Company* (Oxford, Hart Publishing, 2022) 15.

types of wrongdoing on the basis that they were incapable of possessing a *mens rea*.[217] The notion that only natural, and not juridical, persons can be subject to criminal liability still operates in parts of continental Europe, on the basis that 'a legal entity cannot be blameworthy', although this assumption weakened in the late twentieth century.[218]

The reasoning underpinning aggregate theories of the corporation, including the agency theory as it is widely understood, provides even stronger support for focusing on human as opposed to organisational misconduct. According to these theories, corporate personhood is 'a matter of convenience rather than reality',[219] or a mere 'verbal symbol' or 'mathematical expression' to describe its human components.[220] Such models effectively treat the corporation as fictitious, leading to the conclusion that there is 'no such thing as the company'.[221]

Paradoxically, this method of 'privatising' the corporation has sometimes proven advantageous to corporations in the context of rights conferral. Indeed, US courts granted corporations rights before recognising the existence of corporate criminal liability.[222] For example, US Supreme Court case law has employed this reasoning to justify granting constitutional rights to the corporation,[223] on the basis that, as an assemblage of natural persons, it deserves the same protection as its human members.[224] It has also been argued that treating the corporation as an aggregation of individuals, rather than an organisation in its own right, has the effect of humanising, and inviting greater empathy for, the corporation.[225]

The assumption that the corporation is fictitious embedded in contractual theories, including agency theory, also has implications for accountability. These theories sit most comfortably with the view propounded almost a century

[217] See, eg, CD Stone, 'The Place of Enterprise Liability in the Control of Corporate Conduct' (1980) 90 *Yale Law Journal* 1, 3, 70.

[218] EB Diskant, 'Comparative Corporate Criminal Liability: Exploring the Uniquely American Doctrine through Comparative Criminal Procedure' (2008) 118 *Yale Law Journal* 126, 129.

[219] Easterbrook and Fischel (n 34) 1426.

[220] M Radin, 'The Endless Problem of Corporate Personality' (1932) 32 *Columbia Law Review* 643, 658.

[221] *Meridian Global Funds Management Asia Ltd v Securities Commission* [1995] 2 AC 500, [1995] 3 All ER 918, 923 (Lord Hoffmann for the Court).

[222] See generally MH Baer, 'Personhood, Procedure and the Endurance of Corporate Compliance' in E Pollman and RB Thompson, *Research Handbook on Corporate Purpose and Personhood* (Cheltenham, Edward Elgar Publishing, 2021).

[223] *First National Bank of Boston v Bellotti* 435 US 765 (1978) 794–95. See generally Baer (n 222) 335–38, discussing recent case law based on the US Supreme Court's contemporary 'decisive embrace of the aggregate theory': ibid 336.

[224] N Bowie, 'Corporate Personhood v. Corporate Statehood' (2019) 132 *Harvard Law Review* 2009, 2012, 2025.

[225] See S Tang et al, 'The Morality of Organization Versus Organized Members: Organizations Are Attributed More Control and Responsibility for Negative Outcomes Than Are Equivalent Members' (2020) 119 *Journal of Personality and Social Psychology* 901.

ago by Radin, who posited that all legal wrongs are committed by 'flesh and blood' persons,[226] and the goal of the law should be to identify those individuals and bring them to justice.[227]

However, this is not the way contemporary US criminal law has played out. In fact, for several decades prior to the global financial crisis, US prosecutors regularly targeted corporations, rather than senior managers, for liability.[228] In the aftermath of the crisis, Judge Jed Rakoff employed the rhetoric of methodological individualism[229] (albeit to highlight the lack of accountability for senior managers after the global financial crisis) when he criticised this trend in strong terms, describing it as 'technically and morally suspect'[230] because '[c]ompanies do not commit crimes; only their agents do'.[231] An extreme version of this position is to treat entity liability as encompassing 'fictitious offenses perpetrated by fictitious persons'.[232]

This deconstructionist approach is not consistent with contemporary criminal law in common law jurisdictions, such as the US, the UK and Australia, whose legal regimes now assume that corporations can be blameworthy and subject to criminal liability.[233] Entity criminal liability is an important modern legal device, which can enhance accountability in a range of situations, particularly where misconduct occurs due to a defective corporate culture.[234] Recognising the corporation as an entity[235] and an autonomous actor in society enables us to see corporations not only as rights holders, but also as subject to certain responsibilities vis-à-vis society.[236] Lacey argues, for instance, that the emergence of liability for corporate manslaughter in the UK during the twentieth century was emblematic of the ability of societal norms

[226] Radin (n 220) 663.

[227] ibid 661. *cf*, however, the institutional version of the nexus of contracts model of the corporation, where the firm exists 'as a single maximizing unit, not simply as an artifact of transactions among maximizing individuals': see Bratton (n 17) 1480.

[228] This trend was accompanied by the increasing use of deferred prosecution agreements and non-prosecution agreements: see generally JS Rakoff, 'The Financial Crisis: Why Have No High-Level Executives Been Prosecuted?' in RH Huang and N Calcina Howson (eds), *Enforcement of Corporate and Securities Law* (Cambridge, Cambridge University Press, 2017) 11–12.

[229] See B Fisse and J Braithwaite, 'The Allocation of Responsibility for Corporate Crime: Individualism, Collectivism and Accountability' (1988) 11 *Sydney Law Review* 468, 473–75.

[230] Rakoff (n 228) 12.

[231] ibid 11.

[232] Fisse and Braithwaite (n 229) 475.

[233] See generally Micheler (n 13) ch 5.3, noting, however, that the courts in various jurisdictions adopt different tests for when wrongful acts will be attributed to the corporate entity.

[234] See SW Buell, 'The Blaming Function of Entity Criminal Liability' (2006) 81 *Indiana Law Journal* 473, 477–78; SW Buell, 'The Responsibility Gap in Corporate Crime' (2018) 12 *Criminal Law and Philosophy* 471, 473.

[235] See, eg, S Watson, 'How the Company Became an Entity: A New Understanding of Corporate Law' (2015) *Journal of Business Law* 120.

[236] See PI Blumberg, 'The Corporate Entity in an Era of Multinational Corporations' (1990) 15 *Delaware Journal of Corporate Law* 283, 285; Wilson (n 37).

and expectations to affect legal interpretation and doctrine.[237] Entity criminal liability is likely to increase in an era of growing public concern about corporate power, such as that wielded by Big Tech companies, and negative externalities in relation to ESG and climate change.[238]

3.5. CONCLUSION

'I'm now a critic of where we got to.'
Michael Jensen[239]

This chapter argues that, although the economic model has provided valuable insights into the role of incentives within the corporation, its reductionist approach has ultimately provided a myopic, under-inclusive and insufficiently nuanced perspective. The theory, as it has been interpreted (and sometimes misinterpreted) over the ensuing decades, operates as a form of instrumental reasoning designed to address a particular problem, namely the danger of corporate managers preferring their own interests to those of shareholders. When framed as a comprehensive and all-encompassing theory, however, the relatively narrow lens of the agency model creates a form of tunnel vision that obscures other important problems in corporate law and is inconsistent with legal, historical and sociological understandings of the corporation.[240] Agency theory fails to recognise the complexity, distinctive features and diversity of organisations. And, by banishing the state, the theory ultimately fails to recognise 'the importance of intermediating institutions in a pluralist democracy'[241] and to provide a holistic picture of the relationship between government, corporations and individuals.[242]

The chapter argues that are multiple problems in corporate law and different problems may come to the forefront at different times and for different purposes, creating a tension between public and private law. Ultimately, when treated as an all-encompassing paradigm, the agency theory of the firm provides an overly simplified and impoverished depiction of the corporation, which sits uncomfortably with numerous contemporary corporate law and governance developments.

[237] See Lacey (n 215).

[238] See Claassen (n 39).

[239] Jensen was so quoted in J Cassidy, 'The Greed Cycle', *The New Yorker* (New York, 23 September 2002) 75.

[240] See generally Claassen (n 39); Rubin (n 13). See also EW Orts, *Business Persons: A Legal Theory of the Firm* (Oxford, Oxford University Press, 2013), 27–28, stating that agency theory 'flies in the face of a blizzard of perspectives from other disciplines, including law, which reveal and explain the social reality of firms'.

[241] Stewart (n 37) 371.

[242] ibid, 386–87; Buxbaum (n 12) 516, 519–20.

4

The Pathology of Passivity: Shareholder Passivity as a False Narrative in Corporate Law

SARAH C HAAN

4.1. INTRODUCTION

ARE PUBLIC COMPANY shareholders inherently or rationally *passive*? The idea of shareholder passivity gained wide traction after Adolf Berle Jr and Gardiner Means asserted it as fact in their 1932 book, *The Modern Corporation and Private Property*.[1] Decades later, the law and economics movement embraced shareholder passivity and refashioned it as 'rational apathy'. In this now-dominant view, shareholder passivity is taken for granted. It evidences the 'free rider problem' caused by the wide dispersion of stock and is explained by incentives operating on *homo economicus*. The refashioning transformed stockholder passivity from a problem into a *solution* to a problem. In Berle and Means' conception, shareholder passivity was irresponsible and blameworthy but also inevitable in light of the separation of ownership and control; in the law and economics view, it was a rational response by utility-maximising investors and, therefore, a good thing. After shareholder passivity was reimagined by the law and economics movement, it ceased to be a governance problem in need of a legal solution. Instead, corporate law could be narrowly refocused on reducing agency costs.

This chapter argues that, despite its significant influence on corporate law, the evolving 'Passivity Thesis' is deeply flawed, both normatively and descriptively. In both its New Deal-era formulation and its law and economics formulation, the Passivity Thesis located all of the responsibility for passivity in shareholders themselves without considering how corporate law shaped the costs and benefits of shareholders' participation in governance. As a result,

[1] See AA Berle and GC Means, *The Modern Corporation and Private Property* (New York, Macmillan, 1932).

the Passivity Thesis has long deflected attention away from consideration of how law and power shape the participation of shareholders in corporate governance.[2] In fact, there are many reasons to believe that shareholders would have behaved differently – ie, taken a more active role – if corporate law had created structures and mechanisms that made this possible.

In the first decades of the twentieth century, the proxy system and other aspects of corporate law evolved to discourage shareholders from participating meaningfully in shareholder governance. Until Berle and Means popularised the idea of shareholder passivity, the absence of shareholders from the corporate governance project was commonly described as 'absentee ownership', and it was presented as a system-wide problem, not an individual failing. The shift from viewing 'absentee ownership' as a flaw of the emerging corporate law regime, to viewing 'shareholder passivity' as a personal characteristic or choice – one manifesting the small shareholder's lack of suitability for governance – marked an important turning point in the struggle of business law experts to identify a path forward for modern corporate capitalism.

A surge of shareholder activism, organised in many cases as part of a movement for 'corporate democracy', emerged in the 1930s, 1940s and 1950s, only to be defeated by dynamics remaking corporate and securities law and the capital markets themselves. More recently, the rising pitch of shareholder activism, particularly around environmental, social and governance (ESG) matters, challenges the passive shareholder paradigm. Twenty-first-century shareholders are not behaving passively – even though they operate in a framework in which passivity has been reified. The validity of the 90-year-old Passivity Thesis is called into serious question by the emergence of influential shareholder activists who demand an active role in the governance of the public companies in which they invest. At the same time, the public's enthusiasm for active shareholder governance has created demand for innovation in corporate law and new participatory mechanisms.

By habituating a large segment of Americans to passive corporate governance, the Passivity Thesis has helped to define the political economy of citizenship – the arrangements that structure our economy and shape Americans' experiences and aspirations of self-government. The Passivity Thesis advances a normative theory about the proper role of corporate citizens (shareholders) in the governance of important institutions. It teaches shareholders to relinquish power within corporate organisations when doing so is *efficient* or individually *wealth-maximising*. The influence of this 'passive' conception of governance extends beyond the economic sphere, contributing to modern ideas about popular sovereignty and the role of the citizen in democratic governance.

The first section of this chapter traces the history of the Passivity Thesis as an idea – its popularisation during the Great Depression, largely arising out of

[2] See BS Black, 'Shareholder Passivity Reexamined' (1990) 89 *Michigan Law Review* 520, 523. ('The passivity story assumes a benign legal environment.')

the work of Berle and Means, and its reworking through the law and economics movement. The chapter notes possible connections between the emergence of the Passivity Thesis, the rise of investment trusts, and the feminisation of American shareholding. It shows that, by the 1980s, corporate law experts in the law and economics tradition argued that shareholders *should be* passive, turning a descriptive idea into a normative one.

The second section of this chapter contrasts the theory with the evidence. It shows that, at the precise historical moment when Berle and Means were popularising the trope of the passive shareholder, American shareholders were creating a movement for 'corporate democracy' that advocated an active, participatory role for shareholders in corporate governance. Though the corporate law literature has mostly ignored this, attendance at shareholder meetings in the 1940s, 1950s and 1960s grew significantly, even while companies discouraged turnout and rejected offers to broadcast meetings on radio and television. The intermediation of shareholding, changes to proxy regulation, and the emergence of the Friedman doctrine appear to have temporarily suppressed shareholder activism from the 1970s until the early 2000s. More recently, however, shareholder activism has surged back into the headlines. The significant rise in shareholder activism, particularly for the purpose of advancing ESG goals, should put the Passivity Thesis to rest: it appears that shareholders are *not* naturally passive. On the contrary, a meaningful proportion of shareholders appear eager to participate in shareholder governance and are willing to incur costs to do so.

The final section considers the impact of the shareholder passivity norm broadly, on politics and institutional governance. It argues that the main function of the Passivity Thesis was to solidify a certain set of power arrangements in corporate organisations, which then spilled into the political sphere once corporations began engaging in significant political activity. Corporate 'citizens' were taught, in accordance with the Passivity Thesis, to relinquish power for the sake of economic efficiency. Thus, the Passivity Thesis influenced a broader range of norms related to civic virtue, self-rule, and democratic citizenship.

4.2. THE HISTORY OF A POTENT IDEA

The idea of the 'passive shareholder' emerged in American corporate law discourse in the late 1920s and early 1930s and quickly became a lynchpin of modern corporate theory. As noted above, Berle and Means popularised the term in their influential 1932 book, *The Modern Corporation and Private Property*, which suggested that the separation of ownership and control made shareholder passivity inevitable.

The increasing popularity of the passive shareholder trope coincided with a precipitous rise in the proportion of public company shareholders who were women. At the time, sexist stereotypes presented women as a group as inherently passive, submissive and docile. Though earlier corporate law experts had used the term 'absentee ownership' to describe the absence of small shareholders from corporate governance, theorists in the 1920s and 1930s shifted to characterising shareholders as passive, and passivity as a blameworthy quality, one that justified the subordination of the shareholder in corporate organisation. This history suggests that the Passivity Thesis was tainted at its origin by sexism.

When the law and economics movement emerged in the 1970s and 1980s, it reworked the Passivity Thesis, transforming shareholder passivity from a descriptive idea (shareholders were behaving passively) to a normative idea (shareholders *should* behave passively). Law and economics theorists argued that it was rational for shareholders to be passive in corporate governance – to voluntarily relinquish their voting power. By the end of the twentieth century, corporate law scholarship routinely presented shareholder passivity as desirable, efficient, and welfare-maximising. Passivity was no longer a problem for corporate organisations; instead, it had become the standard for shareholder behaviour, a norm widely promoted in business and law schools, helping to cement decision-making control over public companies in a small set of corporate managers.

4.2.1. The Origin of Shareholder Passivity in America

The Passivity Thesis traces its origin to the late 1920s and early 1930s, especially to the work of the two academics, Berle and Means.[3] Yet many of the problems that Berle and Means would ascribe to shareholder passivity in the early 1930s existed in nineteenth-century corporations, especially banks and railroads, which had large numbers of shareholders. By the last quarter of the nineteenth century, even relatively obscure railroad corporations often numbered their shareholders in the thousands – far too many to gather together in a single meeting hall.[4] At these corporations, many shareholders did not attend meetings or otherwise participate in governance but chose

[3] See below nn 33–45 and accompanying text. The 'passive shareholder' appears earlier in British texts than in American ones. See, eg, CT Carr, *The General Principles of the Law of Corporations* (Cambridge University Press, 1905) 111 (using the term 'passive shareholder' in a description of the French *société en commandite*); 'Editorial Notes' (15 July 1908) *Gas & Oil Power* 250 (discussing the proposed formation of an 'Electrical League' that would bring 'to the support of the industry men of standing and influence who at present are merely passive shareholders').

[4] In 1872, for example, the managers of the Lake Shore and Michigan Southern Railroad Company told the Michigan Railroad Commission that it was '[n]ot possible' to quantify its shareholders with precision because '[w]e have about 4,000 stockholders, – changing every day'. First Annual Report of the Commissioner of Railroads of the State of Michigan, For the Year Ending December 31, 1872, 65 (Lansing, WS George & Co, 1874) (Report of the Lake Shore and Michigan Southern Railroad Co).

instead to sign proxies over to corporate managers. In the nineteenth-century and early twentieth-century American literature, these non-participating railroad shareholders were described as 'absent' from governance, not 'passive' in character.

Absentee shareholding was attributed to the distribution of stock across wide geographic regions and to corporate laws and practical considerations that made the participation of far-flung shareholders in corporate governance exceedingly difficult.[5] Indeed, proxy laws passed in Pennsylvania in the mid-nineteenth century suggest that legislators there believed it was reasonable to expect shareholders to attend meetings held within 10 miles of their homes, but not further.[6] Andrew Carnegie decried the absent shareholder in the 1890s.[7] Louis D Brandeis wrote about absentee shareholding before and after joining the US Supreme Court;[8] so did William O Douglas.[9] In 1923, Thorstein Veblen, the social theorist, published *Absentee Ownership and Business Enterprise in Recent Times: The Case of America*, which addressed the problem in detail.[10] By the late 1920s, however, the concept of 'absentee' shareholding was being replaced with new ideas about 'passive' shareholding.

At this time, women were pouring into stockholding as individual shareholders named on stock rolls.[11] Although women had owned corporate stock before then,[12] women's growing shareholding power was becoming culturally salient in the 1920s, particularly after the ratification of the Nineteenth Amendment, which conferred political power on women for the first time.[13] Shareholding expanded in general during the Great Bull Market, but the percentage of women holders rose steeply at many public companies. It was during this period that women shareholders were first reported to outnumber

[5] See, eg, WJ Lauck, *Political and Industrial Democracy 1776–1926* (Funk & Wagnalls Co, 1926) 7 or L Corey, *The Decline of American Capitalism* (New York, Covici, Friede, 1934) 330–32.

[6] 1849 Pennsylvania Act ('no stockholder females excepted, residing within ten miles of the place appointed for such general meeting or election shall vote by proxy').

[7] 'How to Win a Fortune' (2 May 1890) *Brookfield Gazette* (Brookfield, MO) 4 (quoting Andrew Carnegie).

[8] See, eg, LD Brandeis, 'Cutthroat Prices – The Competition That Kills' (15 November 1918) *Harper's Weekly* (describing 'the huge corporation with its myriad of employees, its absentee ownership, and its financial control' as presenting 'a grave danger to our democracy'). Even in his epic dissent in *Louis K Liggett Co v Lee*, in which he repeatedly cited and endorsed Berle and Means' ideas about the separation of ownership and control, Brandeis continued to resist the language of 'passivity'. *See Louis K Liggett Co v Lee*, 288 US 517, 568–69 (1933) (Brandeis, J, dissenting) (retaining the term 'absentee ownership').

[9] See WO Douglas, 'Directors Who Do Not Direct' (1934) 47 *Harvard Law Review* 1305, 1317.

[10] See T Veblen, *Absentee Ownership and Business Enterprise in Recent Times: The Case of America* (New York, BW Huebsch, 1923) 215–16.

[11] See SC Haan, 'Corporate Governance and the Feminization of Capital' (2022) 74 *Stanford Law Review* 515, 542–50.

[12] ibid 531–41 (documenting the rise of women among American shareholders before the 1920s); 'Railroad and Industrial Corporations with $9,000,000,000 Capitalization Owned by 873,000 Shareholders', *Wall Street Journal* (31 August 1911) 6. ('About 50 per cent. of the shareholders of the American Sugar Refining Co. are of the so-called weaker sex.')

[13] The Nineteenth Amendment was ratified in 1920. See Haan (n 11) 539 fns 107–109.

men at leading companies like General Electric (in 1921),[14] the Southern Pacific Railway (in 1927),[15] and the Pennsylvania Railroad (in 1927).[16] At General Motors, women's percentage among shareholders increased from about 22% in 1921 to 40% in 1930.[17] At US Steel, between 1917 and 1927, the number of women stockholders increased by 25.4% – more than double the rate of increase of men.[18] This trend, which was widely covered by the popular and financial press, showed that American shareholding was *feminising*.[19]

Coincidentally, ideas about shareholder *passivity* started appearing in the work of American corporate theorists. The concept of shareholder passivity may have knit together two separate currents of thought: one which described stock held in trust as involving a 'passive' owner or beneficiary,[20] and a second which broadly viewed women – the fastest-growing segment of the shareholder class – as 'passive' in character. During this period, both investment trusts and women investors played greater roles in stock investment, with some overlap. By the 1920s, an increasing amount of corporate stock was held in trust arrangements, expanding beyond the trust's traditional use for estate management. Investment trusts had barely existed before 1921 but grew significantly in number at the end of the 1920s as the stock market soared.[21] The beneficiaries of stock held in trust were often described as 'passive' because they didn't vote their own stock; the trustee voted it.

At the same time, the 'separate spheres' ideology, popular in the 1920s and 1930s, presented women as naturally passive (and weak and emotional), in contradistinction to men, who were described as active (and strong and rational).[22] A dispute over Jay Gould's estate in the 1920s showed how these trends were easily conflated. One of the trustees of Gould's estate, Helen Gould Shepard, argued that because she was a woman, she was a 'passive trustee' and thus should escape liability for acts of the active male co-trustees, her brothers.

[14] General Electric 1921 Annual Report 8.

[15] 'Women Outrank Men Stockholders', *New York Times* (12 August 1927) (45.53% of stockholders of the Southern Pacific were women; 44.99% were men).

[16] 'Woman's Investment Invasion: Overtopping Facts and Figures', *Wall Street Journal* (12 August 1927) 15 (50.38% women in 1927); AK Darby, 'Union Trust Company Directors to Consider Increasing Capital Stock', *Baltimore Evening Sun* (16 December 1927) 50 (50.68% women by the end of the year).

[17] 'Big Concerns' Stockholders All Over U.S.', *Chicago Tribune* (1 May 1932) 29 (40% of GM's common stockholders were women at the end of 1930); 'General Motors Stockholders', *Wall Street Journal* (30 November 1921) 8 (women were 22% of common stockholders and owned almost 8% of common stock); 'Gen. Motors Common Now Owned by 37,787', *New York Times* (29 June 1921) 19 (the number of women common stockholders more than doubled over that period, from 3,459 to 8,110).

[18] 'Women Outrank Men Stockholders' (n 15) 26.

[19] The feminisation of shareholding continued robustly until women became a majority of public company shareholders in the mid-1950s. See Haan (n 11) 558–59.

[20] See EA Harriman, 'Voting Trusts and Holding Companies' (1904) 13 *Yale Law Journal* 109, 109–11. (An early and detailed treatment of 'passive' control through stock held in trust.)

[21] S Livermore and CS Tippetts, *Business Organization and Control* (New York, Van Nostrand, 1932) 553–56.

[22] See Haan (n 11) 576–78.

Shepard's lawyer argued that she was 'a woman without the natural taste or aptitude for managing large business interests'.[23] Though she was 'an intelligent woman,' he argued, 'it would be idle to contend that she had the business acumen and judgment of her brothers and should have taken as active a part in the administration of the estate as they.'[24] The lawyer continued:

> Certainly Jay Gould in naming her a trustee never expected her to become a manager of a great network of railroads. What other course would the objectors have had her take? Equip herself with a desk in railroad offices and go down to business every day? Sit upon the boards of the various roads? Make a show of examining the complicated books of account of the estate and pretend that she understood the entries that she found therein?[25]

Though a trustee's *job* was to actively manage an estate, Shepherd's sex made her a 'passive' trustee.

By the mid- to late-1920s, corporate experts had begun describing American shareholders using language that evoked psychological weakness, such as passivity and docility.[26] John H Sears, who published *The New Place of the Stockholder* in 1929, opined that, 'as a stockholder, your average person today is the most docile, the most shrinking, the most supine of mortals.'[27] Alfred P Sloan Jr, the chairman of General Motors, argued that there was a point beyond which the atomisation of shareholding 'enfeeble[d] the corporation' by 'depriving it of virile interest in management' of one or a few male shareholders.[28]

Harvard economist William Z Ripley published a series of gender-inflected works on corporate law that railed against the 'attempted rape of the voting power' of shareholders[29] and 'the rape of the public stockholder' by corporate managers.[30] In his 1927 book, *Main Street and Wall Street*, Ripley contrasted shareholder voting by proxy with shareholders' 'passive participation in management' and lamented how 'the wide distribution of stock to employees and the consumers of the corporation's product' 'accentuate[d]' the shareholder's 'nullification'.[31] In the same book, Ripley openly demeaned women

[23] 'Calls Mrs. Shepard a Passive Trustee', *New York Times* (4 April 1925) 19.

[24] ibid.

[25] ibid.

[26] See, eg, WHS Stevens, 'Stockholders' Voting Rights and the Centralization of Voting Control' (May 1926) 40 *Quarterly Journal of Economics* 353, 384–85. See also 'Advertisement for the Orange County Trust & Savings Bank', *Santa Ana Register* (Santa Ana, California, 28 June 1924) 11 ('Active Stockholders Build Strongest Banks'). See also EA Guest, 'Just Folks: The Minority Stockholder', *Star Press* (Muncie, Indiana, 18 April 1929) 4 (a poem describing the minority stockholder as 'the meekest man on earth').

[27] JH Sears, *The New Place of the Stockholder* (New York, Harper & Bros, 1929) 62.

[28] A Pritchard Sloan Jr, 'Modern Ideals of Big Business: An Article on the New Leadership', *World's Work* (Oct 1926) 697.

[29] WZ Ripley, *Main Street and Wall Street* (New York, Arno Press, 1927) 77.

[30] WZ Ripley, 'From Main Street to Wall Street', *Atlantic Monthly* (January to June 1926) 99.

[31] Ripley (n 29) 94, 108.

shareholders, judging them 'ill-fitted by training – begging the moot point of sex – to govern' corporations 'directly'.[32] Ripley's book stands out not only as an early articulation of the trope of the passive shareholder, but also for openly endorsing misogynistic stereotypes about women's suitability for a governance role.

4.2.2. The Passive Shareholder in Berle and Means

Berle and Means' important 1932 book, *The Modern Corporation and Private Property*, has been characterised as an extension of Ripley's work.[33] In it, Berle and Means argued that 'the position of [stock] ownership has changed from that of an active to that of a passive agent.'[34] The cause of this change, they wrote, was the dispersion of stock ownership, which led, inevitably, to shareholder passivity.[35] 'When the largest single interest amounts to but a fraction of one per cent,' they wrote, 'no stockholder is in the position through his holdings alone to place important pressure upon the management or to use his holdings as a considerable nucleus for the accumulation of the majority of votes necessary to control.'[36] The inability of a shareholder to exercise control, due to the small size of the holder's stock, was presented as the *condition* of passivity.

Yet as contemporaneous readers understood, the 'passive' label described a *personal* failing of individual shareholders. The term implied that the shareholder had chosen to act meekly and submissively – or, as Berle and Means put it, shareholders had 'surrendered' control.[37] One astute critic observed that Berle and Means had defined 'passive property' as 'passive *because its owner is passive*'.[38] Though Berle and Means generally attached the word 'passivity' to property, the critic observed that, '[p]assivity and activity are not really predicated of property at all, but of two different classes of persons, passive and active, respectively.'[39]

[32] ibid 129–30.

[33] See 'Book Review: The Modern Corporation and Private Property' (1932–33) 18 *Cornell Law Quarterly* 634, 635. Berle's biographer described Ripley as the 'man who figured most importantly in Berle's work'. JA Schwarz, *Liberal: Adolf A. Berle and the Vision of an American Era* (New York, Free Press, 1987) 52.

[34] Berle and Means (n 1) 66; see also ibid 346–47 ('Passive property … gives its possessors an interest in an enterprise but gives them practically no control over it, and involves no responsibility'; it consists 'of a set of relationships between an individual and an enterprise, involving rights of the individual toward the enterprise but almost no effective powers over it').

[35] ibid 84; see also Bernard S Black, 'Agents Watching Agents: The Promise of Institutional Investor Voice' (1992) 39 *UCLA Law Review* 811, 813; FH Easterbrook and DR Fischel, 'Voting in Corporate Law' (1983) 26 *Journal of Law and Economics* 395, 397.

[36] Berle and Means (n 1) 84.

[37] See, eg, ibid 338.

[38] TM Ave-Lallemant, 'Critique of a Revision of Some Fundamental Economic Concepts' (1933) 18 *Marquette Law Review* 20, 28.

[39] ibid.

Berle and Means certainly would have known about the feminisation of shareholding,[40] and parts of their analysis were subtly gendered in meaning.[41] Late in his career, Berle switched to using the term 'passive-receptive' to describe the condition of shareholding.[42] In 1957, the year that the New York Stock Exchange first reported that women outnumbered men among public company shareholders in the United States,[43] Berle wrote that 'the business of stockholders is primarily to receive', and added that the 'passive receptive' side of the corporation was 'functionless'.[44]

After the publication of *The Modern Corporation*, prominent corporate law scholars began incorporating the Passivity Thesis into their work.[45] Among the scholars who did so almost immediately were E Merrick Dodd Jr[46] and Chester Rohrlich.[47] The influential political theorist James Burnham also did so, claiming that the rise of women's stock ownership indicated that capitalists were withdrawing from 'active and direct participation of any sort in the economic process'.[48] Women's stock ownership underscored a growing 'gap' between shareholders and the 'instruments of production,' Burnham wrote, because 'whatever the biological merits, it is a fact that women do not play a serious leading role in the actual economic process.'[49]

Thus, in hindsight, it appears likely that the corporate theorists who created and popularised the idea of shareholder passivity were influenced by the changing demographics of shareholding and by discriminatory stereotypes about women. Berle and Means' view that passivity debased shareholding appears to have echoed themes of gender bias that were common in the first decades of the 1900s. The belief that small shareholders lacked 'aptitude' to participate in corporate governance also was likely coloured by sexism. Over the next decades, shareholder passivity was asserted as fact and used to justify both

[40] The feminisation of shareholding was widely covered in the financial and popular press in the 1920s. See Haan (n 11) 542–50.

[41] See, eg, Berle and Means (n 1) 135 (contrasting the modern, widely-held corporation with an earlier version of corporate capitalism in which '[t]he number of stockholders was few; they could and did attend meetings; they were business-men; their vote meant something').

[42] AA Berle Jr, *Economic Power and the Free Society* (New York, Fund for the Republic, 1957) 7.

[43] See New York Stock Exchange, 'Who Owns American Business?' *1956 Census of Shareowners* 6.

[44] Berle (n 42) 7.

[45] The term also became more common in the popular press. See, eg, 'Salaries of Rail Heads Attacked: Usually Passive Stockholders of Pennsylvania Heckle Management at Meeting' (13 April 1933) *Oakland Tribune* 21.

[46] See E Merrick Dodd, Jr, 'Purchase and Redemption by a Corporation of Its Own Shares: The Substantive Law' (1941) 89 *University of Pennsylvania Law Review* 697, 710 ('[t]he shareholder is a mere passive recipient of dividends'); E Merrick Dodd Jr, 'Statutory Developments in Business Corporation Law, 1886–1936' (1936) 50 *Harvard Law Review* 27, 57.

[47] C Rohrlich, *Law and Practice in Corporate Control* (New York, Baker, Voorhis & Co, 1933) 8.

[48] J Burnham, *The Managerial Revolution: What Is Happening in the World* (New York, John Day Co, 1941) 100–01.

[49] ibid 101. Burnham minimised women's stockholding as instrumental, asserting (without evidence) that the registration of stock in women's names was 'often a legal device to aid in the preservation of wealth'.

the dominance of corporate governance by (male) managers and the shift of the corporate surplus away from shareholders to other interest groups. Experts suggested that shareholders had no one to blame but themselves, for their 'irresponsible' passivity.[50]

4.2.3. Law and Economics and the Rationally Apathetic Shareholder

When the law and economics movement emerged in the 1970s, it embraced shareholder passivity and refashioned it as 'rational apathy'.[51] In this view, the 'natural' passivity of dispersed stockholders evidenced a 'free rider problem' in which shareholders rationally declined to spend resources on governance, expecting other shareholders to bear these costs.[52] Frank Easterbrook and Daniel Fischel explained that:

> Most shareholders are passive investors seeking liquid holdings. They have little interest in managing the firm and less incentive to learn the details of management. … Because other shareholders take a free ride on any one shareholder's monitoring, each shareholder finds it in his self-interest to be passive.[53]

Berle and Means had problematised passivity; the law and economics movement reimagined it as rational decision-making by overextended, welfare-maximising investors.[54] With the rise of portfolio theory and diversification, passivity had become a solution to the problem of 'bounded resources'.[55] If one invested in many companies – as diversification required – how was one to cast an informed vote in every election? Viewed in this light, passivity appeared to be a reasonable, even a desirable choice by the shareholder.[56]

[50] See, eg Berle and Means (n 1) 354.

[51] K Kastiel and Y Nili, 'In Search of the Absent Shareholders: A New Solution to Retail Investors' Apathy' (2016) 41 *Delaware Journal of Corporate Law* 55, 57.

[52] See, eg, KY Testy, 'Linking Progressive Corporate Law with Progressive Social Movements' (2002) 76 *Tulane Law Review* 1227, 1230–31 (summarising the view that '[s]hareholders are passive because share ownership is widely dispersed, leaving shareholders unable to overcome collective action and free rider impediments to effective corporate suffrage'); Black (n 2) 522 ('Most modern corporate scholars, especially those with a law and economics bent, accept shareholder passivity as inevitable.').

[53] FH Easterbrook and DR Fischel, 'The Proper Role of a Target's Management in Responding to a Tender Offer' (1981) 94 *Harvard Law Review* 1161, 1171.

[54] See, eg, LM Fairfax, 'From Apathy to Activism: The Emergence, Impact, and Future of Shareholder Activism as the New Corporate Governance Norm' (2019) 99 *Boston University Law Review* 1301, 1304.

[55] One articulation of the standard view is found in SM Bainbridge, 'In Defense of the Shareholder Wealth Maximization Norm: A Reply to Professor Green' (1993) 50 *Washington and Lee Law Review* 1423, 1430.

[56] See, eg, Bainbridge (ibid) 1430 fn 20 (to 'require shareholders to actively participate in firm management' in a 'large firm' would 'result in chaos'); but see Kastiel and Nili (n 51) 61 (describing '[i]nvestors' rational apathy' as 'a long-standing problem of public firms').

Business law experts argued that shareholders' rational apathy meant that they did not value participation in corporate governance. The only thing a rational shareholder cared about was the stock price.[57] Although this theory was contradicted by real-world evidence[58] – for example, the 1970 proxy season in the US was the most vigorous on record, with a well-publicised shareholder campaign at General Motors (Campaign GM) and rowdy shareholder meetings across the country[59] – law professors pressed ahead with the Passivity Thesis. Future jurist Ralph K Winter told a Senate subcommittee in 1977 that 'the great bulk of shareholders in the United States do not regard shareholder power as being a very important issue to them and certainly do not regard it as anything directly related to the yield on their investments'.[60] At a hearing held by the SEC's Division of Corporation Finance in 1980, the 'vast majority of corporate commentators' expressed the view 'that shareholders have little interest in participating in corporate governance – they are interested primarily in the company's economic performance'.[61]

Meanwhile, the concept of shareholder passivity had developed so much cultural power that it began migrating to other areas of business law and beyond. Easterbrook and Fischel advocated a 'rule of managerial passivity' when a corporate board faced a tender offer.[62] Index investing, in which investments track a stock index, was described as 'passive investing'.[63] The law and

[57] See, eg, Fairfax (n 54) 1312; RJ Gilson and JN Gordon, 'The Agency Costs of Agency Capitalism: Activist Investors and the Revaluation of Governance Rights' (2013) 113 *Columbia Law Review* 863, 895 ('beneficial owners are rationally passive; governance rights are of little value to them').

[58] As one example, in 1978, the *New York Times* reported that AT&T was 'besieged by 1,700 calls and 750 letters a day' from shareholders, hardly the behaviour of apathetic holders. NR Kleinfeld, 'A.T.&T. Stockholders: Valuing Stability and Yield', *New York Times* (17 April 1978) D7.

[59] For a description of the unprecedented events of the 1970 proxy season, see SC Haan, 'Civil Rights and Shareholder Activism: *SEC v. Medical Committee for Human Rights*' (2019) 76 *Washington and Lee Law Review* 1167, 1187–91.

[60] Testimony of Ralph K Winter Jr, Professor of Law, Yale University, in 'The Role of the Shareholder in the Corporate World', Hearings before the Subcommittee on Citizens and Shareholders Rights and Remedies of the Committee on the Judiciary, United States Senate, Ninety-fifth Congress, First Session, Part 1 (27–28 June 1977) 80; see also JD Nelson, 'The Freedom of Business Association' (2015) 115 *Columbia Law Review* 461, 497 (shareholder passivity 'leads individual shareholders to value the corporations in which they invest primarily, if not exclusively, for the instrumental financial returns they promise').

[61] Staff Report on Corporate Accountability, Division of Corporation Finance, Securities and Exchange Commission (4 September 1980) 35. ('Others, however, testified that shareholders are interested in making their participation more meaningful, and several commentators opined that shareholder apathy reflects frustration with the powerlessness of the current role of shareholder/investor, rather than lack of interest.')

[62] FH Easterbrook and DR Fischel, 'The Proper Role of a Target's Management in Responding to a Tender Offer' (1981) 94 *Harvard Law Review* 1161, 1177–78, 1198–99.

[63] See, eg, J Fisch, A Hamdani and SD Solomon, 'The New Titans of Wall Street: A Theoretical Framework for Passive Investors' (2019) 168 *University of Pennsylvania Law Review* 17. More recently, scholars have questioned whether the 'passive' label fits index funds. See, eg, M Barzuza, Q Curtis and DH Webber, 'Shareholder Value(s): Index Fund ESG Activism and the New Millennial Corporate Governance' (2020) 93 *Southern California Law Review* 1243, 1265.

economics approach was even adapted for political democracy in a series of works of political science that questioned why citizens bother to vote.[64] In short, 'passivity' was spotted in a range of corporate and voting contexts, where it was generally viewed as rational and thus desirable.

By the end of the twentieth century, the trope of the rationally passive shareholder had become support for a different normative principle: shareholder wealth maximisation.[65] Shareholder passivity itself was the reason that corporate organisation needed stock prices to do so much heavy lifting – only stock prices could discipline managers because shareholder governance had been trimmed to the bone. Among the problems this created was a strong incentive for corporate managers to manipulate short-term stock prices, which led to a series of major scandals in the early 2000s.[66] It also encouraged companies to ignore externalities, such as environmental harms, whose effects on stock price would emerge only in the long term. By the twenty-first century, both shareholder passivity and shareholder wealth maximisation had become dominant norms in American economic life – not just legal norms, but cultural norms.[67]

4.3. PASSIVITY IN TRUTH AND IMAGINATION

Though a generation of twentieth-century corporate law academics embraced the Passivity Thesis, the historical record does not establish that twentieth-century shareholders meekly surrendered control of the corporation. Evidence that was largely ignored by law and economics scholars showed that twentieth-century shareholders *tried* to participate in shareholder governance but were thwarted by a combination of factors outside their control. Legal scholar Bernard Black made the case in 1990 that '[t]he passivity story' falsely assumed a 'benign legal environment'.[68] In reality, Black asserted, legal obstacles, '[c]ultural norms for proper and improper behaviour' and managerial agenda control discouraged active participation by shareholders.[69]

[64] The original work is A Downs, *An Economic Theory of Democracy* (New York, Harper & Brothers, 1957). See also WH Riker and PC Ordeshook, 'A Theory of the Calculus of Voting' (1968) 62 *American Political Science Review* 25.

[65] See CA Hill and BH McDonnell, 'The Agency Cost Paradigm: The Good, the Bad, and the Ugly' (2015) 38 *Seattle University Law Review* 561, 562–64.

[66] The fall of Enron exemplified this trend. See, eg, GA Mark, 'The Legal History of Corporate Scandal: Some Observations on the Ancestry and Significance of the Enron Era' (2003) 35 *Connecticut Law Review* 1073, 1091 (noting the insufficiency of 'market forces' for curbing wrongdoing by managers).

[67] See Fairfax (n 54) 1314 (describing a 'cultural norm favoring apathy' and asserting that 'most modern corporate scholars on either side of the apathy norm debate accept [its] dominance'); Black (n 2) 562–64 (exploring the informal cultural norms that encouraged passivity).

[68] Black (n 2) 523.

[69] ibid 523–24.

Over time, consensus has built in support of Black's key claim: that corporate law itself discouraged shareholders from participating actively in corporate governance.[70]

Yet the literature still fails to fully appreciate the factors that combined to suppress shareholder participation. This short chapter cannot fully catalogue the actions taken to discourage shareholder participation, but it will sketch some of the main categories. For much of the twentieth century, it was exceedingly difficult for far-flung shareholders to travel to shareholder meetings; communication technology was so rudimentary that participation from a distance was not realistic. When, against these odds, shareholder attendance at meetings rose sharply in the 1950s, corporate managers professed support for the trend but often acted behind closed doors to discourage it. Corporate managers, who controlled all aspects of the shareholder meeting, had many means to make it difficult, costly and unpleasant for shareholders to exercise their voice and vote. It simply is not possible to conclude from this record that twentieth-century shareholders freely chose to abstain from corporate governance. Rather, the law, poor information technology and corporate managers themselves thrust that choice upon shareholders over the vigorous objections of a vocal corps of activists.

Shareholder activism ebbed in the 1980s and 1990s but began rising again in the twenty-first century. This resulted from a re-concentration of shareholding in institutional investors, especially large asset managers, as shareholders moved the bulk of their investments to intermediaries. In the last decade, activism by hedge funds, large asset managers and ESG activists has surged. Changes in information technology have been essential to the rise of activism, as corporate disclosures have become cheaper and more user-friendly, the internet has made information easier to access, and the mechanics of shareholder voting themselves have evolved in tech-enabled ways. The twenty-first-century wave of shareholder participation has been more successful than its twentieth-century antecedent; however, like the twentieth-century wave, this new one has produced a backlash from corporate managers and political actors. The current wave of activism proves that twentieth-century shareholder activism was not an anomaly in the development of corporate capitalism. Instead, it suggests that people *want* to participate actively in corporate governance – and that this impulse can be temporarily suppressed through law and circumstance but not permanently extinguished.

4.3.1. The First Wave: Twentieth-Century Shareholder Activism

Evidence from the 1930s establishes that, at the same moment that Berle and Means declared the condition of shareholding to be passive, small shareholders at large public companies were beginning to awaken. In 1933, a year after

[70] See, eg, Fairfax (n 54).

Berle and Means published *The Modern Corporation*, a young stockholder from Manhattan attended a shareholders' meeting of the Consolidated Gas Company and became infuriated at the dismissive treatment of shareholders by the company's managers.[71] Virtually on the spot, that stockholder, Lewis D Gilbert, committed to a campaign of shareholder activism that rejected passivity and rallied the nation's growing ranks of small shareholders to *active participation* in economic governance.[72] It would consume his professional career.

Gilbert would lead a decades-long movement for corporate democracy, fighting for changes in corporate practice that would have made it easier for shareholders to obtain information, attend meetings, and weigh in on corporate policy. Among his demands were that companies experiment with regional shareholder meetings to encourage attendance. Had this reform been adopted at the time, it might have changed the course of corporate governance. When General Mills experimented with regional shareholder meetings in 1939, for example, about half of its local shareholders showed up – a remarkable turnout considering that shareholders could not vote at regional meetings.[73] Shareholder activists also demanded that companies improve disclosures to shareholders, send them transcripts of shareholders' meetings, and broadcast shareholder meetings via radio and television. Perhaps most importantly, they argued for expanded cumulative voting (which was permitted, but not required, by many states' laws), and for the creation of the shareholder proposal, which the SEC formally promulgated in 1942. Cumulative voting empowered small shareholders to elect representatives to corporate boards, while the shareholder proposal gave small shareholders an opportunity to tee up corporate reforms for a shareholder discussion and vote.

Gilbert advanced his own personal philosophy of corporate democracy, which stressed the self-actualising benefits of participation for the individual.[74]

[71] At the Consolidated Gas meeting, as was typical of this era, the chairman read the company's annual report to the gathering and, then, ignoring shareholders who raised their hands with follow-up questions, adjourned the meeting for lunch. Gilbert had wanted to ask a question and was left hanging. 'There I was, a part owner and I had been treated like a tramp by these people, who were my employees,' he said. R Phalon, 'The Stockholder as a Reformer', *New York Times* (25 April 1965) F1 (quoting Gilbert). For background on Gilbert, see generally J Bainbridge, 'The Talking Stockholder – I', *New Yorker* (11 December 1948) 48.

[72] Gilbert characterised his campaign as a 'counter-revolution' of 'small capitalists' against the very concentration of power that Berle and Means had described and explained. LD Gilbert, *Dividends and Democracy* (New York, American Research Council, 1956) 7. Colleen Dunlavy has pointed out that 1932 was also the year that the term 'corporate democracy' was first used in the *New York Times*. See CA Dunlavy, 'Social Conceptions of the Corporation: Insights from the History of Shareholder Voting Rights' (2006) 63 *Washington and Lee Law Review* 1347, 1363.

[73] General Mills held the first regional shareholder meetings in 1939 and 1940, in major cities like Manhattan, San Francisco, Detroit and Los Angeles; the company reported that about half of its stockholders in the San Francisco area attended the meeting in that city. See L Hughes, 'General Mills, Inc., Stockholders Meet Here', *San Francisco Examiner* (12 December 1939) 29; 'Owners Invited', *Time*, (29 January 1940) 59.

[74] Gilbert (n 72) 16.

He did not endorse shareholder participation merely because it was wealth-maximising (though he argued that it *could* be wealth-maximising); rather, he advocated participation on psychological, moral and political grounds, emphasising its benefits for character-building, for self-government, and for connecting the individual to the burgeoning corporate economy. He spread his philosophy at shareholder meetings, in speaking engagements (including lectures at Harvard Law School), and in a 1956 book, *Dividends and Democracy*.[75] Participation is 'the secret of individual growth as it is the heart of real democracy,' he wrote.[76] Gilbert believed that shareholder participation was essential to self-government and to the American democratic project. 'Participation in the nation's business is the only real democracy,' he asserted, 'in a modern world where it is indisputable that industry and finance are primary even in the field of political decision.'[77]

A surge of shareholder activism during and after World War II confirmed shareholders' interest in *active* shareholder participation in corporate governance – as well as SEC support for such shareholder participation. In the mid-1940s, Gilbert challenged Transamerica Corporation after it refused to publish his shareholder proposals in compliance with the SEC's new Shareholder Proposal Rule; Gilbert was vindicated, and the corporation disciplined, in a 1947 appellate case in federal court.[78] Around the same time, James Peck, Bayard Rustin, and the Congress of Racial Equality (CORE) used shareholder tools to pursue racial desegregation at publicly held busing and variety store companies.[79] At the end of the 1940s, a movement, led by shareholder activist Wilma Soss, grew to nominate and elect women candidates to corporate boards.[80] This activism, which today would be labelled ESG, and a rash of proxy contests in the 1950s, was followed by regulations that disempowered shareholders. Black dated the start of this backlash to 1956.[81]

The regulatory backlash is only half of the story, however. As shareholders' interest in active governance awakened, companies struggled to find meeting venues that could accommodate the growing crowds of attendees. As early as 1945, shareholders of AT&T were being turned away at the door for a lack of space.[82] The management of Standard Oil of New Jersey was surprised when attendance at its annual meeting in Flemington, New Jersey, grew from 400 in 1946 to 600 the following year, forcing some stockholders to stand.[83]

[75] ibid.
[76] ibid.
[77] ibid 229.
[78] *SEC v Transamerica Corp*, 163 F.2d 511 (3d Cir 1947), *cert denied*, 332 US 847 (1948).
[79] See H Wells, 'Shareholder Meetings and Freedom Rides: The Story of *Peck v. Greyhound*' (2021) 45 *Seattle Law Review* 1; Haan (n 59) 1214.
[80] See Haan (n 11).
[81] See Black (n 2) 564.
[82] See 'Labor Group's Plans Lose at A.T.&T. Meet', *Washington Post* (19 April 1945) 14.
[83] *Stenographic Report of the Annual Meeting of the Stockholders of Standard Oil Company* (New Jersey, 4 June 1946) 2; *Stenographic Report of the Annual Meeting of the Stockholders of the Standard Oil Company* (New Jersey, 3 June 1947) 2.

When attendance nearly doubled yet again in 1948, the company put up a tent adjacent to the meeting room and provided space at a nearby courthouse.[84] By 1951, nearly 2,000 stockholders were attending Standard Oil's annual meeting.[85] International Telephone & Telegraph Corp held its 1953 shareholders' meeting in circus tents in Nutley, New Jersey.[86] That same year, American Air Lines held its meeting in a hangar at LaGuardia Field; it was attended by 1,800 shareholders.[87] In 1956, after the Ford Motor Company went public, it held its first annual meeting in a tent and about 2,900 shareholders attended.[88] 'Each year we get more and more stockholders at the annual meeting,' an executive of General Electric said in 1954; the company's 'mammoth' meeting welcomed 2,455 shareholders that year.[89]

In 1961, *20,000* stockholders showed up to AT&T's annual stockholders meeting in Chicago, more than attended the opening of the baseball season.[90] Though that number was unusually large – AT&T had more shareholders than any other American company – high turnout at other companies suggests that shareholders were trying to participate in the governance of big companies, but no clear method presented itself. During this period, most small stockholders held stock in only a few companies.[91] With governance rights in few firms, it would have been possible for shareholders to devote attention to the obligations of economic citizenship. Shareholders were stymied by corporate governance practices that discouraged their participation, and by the lack of transportation and communication technology that might have allowed distant shareholders to attend meetings.

[84] *Stenographic Report of the Annual Meeting of the Stockholders of the Standard Oil Company* (New Jersey, 1 June 1948) 2.

[85] 'Sharp Income Gain for Standard Oil', *New York Times* (9 June 1951) 24. Likewise, attendance at General Motors' annual meetings held at Wilmington, Delaware doubled over the three years from 1948 to 1950. See MM Caplin, 'Proxies, Annual Meetings and Corporate Democracy: The Lawyer's Role' (1951) 37 *Virginia Law Review* 653, 655 fn 5 (citing the Gilberts' report.).

[86] 'I.T.&T. Takes Annual Meeting to Stockholders', *Wall Street Journal* (6 May 1955) 9.

[87] 'The Stockholder's Voice', *Wall Street Journal* (22 May 1953) 4. See also DF Smee, 'Mr. Stockholder: Encouraged by Industry, He Plays a Bigger Part at Annual Meetings', *Wall Street Journal* (19 April 1954) 1.

[88] R Garrett, 'Attitudes on Corporate Democracy – A Critical Analysis' (1956) 51 *Northwestern University Law Review* 310, 328–29 (quoting from the *Wall Street Journal*).

[89] AR Zipser Jr, 'G.E. Profits Set Peak in Quarter At $48,029,000, Up 42% in Year', *New York Times* (21 April 1954) 45; Smee (n 87) 1.

[90] S Porter, 'Sylvia Porter Says: Annual Meetings Taking On More Serious Aspect', *Richmond Times-Dispatch* (28 March 1963) 43.

[91] See, eg, United States Congress House Temporary National Economic Committee, *Investigation of Concentration of Economic Power, Monograph No 29: The Distribution of Ownership in the 200 Largest Nonfinancial Corporations* (Washington, GPO, 1940) XVII. (The average stockholder held shares in 'about two and one-half corporations'.) Almost twenty years later, the NYSE found that the average stockholder held stock from only 3.5 different stock issues – fewer than in 1956, when the average was 4.25. New York Stock Exchange, *Share Ownership in America: 1959* (New York, 1959) 5.

When they were able to attend, shareholders participated robustly at shareholder meetings. The first reported year in which a shareholder challenged AT&T's board to add a woman director was 1933.[92] At AT&T's 1949 meeting, shareholders made more than 75 addresses.[93] At the company's 1950 meeting, an Associated Press reporter counted 105 statements and questions made by shareholders.[94] 'There have been more questions in this meeting than I have had in the last twenty-two years as President,' declared American Sugar's president at its 1951 annual meeting.[95]

Even when they couldn't attend shareholder meetings, shareholders tried influencing management. In 1951, AT&T reported that at least 750 shareholders 'write or phone the company *daily*'.[96] That statistic suggests that, on an annual basis, more than a quarter of the company's million shareholders were reaching out to communicate with the company.[97] Standard Oil of New Jersey received 'a tremendous number of questions from stockholders by mail', according to its president.[98] The SEC itself reported that it received 'thousands' of letters from shareholders in the 1940s, mostly complaining about proxy practices.[99]

To be sure, the crowds at shareholders' meetings represented only a small proportion of the companies' shareholders. As a proportion of total stock, voter turnout at most corporate elections was low.[100] To the extent that shareholders did vote, most did so by signing proxies over to corporate management; shareholders who voted in person often rubber-stamped managerial recommendations. Proxy contests, in which shareholders nominated insurgent candidates for election to the board of directors, were rare. And once the shareholder proposal was introduced in 1942, few proposals were submitted, and those that went to a shareholder vote rarely won. Though this last fact was cited as proof that shareholders didn't support proposals, most proposals were defeated because management voted all the proxies against them. (Shareholder activists

[92] 'Gifford Re-elected by A.T.T.; No One Asks About Dividend', *Chicago Tribune* (29 March 1933) 20.

[93] See 'Owners Arise! Annual Meetings Draw Record Attendance and Pointed Questioning', *Wall Street Journal* (27 April 1949) 1.

[94] 'Pride of Ownership', *Knoxville News-Sentinel* (30 April 1950) 36.

[95] LD Gilbert, *Twelfth Annual Report of Stockholders Activities at Corporation Meetings, 1951* (New York, 1951) 5.

[96] J Beck, 'Meet the Women Stockholders, They Outnumber the Men', *Chicago Tribune* (23 May 1951) 29 (emphasis added).

[97] AT&T had about a million stockholders in 1951; if the company received 750 communications per day (and each shareholder communicated only once per year), more than a quarter of AT&T's shareholders reached out to the company.

[98] Standard Oil Company, *Annual Meeting* (New Jersey, 8 June 1951) 32.

[99] Hearings before Committee on Interstate and Foreign Commerce on HR 1493, HR 1821 and HR 2019, 78th Cong, 1st Sess 20 (1943) (Statement of Hon Ganson Purcell, Chairman, Securities and Exchange Commission) 81.

[100] See Fairfax (n 54) 1307. ('[I]t has been understood that, at least historically, most public company shareholders did not exercise their vote.')

also argued that employee-shareholders often voted with management because there was no secret ballot in corporate elections; voting against their bosses' preferences put workers' jobs at risk.)[101]

Corporate managers had numerous methods for discouraging shareholder attendance at meetings. Holding meetings in hard-to-reach places was common;[102] this was one of the chief complaints of activists in the 1950s and 1960s.[103] Companies could limit attendance by requiring shareholders to jump through hoops to obtain tickets for admittance. Managers discouraged employee-stockholders from attending shareholder meetings by docking their pay for missed work,[104] or by ordering them not to attend.[105] By 1953, AT&T was shunting hundreds of stockholders who showed up into overflow rooms, where they had to watch the proceedings on grainy, black-and-white television sets.[106] Shareholders who were not seated in the meeting room had to communicate with the board chair by telephone.[107] This suggested a strong commitment by the thousands of attendees to the principle of corporate democracy, not just to individual welfare maximisation. Small shareholders understood, of course, that their votes would not determine the result of a corporate election. In fact, the results of the voting were sometimes announced at the *beginning* of the meeting.

Corporations suppressed participation inside meetings by limiting the microphones available in large venues,[108] or by turning off a shareholder's microphone mid-speech.[109] They sometimes sought to embarrass or intimidate shareholders who spoke up. When a shareholder made 'comments and criticisms' from the floor of the 1951 General Foods shareholders' meeting, the

[101] General Motors, *Report of the 53rd Annual Meeting of General Motors Shareholders* (Wilmington, 19 May 1961) 17 (describing 'the case of an employee shareholder at another company who claimed to have been discharged because he voted his shares at that company's annual meeting contrary to the wishes of the management').

[102] For example, Barium Steel moved its 1958 annual meeting from New York City to 'about as inconvenient a location it can find', to discourage attendance when a one-for-four reverse stock split was on the ballot. LD Gilbert and JJ Gilbert, *Nineteenth Annual Report of Stockholder Activities at Corporation Meetings During 1958* (New York, 1959) 18. As another example, FW Woolworth & Co, the national chain store, held its shareholder meetings in Watertown, New York, near the Canadian border. ibid 16–17.

[103] See ibid 15–16.

[104] Radio Corporation of America reportedly docked the pay of workers who missed work to attend shareholder meetings. See ibid 269.

[105] Gilbert and Gilbert (n 102) 268.

[106] 'A.T.&T. Holders View Annual Meeting on TV', *Wall Street Journal* (16 April 1953) 20. Reports of attendance in 1953 ranged from 1,200 to more than 1,800. *cf* 'Wish You Were Here', *Council Compass* (May 1953) 1.

[107] 'S.R.O. Meeting Held by A.T.&T.', *New York Times* (16 April 1953) 45.

[108] For example, only one microphone was made available to the 4,000 shareholders who attended General Electric's 1958 meeting. See ibid 16.

[109] See, eg, 'U.S. Steel Optimistic as Increased Needs Foreseen', *San Bernardino County Sun* (6 May 1958) 30 (describing how shareholder activist Wilma Soss was forced to use a battery-powered megaphone after the management of US Steel denied her access to a company microphone at a shareholders' meeting).

Chairman of the Board retorted that, if she was unhappy with the way the company was run, she should sell her stock.[110] Shareholders were so offended that the Chairman apologised for the remark in the company's annual meeting report.[111] By the 1960s, some companies were paying Pinkerton security guards to stand by during shareholder meetings and occasionally eject activists.[112]

When new technologies arose that could have enhanced shareholder participation, corporations did not adopt them. In the mid-1950s, shareholders of General Motors and AT&T submitted shareholder proposals demanding that the companies broadcast their shareholder meetings around the nation, using closed or open television circuits or even radio or telephony; management voted them down.[113] CBS even offered to televise the AT&T annual meeting for free, but AT&T rejected the offer.[114] The offer itself suggested that CBS believed there would have been a sizeable audience for the broadcasts, but public companies never agreed to televise their meetings.

Thus, by the time the 'deretailization'[115] of shareholding began in earnest in the last decades of the twentieth century, shareholders had become habituated to passivity – even those who were inclined to participate actively.

4.3.2. The Second Wave: Twenty-First-Century Shareholder Activism

The twenty-first century has witnessed a resurgence of shareholder activism driven by hedge funds,[116] ESG activists[117] and large asset managers[118] and a

[110] Gilbert (n 95) 16.

[111] ibid.

[112] See SF Green, 'The Heckler Has Had It', *Record* (Hackensack, 13 May 1965) 36 (describing how Pinkerton guards ejected Wilma Soss and Lewis D Gilbert from the Communications Satellite Company shareholders meeting).

[113] General Motors Corporation, *Summary of Proceedings, 48th Annual Meeting of General Motors Stockholders* (25 May 1956) 14–15 (describing the defeat of the shareholder proposal at GM); LD Gilbert and JJ Gilbert, *Eighteenth Annual Report of Stockholder Activities at Corporation Meetings During 1958* (New York, 1959) 32–33 (describing the defeat of the shareholder proposal at AT&T).

[114] 'The Bold and the Bell', *Council Compass* (May 1956) 11.

[115] See DC Langevoort, 'The SEC, Retail Investors, and the Institutionalization of the Securities Markets' (2009) 95 *Virginia Law Review* 1025, 1026 (quoting Brian G Cartwright, 'The Future of Securities Regulation' speech at the University of Pennsylvania Law School Institute for Law and Economics (24 October 2007), using the term 'deretailization').

[116] See, eg, LA Bebchuk, A Brav and W Jiang, 'The Long-Term Effects of Hedge Fund Activism' (2015) 115 *Columbia Law Review* 1085; BR Cheffins and J Armour, 'The Past, Present, and Future of Shareholder Activism by Hedge Funds' (2011) 37 *Journal of Corporation Law* 51.

[117] See P Michaels and A Scruggs, 'The Rise of Shareholder Activism and Litigation Related to Environmental, Social, and Governance Investing' (2021) 31 *Securities Litigation* 18, 18.

[118] See FJ Aquila and LS Boehmke, 'The Shareholder Rights and Activism Review: USA' (18 August 2022) *Law Reviews*, https://thelawreviews.co.uk/title/the-shareholder-rights-and-activism-review/usa; Sullivan & Cromwell LLP, 'Review and Analysis of 2022 U.S. Shareholder Activism and Activist Settlement Agreements' (13 December 2022) 5 (reporting that '[t]he first quarter of 2022 represented the busiest quarter for U.S. activism on record …'). Jeffrey Gordon asserts that this activism can

growing trend of shareholder stewardship.[119] Shareholders are engaging in a range of methods to shape corporate policy and the composition of boards, including pressure campaigns, proxy contests and shareholder proposals. Engine No 1's 'watershed victory' at ExxonMobil in 2021 grabbed headlines and demonstrated the assertiveness of shareholders in this new climate.[120] As part of this overall trend, major asset managers have begun experimenting with pass-through voting, which is a response to the demands of their clients, especially pension funds, to participate more fully in shareholder governance.[121]

Lisa Fairfax has argued that this shift 'from apathy to activism' embodies 'a radical departure from the traditional corporate governance norm' of passivity.[122] Certainly, it defies the standard law and economics catechism about the proper role of the shareholder. As Fairfax observes, the rise in activism has been accompanied by a normative shift in which both shareholders and corporate managers now view shareholder activism as appropriate and desirable.[123] Shareholder activism has replaced passivity as 'the new corporate governance norm' and appears to have staying power.[124]

The new activism has been driven by institutional investors rather than retail investors; the latter group continues to vote infrequently. In fact, Kobi Kastiel and Yaron Nili found that the proportion of stock that is not voted has *increased* since 2008 due to a rule change that now prohibits brokers from voting clients' stock under certain circumstances.[125] Kastiel and Nili argue that this trend has revealed 'the true scope and impact of retail investors' apathy', which was previously masked by broker voting of retail investors' stock.[126] Though their

be divided into three rough categories: governance entrepreneurship, which uses activism to push board accountability; ESG activism in pursuit of environmental and social reforms; and 'performance activism' by investors seeking to make financial gains. JN Gordon, 'The Rejected Threat of Corporate Vote Suppression: The Rise and Fall of the Anti-Activist Pill' (2022) *Columbia Business Review* 206, 211.

119 See T Bowley and JG Hill, 'The Global ESG Stewardship Ecosystem', ECGI Law Working Paper No 660/2022 (October 2022) 34 (draft on file with the author); D Katelouzou, 'The Rhetoric of Activist Shareholder Stewards' (2022) 18 *New York University Journal of Law & Business* 665, 671–72.

120 E Klein, M Weingarten and B Gold, 'A Pivotal Year' (2022) *Activist Investing Annual Review* (New York, Insightia and Schulte Roth & Zabel) 3. See also JC Coffee Jr, 'The Coming Shift in Shareholder Activism: From "Firm-Specific" to "Systemic Risk" Proxy Campaigns (and How to Enable Them)' (2021) 16 *Brooklyn Journal of Corporate, Financial & Commercial Law* 45, 54–59 (describing the Engine No 1 campaign).

121 See Sullivan & Cromwell LLP (n 118) (describing BlackRock's 'Voting Choice' policy and similar policies at Vanguard and State Street).

122 Fairfax (n 54) 1305.

123 ibid (adding that '[i]n light of the long-held belief in the viability and validity of shareholder apathy, this [normative] shift is remarkable'). See also Kastiel and Nili (n 51) 67. ('Over the past decade there has been a pivotal shift in corporate governance thinking toward a "shareholder franchise" approach …')

124 Fairfax (n 54) 1305. (Shareholder activism 'likely will remain a fixture of corporate governance in the future'.)

125 See Kastiel and Nili (n 51) 61. ('Since 2008 the percentage of non-voting shares has jumped by 42% from 15.2% in 2008 to 21.7% in 2015.')

126 ibid 62.

research suggests that the problem of retail shareholder non-voting is worse than previously understood, Kastiel and Nili have joined the ranks of corporate law scholars seeking to solve the 'problem' of shareholder passivity, underscoring the normative shift that has occurred within the corporate law academy. Today it is common to find corporate law professors treating shareholder activism as proper and desirable in governance.

Evidence of the new activism is significant. Investors have channelled trillions of dollars into ESG funds that pursue social and environmental goals, often through voting and active engagement with management.[127] Funds are more activist than ever before, as evidenced by their voting behaviour and by the rise in shareholder proposals. Shareholder proposals are winning in an unprecedented trend.[128]

The norm shift (from apathy to activism, as Fairfax puts it) should be recognised as a *renewal* of past governance trends, which the law and economics movement mostly ignored. It reveals that shareholder activism is hydraulic, responding to changes in law and technology. Shareholders' engagement in active governance rises until it is met with countervailing pushback from corporate managers, law-makers and regulators. This suggests, in short, that a subset of shareholders values active participation in corporate governance and will pursue it, regardless of whether this increases their wealth. This history refutes the descriptive Passivity Thesis by showing that passivity is not the default condition of shareholding.

4.4. THE PASSIVE CORPORATE CITIZEN

As discussed in the above section, the normative Passivity Thesis encouraged shareholders to take a passive role in corporate governance. Shareholder passivity was said to create efficiencies at the firm level by, for example, streamlining decision-making. When shareholders took themselves out of the governance picture, stock prices could function frictionlessly to steer capital toward its highest and best use and to yoke managers to short-term stock gains in the name of shareholder value. Thus, shareholder passivity was efficient at the market level, too, and served social welfare by promoting efficient capital allocation. In reality, however, when shareholders stepped back, managers were free to direct the corporate surplus in whatever direction they liked, with little accountability.

[127] See, eg, PWC, *Asset and Wealth Management Revolution 2022* (2022) 3, www.pwc.com/gx/en/financial-services/assets/pdf/pwc-awm-revolution-2022.pdf (estimating that, in 2021, $4.5 million in ESG assets were under management in the US and predicting that this will more than double by 2026 to $10.5 trillion).

[128] See *Proxy Preview 2022* (Berkeley, As You Sow, 2022) 88–89 (reporting that 39 shareholder proposals won a majority vote in 2021 and that average support for 185 ESG proposals was 33.8%, compared to less than 19% in 2011).

Executive compensation rose steadily. Particularly where matters were deemed immaterial under existing law, shareholders could not even learn about them, much less discipline managers for the agency costs they created. The passivity norm subordinated shareholders to managers, but it also made public companies' largest – and in some cases, their most diverse – constituency, their shareholders, voiceless in the conversations that produced companies' policies and political activity. One of the most significant accomplishments of the Passivity Thesis was to cement these power relationships by embedding them in the catechisms taught in business and law schools.

What were the big-picture consequences of these choices? This section connects the false narrative of shareholder passivity to broader themes in American life and politics during the last quarter of the twentieth century. As corporations became increasingly active in politics during those decades, the political consequences of shareholder passivity, and the empowerment of corporate managers to make all political decisions on behalf of the firm, extended passive values beyond the corporate realm into the wider political sphere. By shaping Americans' views about when it is appropriate to exercise power in governance, shareholder passivity has influenced the political economy of citizenship and our most fundamental ideas about the purpose and value of voting in a democratic system.

During the years when the normative Passivity Thesis was becoming dominant, American constitutional law was expanding the permissible role of corporations in politics. The 1978 decision of the US Supreme Court, *First National Bank of Boston v Bellotti*, set this trend in motion by granting corporations significant political spending rights.[129] Thereafter – and particularly after *Citizens United v FEC*[130] and the growth of outside spending in federal elections[131] – corporate political activity has expanded.[132] Today, it is common for corporations to spend millions of dollars to influence elections and ballot initiatives.

As corporate political activity expanded, shareholders were side-lined from it and forced into a passive role. They were not given a vote on the company's political activity, unlike in the UK, where shareholder authorisation is required.[133] In 1975, in *Cort v Ash*, the Supreme Court held that shareholders

[129] 435 US 765 (1978).

[130] 558 US 310 (2010).

[131] See WL Hansen and MS Rocca, 'The Impact of *Citizens United* on Large Corporations and Their Employees' (2019) 72 *Political Research Quarterly* 403, 403 (describing a 426% increase in independent expenditures in presidential elections from 2008 to 2012, and attributing 'dramatic increases' in outside spending after *Citizens United* to expenditures by individuals).

[132] Corporate political activity extends beyond electoral expenditures and includes any activities in which corporations seek to shape law or policy. See, eg, M Hadani et al, 'Corporate Political Activity, Public Policy Uncertainty, and Firm Outcomes: A Meta-Analysis' (2017) 15 *Strategic Organization* 338, 338–39.

[133] See Companies Act 2006 (c 7), s 366 (UK); C Torres-Spelliscy and K Fogel, 'Shareholder-Authorized Corporate Political Spending in the United Kingdom' (2011) 46 *University of San Francisco Law Review* 525, 577.

have no private right to prosecute violations of the federal Corrupt Practices Act, which regulates corporate campaign finance expenditures; shareholders do, however, enjoy a private right of action to enforce federal laws against securities fraud.[134] But to sue about a company's political spending, shareholders would have to know about it; disclosure laws did not keep pace with the deregulation of corporate political speech. Corporate campaign finance expenditures are virtually never so large in relation to the corporation's finances that they would be 'material', as that concept is defined in securities law.[135]

As a result, managers – in whom virtually all power over corporate operations resides for efficiency purposes – also acquired all the corporation's political power. Managers determined everything about the corporation's political activity, including the candidates and causes that would receive the corporation's financial support and the policy positions the corporation would publicly espouse. Shareholders' decision to 'rationally' cede power to managers meant that they were also ceding any role in directing the corporation's political power. Shareholders' passivity in the corporate sphere became passivity in the political sphere.

The political philosopher Michael J Sandel has argued that, throughout much of American history, a 'civic strand' in debates about economic policy advocated for economic arrangements that were necessary for, or most beneficial to, political self-government.[136] Political leaders sought to give deliberate shape to what Sandel calls the 'political economy of citizenship':[137] an economy with attributes that nurture, rather than undermine, the *sine qua non* of democracy – democratically minded citizens.[138] From the Great Depression to the 1960s, American thought leaders promoted self-actualisation through participation in corporate governance. In his impassioned dissent in *Louis K Liggett Co v Lee*, Justice Brandeis wrote that Americans could 'secure the moral and intellectual development which is essential to the maintenance of liberty' only through 'participation by the many in the responsibilities and determinations of business'.[139] Shareholder activist Lewis D Gilbert drew a direct connection between his participation in shareholder governance and modern democracy: 'Participation in the country's business,' he wrote, 'is at once and the same

[134] Compare *Cort v Ash*, 422 US 66, 68 (1975) with *JI Case v Borak*, 377 US 426, 430–31 (1964).

[135] Obviously, at some point, very large political expenditures would become financially material, as that term is understood in federal securities law. However, corporate political expenditures do not need to be particularly large in relation to a company's assets or income to influence a federal or state election. Thus, there is no case on record in which a public company has been determined to have spent so much money on political activity that it crossed the materiality threshold.

[136] MJ Sandel, *Democracy's Discontent: America in Search of a Public Philosophy* (Cambridge Mass, Belknap Press, 1996) 124.

[137] ibid 144.

[138] For example, Sandel wrote (ibid 320), 'the political economy of citizenship that informed nineteenth-century American life sought to cultivate not only commonality but also the independence and judgment to deliberate well about the common good.'

[139] 288 US 517, 580 (1934) (Brandeis, J, dissenting).

time the secret of individual growth and the foundation of real democracy.'[140] Henry Ford II proclaimed 'participation' to be the fundamental principle of democracy, observing, in an address to automotive executives in 1950, that the 'basic idea of dictatorships is to reduce and even eliminate participation'.[141]

Sandel suggests that American politics should seek 'to revitalise the civic strand of freedom,' a project that would seem to require some attention to the governance of corporations, a dominant institution in the twenty-first century, and especially to the behaviours and practices promoted by corporate governance.[142] Is it possible that our dominant theory about the optimal role played by corporate 'citizens' (ie, shareholders) in corporate governance has influenced our ideas about the optimal role played by voting citizens in our democracy? In fact, one prominent scholar, Mark Tushnet, has argued that the 'real source' of the modern discontent Sandel identified is our inability to 'exercise effective control over transnational corporate power'.[143]

Passivity is not a characteristic of robust self-rule or civic engagement. Because it involves shrinking from decision-making and deferring to others in governance, passivity is the opposite of democratic self-governance. Passivity and docility discourage people from *doing* and *acting*, from expressing themselves or engaging in debate, from creating and actualising preferences in pursuit of social welfare, and from forming relationships and coalitions that are action-oriented. In fact, the historical connection of passivity to women is rooted in the politics of womanhood, connecting back to a time when women could be both virtuous and docile *because* they were excluded from democratic citizenship. A question we might reasonably ask is whether the normative Passivity Thesis has taught passive governance to Americans on a wide scale, thereby contributing to a political economy that habituates us to passive citizenship or acceptance of autocratic leadership, not only in corporate organisations but in other types of institutions, too.

4.5. CONCLUSION

Shareholder passivity is a false narrative of corporate law – descriptively wrong and normatively flawed. It is an idea that has proved as flexible as it was powerful for pushing shareholders to give up their own power in corporate organisation. The Passivity Thesis deflected attention away from the role of law in shaping corporate governance and obscured how corporate managers used strategies to

[140] See Gilbert (n 72).

[141] 'Wilson Stresses Personal Freedom', *New York Times* (4 October 1950) 22.

[142] Sandel (n 136) 203.

[143] M Tushnet, 'Book Review: A Public Philosophy for the Professional-Managerial Class' (1997) 106 *Yale Law Journal* 1571, 1597, 1599 (reviewing Sandel (n 136) ibid 1590–91).

discourage shareholder participation. History suggests that shareholders would have taken a more active role in corporate governance if corporate law had made this possible. In fact, history suggests that a subset of shareholders was making significant efforts to participate and incurring costs to do so. The philosophy of participation advanced by twentieth-century shareholder activists like Lewis D Gilbert appealed to many investors and has been taken up anew by twenty-first-century actors.

The current resurgence of shareholder activism shows that some Americans – a substantial minority – truly value active participation in corporate governance. In the mid-twentieth century, corporate democrats argued that activism promoted self-actualisation and civic virtue; today, in light of the corporation's major role as a political actor, we must add that shareholder activism is necessary as a democratic safeguard, to prevent enormous political power from being wielded by a tiny group of unaccountable corporate managers.

The existence of powerful shareholder activists, demanding a participatory role in the governance of public companies, calls the validity of the 90-year-old Passivity Thesis into serious question. It has created demand for corporate law to innovate and to produce new forms of participatory shareholder governance.

5

The Corporation and the Fallacy of the Public-Private Divide

CHERIE METCALF[1]

5.1. INTRODUCTION

DEBATE OVER THE nature of the modern corporation is not new. The current clash between proponents of shareholder value maximisation (SVM) and stakeholder theory highlights the potential gap between competing visions of what a corporation is and *ought* to be. While corporations are incredibly diverse in size and structure, the focus of debate is on the largest, usually public, corporations that exert meaningful influence on the national and international stage. The size and impact of these corporations raise the significance of how we conceptualise their purpose and structure enabling law.

Stakeholder theorists adopt a more pluralistic view of the corporation's aims that can include the interests of employees, suppliers, customers and other more general public concerns like the environment.[2] Stakeholder theory takes explicit account of the broad reach of corporations' actions by embedding a duty to consider certain direct impacts on public welfare within the firm's otherwise traditional governance structure.

[1] Research assistance provided by Sophia D'Souza and Isaac Wai Hin Tsang and financial support from the Social Sciences and Humanities Research Council of Canada is gratefully acknowledged. Special thanks to participants and paper commentators at the 'Hidden Fallacies in Corporate Law and Financial Regulation: Reframing the Mainstream Narratives' Conference (2023).

[2] See EM Dodd Jr, 'For Whom Are Corporate Managers Trustees?' (1932) 45 *Harvard Law Review* 1145–63; M Blair and L Stout, 'A Team Production Theory of Corporate Law' (1999) 85 *Virginia Law Review* 247; L Stout, 'The Shareholder Value Myth' (2013) 771 *Cornell Law Faculty Publications*; E Elhauge, 'Sacrificing Corporate Profits in the Public Interest' (2005) 80 *New York University Law Review* 733; S Deakin, 'The Corporation as Commons: Rethinking Property Rights, Governance and Sustainability in the Business Enterprise' (2012) 37 *Queen's Law Journal* 339; RE Freeman, *Strategic Management: A Stakeholder Approach* (Cambridge, Cambridge University Press, 1984) 53; C Mayer, *Prosperity* (Oxford, Oxford University Press, 2019) 39; A Edmans, *Grow the Pie: Creating Profit for Investors and Value for Society* (Cambridge, Cambridge University Press, 2020); LE Strine Jr, 'Restoration: The Role Stakeholder Governance Must Play in Recreating a Fair and Sustainable American Economy – A Reply to Professor Rock' (2020) 76 *Business Lawyer*; M Lipton, AO Emmerich, KS Schwartz, SV Niles and AM D'Ginto, 'ESG, Stakeholder Governance, and the Duty of the Corporation' (2022) *Harvard Law School Forum on Corporate Governance*.

Shareholder value maximisation adherents instead conceptualise the corporation as a fundamentally private entity. The corporation is constituted to serve its own private ends, and the corporation's role is separate and distinct from that of the state as a regulator. The corporation is not obligated to weigh the social impacts of its actions or to incorporate public law values in exercising its authority, except when doing so overlaps with its legal obligations and the interests of the corporation and its shareholders. The privateness of the corporation leads to a focus on regulating the internal governance challenges that might hamper its efficiency and competitiveness since these are the major challenges to corporations maximising their contribution to social welfare – through efficient, productive, market-driven activity.[3]

In this contribution, I argue that the vision of the corporation reflected in the two poles of the corporate purpose debate misses forms of fluidity and hybridity between corporations and regulators. There are many ways in which public interests may be integrated into the corporation. Modern corporations in important contexts involve tight alignment of public and private objectives within the entity, serve as active participants in regulation, and are institutional mechanisms for transmission of public values. Neither the SVM nor the stakeholder model captures this reality. The idea of neatly separating private corporations from public regulators in the SVM model is a fallacy. However, the stakeholder model is underinclusive, failing to recognise the range of ways public and private objectives and impacts can attach to corporations. In designing mechanisms for governance, the more complex problem of accountability in both public and private spheres must be considered. This is an aspect of protecting the public interest in government and corporations' accountability in cases where corporations' private activity merges with public functions and welfare.

I develop this argument by first looking to economic theory to help explain the pull of the (dominant) private vision of the corporation and the clean divide from government regulators. Despite theoretical and normative aspects that can seem attractive, I argue that this theory fails to capture important aspects of the public-private divide in practice.

One aspect of this is the blurring of public-private objectives and functions within the corporate entity. To illustrate this, I employ historical examples from the colonial period and from the early history of the US, as well as contemporary examples that display some of the same functional public-private hybridity. These examples help reveal the potential for fusion between the private interests of the corporation and its investors and the public interests and need for accountability that attach to public actors. In the modern context, I discuss

[3] See, eg, SM Bainbridge, *The Profit Motive: Defending Shareholder Value Maximization* (Cambridge University Press, 2023); LA Bebchuk and R Tallarita, 'The Illusory Promise of Stakeholder Governance' (2020) 106 *Cornell Law Review* 91; H Hansmann and R Kraakman, 'The End of History for Corporate Law' (2001) 89 *Georgetown Law Review* 2, 439; M Jensen and W Meckling, 'Theory of the Firm: Management Behavior, Agency Costs, and Ownership Structure' (1976) 3 *Journal of Financial Economics* 305.

public-private hybrids in areas including military and defence firms, banking, and public services and utilities. Beyond these hybrids, there is a range of public-private blending within corporations that includes the adoption of voluntary ESG (environmental, social and governance) commitments and participating in the articulation of public values.

I then consider ways the public-private divide blurs in practice in corporate consideration of 'external' public welfare effects. Legal liability, uncertainty and the potential for outrage and reputation effects to drive legal evolution mean that, in practical terms, firms *ought* to engage in public interest weighing when negative externalities are significant.

I next illustrate the fallacy of the public-private divide by examining the ideal of the public government regulator, contrasting it with the reality of corporate influence on legal and political decision-making. Corporations are often *directly* engaged in 'public' regulation. They do not serve only as (private) objects of government regulation but participate actively in its development and in the implementation of government regulatory policy.

Finally, I briefly look at climate change as a context to illustrate the many ways in which the public-private divide in relation to the corporation breaks down, drawing on discussion throughout the earlier sections. Climate change provides one, but far from the only example illustrating the need to expand the vision of the corporation beyond the two poles in the current debate to recognise the complex mix of public and private that the modern corporation can involve. Discarding the fallacy that the traditional economic account/SVM model provides *the* baseline paradigm is especially important. Placing it at the centre of corporate regulation risks over-emphasis on private, internal governance challenges at the expense of accountability for public dimensions of corporate activity.

5.2. THE CLASSIC ECONOMIC MODEL OF THE CORPORATION

That the corporation is often seen as a fundamentally private entity, that *should* focus on its private interests and the goal of maximising profits, likely owes a lot to economic theory. Foundational theories of the firm in standard economic models are built around the objective of profit maximisation.[4] This objective drives firm choices across a range of inputs and strategies, from investment to hiring to how much to produce. When markets are competitive and complete, the pursuit of profit maximisation by the firm leads to efficient use of all available resources.

[4] See, eg, G Debreu, *Theory of Value: An Axiomatic Analysis of Economic Equilibrium* (New Haven and London, Yale University Press, 1959) 43; G Mankiw, *Principles of Economics* (Boston, Cengage Learning, 2021) 9; DM Kreps, *Microeconomic Foundations I: Choice & Competitive Markets* (Princeton, Princeton University Press, 2013).

What gives this efficiency result even more normative pull is that when consumers are incorporated into the perfectly competitive market model, the equilibrium in the market will be 'optimal'.[5] It is not possible to make anyone better off without making someone else worse off. The economy is at its highest potential to produce outputs from available resources to satisfy demand driven by consumers' preferences. This is the first fundamental welfare theorem in economics – a perfectly competitive equilibrium (in which firms' choices are driven by profit maximisation) will be Pareto-optimal.[6] This 'optimal' competitive market equilibrium may not reflect important social values around the distributive aspects of equilibrium. Economists have long recognised that social welfare can depend on the distribution of utility (usually proxied by income), even if society is on the efficiency frontier.[7] However, the second theorem of welfare economics establishes that any preferred distribution can be achieved with the use of lump sum taxes and transfers.[8]

At the same time the virtues of the competitive equilibrium were recognised, so were a range of 'market imperfections' that could threaten its realisation. Problems like imperfect competition (monopoly, oligopoly), returns to scale, incomplete information, the imposition of unpriced costs on 'outsiders' to the firm (externalities), the existence of 'public goods', and incomplete markets are among those identified.[9]

A common response in the literature was to suggest this opened up a role for the government to employ regulatory responses that would 'fix' the problems in the market to move toward a more competitive outcome. For example, in the environmental realm, multiple government solutions were proposed for environmentally harmful 'externalities' created by firms' private activities. Pigouvian taxes could put a price on pollution, property rights could be created to complete the missing element of the market and force internalisation of the costs, or command and control regulations could directly constrain firms' choices.[10] Foundational economic theory also puts the focus on the state to use its public powers to address the social welfare consequences of competitive market capitalism. It is the government's job to regulate and redistribute income

[5] ibid, *Theory of Value* at 90.

[6] ibid, *Theory of Value*; see also J Stiglitz, 'Information and the Change in the Paradigm in Economics' (2002) 92 *American Economic Review* 460, 477.

[7] A Bergson 'A Reformulation of Certain Aspects of Welfare Economics' (1938) 52 *Quarterly Journal of Economics* 310, 314.

[8] Stiglitz in his Nobel lecture describes the role of the fundamental theorems in establishing the belief that competitive markets will lead to Pareto optimal outcomes and that the role for government can be confined to redistributive transfers, so that there is a neat separation between efficiency and equity. He goes on to explain how the economics of information have undermined these basic claims; market failure is much more pervasive, there are more opportunities for government intervention to improve welfare of all parties, and even 'competitive' markets (eg stock markets) might not be Pareto efficient. See J Stiglitz (n 6) 477, http://www.jstor.org/stable/3083351.

[9] O Hart and L Zingales, 'The New Corporate Governance' (2022) 1 *The University of Chicago Business Law Review* 195, 198–204.

[10] See RH Coase, 'The Problem of Social Cost' (1960) 3 *The Journal of Law & Economics* 44.

to maximise social welfare, while firms should maximise profits.[11] This standard economic model provides a paradigmatic account that lurks in the background of modern debates about the nature of the corporation and its relationship to the public interest.

The legal debate over the purpose of the corporation has long roots and has generally been well covered in other contributions, including within this volume.[12] Among participants are those who view the corporation as aligning with this fundamentally private account.[13] This view sees the separation of ownership and control in the modern corporation generating risks to profit maximisation from within the corporation as the major challenge for corporate regulation.[14] Shareholders are vulnerable, either as owners who are separated from managerial control or as residual claimants in the 'nexus of contracts' that is the corporation. Their inability to protect themselves adequately gives rise to risks that managers can prefer their own interests in a way that reduces the value of profits and shareholder claims.[15] The adoption of SVM as the anchor for corporate purpose and the fiduciary duties of directors provides the best corrective.[16] The interests of other parties affected by corporations' decisions, such as stakeholders and the general public, should be protected in other ways, and in particular through 'public interest' regulation by the state. The 'internal' threats to aligning the interests of managers and shareholders and addressing agency costs of the structure of the corporation have become a predominant focus of corporate governance law. The common theme is that the problems identified relate to departures from the benchmark competitive firm and the inefficiencies that result.[17]

The naïve economic model of the corporation provides one important theoretical lens on the private internal challenges to corporate efficiency and

[11] M Friedman 'The Social Responsibility of Business Is to Increase Its Profits' *New York Times* (13 September 1970, section SM, p 17).

[12] See, eg, chapter 3 (JG Hill, 'Hidden Fallacies in the Agency Theory of the Corporation'); CA Hill, 'The Rhetoric and Reality of the Corporate Purpose Debate' (2024) *Chicago-Kent Law Review* (forthcoming).

[13] See, eg, Bainbridge (n 3); Bebchuk and Tallarita (n 3). For a detailed history of economic theories of the corporation, their evolution over time and link to corporate law doctrine, see W Bratton Jr, 'The New Economic Theory of the Firm: Critical Perspectives from History' (1989) 41 *Stanford Law Review* 1471.

[14] Jensen and Meckling (n 3) identify the agency costs that come from separation of ownership and control, such as opportunistic behaviour by management (preferring their interests to those of shareholders), costs associated with trying to monitor the agent (management) and costs that agents (management) may face to convince principals (shareholders) to rely on them.

[15] See, eg, FH Easterbrook and DR Fischel, 'Voting in Corporate Law' (1983) 26 *Journal of Law and Economics* 395 identifying voting rights as a way to protect shareholders; E Fama, 'Contract Costs and Financing Decisions' (1990) 63 *The Journal of Business* 71 arguing shareholders' interests must be at heart of fiduciary duties; see also Bainbridge (n 3) 88–90.

[16] See, eg, Bebchuk and Tallarita (n 3); Bainbridge (n 3) 88–90.

[17] Threats to the efficiency of capital markets, such as asymmetric information and moral hazard also underpin conventional purposes for legal regulation of securities markets to provide corrective transparency and information forcing for markets. However, the focus of this chapter is more narrowly on the corporation.

highlights the role of incentives in driving the behaviour of actors within the 'black box' of the corporation. However, the private nexus of contracts model of the corporation, combined with a social welfare maximising government, is not a descriptively accurate account of either the corporation or governments as regulators. It promotes a simplistic view of the public-private divide, missing important ways corporations can embody hybrid public-private objectives and reflect public interests and values. It also neglects the blurring of public and private interests in developing and implementing government regulation. This is not only because of the potential for political rent-seeking by private actors but because there is often a public-private partnership of some degree in designing and implementing regulation. The traditional economic account, while providing some powerful insights, encourages an overly narrow view of 'profit maximisation' as a virtue, and efficiency as the focal outcome of private corporate activity. It fails to acknowledge persistent variation in the public-private divide in corporate activity and government regulation.

Public-private intersections are embraced somewhat more by proponents of stakeholderism, but it too provides a fairly restrictive view of the landscape. The model essentially inserts a hypothetical public interest mandate into the corporation at the board level. While this captures some ways in which a corporation might integrate a public dimension, it fails to account for many of the other forms of public-private blending outlined above.

Below, I examine three main ways that the public-private divide in practice can differ from these theoretical poles before turning to the example of climate change as a further general illustration.

5.3. THE CORPORATION AND THE STATE: A (CONTINUING) HISTORY OF BLURRED LINES

5.3.1. Historical Origins and the Public-Private Character of the Corporation

Historical antecedents to the modern transnational corporation can be found in the chartered companies of the heroic age of commerce. States granted monopolies to companies such as the Dutch East and West India Companies, English East India Company and Hudson's Bay Company, among others.[18] These historic enterprises illustrate the potential for combining public and private goals and roles within the corporate form. Although ostensibly serving the interests of their shareholders and directors, the companies were often created to advance strategic national economic and military objectives, acting as proxies for national governments while relieving them of direct accountability.

[18] See generally SR Bown, *Merchant Kings: When Companies Ruled the World, 1600–1900* (Vancouver, Douglas & McIntyre, 2009).

The companies' activity carried them into complex blends of commercial enterprise and governance. The combination of business and government did not always work well, and ultimately these companies were replaced by state governments in the expansion of empire. However, for extended periods, these corporations served hybrid purposes that blurred the lines between public and private actors.

The early history of what was to become New York provides one illustration. The area first came to the attention of the Dutch during Henry Hudson's (unsuccessful) search for a passage to the Indies.[19] Initially, his 'discovery' generated little interest, although some Dutch merchants and early settlers took up agricultural and fur trade opportunities.

Dutch interest in the region picked up as part of a strategy to support the prospective war against Spain in the early 1600s. The Dutch West India Company was granted a monopoly charter in 1621, giving it exclusive rights to trade in the 'New Netherlands'. The company also exercised its authority to conduct raids on Spanish shipping and colonial/corporate possessions in the West Indies and North America. The Dutch government could thus advance strategic and military aims without directly going to war while leveraging private capital. The Dutch West India Company enjoyed success, capturing valuable ships and cargo, establishing trading posts and wresting territory from other nations' possessions in the plantation and slave trading regions of West Africa, Brazil and the Caribbean.[20] The Company pursued its interests in North America, bringing employees/settlers to New Amsterdam to secure both trade and an important port that would also serve company ships *en route* to the Caribbean.

The Dutch West India Company then occupied the difficult position of running an emerging colonial settlement and a commercial trading outpost rolled into one in the New Netherlands. The Company's Board was focused on profits for investors. It was reluctant to have the company take on the more public tasks of providing infrastructure for settlers, such as schools, laws or military defences.[21] Nevertheless, a series of risks to the security of the territory led to the installation of a company governor who began to provide basic elements of government: declaring bylaws, constructing streets, establishing a monetary system with legal tender, building infrastructure to strengthen defences (ultimately becoming Wall Street), constructing churches, and developing the port facility.[22]

The tension of the corporate mandate was reflected in challenges governing the colony. The company adopted a corporatist, authoritarian style of governance for both employees of the Dutch West India Company and settlers. Discontent

[19] ibid 66–70.

[20] ibid 72–73.

[21] ibid 75.

[22] ibid 76–78, describing threats in the form of the presence of French and English in adjacent settled areas, and impacts on trade and settlement from incompetent governors who provoked hostilities with Indigenous peoples.

among settlers led to demands that the Company provide a form of responsible municipal government. The Dutch government was initially receptive, as the end of the Thirty Years' War had decreased the benefits of the corporate model for the New Netherlands.[23] However, the onset of the first Anglo-Dutch war revived the Company's value as a strategic ally. Orders to establish responsible government were rescinded, and the Company's profit-seeking objective again took precedence.[24] The uneasy balance between corporate structure and profit-seeking and the demands of running a settlement continued to cause friction in the New Netherlands.

The failure to transition to a more public model for managing the New Netherlands ultimately contributed to the loss of the territory. In 1664, King Charles II of England granted his brother, James the Duke of York, a secret charter for a proprietary colony covering the New Netherlands and authorising the use of military force to compel its surrender.[25] James' military strike surprised the Dutch West India Company, but ongoing settler dissatisfaction over the lack of responsive public government assured the surrender.[26] English rule came with commitments to freedom of religion, property rights, inheritance laws, and continued trade with the Netherlands – public rights that attracted the loyalty of the settlers.[27] The New Netherlands became New York, and New Amsterdam became New York City.

This extremely early history illustrates how 'public' government objectives related to territorial acquisition, military, strategic and economic goals were pursued through the vehicle of monopoly-chartered companies.[28] The corporate form allowed states to leverage private capital and action driven by profit-seeking to achieve state aims while limiting direct state engagement and accountability. At the same time as these companies pursued private profit, they were charged with significant public functions and responsibilities.

The early history of corporations in the US continued to reflect the hybrid blending of public objectives and constraints within the private corporate form. In the early nineteenth century, states granted corporate charters on an individualised basis, commonly conditioning them to provide various types of public services.[29]

[23] ibid 93–94.

[24] ibid 95.

[25] James was also Governor of the Company of Royal Adventurers Trading into Africa, which was conducting an informal proxy war with the Dutch through the Dutch West India Company on the coast of West Africa. 'New York Colony Secretary Charter of the Proprietary Colony from Charles II to the Duke of York' (New York Archives Records, 1664), https://iarchives.nysed.gov/xtf/view?docId=ead/findingaids/B1371.xml.

[26] Bown (n 18) 98.

[27] ibid 63–64.

[28] See also M Blair, 'Corporate Personhood and the Corporate Persona' (2013) 2013 *University of Illinois Law Review* 785, 788 and E Pollman, 'Corporate Personhood and Limited Sovereignty' (2021) 74 *Vanderbilt Law Review* 1727, 1736 discussing the Dutch East India Company's structure as a private commercial vehicle for spice merchants that also simultaneously possessed and executed state-like powers on behalf of the Netherlands.

[29] See, eg, M Blair, 'Locking in Capital: What Corporate Law Achieved for Business Organizers in the Nineteenth Century' (2003) 51 *UCLA Law Review* 387; JW Hurst, *The Legitimacy of the*

For example, corporate charters were awarded to facilitate the creation of transportation infrastructure, utilities and banks.[30]

In this early era, the state granted a 'concession'; the ability to operate under a corporate form that came with limited liability and often other quasi-public powers, such as the ability to expropriate land or enjoy monopoly over the provision of critical public infrastructure.[31] Special charter regimes were associated with using state power to extend economic advantages to elites and distribute political rewards, even while providing a popular means to facilitate economic development without the need for raising tax revenue.[32] However, concerns over the potential for exploitation and concentration of power in corporations led to various restrictions, such as limits on corporate purpose and activities, restricting shareholding, and limited lifespans for the entity's special charter.[33]

In this early era, the 'concession theory' of the corporation was dominant. Under this view, the corporation's very existence was at the state's pleasure and could thus be conditioned on requirements for corporations to serve the public interest. This view was well articulated in the *Dartmouth College*[34] decision, in which Justice Marshall famously declared that 'a corporation is an artificial being … existing only in contemplation of the law' and that, as such, 'it possesses only those properties which the charter of its creation confers upon it …'[35] While this case affirmed the contingent nature of the corporation and its privileges, it simultaneously characterised the corporate charter as a contract. It protected the private interests granted from *ex post* regulation that would eliminate the benefits or fundamentally alter the terms.[36] However, rather than tending toward a purely private view of the corporation, the immediate result was a tendency to embed potential regulatory restrictions within the charter at the outset. Courts also took the view that the public interest required a narrow interpretation of the private benefits, leaving more room for regulation.[37]

Eventually, pressure to democratise access to incorporation led to the adoption of general incorporation statutes. While individualised action by the legislator was no longer needed, statutes continued to permit the embedding of restrictions and regulations within the corporate charter. Early efforts to promote general incorporation proved ineffective, as parties pursued special

Business Corporation in the Law of the United States 1780-1970 (Charlottesville VA, University of Virginia Press, 1970); E Pollman 'Reconceiving Corporate Personhood.' (2011) 2011 *Utah Law Review* 1629.

[30] N Lamoreaux and W Novak, 'Corporations and American Democracy: An Introduction' in N Lamoreaux and W Novak (eds), *Corporations and American Democracy* (Cambridge MA, Harvard Press, 2017) 8.

[31] ibid, noting the monopoly right to impose tolls that accompanied bridge, canal and turnpike charters, and the right of banks to issue private notes.

[32] ibid 7 and Pollman (n 29) 1640.

[33] Pollman (n 29) 1635.

[34] *Trustees of Dartmouth College v Woodward* 17 US (4 Wheat) 518 (1819).

[35] ibid 636.

[36] Pollman (n 29) 1636.

[37] Lamoreaux and Novak (n 30) 9, citing *Charles River Bridge v Warren Bridge* 36 US 420 (1837).

charters to avoid regulatory limitations and gain more advantageous terms.[38] Over time, concerns over the impact on democracy of special terms combined with competitive pressure between states led to more standard terms for general corporate charters.[39] Courts also became more receptive to regulatory limits imposed through general legislation.

Despite this trend, some examples persisted in which corporate structures and restrictions reflected a tight alignment of public and private interests within the entities' operations. Banking provides an example. Early banking history reflected use of the special charter regime to both mobilise private capital to facilitate investment in the early republic, as well as to provide political rewards through these potentially valuable monopolies in a credit-constrained environment. For example, corporate bank charters were valuable political rewards in New York, and incumbents could leverage the political system to preserve their monopolies.[40] However, profit opportunities led to 'banking' and note issues by non-chartered institutions, and shifts in government led to more expansion. Crises caused by the failure of significant numbers of these institutions, combined with concerns over corruption in allocating bank charters, created pressure for 'free banking' statutes that would democratise access.[41] However, some early free banking statutes failed to incorporate sufficient capitalisation and other requirements and led to dramatic expansions, then failures of the new institutions.[42] The New York free banking statute, which became a model for many other states and ultimately the National Banking Acts of 1863–64, included both a high capitalisation requirement and full collateralisation of bank notes with bonds.[43] The importance of banks for access to credit and to facilitate key economic transactions meant that their stability was a matter of significant public macroeconomic interest. Restrictions inherent to these charters reflected the hybrid public-private role of banks, even as they offered a 'general' path to bank incorporation.

These early examples illustrate close relationships of dependency between corporations and government, and the mixing of private means and objectives with public goals and interests. Early 'concession theory' is clearly at odds with the private vision of the modern SVM model, instead conditioning the existence of the corporation on varying public interest obligations combined with a private profit opportunity. But neither does this history reflect the idea that companies were simply charged with a discretionary duty to have regard to broader public interests, akin to the stakeholder approach. The historical examples above reflect more explicit and intentional structuring of both public and private interests within the corporation – at least in certain key areas.

[38] Eric Hilt, 'Early American Corporations and the State' in Lamoreaux and Novak (n 30) 52–54.
[39] Pollman (n 29) 1640.
[40] Hilt (n 38) 61–63.
[41] Hilt (n 38) 63–65.
[42] ibid 68, discussing experience with free banking in Michigan in 1837 in which nearly all of the 40 new banks created failed.
[43] ibid 66–67.

5.3.2. The Modern Corporation and Public-Private Hybridity

Early history offers examples of ways in which multiple objectives were integrated within the corporation – blending the public and private. Access to modern general incorporation regimes has weakened the concession theory of the corporation, and it might seem that the historical examples are of limited current relevance.[44] However, there are modern analogues.

As with the earliest historical examples, modern counterparts are implicated in areas of strategic and military importance for states. Private Military Firms (PMFs) are a form of corporate enterprise spanning the public-private divide in this area. These firms have grown in number and scale and provide a global market in military capability for hire. PMFs have become increasingly relied upon by states in strategic and military conflicts since the end of the Cold War and the dramatic reductions in government military forces that followed.[45] The firms have featured in numerous international conflicts, including Iraq,[46] the Central African Republic,[47] Syria[48] and Ukraine,[49] among others.

In these conflicts, PMFs have maintained cloudy relationships with states. While ostensibly serving as military capacity for hire, the degree of control over the operations of PMFs is sometimes opaque. The use of the Blackwater private security company by the US in Iraq and Afghanistan led to scrutiny by the House Committee on Oversight and Accountability, probing whether the firm was advancing or hindering US interests, whether the State Department had responded appropriately to shooting incidents associated with these private forces, and cost implications for taxpayers of relying on these PMFs.[50] In the Central African Republic (CAR), military support by the Wagner Group has served as a means for Russia to strengthen ties with the government of the resource-rich country. Russian support via Wagner forces has been credited with preserving the CAR government from threats by rebel groups and

[44] Bainbridge (n 3) 12–13 on transition away from restricted corporate purpose under modern regimes; Pollman (n 29) 1640.

[45] PW Singer, 'Corporate Warriors: The Rise of the Privatized Military Industry and Its Ramifications for International Security' (2001-2002) 26 *International Security* 186 ('Corporate Warriors').

[46] PW Singer, 'Warriors for Hire in Iraq', *Salon Magazine* (15 April 2004), www.salon.com/2004/04/15/warriors/; PW Singer, 'The Dark Truth about Blackwater', *Brookings Institute: Commentar*, (2 October 2007), www.brookings.edu/articles/the-dark-truth-about-blackwater/.

[47] R Chason and B Debout, 'In Wagner's largest African outpost, Russia looks to tighten its grip', *Washington Post* (18 September 2023), www.washingtonpost.com/world/2023/09/18/wagner-central-african-republic-touadera/.

[48] I Tharoor, 'The battle in Syria that looms behind Wagner's rebellion', *Washington Post* (30 June 2023), www.washingtonpost.com/world/2023/06/30/wagner-syria-russia-battle-united-states/.

[49] M Mirovalev, 'Who is the Wagner Group officer Putin asked to form "volunteer battalions"? And what could be next for the Russian mercenary group in Ukraine, after Yevgeny Prigozhin's death?' (*Al Jazeera*, 3 October 2023), www.aljazeera.com/news/2023/10/3/who-is-the-wagner-group-officer-putin-asked-to-form-volunteer-battalions.

[50] House Committee on Oversight and Accountability, Hearing on Private Security Contracting in Iraq and Afghanistan, *Blackwater USA* (2 October 2007), https://oversightdemocrats.house.gov/legislation/hearings/hearing-on-private-security-contracting-in-iraq-and-afghanistan-0.

restoring security.[51] Yet Wagner's activities extended beyond this to intervening in CAR politics, securing concessions for associated companies to mineral and timber resources.[52] The US Treasury has moved to sanction the companies used to extract CAR resources and Wagner itself, recognising both brutality and violations of fundamental rights in its operations and its role as a 'proxy military force of the Kremlin'.[53] Disagreement between the Wagner principal, Yevgeny Prigozhin, and Russia over the war in Ukraine led to a revolt against the Kremlin, a formal breach between Russia and the group, and the apparent assassination of Prigozhin in late summer of 2023.[54]

While the potential for a direct line between PMFs like Wagner and state governments acting as principals is clear, PMFs can pursue their own agendas that include generating destabilising conflict, deviating from a state principal's objectives to protect PMF's private interests and stripping resources for private gain.[55] The very gaps in control by states can be a rationale for the use of PMFs – as a way to claim 'plausible deniability' associated with their actions.[56] The use of PMFs can also allow states to avoid legal and policy limits and cloak the policy consequences of the use of force. For example, it has been argued that US use of PMFs in Iraq allowed for a dramatic increase in the size of combat forces, without formal increases in troop deployment or mobilisation of additional US forces (eg by calling up National Guard), and concealed casualty costs, by privatising PMF dead and wounded, ultimately undercutting the Abrams Doctrine – that US military operations should have the public support of the nation.[57]

While some PMFs are (illegal) military mercenaries, many are legitimate business enterprises. Connections between public military and strategic actors and these enterprises in countries like the US provide confirmation.[58] The very existence and role of PMFs depend on a tight public-private connection. A degree of partnership is implicit, given the state's monopoly on the legitimate use of military force. Echoes of the blurred public-private nature of the historic empire-building monopolies can be seen in these modern corporate PMFs and

[51] See n 47.

[52] See n 47.

[53] US Department of the Treasury, 'Treasury Sanctions Illicit Gold Companies Funding Wagner Forces and Wagner Group Facilitator' (US Department of the Treasury, 27 June 2023), Press Release, https://home.treasury.gov/news/press-releases/jy1581.

[54] D Alperovitch, 'Prigozhin's Assassination Was Business, Not Revenge', *Foreign Policy* (5 September 2023), https://foreignpolicy.com/2023/09/05/yevgeny-prigozhin-assassination-vladimir-putin-wagner-deal-revenge/.

[55] 'Corporate Warriors' (n 45) 204, summary table of impacts from PMFs; Alperovitch (n 54) suggesting that Prigozhin's downfall was the result of his appropriation of wealth from African theatres, including CAR, that Russia wanted to capture itself.

[56] 'Corporate Warriors' (n 45) 218.

[57] See Singer (n 46).

[58] See Singer (n 46) on the connection between Dick Cheney and PMF Haliburton; see E Lipton, 'New Spin on a Revolving Door: Pentagon Officials Turned Venture Capitalists', *New York Times* (30 December 2023), www.nytimes.com/2023/12/30/us/politics/pentagon-venture-capitalists.html.

their relationships with state principals. As with the historical examples, PMFs fit awkwardly with the model of the corporation in either SVM or stakeholder approaches. There is a conditionality and need for public participation inherent in the activities of the corporation that is at odds with a purely private view, and yet private profit motives clearly drive these actors. Their behaviour is far from the stakeholder ideal of a corporation using discretionary power to take into account the broader social welfare impacts of its activity. PMFs are corporate entities with deliberately blurred public-private boundaries built into their purpose and structure.

However, it is not only in the direct use of PMFs for military action that the boundaries of corporate and state interests become unclear. Reliance on using private corporate networks and communication platforms for crucial strategic communications has become an issue in the telecommunications industry. A decision by Elon Musk's Starlink satellite communication firm to refuse the use of the network for military action by Ukraine during the conflict with Russia raised questions for US defence officials about the company's potential role and reliability in supporting US foreign relations and military strategy.[59] Ostensibly a private, corporate decision, the centrality of the network and potential strategic impact meant it was inextricable from critical public interests. Concerns about the mixed public-private character of large telecommunications firms have led to strategic decisions to exclude the Chinese company Huawei from the 5G networks of the 'Five Eyes' allies and Canada.[60] Similar efforts have been made to ban the popular app TikTok over concerns that its Chinese parent company ByteDance could share sensitive data with the Chinese government, posing a threat to national security.[61] In the latter examples, the fundamental concern is driven by questions about the 'privateness' of these entities vis a vis the Chinese government, combined with the ubiquity of the platforms for communication. In the first example, it is the privateness of critical communications infrastructure that raises public interest concerns about choices around access and operations.

These rather dark blurrings of public and private in the corporation provide modern examples that fit uncomfortably with the visions of corporate form and purpose at the heart of the modern legal debate. In some examples, such as PMFs or companies like Huawei, there is a fundamentally hybrid public-private character to both the entities and their operations, at odds with both SVM and stakeholder theory. In other respects, while companies can seem more purely

[59] T Copp, 'Elon Musk's refusal to have Starlink support Ukraine attack in Crimea raises questions for Pentagon', *Associated Press* (11 September 2023), https://apnews.com/article/spacex-ukraine-starlink-russia-air-force-fde93d9a69d7dbd1326022ecfdbc53c2.

[60] D Ljunggren and S Scherer, 'Canada to ban Huawei/ZTE 5G equipment, joining Five Eyes allies', *Reuters* (20 May 2022), www.reuters.com/business/media-telecom/canada-announce-ban-use-huawei-zte-5g-equipment-source-2022-05-19/.

[61] S Maheshwari and A Holpuch, 'Why Countries Are Trying to Ban TikTok', *New York Times* (16 August 2023), www.nytimes.com/article/tiktok-ban.html.

private (eg Starlink), the nature of their business entails significant embedded public welfare consequences for corporate choices. Akin to recipients of historic corporate charters, their business is providing infrastructure critical to the delivery of services for the public. As in the Ukraine example, their choices consequently implicate significant public interests. Yet again, there is little to suggest that any private discretionary power is exercised in a way that necessarily overlaps with public welfare rather than shareholder interests. While the context of national defence and military action may seem unique, it is not the only modern example.

Hockett and Omarova have written a persuasive account of the hybrid public-private character of modern banking and finance enterprises.[62] The public welfare costs of risky private innovation by financial sector firms during the global financial crisis of 2008 are highlighted in Omarova's contribution to this volume.[63] As with banks in the historical era, the spillover effects on the macroeconomy and individuals' welfare lend these actors' private choices extraordinary public impact.[64] As Omarova argues, the intuition that private financial innovation is inherently efficient and welfare-enhancing is a fallacy. However, the hybridity that Hocket and Omarova outline involves a much closer symbiotic public-private relationship inherent in these 'private' actors' business. They challenge the account in which these firms are simply engaged in the 'intermediation' of credit through channelling scarce supplies of private capital from lenders to borrowers. Instead, Hockett and Omarova see these firms as engaged in the process of money and credit creation, which is fundamentally facilitated by state backing of the private liabilities central to the process.[65] The state extends sovereign full faith and credit through actions of the Federal Reserve in accommodating private debt liabilities, allowing for monetisation of these same debts by the private entities.[66] Hockett and Omarova describe the state, as the provider of the critical foundational guarantee, as a 'franchisor' that enables banks and financial market actors to operate as 'franchisees', essentially 'dispensing' sovereign full faith and credit via their credit expanding private liabilities.[67] They argue that this public-private partnership permeates the financial sector – from banking to high-tech finance.[68] Hockett and Omarova stress the importance of their account for understanding the roles of public and private actors in the financial system, and better regulation.[69]

[62] See RC Hockett and ST Omarova, 'The Finance Franchise' (2017) 102 *Cornell Law Rev* 1144.

[63] See chapter 2 (ST Omarova, 'Financial Innovation: Three Fallacies in the Debate').

[64] See J Armour and JN Gordon, 'Systemic Harms & Shareholder Value' (2014) 6 *Journal of Legal Analysis* 35, arguing that banks are systemically important institutions, due to spillovers from their excessive risk taking, so alteration of SVM is required.

[65] Hockett and Omarova (n 62) 1147–48.

[66] ibid 1155–64, developing the details of the argument in the context of banking.

[67] ibid 1147.

[68] ibid 1148 stating the claim, developed in detail in sections II–VI of the article.

[69] ibid 1218.

Here, I abstract from some of their more specific implications and simply use their work to illustrate these economically significant corporations' fundamentally public-private hybrid character.[70]

Hockett and Omarova's work again raises two distinct types of mismatch with the dominant theories of the corporation. The first, reflecting the historical context, lies with an implicit public-private connection driven by the foundational role large banks and financial corporations play in the macroeconomy. Private choices inevitably have outsized public welfare consequences. The second lies in the nature of the entity; as Hockett and Omarova point out, the corporation is fundamentally a hybrid, relying on direct participation by the state. In both cases, the public and private in the nature and operation of large banks and financial institutions cannot by captured by a purely private SVM model of the corporation. Stakeholder theory also poorly reflects the hybrid structure and does not reflect the behaviour of many large banks and financial institutions, whose pursuit of risky profit strategies has precipitated financial crisis, rather than accounting for public welfare consequences of their actions.

A final example of public-private hybridity also echoes historical areas of overlap in the provision of public services and utilities. The North American Electric Reliability Corporation (NERC) is generally an obscure entity except when it is spotlighted in relation to high-profile electric grid failures, such as the 2021 blackout in Texas and parts of the US Midwest and Southeast.[71] Macey, Welton and Wiseman have recently provided a detailed analysis of NERC, contributing to a sparse literature.[72] NERC is a private (non-profit) corporation that currently serves as the statutory 'electric reliability organisation' (ERO) under the federal framework structuring national grid reliability in the US, overseen by the Federal Electric Reliability Commission (FERC).[73] In practice, NERC is responsible for developing and enforcing the various standards that ensure overall grid reliability across much of North America. Standards are developed by NERC's elected Standards Committee and voted on by its Registered Ballot Body, which includes representatives from all industry segments.[74] In practice, both the development of standards and their

[70] This is not the only way in which the public-private divide blurs in banking and finance. See, eg, RC Hockett and ST Omarova, '"Private" Means to "Public" Ends: Governments as Market Actors' (2014) 15 *Theoretical Inquiries in Law* 53, discussing government taking 'private' actions in markets to support public functions of market-making, market-moving, market-levering and market-preserving.

[71] See FERC, NERC and Regional Entities, *FERC-NERC-Regional Entity Staff Report: The February 2021 Cold Weather Outages in Texas and the South Central United States* (9 November 2021), https://ferc.gov/media/february-2021-cold-weather-outages-texas-and-south-central-unitedstates-ferc-nerc-.

[72] See JC Macey, S Welton and H Wiseman, 'Grid Reliability in the Electric Era' (2024) 41 *Yale Journal of Regulation* 164.

[73] ibid 188.

[74] ibid 201–02. Note that development of standards and enforcement is often further delegated to regional entities (ibid, 199).

approval are dominated by large industry incumbents, including for-profit private utilities. However, representatives include a wide range of both public and private industry actors.[75] As Macey, Welton and Wiseman point out, NERC grew out of a self-regulatory model justified by expertise and mutual incentives for efficient standards and high reliability among all its original members. Self-regulation worked well, as both public and private objectives aligned.[76] More recently, tension between the private objectives of dominant incumbent members and the broader public policy objective of facilitating the energy transition has emerged. NERC standards, developed and used by private actors, appear increasingly tilted toward the preservation of 'extensive, centralised, fossil-fuel-fired generation' at the expense of integration of renewables.[77] While a detailed discussion of the structure of grid reliability governance is beyond this chapter's scope, it is clear that the organisational form currently at its heart is a hybrid blend of public and private interests and actors.[78]

As with the two prior examples, NERC's business and structure fail to match well with the dominant models of the corporation in the literature. There is a fundamentally mixed public-private character to the organisation, and its 'private' choices have enormous social welfare impacts. While NERC is formally a non-profit corporation, its governance structure allows for a range of both public interest and private profit-driven considerations to inform its basic functions. This is not necessarily a criticism since there is potential for complementarity. However, as Macey, Welton and Wiseman point out, failure to align the governance structure with the need for accountability along both dimensions is problematic.

5.3.3. The Modern Corporation and the Public-Private Spectrum

The examples above involve entities that have a fundamentally hybrid public-private character. Corporate actors are engaged in inherently partnered activity with public authorities, simultaneously reflecting both private and public interests and purposes in corporate activity. While this provides a strong form of departure from a neat public-private divide, the line blurs in other important

[75] ibid 202. Representatives in the ballot body come from categories including: transmission owners, electric generators, load-serving entitles, electricity brokers, transmission dependent utilities, regional transmission organisations, electricity users, and government entities, among others.

[76] ibid 181.

[77] ibid 213.

[78] See also E Hammond, 'Double Deference in Administrative Law' (2016) 116 *Columbia Law Review* 1705, discussing NERC as an example of a self-regulatory organisation exercising delegated government regulatory authority; HM Osofsky and H Wiseman, 'Hybrid Energy Governance' (2014) 2014 *University of Illinois Law Review* 1 discussing NERC as an organisation composed of both public and private actors.

ways. Below I discuss examples in which corporations adopt voluntary commitments that overlap with public law norms. In these and other cases, firms deliberately enter debates involving the articulation of public values, despite lack of certainty around a business case for doing so. There is a complex interplay between private interests and public values in this voluntary activity.

The current movement to address 'environmental, social and governance' (ESG) interests provides an obvious example. While the label 'ESG' can cover a wide range of activity by corporations, one element relevant to the public-private divide is the deliberate overlap between firms' voluntary ESG activity, normative commitments in public law and efforts of public actors to foster the connection. The OECD and UN have focused on directly engaging transnational corporations through instruments like the Global Compact and OECD Guidelines.[79] The UN Global Compact requires firms to adopt and support 10 principles directly linked to UN-supported instruments, including the Universal Declaration of Human Rights, ILO Core Labour Conventions, the Rio Declaration on Environment and Development, and the UN Convention against Corruption. The OECD Guidelines focus on a similar but slightly expanded set of substantive areas, including 'human rights, labour rights, environment, bribery and corruption, consumer interests, disclosure, science and technology, competition, and taxation'. The normative commitments in both the Global Compact and OECD Guidelines reflect instruments of state-centred public international law. The focus on transnational corporations is a deliberate strategy to overcome gaps in support by sovereign states, backfilling the lack of public adhesion and implementation with voluntary private activity by these powerful global firms.

Firms making ESG commitments and reporting on them often voluntarily choose to reference norms and goals drawn from public international law.[80] For example, in the environmental realm, both Amazon and Walmart have greenhouse gas (GHG) reduction commitments that link to the Paris Agreement and its goals.[81] Efforts of private associations such as the Global Reporting Initiative and Carbon Disclosure Project to establish common third-party

[79] The Guidelines are 'recommendations addressed by governments to multinational enterprises'; an updated version was released in June 2023 (prior version 2011). See UN, *UN Global Compact, Business as a Force for Good, 10 Principles* (United Nations Global Compact), https://unglobalcompact.org/what-is-gc/mission; see OECD, *Guidelines for Multinational Enterprises* (Responsible Business Conduct: OECD Guidelines for Multinational Enterprises), https://mneguidelines.oecd.org//MNEguidelines/.

[80] C Metcalf, 'Corporate Social Responsibility as Global Public Law: Third Party Rankings as Regulation by Information' (2010) 28 *Pace Environmental Law Review* 145, 150.

[81] See Amazon Climate Pledge, with its direct incorporation of the Paris Agreement: 'Driving Climate Solutions' (Amazon, Sustainability), https://sustainability.aboutamazon.com/about/the-climate-pledge#section-nav-id-0>. Walmart also has initiatives linked to the Paris Agreement, including a commitment to reach net zero emissions by 2040 and its 'Project Gigaton' for removal of GHG emissions driven by private business, https://corporate.walmart.com/medialibrary/document/walmart-sets-goal-to-become-a-regenerative-company/_proxyDocument?id=00000174-ae08-dcf3-a7fc-afdcca070000.

reporting standards have filled a quasi-regulatory role by creating mechanisms for benchmarking corporate ESG performance.[82] Some form of standardisation and transparency is needed for ESG commitments to be effective and subject to public scrutiny and accountability. Reporting standards serve as a bridge between the private ESG commitments of firms and accountability in relation to the substantive public norms through incorporation of those norms into the standards. The evolution of the international landscape is toward the transformation of private voluntary commitments and disclosure toward one of state-enforced ESG accountability. This is apparent in the development of more state-centric ESG reporting frameworks. States have drawn on work to harmonise standards privately at the global level by the Task Force on Climate-Related Financial Disclosure (TCFD) and International Financial Reporting Standards (IFRS) to formulate public disclosure regimes, such as the EU Corporate Sustainability Reporting Directive, and in efforts by securities regulators to establish climate risk disclosure standards in Canada and the US.[83] Failure to meet voluntary ESG commitments is increasingly exposing firms to litigation.[84]

The extent to which the ESG 'commitments' of transnational firms really reflect the integration of public interest commitments and public values is hotly debated.[85] Some argue that this is simply an evolution of a profit-maximising strategy. Significant demand for ESG is driven by markets for both labour and capital.[86] Failure to address risks around ESG performance can potentially expose firms and their management to punishing consequences; to achieve sustainable, long-run profitability, corporations must consider the risks that ESG factors embody.[87] However, at least some proponents of this engagement

[82] See description of CDP reporting goals and standards: www.cdp.net/en; description of GRI: www.globalreporting.org/about-gri/.

[83] See TCFD: www.fsb-tcfd.org/about/; on the EU Corporate Sustainability Reporting Directive, see KPMG, *A brief overview of the key changes and impacts from the CSRD*, https://kpmg.com/nl/en/home/topics/environmental-social-governance/corporate-sustainability-reporting-directive.html.

[84] See, eg, J Hijazi, 'Shell Greenwashing Challenge Highlights Risk of ESG Claims', *Bloomberg Law* (16 February 2023) on suits brought against large corporations including Shell, Coca-Cola, Exxon-Mobil and Nestle for failure to meet voluntary ESG climate-related commitments. See also, J Sarra, 'Canada's securities regulators must finalize climate-disclosure rules without delay', *Globe & Mail* (11 February 2024), arguing that lack of clear regulatory standards in Canada is increasing litigation risks to corporations, pointing to over 900 cases globally, and urging adoption of IFRS standards, already adopted by 63 other jurisdictions and basis for proposed SEC disclosure rules in US.

[85] See, eg, Bebchuk and Tallarita (n3) and Bainbridge (n 3), who argue that these commitments are insubstantial at best. But see Q Curtis, J Fisch and AZ Robertson, 'Do ESG Funds Deliver on Their Promises?' (2021) 120 *Michigan Law Review* 393, https://repository.law.umich.edu/mlr/vol120/iss3/2, finding ESG mutual funds do generally deliver on promises.

[86] See, eg, M Barzuza, Q Curtis and DH Webber, 'The Millennial Corporation: Strong Stakeholders, Weak Managers' (2023) *Stanford Journal of Law, Business, and Finance*, https://doi.org/10.2139/ssrn.3918443; H Kim, 'Expecting Corporate Prosociality' (10 October 2022) University of Chicago Coase-Sandor Institute for Law & Economics Research Paper No 978, https://ssrn.com/abstract=4282358.

[87] See, eg, M Delikat, S Kray and C Frantz, 'Trends in ESG Litigation and Enforcement' (2023) *Harvard Law School Forum on Corporate Governance*; M Lipton, 'Further on the Purpose of the Corporation' (2022) *Harvard Law School Forum on Corporate Governance;* M Lipton,

see it as an evolution in corporate purpose and responsibility that extends beyond the baseline private model and engages more public responsibilities for the corporation.[88] The extent to which there is a neat separation between profitability concerns and genuine articulation of public values and commitments is often unclear. Fisch and Solomon discuss this uncertainty, referring to the example of Dick's Sporting Goods (a very large US sports store chain) deciding to stop carrying guns in response to school shootings.[89] Initially, the decision was framed as one driven by moral or public-welfare concerns at the expense of profit, with the CEO declaring he didn't 'care what the financial implication is'.[90] However, subsequently, it appeared that removing guns from its stores increased sales and was a value-enhancing strategy.[91] Certainly, in some cases, corporate choices are *perceived* as reflecting a mixture of business, political and social action. The overlap between ESG and public normative commitments in areas like human rights and climate change provide examples.

In the US, the public/political dimension of ESG has been emphasised in polarised push-back from a number of Republican-controlled states, seeking to limit firms' pursuit of ESG through regulation. For example, Attorneys General have initiated investigations into banks participating in the UN Global Financial Alliance for Net Zero and launched anti-trust claims against investment companies for prioritising a climate agenda. Various states have divested from investment powerhouse BlackRock because of its climate change, 'anti-fossil fuel' agenda. Texas passed legislation requiring state pension and school funds to divest from financial institutions that 'boycott energy companies'.[92]

Complex intersections between private corporate choices and public values are also apparent in the ongoing dispute between Disney and Florida Governor, Ron DeSantis. When Disney publicly criticised Florida's Parental Rights in Education Bill ('Don't say gay' law) and called for its repeal, DeSantis argued that the company had illegitimately tried to use its 'economic might to attack the parents of my state'.[93] The state retaliated by eliminating the special self-governing district designation that had allowed Disney to operate its resort independently as a quasi-municipality, potentially leaving the area's actual municipalities to pick up significant service expenses and debt that Disney had assumed in managing its resort. The legal battles are ongoing, and the costs

AO Emmerich, KS Schwartz, SV Niles and AM D'Ginto, 'ESG, Stakeholder Governance, and the Duty of the Corporation' (2022) *Harvard Law School Forum on Corporate Governance*.

[88] See, eg, JG Ruggie, 'Corporate Purpose in Play: The Role of ESG Investing' (7 November 2019) M-RCBG Faculty Working Paper Series, 2019-05, https://ssrn.com/abstract=3483205.

[89] See JE Fisch and SD Solomon, 'Should Corporations have a Purpose?' (2021) 99 *Texas Law Review* 1309.

[90] ibid 1332.

[91] ibid.

[92] *See* Lipton et al (n 87).

[93] See A Atterbury, 'DeSantis revokes Disney's special status after 'Don't Say Gay' opposition', *Politico* (22 April 2022), www.politico.com/news/2022/04/22/desantis-disney-special-status-dont-say-gay-00027302.

of the dispute for both parties are significant.[94] The extent to which Disney's original actions reflect a profit-driven strategy is unclear, but the perception that the company is participating in the articulation of public values is hard to ignore.

These examples differ from public-private hybrid entities, such as NERC, PMFs or large financial institutions. They are a potentially better fit with the SVM model of the corporation, and yet the deliberate choice to voluntarily engage in public-law related commitments and (ostensibly) align the company's business with contested public values does not always fit clearly with a profit-focused strategy. The examples in this way perhaps overlap with stakeholder theories of the corporation. However, the limits of this model are reflected in the decision by some firms to retreat from ESG commitments in the face of state push-back on the political front that raise threats to profits.[95] The examples reflect a genuine blending of public and private interests and actions that falls along a spectrum between the two poles of the corporate purpose debate. They also illustrate the need for forms of accountability that are responsive to both the firm's public and private roles. The engagement by corporations in articulating and advancing public objectives and values through corporate activity requires some form of accountability for this public aspect. In the case of climate emissions disclosure and ESG, the articulation of these standards also takes the form of a public-private hybrid collaboration, which is both international and transnational in scope.

5.4. THE CORPORATION AND SOCIAL COSTS: FORMS OF ACCOUNTABILITY

Corporate law scholars all recognise that divergence between corporate action and public welfare can arise due to 'externalities' – impacts on the public that don't form part of the firm's private decision-making calculus.[96] However, there is disagreement about where the responsibility to address these should rest.

Proponents of 'stakeholderism' argue that at least some responsibility should be placed within the firm, giving it a public-interest mandate to address these social impacts. Corporate choices should account for at least some of the most direct impacts on proximate stakeholders, rather than just shareholders. SVM proponents advance the traditional economic view that the government should take on the public role of regulating. Prominent critics, such as Bebchuk

[94] B Barnes, 'Disney Pulls Plug on $1 Billion Development in Florida', *New York Times* (18 May 2023), www.nytimes.com/2023/05/18/business/disney-ron-desantis-florida.html.

[95] See, eg, S Kishan, 'BlackRock Sued by Tennessee Over "Misleading" ESG Strategy', *BNN Bloomberg* (18 December 2023); E Halper, 'Is BlackRock's Larry Fink blowing it for the climate?', *Washington Post* (6 May 2023).

[96] See, eg, Bainbridge (n 3) 9. Note that 'externalities' can be both positive and negative, and the reference point for classification can be challenging; see, eg, CA Hill, 'The Rhetoric of Negative Externalities' (2016) 39 *Seattle University Law Review* 517.

and Tallarita, argue that placing discretionary responsibility within firms will exacerbate agency problems, lead to little substantive improvement for affected stakeholders, and potentially dull 'legal, regulatory and policy reform' that could 'provide real, meaningful protection'.[97] Similarly, Bainbridge, in his review of the Business Roundtable's 2019 statement on corporate purpose, argues that embracing stakeholder interests is 'puffing' to tap into market benefits of a socially responsible image and to ward off regulation, and/or a return to enhanced discretion that allows management to advance its own interests.[98] Instead, these scholars suggest that the firm should focus on its private interests, maximising value for shareholders, while the government implements legal constraints to reflect external social costs and benefits. Under the *Caremark* doctrine, the pursuit of profits cannot take priority over these legal constraints, and directors must exercise reasonable compliance oversight.[99]

However, such a neat separation of public and private responsibility for social costs is unrealistic. The idea that firms can maximise profits, only accounting for the social impacts of their choices when there are explicit legal constraints that force internalisation, fails to capture the complex means by which accountability can be created. It also neglects the dynamic through which public awareness of significant social harms caused by firms' private choices can lead to legal change. While this can occur through public regulation, it can also extend to evolution in private law.

Purely private tort action can provide a weak mechanism for internalising externalities. For example, early litigation on the dangers of asbestos failed around challenges of proving causality,[100] and the advantages of class proceedings were often unavailable due to the fact-specific nature of claims leading to a denial of certification.[101] However, some claims did succeed, and large punitive damages were driven by jury perceptions of corporate indifference to the

[97] See Bebchuk and Tallarita (n 3); but see H Kim, J Macey and K Underhill 'Does ESG Crowd Out Support for Government Regulation?' (2023) University of Chicago Coase-Sandor Institute for Law & Economics Research Paper No 983, empirically testing the claim, weak evidence for crowding out effect; DA Dana and J Nadler, 'Regulation, Public Attitudes, and Private Governance' (2019) 16 *Journal of Empirical Legal Studies* 1, 69, finding that voluntary ESG can increase support for regulation.

[98] S Bainbridge, 'Making Sense of the Business Roundtable's Reversal of Corporate Purpose' (2021) 46 *Journal of Corporation Law* 285, 316.

[99] S Bainbridge, 'Don't Compound the *Caremark* Mistake by Extending it to ESG oversight' (2021) UCLA School of Law, Law & Economics Research Paper No 21-10, 9.

[100] See, eg, *Lohrmann v Pittsburgh Corning Corp Eyeglasses*, 782 F.2d 1156 (4th Cir 1986), a claim against manufacturers for harm from exposure to asbestos dust, failure to warn, strict liability, dismissed on causation; *Cipollone v Ligget Group Inc*, 112 S Ct 2608 (1992), a case initially successful at trial but repeatedly appealed and ultimately dropped, scientific complexity of proving claims, litigious strategy of defendants increased cost of bringing claims).

[101] See, eg, *Georgine v Amchem Products, Inc*, (83 F.3d 610) (3d Cir 1996); affirmed in *Amchem Products, Inc v Windsor*, 521 US 591 (1997), denial of certification in class action seeking damages for exposure to asbestos manufactured by defendants, liability theories include strict liability, negligent failure to warn, etc.

risk created. Evidence that corporate defendants were aware of risks, failed to warn and pursued strategies that would increase exposure through product sales served to increase culpability.[102] Jury awards for punitive damages sometimes served as a vehicle for public outrage over corporations' pursuit of profit causing failure to mitigate significant harms, even in cases where a plausible cost-benefit justification might be argued.[103] A canonical example of this dynamic can be found in automobile design cases, where cost-benefit analysis was used to justify tolerating known accident risks. Ford's Pinto is famous for grounding a media and business ethics narrative around the blameworthiness of the company's actions lying in the willingness to trade-off the value of lives against pursuit of profits.[104] However, there are multiple examples of cost-benefit analysis supporting failure to address design defects, and consequent framing of the choices as a morally repugnant pursuit of profit forming a basis for large punitive jury awards.[105] Although one could argue that these cases simply reflect the ordinary private imposition of liability for failure to follow the law, the awarding of punitive damages underlines an enhanced objection to the choice of these private corporations to pursue profit at the expense of costs imposed on the public.

Public actors have also begun to use the tort system to bring claims against corporations to recoup public expenditures for widespread harms and direct costs to the public attributable to corporate action. Mississippi initiated this movement in tobacco litigation, arguing that American Tobacco was liable for the medical expenses of harmed smokers covered by state Medicaid.[106] The state argued that the company had created a public nuisance by questioning scientific evidence linking smoking and cancer to increase the number of addicted smokers. Injunctive relief was also sought to limit strategies to recruit young smokers and create future demand. Mississippi was ultimately joined by numerous other

[102] See, eg, *Izell v Union Carbide Corp*, 231 CalApp4th 962 (Cal Ct App 2014), punitive damages against Union Carbide for knowing low level exposure to asbestos could cause mesothelioma, but choosing not to warn; *Engle v Liggett Group*, Inc, 945 So.2d 1246 (Fla 2006), personal injury litigation against tobacco manufacturer, addictive properties of nicotine known and manipulated to promote smoking, defendant concealed information about dangers of smoking, large punitive damage award ($140bn) – verdict vacated but key factual findings could be relied upon in individual litigation.

[103] See, eg, GT Schwartz, 'The Myth of the Ford Pinto Case' (1991) 43 *Rutgers Law Review* 1013, discussing the Ford Pinto case in which the jury awarded $125 million in punitive damages, suggesting that secrecy of deliberations on risk, failure to convey risks to consumers and inform expectations led to outrage in jury.

[104] See, eg, MT Lee and MD Ermann, 'Pinto "Madness" as a Flawed Landmark Narrative: An Organizational and Network Analysis' (1999) 46 *Social Problems* 30, 31, citing extensive media and academic literature consistent with this narrative.

[105] See, eg, WK Viscusi, 'Corporate Risk Analysis: A Reckless Act?' (2000) 52 *Stanford Law Review* 547, discussing cases and also performing experiments identifying the tendency of mock-jurors to award punitive damages more often if companies did cost-benefit analysis of risks.

[106] GW Traylor, 'Big Tobacco, Medicaid-Covered Smokers, and the Substance of the Master Settlement Agreement' (2010) 63 *Vanderbilt Law Review* 1081.

states, leading to a Master Settlement Agreement reportedly for $206 billion, including all US states, DC, and the five territories.[107]

Here again, while it is possible to see the results as simply private liability for a private fault, there are significant public dimensions. The nature of the wrong, at least partly, is in corporate action related to established public values. While simply lying or concealing evidence from regulators is clearly off-side, the boundaries of legitimate contestation of science within regulatory processes may not always be clear *ex ante*. The fault (public nuisance) lies partly in exploiting this public expressive value for private gain, neglecting the public costs in doing so. US tobacco litigation inspired public actors in other jurisdictions and legal changes. In the Canadian province of British Columbia, legislation to facilitate government claims by altering tort law was passed and survived constitutional challenges.[108] Regardless of any legal ambiguity tobacco executives may have believed existed while forming their strategy, *ex post*, the significant social costs *ought* to have been considered.

A similar pattern can be seen in recent suits by public plaintiffs concerning the opioid epidemic. The 'first wave' of this current public health crisis began with the reformulation of opioid pain medication aggressively marketed as prescription drugs for pain management.[109] An explosion in use and abuse led to a doubling of the opioid overdose death rate between 1999 and 2010.[110] In addition to the direct costs of overdose deaths, addiction and related medical treatment, the prescription opioid epidemic had significant negative economic impacts, through labour force participation, productivity and the well-being of workers.[111] States, municipalities and other institutional claimants drew on the successful tobacco litigation to pursue cost-recovery from pharmaceutical manufacturers and distributors of prescription opioids.

These public claims generally targeted manufacturers and distributors of prescription opioids for misrepresenting addiction risks and failure to monitor distribution that allowed drugs to enter the illegal market.[112] States claimed under *parens patriae* jurisdiction and public nuisance, as well as advancing statutory claims. The equitable actions under *parens patriae* allowed states to

[107] ibid.

[108] *British Columbia v Imperial Tobacco Canada Ltd* [2005] 2 SCR 473, 2005 SCC 49.

[109] See 'The Opioid Crisis in the US: A Brief History', *Congressional Research Service* (30 November 2022), https://crsreports.congress.gov/product/pdf/IF/IF12260.

[110] ibid, the shift was from 2.9 to 6.8 deaths per 100,000 population.

[111] See, eg, AB Krueger, 'Where have all the Workers Gone: An Inquiry into the Decline of the U.S. Labor Force Participation Rate', *Brookings Papers on Economic Activity* (7–8 September 2017), www.brookings.edu/wp-content/uploads/2017/09/1_krueger.pdf, finding that half of non-labour force participating prime aged males were taking pain medication daily, 66% of which was prescribed. Labour force participation had declined more precipitously in areas exposed to opioids, and well-being was reported as lower in these areas as well, with respondents saying they derived little meaning from daily activities.

[112] See E Aliferov, 'The Role of Direct-Injury Government-Entity Lawsuits in the Opioid Litigation' (2018) 87 *Fordham Law Review* 1141, 1159, providing examples of claims raising allegations.

pursue damages to 'quasi-sovereign interests', such as harm to the 'health and well-being' (physical and economic) of its residents flowing from the corporate actions.[113] Nuisance claims supported recovery of state costs associated with the addiction crisis, such as increased medical, police, and social support services. Ultimately, thousands of claims by states and local political subdivisions were consolidated into an MDL (Multi District Litigation), and in 2021 and 2022, National Settlements were reached against key manufacturers and distributors. Firms' contributions to public harm from opioids led to obligations to pay billions of dollars in almost all cases.[114]

In these cases, the claims (public nuisance, unjust enrichment, *parens patriae*) subject companies to liability for widespread and significant harms from their products, contributed to by what companies likely thought were 'profit-maximising' strategies. Despite any possible ambiguity over regulatory constraints or potential for tort claims, there can be *ex post* liability for creating significant negative externalities. Attempts to conceal or contest the social impact of corporate actions (perhaps with a view to preserving short-term shareholder value) can be seen as exacerbating factors and even a basis for liability. The very scope and scale of the harm can push governments toward *ex post* cost-recovery litigation.

It is a fiction to say that a corporation can safely ignore the negative impacts of its operations on the public in the absence of current regulation/legal cost-internalisation mechanisms. Firms often possess the best information to gauge the risks from their activities and products and make decisions to address negative externalities. Failure to account for these, to pursue profits that firms know come at the expense of imposing substantial social costs, is likely to increase the potential for *ex post* liability. The actions above illustrate that this can be in the form of direct tort liability for damages. Litigation also has the potential to negatively affect firms' reputations, which can create an additional rationale to address externalities.[115]

Another influence are *Caremark* duties. While some scholars suggest that *Caremark* should be interpreted narrowly, others argue that although any liability under the doctrine could easily be avoided, *Caremark* created a much broader obligation for companies to consider the social costs of their actions.[116] Hill argues that *Caremark* has a 'penumbral' effect that encourages companies to go beyond monitoring and minimal legal compliance. The perceived uncertainty and costs of liability encourage firms to go beyond this to promote compliance

[113] ibid 1158, citing *Alfred L Snapp & Son, Inc v Puerto Rico ex rel Barez*, 458 US 592 (1982).

[114] 'Executive Summary of National Opioid Settlements' (National Opioid Settlement, 9 August 2023), https://nationalopioidsettlement.com/executive-summary/.

[115] Fisch and Solomon (n 89) 1331, citing D Lund on importance of reputation, impact on prospective regulatory environment, market demand for firms to consider public-interest stakeholder concerns.

[116] See Bainbridge (n 99); CA Hill, 'Caremark as Soft Law' (2018) 90 *Temple Law Review* 681.

with both the letter and spirit of the law and integrate ethical and reputational impacts. A company cannot 'compute costs and benefits narrowly as it would in other contexts, quantifying its ability to avoid detection or ameliorate harms (via greenwashing or other techniques) to justify taking the risk as a profit-maximising strategy'.[117] Hill points to the example of *Bank of America v City of Miami*,[118] in which the court upheld an expansive interpretation of the US Fair Housing Act permitting municipalities to sue lenders for lost property taxes from blighted areas caused by fallout from discriminatory lending practices during the financial crisis.[119] Reflecting on the role of public outrage in the tort litigation above, Hill argues that the scope and scale of losses caused by corporate choices around risk helped fuel this legal outcome.

The line between private value maximising choices and public interest consideration of potential negative externalities from corporate action can be thin and indeterminate. Rational firms *should* often consider these impacts and try to mitigate them, notwithstanding that they fall on 'stakeholders' outside the firm, can overlap with the public welfare, and strict legal requirements or liability are unclear. The idea that firms should adhere to a strict SVM model fails to reflect the complexity of the risk calculations required in practice, as well as the evolving nature of legal constraints that are likely to shift in response to the scale of externality harms. However, while a duty to consider externality effects would align with a stakeholder theory of the firm, the examples above illustrate that left to their own discretion, firms may seriously underperform. A combination of private liability, public regulators enforcing liability, legal duties for firms and the impact on prospective profits works to force firms to have regard to public-interest externalities.

5.5. THE CORPORATION VS THE REGULATOR: ENEMY WITHIN THE GATES?

The public-private division of labour that sees protection of the public interest as the government's role relies on an optimistic assumption that the government acts as a social welfare maximiser.[120] This is implicit in critiques of expanded corporate purpose by scholars like Bebchuk and Tallarita and Bainbridge, who argue that government regulation is what will provide meaningful protection for stakeholders.[121] In practice, regulation emerges from a process that is political

[117] ibid 688.
[118] *Bank of America Corp v City of Miami*, 137 S Ct 1296, 1307 (2017).
[119] Hill (n 116) 690–91.
[120] See Coase (n 10) critiquing this view ascribed to Pigou.
[121] Note that they recognise that government does *not* always act in the public interest, but still leave government this role as more promising compared with allocating responsibility to corporations via stakeholder theory.

and involves potential for group dynamics that do not promote either efficiency or social welfare.[122] The neat separation of public and private breaks down here as well, as we find corporations embedded within the regulatory process to varying degrees.

The largest firms are of particular concern. In the same way anti-trust recognises that firms can achieve a size and scale that gives then the ability to manipulate the market, a similar effect can be present in the politics of regulation, allowing firms to influence the law they face. Large firms, as a result of their impact in the market, their role in providing key infrastructure/acting as central nodes in economic networks, and their specialised knowledge and expertise, can also become directly involved in assisting with regulatory activity. These firms operate along a spectrum of involvement, from helping to design and enforce standards through public regulatory processes to being charged with partnering with regulators to create and enforce 'regulation' through their private activity. Both the potential for social welfare externalities from large corporations' influence in the regulatory arena and the role these firms play in undertaking public regulatory functions through their activity contribute to blurring the public-private divide.

5.5.1. Corporations and the Politics of Regulation

Sometimes, corporations' impact on regulation comes through indirect influence on the workings of government. For example, scholars have documented complex networks seeking influence, constructed by fossil fuel proponents, attempting to forestall climate change law and policy and entrench the industry. Tactics such as campaign contributions, use of foundations for funding of politicians and lobbies, and generation of misinformation have played a role.[123] Results include preservation of substantial subsidies for the industry and delays in adopting climate mitigation strategies, such as moving away from coal-fired electricity generation.[124] A general lack of transparency in relation to corporate expenditures for indirect lobbying and political influence has been criticised for allowing the extent of corporate involvement in the regulatory process to remain obscured.[125]

[122] See, eg, M Olsen, *The Logic of Collective Action: Public Goods and the Theory of Groups* (Cambridge MA, Harvard University Press, 1965).

[123] See, eg, J Farrell, 'Network structure and influence of the climate change countermovement' (2016) 6 *Nature Climate Change* 4, 370; RJ Brulle, 'Institutionalizing delay: foundation funding and the creation of US climate change counter-movement organizations' (2014) 122 *Climatic Change* 681.

[124] See, eg, A Lucas, 'Investigating networks of corporate influence on government decision-making: The case of Australia's climate change and energy policies' (2021) 81 *Energy Research & Social Science*.

[125] See, eg, Union of Concerned Scientists, 'A Climate of Corporate Control, How Corporations Have Influenced the U.S. Dialogue on Climate Science and Policy: Executive Summary' (Union of Concerned Scientists, 31 May 2012), www.ucsusa.org/resources/climate-corporate-control.

Obscured connections between corporate interests and parties bringing litigation focused on regulations and rule-making are another way the public and private influences on regulation are mediated. The recent *Loper Bright Enterprises v Raimondo* case at the US Supreme Court fundamentally challenges the scope of federal administrative regulatory authority according to the *Chevron* doctrine, which extends deference to agencies' understanding of their statutory mandates.[126] While on its face, the case is about claims of individual commercial fishermen and costs to have monitors on their boats, indirect links between companies funding the litigation, the law firm, and Koch Industries have been highlighted in the press. Legal scholars have described a private, deregulatory agenda advanced by Mr Koch, who also chairs Koch Industries, the US's second-largest privately held corporation.[127]

The indirect influence of corporate interests in regulation and policy can have serious consequences. The Canadian provincial government of Alberta made a surprising decision in 2023 to put a moratorium on the approval of renewable energy projects in the province. The objective was ostensibly to study land use implications, environmental risks and reclamation costs.[128] The move abruptly shut down a rapidly growing renewables sector, important for reaching climate mitigation targets. Concerns for renewables' end-of-life remediation were surprising, as little progress has been made to curb substantial environmental impacts from orphan oil and gas wells in the province.[129] Significant support for the moratorium appears to have come from landowners concerned with the construction of renewables near their property, an issue that has stalled projects in the US as well.[130] Unfortunately, misinformation appears to play an important role in community scepticism, and involvement by fossil fuel-related advocacy is part of the problem.[131] Local approval is required for the siting of renewable projects, a regulatory structure that sets up an accessible veto point for interests opposed to seeing the industry advance.

At some level, the participation of corporate actors in the political and legal arena to influence regulation is consistent with their character as private actors, motivated by their own interests. However, the degree and nature of involvement raise serious questions about the ability of government to use regulation

[126] See H Tabuchi, 'A Potentially Huge Supreme Court Case Has a Hidden Conservative Backer', *New York Times* (16 January 2024).

[127] ibid.

[128] See J French, 'Renewables industry feels burned by Alberta's sudden pause on project approvals', *CBC News* (3 August 2023), www.cbc.ca/news/canada/edmonton/renewables-industry-feels-burned-by-alberta-s-sudden-pause-on-project-approvals-1.6926094.

[129] ibid.

[130] J Simon, 'Misinformation is derailing renewable energy projects across the United States', *NPR* (28 March 2022), www.npr.org/2022/03/28/1086790531/renewable-energy-projects-wind-energy-solar-energy-climate-change-misinformation.

[131] See, eg, JT Fergen, JB Jacquet and R Shukla, '"Doomscrolling" in my backyard: Corrosive online communities and contested wind development in rural Ohio' (2021) 80 *Energy Research & Social Science* 1.

to protect the public interest. Extremely large, well-resourced corporations have the potential to significantly shape the regulatory environment they face through indirect influence on government and public regulatory processes. Although advancing their private interests, significant public consequences attach to their efforts. As with large banks and financial institutions, the pursuit of private interest by large corporations generates potential for substantial public welfare externalities, here within 'markets for regulation'. Their activity has an inherently public quality, important to capture when thinking about the nature of these firms. The SVM model's assumption that corporate law can focus on governing the private aspects of the corporation, leaving regulators to protect the public interest, fails to grapple with this reality. The stakeholder model, placing public interest duties within the firm, avoids the problem to some degree, since firms should self-regulate under the duty. However, this model fails to address the reality of financially self-interested regulatory action by large corporations that better reflects the incentive pressures inherent in SVM.

5.5.2. Regulatory Partnership: Corporations as Regulators

The involvement of corporate parties in regulatory processes can be much more open and direct. Negotiation with 'industry partners' is often an element of crafting regulation and can be important for effective regulatory design. Top-down directives from government can be inefficient and costly to implement; information about the context within which regulated entities are operating, details around implementation challenges, competitive concerns – can all be inputs that lead to better regulation. The case of NERC, discussed above, provides an example of this theory. Responsive regulation or co-regulation recognises the important positive ties between government and firms in the regulatory process.[132] However, the extent to which industry participation in regulatory design reflects this ideal, as opposed to regulatory capture, is not always clear.

We can see concerning examples in the context of climate change/the energy transition. Libby Dimenstein and Burçin Ünel have considered the process for approval of natural gas pipeline capacity expansion under FERC.[133] The US is heavily reliant on natural gas for electricity generation; however, reaching US climate goals for GHG reductions will require a transition away from natural gas generation. Dimenstein and Ünel critique the FERC process for review of proposals to expand natural gas capacity through pipeline construction, arguing

[132] See, eg, I Ayres & J Braithwaite, *Responsive Regulation* (Oxford, Oxford University Press, 1992).

[133] L Dimenstein and B Ünel, 'Regional Planning for Just and Reasonable Rates: Reforming Gas Pipelines Review' (2024) 49(1) *Columbia Journal of Environmental Law* 1.

that despite a statutorily robust process for public interest evaluation, actual approval delegates much of the process to proponents:

> FERC approves pipelines on an ad hoc basis that is driven by the business decisions of individual developers. When a pipeline applies to the Commission, instead of asking for market-based evidence that the proposed pipeline would satisfy unmet regional demand or enhance reliability, the Commission bases its decision largely on the existence of a precedent agreement: a contract between the developer and a client who wants to purchase pipeline capacity. If the developer can show FERC a precedent agreement, the Commission will approve the pipeline, effectively substituting the existence of private contracts for a demonstration of public interest.[134]

This is an important example, particularly as FERC has approved over 400 interstate natural gas pipelines in the last 25 years, representing substantial potential for stranded infrastructure and strengthening industry incumbency claims that can slow the energy transition.[135] While, ideally, the approval process would harness the expertise and knowledge of regulated entities to make a public interest decision, in this instance it seems that there is simply an assumption that a private agreement *is* evidence that the public interest criterion is met.

In a similar vein, Joshua Macey has highlighted problematic 'outsourcing' of energy market rules to regulated parties in electricity generation and transmission.[136] Macey argues that the regulatory structure has allowed generators to embrace climate transition policies – such as GHG charges and support for renewables capacity – because they control important elements of regulatory design that insulate them from the impacts of these initiatives and ultimately frustrate the achievement of the policy goals. For example, generators are permitted 'fuel adjustment clauses' that allow them to pass the cost of GHG charges onto captive ratepayers, who are prevented by regulators from switching suppliers.[137] Regulated utilities also hold the power to file tariffs outlining conditions of electricity service, propose which transmission resources are constructed, and provide information on costs to meet future demand.[138] These statutorily entrenched rights allow industry incumbents to protect their private interests from losses that a full-scale energy transition would involve. While the presence of these regulated parties within the design structure is likely intended to harness their expertise and respect technical, capacity or other constraints, the results seem to be public-privately crafted rules that favour private interests.

Both the examples above appear to involve hazards of regulatory capture by private, corporate interests. In other cases, the potential for more cooperative engagement between regulators and regulated entities may be significant.

[134] ibid 3.
[135] ibid.
[136] J Macey, 'Outsourcing Energy Market Design' (2024, forthcoming) 91 *University of Chicago Law Review* (draft on file with author).
[137] ibid 6.
[138] ibid 10.

Rory van Loo has described a new category of private 'enforcer firms' – among the largest companies in the US.[139] Van Loo uses a series of case studies to illustrate how these firms have been 'deputised' by regulators to act as monitors and enforcers for third-party firms they contract with. For example, in the wake of the Cambridge Analytica scandal in which Facebook users' data was accessed and used to promote Donald Trump's election campaign, the Federal Trade Commission (FTC) required Facebook to take a direct role in overseeing the security practices of third-party service providers such as app developers.[140] Facebook was required to develop an oversight policy and a robust monitoring network that included targeted security audits. Van Loo details similar case studies in which large firms in the financial, oil, and pharmaceutical industries were required to take on obligations by regulators to monitor third-party firms for compliance with regulatory standards, for example, including clauses mandated by regulators to set compliance obligations into their contracts.[141] Enforcer firms then become the target of regulatory enforcement if they fail to oversee these third-party regulatory mandates effectively. While firms like the targeted 'enforcers' have private incentives to oversee and monitor the operations of contract parties, van Loo persuasively argues that this development is a more public function embedded within firms. Regulators are leveraging firms' private information and contractual bargaining power to produce a new tier of private, delegated administrators for public regulatory policies. Firms are engaged in the public administrative functions of 'rule-making' through drafting contract clauses to structure third-party regulatory compliance[142] and mandated enforcement through ongoing monitoring and imposing 'penalties' on non-compliant third-parties in the form of exiting the business relationship.[143] This arrangement means 'appeals to the private nature of the firm are less persuasive' and raises questions about mechanisms for accountability of both public agencies and enforcer firms in exercising these public mandates.[144]

The rapid emergence of AI (artificial intelligence) capability and the potential for largely unregulated uptake provide a possible example of more voluntary public-private regulatory collaboration. Industry participants have recently called for regulatory intervention to help structure this market and

[139] R Van Loo, 'The New Gatekeepers: Private Firms as Public Enforcers' (2020) 106 *Virginia Law Review* 467, https://scholarship.law.bu.edu/faculty_scholarship/800.

[140] ibid 14–15.

[141] ibid 17–24, outlining details of case studies related to the Consumer Financial Protection Bureau (CFPB), Environmental Protection Agency (EPA) and Food and Drug Administration (FDA), and at 27 discussing contract clauses the FTC required Facebook to include regarding third-party privacy protection. The use of private contracts as a regulatory modality is also discussed by Anna Gelpern in her contribution to this volume, in relation to 'too big to fail' financial institutions and state bailouts; see chapter 11 ('Boilerplate against Bailouts: A Regulatory Ride Fallacy').

[142] Van Loo (n 139) 27–28.

[143] ibid 30–32.

[144] ibid 38, 44.

create guardrails to avoid potentially significant social harm.[145] The novelty and technical nature of the technology pose a barrier to independent government regulation, as regulators appear to lag far behind the industry in understanding the nature and risks of AI and its applications. Tallarita has recently recognised the need to incorporate safety and public interest within AI corporate governance. While he suggests that unique governance structures could potentially facilitate this, he cautions that 'even the most creative corporate governance innovations cannot be a long-term substitute for the public governance of catastrophic risks'.[146] He argues that the government will need to step in to create a body incorporating public and private actors to work collaboratively on the project, with public investments in research and prioritisation of safety.

However, the sheer size and global market dominance of tech platform companies involved can make it difficult for the government to pursue public interest regulation. Recent attempts to regulate the provision of news via Meta and Google platforms by regulators in Canada and Australia have taken the form of hard-ball negotiations.[147] Passage of the Online News Act (Bill C-18)[148] in Canada was preceded by negotiations between Meta and Google and federal regulators to try to secure agreement over the scope and extent of financial transfers to compensate the news industry for linking to their content. While an agreement was reached with Google, Meta continues to exercise its threat point option of simply withdrawing from the market and banning news on its platforms.[149] Given the dependence on these platforms by the public for information access, this stance represents a serious threat that could dramatically curtail meaningful dissemination of traditional news media output.

The nature of these regulatory debates helps further illustrate the blurred distinction between public and private, since these platforms have become critical vectors for individuals exercising free expression. Private choices of firms impact the practical ability for the public to enjoy these rights, and content moderation policies (or their absence) have profound implications for the reach of public harms from disinformation and deliberate dissemination of 'fake news' likely to be accelerated by the emergence of accessible AI. Commentators have

[145] See, eg Statement on AI Risk | CAIS (safe.ai); 'U.S. Chamber of Commerce calls for AI regulation' (*Reuters*, 9 March 2023) www.reuters.com/technology/us-chamber-commerce-calls-ai-regulation-2023-03-09/; C Kang, '*OpenAI's Sam Altman Urges A.I. Regulation in Senate Hearing*' (*New York Times*, 16 May 2023) www.nytimes.com/2023/05/16/technology/openai-altman-artificial-intelligence-regulation.html.

[146] R Tallarita, 'AI is Testing the Limits of Corporate Governance' (*Harvard Business Review*, 5 December 2023).

[147] J Mundle, 'Canadians will no longer have access to news content on Facebook and Instagram, Meta says' (*CBC News*, 22 June 2023) www.cbc.ca/news/politics/online-news-act-meta-facebook-1.6885634.

[148] SC 2023 (c 23).

[149] See N Yousef, 'Meta's News Ban in Canada remains as Online News Act goes into Effect' (*BBC*, 19 December 2023) www.bbc.com/news/world-us-canada-67755133. Meta's policy had not changed at the time of writing.

raised concerns over the potential for election misinformation to sway global elections, potentially tilting the world toward authoritarian governments.[150] While platforms themselves have been considered private entities with no First Amendment constraints on their content moderation policies, some, like Meta, have adopted special independent governance measures for this quasi-public function that clearly engages public values and the public interest.[151]

In many ways, the traditional perception of government as a public-interest regulator, to which the public interest can safely be delegated, is breaking down. Corporations are not necessarily ideally motivated guardians of the public interest. However, strict separation of public and private in the realm of regulation does not reflect regulation 'on the ground' and fails to recognise that, in some cases, corporate engagement can have public interest considerations in view when participating in establishing regulations or acting in self-regulation. The pervasive engagement of the largest corporations in the realm of regulatory creation, design and enforcement is an important public dimension of their existence. Neither of the two dominant theories in the corporate purpose debate adequately capture this aspect. Accountability for this public aspect of large corporations' activity cannot simply be viewed as a failure of public regulation, because of the inherently endogenous public-private means through which regulation emerges. Maintaining the fallacy of the public-private divide leaves a critical gap in thinking about how to govern the active regulatory role played by large corporations.

5.6. CLIMATE CHANGE AND THE CORPORATION: ILLUSTRATING THE FALLACY OF THE PUBLIC-PRIVATE DIVIDE

Climate change is a global externality characterised as an 'existential threat' by the Intergovernmental Panel on Climate Change (IPCC). Failure to successfully implement mitigation and adaptation strategies poses an increasingly serious risk of high economic, human and ecological costs.[152] Climate change is also a context that illustrates the fallacy of a neat regulatory-corporate mapping onto the public-private divide.

Climate policy initiatives such as the energy transition, pricing emissions and generation of adaptation risk information implicate public-private hybrids in the regulatory arena. In addition to the hybrid role of NERC, issues around public-private regulatory pipeline approval and energy market design that affect

[150] T Hsu, S Thompson and S Myers, 'Elections and Disinformation Are Colliding Like Never Before in 2024', *New York Times* (11 January 2024), www.nytimes.com/2024/01/09/business/media/election-disinformation-2024.html.

[151] E Douek, 'The Meta Oversight Board and the Empty Promise of Legitimacy' (forthcoming 2024) 37 *Harvard Journal of Law & Technology*, https://ssrn.com/abstract=4565180.

[152] See, eg, IPCC AR6 Synthesis Report: Climate Change 2023, www.ipcc.ch/report/ar6/syr/.

the energy transition discussed above, hybridity is also found in climate adaptation. Both public decision-makers like municipalities and private actors like financial institutions are increasingly relying on localised climate risk information in decision-making about investments affected by extreme weather events linked to climate change.[153] The need for risk data has spurred steep growth in corporate entrants providing localised risk data. While the use of this private risk information has enormous consequences for the allocation of both public and private capital, there is little methodological transparency to test the accuracy of private climate risk information.[154] Forecasts, while currently an expensive private product, draw on extensive information sources, many of which are publicly provided by government scientists. Investment in basic science and generation of scientific information as a public good provide the necessary foundation for private climate risk products. Climate risk information is a basic input into networked economic, social and political decision-making around climate policy and regulation. The emerging role of dominant corporate actors at the centre raises important questions about how the public and private interests will be accommodated and how accountability for both public and private aspects will be achieved.

Corporate actors and their climate actions engage public law objectives and values held by many investors, employees, consumers and members of the public. The overlap between public law climate change goals and the private climate actions of large corporations is discussed above; the adoption of the Paris Agreement targets by industry giants from BlackRock to Walmart illustrates this alignment. Authors have highlighted the integration of climate change concerns into investors' decision-making, both in terms of assessing the risk of investments and reflecting investor commitments as a matter of morals or values.[155] The pervasive impacts of climate risk on the market have led some academics to theorise that extremely large investment 'market movers' will effectively internalise these social costs in decision-making, blurring the divide between public and private around the costs of climate inaction.[156] Some have argued that institutional investors have effectively become 'regulators' on climate change and other ESG mandates through their influence over corporate actors.[157]

Private action by large transnational corporations and institutional investors is likely to be an important element of achieving climate goals. Many of these

[153] See M Condon, 'Climate Services: The Business of Physical Risk' (2023) 55 *Arizona State Law Journal* 147, https://ssrn.com/abstract=4396826; J Mankin, 'The People Have a Right to Climate Data', *New York Times* (20 January 2024), www.nytimes.com/2024/01/20/opinion/climate-risk-disasters-data.html.

[154] Condon (n 153).

[155] See M Barzuza, Q Curtis and D Webber, 'Shareholder Value(s): Index Fund ESG Activism and the New Millennial Corporate Governance' (2020) 93 *Southern California Law Review* 1243.

[156] See, eg, J Gordon, 'Systemic Stewardship' (2022) 47 *Journal of Corporation Law* 627; M Condon, 'Externalities and the Common Owner' (2020) 95 *Washington. Law Review* 1.

[157] See D Lund, 'Asset Managers as Regulators' (2023) 171 *University of Pennsylvania Law Review* 77.

private actors have publicly committed to mitigation goals aligned with the international law targets for states under the Paris Agreement.[158] Progress on these goals and the degree of firms' commitment is less clear.[159] These companies' actions are independent of those of their home states but often align with the overall framework of international climate law that structures state ambitions and Nationally Determine Contributions (NDCs). They feed into the ability of states to achieve their own goals, particularly as these private actors can have an outsized impact on emissions.

Even absent the evolution of domestic public reporting standards, such as the proposed SEC climate disclosure rules, there are public and market pressures for firms to demonstrate their commitments. As discussed previously, building credible commitments is aided by the work of third parties who design benchmarking standards and provide assurance. These structures often do not follow a neat public-private divide but feed into constructing public accountability standards.

The private actions of firms are increasingly exposed to risks associated with failure to internalise and mitigate climate change impacts. Following the pattern in tobacco and opioid litigation, there has been an explosion in private litigation seeking damages from corporations (particularly those in the fossil fuel industry) for damages associated with their emissions.[160] Many of these have been brought by states or municipalities seeking contributions for the cost of climate impacts and financing of required adaptation.[161] Evolution in attribution science is making the prospect of successful suits much higher. While in the past courts have tended to shy away from claims, in part due to the global nature of climate change, researchers are now prepared to offer much more precise estimates of corporate emissions profiles and to link these causally to damages from specific events.[162] With such liability looming, the public externality impacts of climate change from a firm's operation become private interests of the firm.

While firms may be targeted in suits as private contributors to climate change harms, this activity also has a public dimension. It contributes to global emissions and has implications for states' own emissions profiles and contributions to climate change harms. The same attribution science that is sharpening causal connections to private firms' GHG emissions is providing a basis to assign liability to states for the costs of their failures to meet international mitigation targets.[163] Developing states, especially those in the global south, are experiencing high costs of climate change impacts, imposed on already vulnerable populations, and are growing weary of waiting for assistance from G20 states

[158] See n 81 (Amazon, Walmart pledges).

[159] See, eg, Halper (n 95).

[160] AI Saad, 'Attribution for Climate Torts' (2023) 64 *Boston College Law Review* 867.

[161] ibid 876.

[162] ibid 877–79.

[163] CW Callahan and JS Mankin, 'National attribution of historical climate damages' (2022) 172 *Climatic Change* 40, https://doi.org/10.1007/s10584-022-03387-y.

under the UN loss and damage and other climate adaptation funds.[164] States are seeking an advisory opinion from the ICJ that may implicate an obligation for responsible states to provide climate reparations.[165] While the enforceability of international law is always in play, the political and moral implications of such international legal developments are likely to involve some costs borne by home states for private corporate emitters, whose private actions are ultimately ascribed to the state.

5.7. CONCLUSIONS

Current debates about the nature and purpose of the corporation focus on two distinct models. One is the stakeholder model. This imbues the corporation with a duty to look beyond shareholders to the interests of a broader group in a way that can make the firm responsive to certain direct public welfare aspects of its operations. In contrast, the (more dominant) SVM model characterises the firm as a fundamentally private entity, anchored by an economic account that prioritises efficiency and minimising agency costs to best enhance welfare through corporate action. Both incorporate a relatively specific vision of the public-private divide, and the SVM, in particular, draws a clean line between the private actions firms *ought* to focus on and the role of government in addressing public interest concerns.

The thrust of this contribution is that neither fully captures the reality of the corporation and the balance of public and private interests and functions. There are diverse ways that the public and private intersect in the corporation. In some economically significant sectors, large corporations play a hybrid public-private role. Examples track historical cases, such as military and strategic activity, banking and finance, and utilities and public services. Despite the passage of time and significant changes in the law and theory of the corporation, some functional public-private blending persists in these areas.

The public-private divide also blurs in other less direct ways. The explosion in voluntary ESG illustrates a degree of engagement in quasi-regulatory activity and in the articulation of public values. Various factors, including market pressure from consumers and investors, third-party standard-setting, and potential for legal liability in tort or corporate law (*Caremark*) create practical if not legal obligations for the largest corporations to consider the social impacts of their actions. This reality fails to match theories of either the stakeholder-specific

[164] See, eg, N Lakhani, 'Why loss and damage funds are key to climate justice for developing countries at Cop28', *The Guardian* (29 November 2023), www.theguardian.com/environment/2023/nov/29/why-loss-and-damage-funds-are-key-to-climate-justice-for-developing-countries-at-cop28.

[165] See, eg, M Tigre and J Bañuelos, 'The ICJ's Advisory Opinion on Climate Change: What Happens Now?', *Columbia Law School Sabin Center blog* (29 March 2023), https://blogs.law.columbia.edu/climatechange/2023/03/29/the-icjs-advisory-opinion-on-climate-change-what-happens-now/.

social impact responsibility or a responsibility simply to obey the law and follow regulations implicit in the SVM model.

Corporations are not simply the private subjects of public interest legal constraints. The process of generating public regulation often involves active participation by firms – more and less directly. In important cases, firms are participating in both setting and implementing public regulatory mandates. Firms can be charged with engaging in public interest regulatory activity, participating in a less formal partnered way to coordinate and facilitate public regulation, or providing quasi-public regulation themselves. The largest corporations are actively involved in political 'markets' for regulation, and their size and potential to move outcomes creates a significant public welfare dimension to their private choices.

While the dominant SVM theoretical framework provides a persuasive account of ways in which the corporation's efficiency can falter from a private perspective, it provides an incomplete picture where firms have a hybrid public-private character or are engaged in playing a significant public role. Continuing to place the private SVM model at the centre of corporate law is likely to lead to blind spots over how to address accountability for the public activity that firms *are* engaged in. Stakeholder theory may seem a better fit for the public-private blending that can be present in large corporations by creating a duty to consider some of these public interests in corporate decision-making. However, it is an underinclusive vision of ways that the corporation can require accountability for public dimensions of its activity, such as partnership in regulation. The stakeholder model, as many critics have noted, also lacks a clear accountability metric.[166] As this contribution shows, discretionary choices by corporations can diverge from consistency with the public-welfare attentive vision of stakeholder theory.

Developing a normative account of how the public dimensions of the corporation should be reflected in corporate law is a complex issue beyond the scope of this contribution. Scholars have suggested a range of possible mechanisms to better align corporate governance with corporations' public role.[167] More attention should be given to addressing this gap in corporate governance and accounts of the corporation. In interpreting existing mechanisms for corporate accountability and transparency, we should take care not to buy into the fallacy of a clean public-private divide that leaves corporations in the purely private realm.

[166] See, eg, Bainbridge (n 3); Bebchuk and Tallarita (n 3).

[167] See, eg, B Clarke and GE Henderson, 'Directors as Guardians of the Public Interest: Lessons from the Irish Banking Crisis' (2016) 16 *Journal of Corporate Law Studies* 187, discussing the role of public interest directors; Fisch and Solomon (n 89) 1335, discussing options for revising board structure to reflect stakeholder constituency interests along with other mechanisms to enforce non-SVM objectives.

6

The False Narrative of 'Responsible Investment'

ELLEN QUIGLEY

6.1. INTRODUCTION

THIS CHAPTER ARGUES that responsible investment – or indeed sustainable, ethical, or environmental, social and governance (ESG) investing – does not warrant the use of the terms employed to describe it. What follows illustrates the ways in which these (closely related) ways of investing largely fail to be responsible, sustainable, ethical, or environmentally and socially focused. It also demonstrates that the activities associated with this field very rarely constitute 'investing' or 'financing' in that they do not tend to deploy primary market flows towards desirable ends, nor do they prevent the flow of capital towards undesirable ends or prompt significant company-level behaviour change as a result of responsible investors' work. Accordingly, responsible investment can be considered neither responsible nor investment.

For the purposes of this chapter, the phrase 'responsible investment' will be used as an umbrella term to refer to responsible investment (RI), ethical investing, ESG investing, sustainable finance, and socially responsible investing (SRI). Some of these terms more typically refer to the use of exclusions/divestment to avoid exposure to companies deemed harmful on ethical grounds, while others have more of a focus on financial risk reduction from environmental and social harms. Ethical and socially responsible investing are often considered interchangeable, with the former term having been used until the 1990s, when SRI came into more popular use,[1] and both of these tend to be understood as investment strategies that avoid exposure to companies engaged in unethical behaviour (eg weapons, alcohol, pornography, gambling), although

[1] See R Sparkes, 'A Historical Perspective on the Growth of Socially Responsible Investment' in R Sullivan and C Mackenzie (eds), *Responsible Investment* (London, Routledge, 2017).

debates about definitions in this space are ongoing.[2] Elizabeth Pollman[3] suggests that ESG is variously used to describe the use of environmental, social and governance factors in investment analysis; risk management; promoting sustainability or other social and environmental goods; and investor ethical preferences (akin to voting or expressing a partiality for certain companies or values). Activities associated with responsible investment can encompass a range of strategies, including tilts, best-in-class security selection, shareholder engagement and voting, and others. 'Sustainable finance' can refer to all of the above, in addition to impact-driven approaches across asset classes (for example, denying debt to problematic companies while using shareholder power to vote against the board of directors on the equity side), in contrast to ESG, which was originally coined as a means to incorporate ESG factors into investment analysis (eg, to attempt to assess or reduce environmental, social and governance risks *to* the portfolio). Although some would dispute the lumping-together of these terms, 'responsible investment' is already often used as an umbrella term to describe a variety of them, and the critiques raised in this chapter apply to all. Ultimately, equating aspirational rhetoric with practical impact renders the current understanding of what responsible investment entails fundamentally misleading – and, in that sense, a fallacy – regardless of which term is used.

What follows will detail the contours of this fallacy. We begin with a brief history of responsible investment and an outline of the myriad systemic risks – the polycrisis, as some call it – that characterise our current era. In the ensuing two sections, we examine the two main expectations associated with responsible investment – that it decreases portfolio risk and/or outperforms the market, and that it contributes to environmental and social well-being – concluding that it does not meet either of them. The penultimate section addresses the fallacy of responsible investment as 'investment', showing that most responsible investment activity is confined to secondary market securities swapping, not primary market financing with 'additionality' (where additional investments have an impact by increasing how much a company can raise and at what price, for example). We conclude with an overview of the arguments and suggestions for improving the practice of responsible investment, including the greater use of certain impact-oriented tactics – such as voting against the (re-)election of company directors – that have already been found to be more effective than those in most common use, with the hope of encouraging the field of responsible investment to live up to its many names.

[2] See A Martini, 'Socially Responsible Investing: From the Ethical Origins to the Sustainable Development Framework of the European Union' (2021) 23 *Environment, Development and Sustainability*.

[3] See E Pollman, 'The Making and Meaning of ESG' (2022) *SSRN Electronic Journal*, https://papers.ssrn.com/abstract=4219857.

6.2. HISTORICAL AND CURRENT CONTEXT

'The earliest "ethical investors" were the churches on both sides of the Atlantic'[4] who termed their activities 'ethical investment', which stemmed from the moral concerns of religious groups – such as the Methodists and Quakers[5] – that were intent on aligning their investment practices with the values they promoted. In its earliest recognisable guise, responsible investment centred on human and civil rights struggles and Apartheid South Africa in the 1960s and 1970s[6] in the US, although shareholder activist 'gadflies' from the 1940s onwards had pushed for progress on racial and sex discrimination previously.[7] Although many ethical investors throughout this period may have wished merely to avoid profiting from products and services they found morally objectionable, many others clearly aimed to deploy ethical investment towards social change and undertook additional non-investment actions to attain political or social ends. For example, tactics deployed in the campaign against Apartheid in South Africa included pressuring investors to divest, companies to withdraw from the country, and banks to withhold financing.

ESG emerged in the early 2000s as a result of engagements between the UN and the financial community, resulting in the creation of the United Nations-supported Principles for Responsible Investment (PRI) in 2006. The use of ESG factors in investment decision-making,[8] not necessarily with an ethical underpinning, began to take hold around this time. Accordingly, much ESG-related activity continues to centre on efforts to optimise portfolio performance – by, for example, excluding companies exposed to environmental-, social- and governance-related risks or tilting towards companies exposed to environmental or social opportunities, as opposed to by undertaking efforts to make real-world change according to these same metrics. It is ESG that has become mainstream, engendering its own backlash[9] and now accounting for a third of all assets under management globally.[10]

As ESG has risen in popularity, so too have major global systemic risks intensified. These include climate change, which is slated to cause the displacement of up to a billion people by 2050,[11] with all of the attendant social and political conflict and instability this would engender[12] – and, in many places,

[4] See Sparkes (n 1).

[5] See Martini (n 2).

[6] M Welker and D Wood, 'Shareholder Activism and Alienation' (2011) 52 *Current Anthropology* 57, 69.

[7] R Marens, 'Inventing Corporate Governance: The Mid-Century Emergence of Shareholder Activism' (2002) *Academy of Management Proceedings*.

[8] See Pollman (n 3).

[9] ibid.

[10] See Global Sustainable Investment Alliance, 'Global Sustainable Investment Review 2020' (2021).

[11] See International Organization for Migration, 'Migration and Climate Change' (2019).

[12] See GJ Abel and others, 'Climate, Conflict and Forced Migration' (2019) 54 *Global Environmental Change* 239.

inequality, which a substantial global dataset has linked to the erosion of democracy worldwide,[13] among other ills. Biodiversity supports 50% of GDP,[14] and its loss is already increasing the risk of pandemics[15] and the death and disruption that results. Antimicrobial resistance (AMR) could result in 100 trillion dollars of whole-economy costs by 2050[16] as well as the growing risk that basic infections could no longer be treated with the medicines we have available.[17] Emissions are still rising; extreme weather events are intensifying; inequality is increasing (or simply remaining unacceptably high); food systems are becoming ever more vulnerable. Although previous generations faced war, pestilence and other tribulations, it is only in our current era that there are so many externalities – costs that companies impose on society and other companies – that are truly global in scale and reach. One might have wondered whether responsible investment was an appropriate tool even before climate change, international flights, complex supply chains and the internet rendered human societies – and systemic risks – so interconnected, but doubts are surely warranted today.

The evolution of responsible investment is rooted in a history of ethical concern, often religious, while its adoption by the mainstream has coincided with a growing recognition of the profusion of truly global and interconnected systemic risks we currently face. Yet responsible investment in its current guise does not appear to achieve ethical ends, nor does it address these growing environmental and social systemic risks. Depending on whom one asks, responsible investment is supposed to protect returns, do good in the world, provide new capital to responsible businesses, or all of the above. In the next section, we explore in turn whether responsible investment meets any of these expectations – especially given the context in which we now find ourselves.

6.3. IS RESPONSIBLE INVESTING RESPONSIBLE?

A common view is that of responsible investment as a risk management tool.[18] The argument goes that responsible investment analysis can help investors to

[13] See RS Foa and others, 'The Global Satisfaction with Democracy Report 2020' (University of Cambridge, 2020).

[14] See World Economic Forum, 'Nature Risk Rising: Why the Crisis Engulfing Nature Matters for Business and the Economy' (2020).

[15] See A Afelt, R Frutos and C Devaux, 'Bats, Coronaviruses, and Deforestation: Toward the Emergence of Novel Infectious Diseases?' (2018) 9 *Frontiers in microbiology* 702; L Bloomfield, TL McIntosh and EF Lambin, 'Habitat Fragmentation, Livelihood Behaviors, and Contact between People and Nonhuman Primates in Africa' (2020) 35 *Landscape Ecology* 985; F Keesing and others, 'Impacts of Biodiversity on the Emergence and Transmission of Infectious Diseases' (2010) 468 *Nature* 647.

[16] See S Davies and J Pearson-Stuttard, *Whose Health Is It, Anyway?* (Oxford University Press, 2021), https://academic.oup.com/book/36136; J O'Neill, 'Tackling Drug-Resistant Infections Globally: The Review on Antimicrobial Resistance' (2016).

[17] See S Davies, J Grant and M Catchpole, *The Drugs Don't Work: A Global Threat* (Penguin Books, 2013).

[18] See Pollman (n 3).

underweight or exclude companies that are likely to encounter physical climate effects, litigation or legislation risk, or public opprobrium in the future. In doing this, the thinking goes, investors can improve portfolio performance relative to the market or protect the portfolio from downside risk. Whether responsible investors have been successful at improving performance or reducing portfolio risk in a relative sense will be addressed below. Whether they have been or can be successful in absolute terms, however, is doubtful. This is because most of investors' returns do not come from outperformance of the market. Most of investors' returns *track* market returns, whether they are passively invested or not. Estimates vary, but an overwhelming proportion of institutional investors' returns come from overall market performance,[19] not active management security selection, which is logical given that portfolios tend to only marginally over- or underperform the market as a whole.

The implications of this are enormous. The top concern of responsible investors – climate change – could easily impair overall market performance and likely already has. A world with multiple breadbasket failures and hundreds of millions of (or even a billion) climate refugees – a fate we face by 2050 or significantly earlier[20] – quite quickly calls into question the resilience of governments, international governance, and supply chains, let alone the hearty financial returns of old. The idea that clever stock-picking can allow a pension fund to pay out its promised dividends in the face of extreme and interconnected systemic externalities is overly optimistic at best. Even some of the most favourable findings from studies on the subject only suggest responsible investment outperformance of under 3% on the high end;[21] this pales in comparison to the significant majority of returns that rely on functioning markets and the natural and social systems that underpin them. Indeed, half of GDP already relies on biodiversity.[22] Historical market crashes have led to investment losses of over 80%, requiring around 15 years for full recovery.[23] Mounting costs associated with climate change – in real estate, insurance, agriculture, and more – are, in

[19] See RG Ibbotson, 'The Importance of Asset Allocation' (2010) 66 *Financial Analysts Journal* 18; GP Brinson, LR Hood and GL Beebower, 'Determinants of Portfolio Performance' (1986) 42 *Financial Analysts Journal* 39; JP Hawley and J Lukomnik, 'The Long and Short of It: Are We Asking the Right Questions? Modern Portfolio Theory and Time Horizons' (2018) 41 *Seattle University Law Review*; J Lukomnik and JP Hawley, *Moving beyond Modern Portfolio Theory: Investing That Matters* (Taylor and Francis, 2021).

[20] See International Organization for Migration (n 11).

[21] See G Filbeck, TA Krause and L Reis, 'Socially Responsible Investing in Hedge Funds' (2016) 17 *Journal of Asset Management* 408; R Bauer, R Otten and ATourani-Rad, 'Ethical Investing in Australia: Is There a Financial Penalty?' (2006) 14 *Pacific-Basin Finance Journal* 33. One study finds *under*performance of up to 7%: L Renneboog, J Ter Horst and C Zhang, 'The Price of Ethics and Stakeholder Governance: The Performance of Socially Responsible Mutual Funds' (2008) 14 *Journal of Corporate Finance* 302.

[22] See World Economic Forum, 'Nature Risk Rising: Why the Crisis Engulfing Nature Matters for Business and the Economy' (2020).

[23] See SM Bartram and GM Bodnar, 'No Place to Hide: The Global Crisis in Equity Markets in 2008/2009' (2009) 28 *Journal of International Money and Finance* 1246.

contrast, not temporary; if anything they will continue to rise and compound year on year, potentially impairing GDP by 20% or more by 2066.[24] Already, human efforts are not keeping up with the increasing harms from externalities; while we have substantially improved human survival rates in extreme weather events, costs stemming from physical damage have skyrocketed[25] – to USD 145 billion in the US and USD 63 billion in the European Union in 2021 alone relative to USD 190 billion and USD 85 billion in the entirety of the decade from the 1980s onwards, respectively.[26] As unmitigated climate change worsens physical damage and its social and political consequences, investors will all feel the effects.

Those investors who tried to stock-pick away from the more obvious harms may simply have paid more to do so – either by keeping demand (and therefore prices) for more 'responsible' securities high, through the additional fees responsible investors pay (more on this below), or both. Indeed, evidence suggests that investors can generate excess returns from a declining industry,[27] and if responsible investors avoid problematic companies to a great enough extent as to move the share price, non-responsible investors will gain from buying underpriced shares. The shares of companies with positive environmental or social credentials, on the other hand, should logically remain overpriced if affected at all; this arguably only directly benefits investors if these companies' growth outstrips that of the market average to the same extent.

A related ongoing debate rages as to whether responsible investment improves financial performance relative to the market; indeed, a large proportion of academic articles on the subject of responsible investment aim to address this question. As discussed above, this debate is beside the point given that outperformance and underperformance account for such a small share of investors' overall returns. Climate change and other systemic risks could easily dwarf these effects by impairing returns across the board to a greater extent than responsible investment outperformance could compensate for. But even by more modest standards, the claim of outperformance is difficult to defend.

[24] See RS Pindyck, 'The Social Cost of Carbon Revisited' (2019) 94 *Journal of Environmental Economics and Management* 140.

[25] See World Meteorological Organization, 'WMO Atlas of Mortality and Economic Losses from Weather, Climate and Water Extremes (1970–2019)' (World Meteorological Organization, 2021), https://library.wmo.int/index.php?lvl=notice_display&id=21930.

[26] See www.climate.gov/news-features/blogs/beyond-data/2021-us-billion-dollar-weather-and-climate-disasters-historica and https://ec.europa.eu/eurostat/cache/egd-statistics/.

[27] See V Atta-Darkua and E Dimson, 'Sector Exclusions' in NOU (ed), *Energiaksjer i Statens pensjonsfond utland* (Norwegian Ministry of Finance, 2018).

Many studies find that responsibly invested public equity funds outperform or match the benchmark.[28] Other studies contradict these findings.[29] Overall, the argument seems to fall on the side of modest outperformance. But these studies have, by definition and by necessity, only looked at a relatively short time period since responsible investment in its current guise is fairly young. What we do know is that for companies or sectors that are volatile – such as fossil fuels – the time frame is the most important methodological choice one can make in assessing relative performance.[30] Over a 118-year time frame, fossil fuels perform about as well as the market (so, exclusions over that time frame would have had little effect),[31] with coal performing the worst of all sectors in the UK over the full study period. Studies assessing performance from 1950 onwards would find that fossil fuels outperformed the market, however, while studies examining the years from 2010 onwards would find the opposite.[32] It may seem logical that identifying and acting on unpriced or underpriced social and environmental risks in the market would have resulted in outperformance in the past, although even this is disputed; it seems doubtful, however, that a responsible investment premium would persist in the coming years even as responsible investment becomes all the more mainstream – especially if the associated practices do not tend to be successful in prompting companies to change real-world behaviour, as we shall discuss below – as these factors are unlikely to remain un- or underpriced.

One last note about the risk-return debate, an important one: *responsible investment typically incurs greater fees*,[33] which eat into returns and compound these losses year on year. Some investors go so far as to claim that 'ESG saved active management' since fund managers stood to lose out on fees with the move towards low-cost passive investing. If responsible investment lived up to its promise – either of outperformance/risk management or of real-world impact – the extra fees might seem worth it. Given the lack of evidence for these claims, however, these fees have the effect of doubly harming investors – by achieving

[28] See G Friede, T Busch and A Bassen, 'ESG and Financial Performance: Aggregated Evidence from More than 2000 Empirical Studies' (2015) 5 *Journal of Sustainable Finance & Investment* 210; M Orlitzky, FL Schmidt and SL Rynes, 'Corporate Social and Financial Performance: A Meta-Analysis' (2003) 24 *Organization Studies*; J Allouche and P Laroche, 'A Meta-Analytical Investigation of the Relationship between Corporate Social and Financial Performance' (2005) 57 *Revue de Gestion des Ressources Humaines* 18.

[29] See W Azmi, S Mohamad and ME Shah, 'Ethical Investments and Financial Performance: An International Evidence' (2020) 62 *Pacific-Basin Finance Journal* 101147; Renneboog, Ter Horst and Zhang (n 21).

[30] See E Quigley, E Bugden and A Odgers, *Fossil Fuel Divestment: Advantages and Disadvantages for the University of Cambridge* (Cambridge University Press, 2020).

[31] See Atta-Darkua and Dimson (n 27).

[32] ibid.

[33] See CS Kim, 'Can Socially Responsible Investments Be Compatible with Financial Performance? A Meta-Analysis' (2019) 48 *Asia-Pacific Journal of Financial Studies* 30.

none of the stated goals of the strategy while charging more all the same. For a fiduciary charged with ensuring the long-term health of a pension fund or foundation, combining high fees and little to no risk attenuation or positive impact does not seem responsible or sustainable.

Regardless, the evidence for the argument that responsible investment shields portfolios from environmental or social risks, or that it consistently improves performance,[34] is scant. Even if these claims hold true, their effect is dwarfed by the harms posed by environmental and social systemic risks to investors' overall performance as linked to the health of the whole economy. To affect the health of the whole economy, responsible investment would have to have an impact on companies in the real economy; we turn to this next.

6.4. DOES RESPONSIBLE INVESTMENT DO ANY GOOD?

A careful parsing of the text in many fund managers' promotional materials reveals the language used to describe the purpose of a fund bearing labels like 'responsible investment', 'green', 'SDG-linked', and others. Some boldly claim that investing in such a fund has the equivalent effect on emissions as avoiding a certain number of car trips or flights,[35] for example, although this is probably becoming rarer due to high-profile regulatory crackdowns on greenwashing.[36] Most ordinary people appear to assume that responsible or sustainable investing does some good in the world, though[37] – an easier assumption for the layperson than that the purpose of such investing is to attenuate financial risk to the portfolio. Doing good in the world through responsible investing turns out to be a difficult claim to substantiate, however, in the ways it is normally practised.

Most responsible investing is confined to security selection in the secondary market – buying or selling, screening or tilting the shares of publicly listed

[34] Meta-analyses tend to find a mix of modest outperformance and no effect; see L Hornuf and G Yüksel-Gundlach, 'The Performance of Socially Responsible Investments: A Meta-Analysis' (2023) *European Financial Management*; C Revelli and JL Viviani, 'Financial Performance of Socially Responsible Investing (SRI): What Have We Learned? A Meta-Analysis' (2015) 24 *Business Ethics: A European Review* 158; Kim (n 33); M Orlitzky, FL Schmidt and SL Rynes, 'Corporate Social and Financial Performance: A Meta-Analysis' (2003) 24 *Organization Studies*; J Allouche and P Laroche, 'A Meta-Analytical Investigation of the Relationship between Corporate Social and Financial Performance' (2005) 57 *Revue de Gestion des Ressources Humaines* 18.

[35] See, eg, www.deutschebank.be/dam/belgium/fr/pdf/Regnestykke-baggrund.pdf or https://pressreleasehub.pa.media/article/greening-pensions-reduces-carbon-footprint-more-than-stopping-flying-7877.html.

[36] See A Klasa and others, 'ESG's Legal Showdown: "There's Nothing to Suggest DWS Is a One off"', *Financial Times* (14 June 2022), www.ft.com/content/1094d5da-70bf-40b5-98f4-725d50620a5a.

[37] See S Dupre, C Bayer and T Santacruz, 'A Large Majority of Retail Clients Want to Invest Sustainably: Survey of French and German Retail Investors' Sustainability Objectives' (2° Investing Initiative, 2020).

companies – which has little to no additionality.[38] That is, stock-picking has little to no impact on the companies that are included in or excluded from the portfolio, especially when it comes to the small number of companies that disproportionately contribute to harms such as climate change. For this reason alone, it would be surprising if responsible investment could result in positive societal outcomes. Indeed, multiple studies find that stock-picking has neither affected companies' cost of capital nor share price (except perhaps in the very short-term),[39] and it is therefore no surprise that such a practice has failed to produce much if any change on the part of the companies targeted.[40] This is because primary market transactions are what provide new capital to companies, while in secondary market trades investors exchange capital and shares with no new money flowing to the company. *New* capital is what allows both 'good' or 'problematic' new infrastructure to be built, for example, or for new business lines to be developed or advertised. For this reason, primary market capital is more likely to contribute directly to the harm or benefit a company generates, while secondary market transactions are unlikely to do so. This will be discussed in further detail in the following section.

Engagement and voting strategies represent a minority of the responsible investment tactics responsible investors use, and these are typically deployed in public equity holdings where the ownership of shares normally comes with the ability to vote on director elections, shareholder resolutions, auditor appointments, remuneration packages, and more. These strategies account for a significantly lower proportion of responsible investment activities – about 18% – relative to ESG integration, positive and negative screens, and other stock-picking strategies.[41] Some studies suggest that private engagements[42] and shareholder resolutions[43] are both capable of achieving their stated goals

[38] See E Quigley, 'Universal Ownership in Practice: A Practical Investment Framework for Asset Owners' (Thomas Clarke (ed), Cambridge, Cambridge University Press, forthcoming 2025), https://papers.ssrn.com/sol3/papers.cfm?abstract_id=3638217.

[39] See V Atta-Darkua, 'Corporate Ethical Behaviours and Firm Equity Value and Ownership: Evidence from the GPFG's Ethical Exclusions' (2020) 69 *SSRN Electronic. Journal*, https://papers.ssrn.com/sol3/papers.cfm?abstract_id=3388868; E Quigley, 'Evidence-Based Climate Impact: A Financial Product Framework' (2023) 105 *Energy Research & Social Science*; D Heath and others, 'Does Socially Responsible Investing Change Firm Behavior?' (2023) *Review of Finance*; A Ansar, B Caldecott and J Tilbury, 'Stranded Assets and the Fossil Fuel Divestment Campaign: What Does Divestment Mean for the Valuation of Fossil Fuel Assets?' (SSEE, 2013); JF Kölbel and others, 'Can Sustainable Investing Save the World? Reviewing the Mechanisms of Investor Impact' (2020) *Organization & Environment*.

[40] See T Busch, R Bauer and M Orlitzky, 'Sustainable Development and Financial Markets: Old Paths and New Avenues' (2016) 55 *Business & Society* 303.

[41] See Global Sustainable Investment Alliance, 'Global Sustainable Investment Review 2020' (2021).

[42] See E Dimson, O Karakaş and X Li, 'Active Ownership' (2015) 28 *Review of Financial Studies* 3225, 3268; E Dimson, O Karakas and X Li, 'Coordinated Engagements' (2019), https://ssrn.com/id=3209072.

[43] See W Proffitt and A Spicer, 'Shaping the Shareholder Activism Agenda: Institutional Investors and Global Social Issues' (2006) 4 *Strategic Organization* 165; P Tkac, 'One Proxy

(more on the goals below, as these are unlikely to be linked to genuine substantive reductions in systemic risks). However, a closer examination of the underlying data suggests that engagements and shareholder resolutions classified as a 'success' cannot be tied reliably to actual company-level behaviour change, and certainly not on the scale or at a speed commensurate with the crises at hand. Indeed, the world's largest shareholder engagement collaboration is Climate Action 100+, currently with institutions representing USD 68 trillion[44] in assets under management as signatories, which emerged in 2017 and has yet to deliver significant results. The initiative's 170 target companies account for a large majority of emissions from all listed companies globally, and these are still rising despite the multi-year efforts of the largest shareholder engagement coalition in history.

Sadly, current responsible investment approaches tend to allow or encourage companies to slice and dice commitments so as to cede as little ground as possible. Most engagement, voting, shareholder resolutions, and ESG data providers choose indicators or demands that centre around reporting, disclosure, or policy changes that are unlikely to change company behaviour. Disclosure has been found to be ineffective as a mechanism for behaviour change in a variety of realms.[45] Specifically, evidence suggests that improved environmental disclosure is not associated with improved environmental performance; in fact, although studies differ in their findings, a greater proportion find a negative correlation between improved environmental disclosure and environmental performance than the inverse.[46] In other words, companies that cause significant environmental harms are *more* likely to make environmental disclosures than those with a smaller environmental footprint – perhaps because some of the most inveterate emitters disclose as a concession to investors instead of taking action on emissions themselves. One study found that, *even among companies with a climate change policy*, a minority of them had convened even a single board discussion on the topic of climate risk, and many fewer had discussed climate opportunities,[47] let alone undertaken substantive actions to address environmental issues at the source.

Requests for disclosure or reports account for a significant majority of responsible investment activities, including shareholder resolutions,[48] but the rest are likely insufficient to produce company-level behaviour change as well.

at a Time: Pursuing Social Change through Shareholder Proposals' (2006) *Federal Reserve Bank of Atlanta Economic Review* 1.

[44] With double-counting due to the participation of asset owners and their managers.

[45] See SD Solomon and CA Hill, 'Limits of Disclosure' (2013) 36 *Seattle University Law Review* 599.

[46] See MH Doan and R Sassen, 'The Relationship between Environmental Performance and Environmental Disclosure: A Meta-Analysis' (2020) 24 *Journal of Industrial Ecology* 1140.

[47] See PS Shrivastava and A Addas, 'The Impact of Corporate Governance on Sustainability Performance' (2014) 4 *Journal of Sustainable Finance & Investment* 21.

[48] See Dimson, Karakas and Li, 'Coordinated Engagements' (n 42).

Green bonds can finance the green activities of even extremely dirty companies – including those that are still building new fossil fuel infrastructure that will lock in decades' worth of emissions and the attendant reliance on the oil and gas supply of autocratic regimes – and sustainability-linked bonds or loans are often tied to distinctly low-ambition targets.[49] Indeed, the Royal Bank of Canada promoted a syndicated sustainability-linked loan it had participated in for pipeline company Enbridge as part of a document touting its sustainable finance commitment in 2021.[50] Investors and bankers tend to impose restrictions on project financing when responding to stakeholder pressure, even though most fossil fuel expansion is in fact paid for through general corporate financing or underwriting (or company cash flows).[51]

Requests for the inclusion of ESG factors in executive pay usually result in ambiguous indicators tied to a vanishingly small share of executives' total remuneration; indeed, ESG-linked targets tend to be set to be easy to meet, and these indicators pay out at higher rates than other variable pay indicators do,[52] suggesting that they are easier to achieve. Taken together, it is simple enough to see how executives can avoid or evade enacting changes that would have a meaningful effect on reducing emissions, pay disparities, or other social and environmental harms.

This is not to say that impact on companies can only be achieved through investments/exclusions or engagement; other channels are available. The divestment movement's aim is usually not to affect a company's cost of capital nor to change its behaviour directly; it is to stigmatise an industry to the point at which it becomes socially acceptable to legislate it.[53] This occurred in the historical case of Apartheid South Africa, where 'it was the alignment of international condemnation, internal resistance, and corporate withdrawal … that finally convinced the [South African] government that the human rights violations that apartheid embodied were not acceptable to the world community'.[54] Divestment and boycott campaigns aimed to put pressure on the South African government and to persuade international peer countries and companies to enact sanctions and other penalties against the Apartheid regime.

In the case of fossil fuels, the main contributor to climate change-inducing greenhouse gas emissions, governments continue to provide subsidies to the

[49] See G Vulturius, A Maltais and K Forsbacka, 'Sustainability-Linked Bonds – Their Potential to Promote Issuers' Transition to Net-Zero Emissions and Future Research Directions' (2022) *Journal of Sustainable Finance & Investment*.

[50] See www.rbc.com/community-sustainability/_assets-custom/pdf/OurCommitment_EN.PDF.

[51] See B Steffen, 'The Importance of Project Finance for Renewable Energy Projects' (2018) 69 *Energy Economics* 280.

[52] See P O'Connor, L Harris and T Gosling, 'Linking Executive Pay to ESG Goals' (2021), www.pwc.com/gx/en/issues/reinventing-the-future/take-on-tomorrow/download/Linking-exec-pay-ESG.pdf.

[53] See Quigley, Bugden and Odgers (n 30).

[54] MP Mangaliso, 'South Africa: Corporate Social Responsibility and the Sullivan Principles' (1997) 28 *Journal of Black Studies* 219, 236.

very companies whose expansionary activities must be curtailed to preserve any hope of restricting warming to safe levels. These are highly-regulated industries in one sense, in that they are subject to health and safety guidelines and the like, but these and other companies that cause significant environment- or climate-related harms typically remain under current legal or regulatory regimes that are not sufficient to reduce emissions in line with the recommendations of scientists.

Accordingly, it is clear that the current level of regulation/legislation is as yet insufficient. The divestment movement acknowledges that societies tend to legislate activities or products once they are viewed as bad; in other words, stigma is one of the ways in which we get new laws. This may seem harsh or undesirable for those who prefer the carrot to the stick, but social stigma appears to be more powerful than social esteem in prompting behaviour change.[55]

Responsible investment makes use of some of the same tools as divestment – exclusions, mainly – but denudes them of their political utility and potential to influence public discourse and norms. Divestment advocates know that stigmatisation will not work if neither the company nor the public is made aware of – nor told the reason for – the exclusion of a company's stock from an investor's portfolio, and responsible investment was not designed to include a public discourse element. Responsible investment is quiet divestment, as it does not name and shame (or even publicise) its exclusions or tilts; it lacks the power of divestment's theory of change while also confining itself to inherently low-impact tactics and strategies more generally.

6.5. IS RESPONSIBLE INVESTMENT EVEN … INVESTING?

Part of the thought process supporting claims of responsible investment impact has to do with the idea of providing incentives to 'good' companies – or 'bad' companies that sincerely want to change – and disincentives to those that are unrepentant in causing harm. Elaborations on this argument tend to entail discussions of suppressed stock prices, higher cost of capital, and voluntary company adjustments to bring investors back into the fold.

This argument does not appear to hold in reality, however. As discussed above, most responsible investment involves stock-picking among publicly listed holdings, and exclusions, tilts, screening and ESG integration – mostly involving asset allocation in public equity portfolios – account for a large majority of responsible investment strategies:

[55] See S Casal and L Mittone, 'Social Esteem versus Social Stigma: The Role of Anonymity in an Income Reporting Game' (2016) 124 *Journal of Economic Behavior & Organization* 55.

Figure 6.1 Sustainable Investing Assets by Strategy and Region 2020 (billions USD)

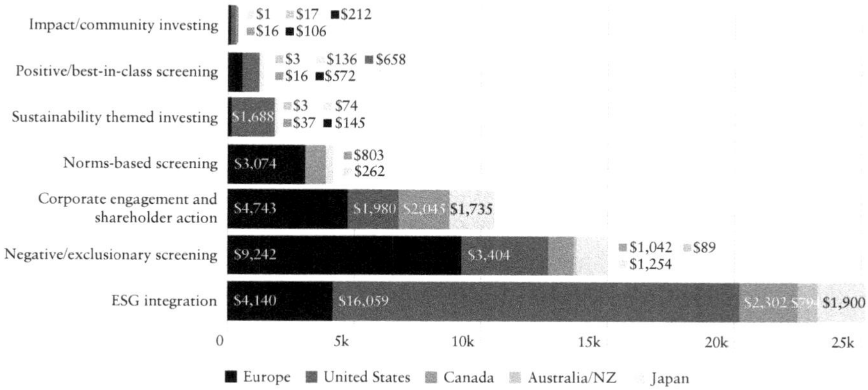

Source: Global Sustainable Investment Alliance, 2021.

In effect, the vast majority of responsible investment practices involve secondary market trades, and, as expected, they do not tend to have an effect on the company if the underlying value of the assets remains unchanged. Indeed, a large and growing body of evidence finds little to no 'additionality' in public equity, where there is a buyer for every seller of a share.[56] If the stock price is affected at all, it is very temporary;[57] the effect on cost of capital is negligible;[58] and the effects on company behaviour are even more difficult to find.[59] The money, in this case, flows from one investor to the other; the company does not receive any fresh capital. Logic aligns with evidence, then, in finding little to no effect from stock-picking among the shares of publicly listed companies.[60]

Where does fresh capital for, say, fossil fuel expansion come from? *Debt*, largely – bank loans and bonds. These sources account for approximately 90% of fossil fuel financing,[61] and the rest comprises primary market capital raises such as new equity issues and initial public offerings (IPOs). These primary market investments – from bank loans, bonds, IPOs, and the like – represent new money flowing into companies' coffers. This is in contrast to secondary market investments such as those in the shares of publicly listed companies; as noted above, the shares change hands between and among investors and therefore do not provide new capital to the companies in question, hence the negligible effect on stock prices or the cost of capital when shares are bought

[56] See Quigley (n 38).

[57] See V Atta-Darkua, 'Corporate Ethical Behaviours and Firm Equity Value and Ownership: Evidence from the GPFG's Ethical Exclusions' (Working Paper, 2020), https://papers.ssrn.com/sol3/papers.cfm?abstract_id=3388868.

[58] See Quigley (n 39).

[59] See Quigley (n 38).

[60] ibid.

[61] See TF Cojoianu and others, 'Does the Fossil Fuel Divestment Movement Impact New Oil and Gas Fundraising?' (2021) 21 *Journal of Economic Geography* 141.

or sold. Perhaps unsurprisingly, withholding primary market financing *is* associated with increases in a company's cost of capital and the total amount of capital the company can raise. This is not where responsible investors tend to apply exclusions, however;[62] these are typically confined to public equity, where they have little to no effect on the cost or volume of capital raised.

For the lay public, the terms 'investing' or 'financing' imply support for the financed entity; it helps a company when you invest in it, and if you do not it hurts the company. Indeed, the aforementioned 2° Investing Initiative study found that respondents believed that responsible investment in public equity would have a positive impact on society.[63] Even within a sample of unusually financially literate respondents, the United Kingdom's Financial Conduct Authority found that a bare majority was able to distinguish between investments aimed at reducing the portfolio's *exposure to* certain environmental or social risks versus those that were designed to *contribute to* positive environmental or social outcomes,[64] suggesting that even sophisticated investors may have greater faith in the efficacy of responsible investment (as it is usually practised) than is in fact warranted.

Interestingly, the French language distinguishes between 'investissement' – loosely corresponding to our understanding of primary market financing – and 'placement', which speaks to the passive holding of secondary market instruments that are expected to earn a profit.[65] This understanding of 'investissement' is not reflected in most responsible investment, where stock-picking is the norm. True financing – provision of primary market capital through new bond issues, bank loans or IPOs – is mainly absent from responsible investing. Accordingly, one could say it is neither responsible nor does it qualify as 'investing'.

6.6. TO WHAT END: IS RESPONSIBLE INVESTMENT RESPONSIBLE? DOES IT INVEST RESPONSIBLY?

Fallacies do not always cause harm, especially when they are crimes of omission. But where they replace strategies that could contribute to mitigating some of society's greatest harms, they can be what former BlackRock executive (and current responsible investment critic) Tariq Fancy calls 'a dangerous placebo'. The danger here is in performing responsible investment when more effective treatments are available.

[62] See A Ansar, B Caldecott and J Tilbury, 'Stranded Assets and the Fossil Fuel Divestment Campaign: What Does Divestment Mean for the Valuation of Fossil Fuel Assets?' (University of Oxford, 2013); JF Kölbel and others, 'Can Sustainable Investing Save the World? Reviewing the Mechanisms of Investor Impact' (2020) *Organization and Environment* 34.

[63] See S Dupre at al (n37).

[64] See CG Gilchrist and others, 'Matter of Fact-Sheets: Improving Consumer Comprehension of Financial Sustainability Disclosures' (Financial Conduct Authority, 2022) 62.

[65] See PH Dembinski and others, 'The Ethical Foundations of Responsible Investment' (2003) 48 *Journal of Business Ethics* 203.

What are these treatments? As Fancy notes, and as the divestment movement argues, legislation is one. Investors could seed the ground for supportive legislation by advocating for it directly and by imposing bold penalties – voting against directors, denying debt (refusing to participate in new bond issues), even taking legal action – upon companies that lobby against evidence-based legislation to mitigate climate change or income/wealth inequality, or that belong to trade associations that do the same. Lobbying for fossil fuels still far outweighs lobbying for renewables,[66] and it is difficult to envision suitable environmental laws and regulations being enacted until this has been remedied.

To date, responsible investors may have in fact – largely unwittingly – undermined efforts to regulate this conduct and address the issues they purport to concern themselves with. Responsible investment both explicitly and implicitly favours voluntary frameworks. For example, the largest responsible investment membership organisation, the UN-supported Principles for Responsible Investment (PRI), asks that signatories voluntarily commit to six principles,[67] most of which are disclosure-based, and the organisation has not yet taken much action against firms that do not comply. Indeed, only five firms – out of thousands of signatory organisations – have ever been asked to leave the initiative as a result of failing to meet the minimum criteria.[68] PRI members could lobby *against* sensible environmental and social legislation and regulation while remaining signatories, as indeed some of them have.[69]

The responsible investment field has conjured official efforts such as the Task Force for Climate-Related Financial Disclosures (TCFD), initially a voluntary disclosure regime that largely focuses on single materiality – the impact climate-related risks have on companies financially.[70] The International Sustainability Standards Board (ISSB), an attempt at combining existing standards so as to create a common sustainability disclosure framework for companies, has begun to gain traction after many years of divergent and competing efforts in this area. But again, the emphasis has been on disclosure, often purely voluntary disclosure, even as the evidence continues to point to a disconnection between improved environmental disclosure and improved environmental performance.[71] And the daily practice of responsible investment is largely to the same end: much of it involves asking companies to reveal information that they could have been legally required to provide in the first place. After nearly two decades of

[66] See S Trachtman and J Meckling, 'The Climate Advocacy Gap' (2022) 172 *Climatic Change* 1.

[67] See Pollman (n 3).

[68] See www.unpri.org/reporting-and-assessment/signatories-delisted-for-not-meeting-the-minimum-requirements/6480.article?adredir=1.

[69] See InfluenceMap, *Finance and Climate Change* (2022), https://influencemap.org/report/Finance-and-Climate-Change-17639.

[70] Double materiality, on the other hand, addresses a company's climate-related *impacts* – including harms – as well.

[71] See Doan and Sassen (n 46).

requesting voluntary disclosure and failing to achieve this or much of anything else, it is reasonable to wonder whether well-meaning responsible investors have unintentionally contributed to replacing or delaying needed legislation and regulation that could have driven meaningful change in this critical era – a dangerous placebo indeed.

Thankfully, the European Commission's Sustainable Finance Disclosure Regulation (SFDR) and the European Parliament's Corporate Sustainability Reporting Directive (CSRD) have rendered climate-related disclosures – by large corporations and investors – mandatory in the EU at long last, a welcome development. Upon full implementation, however, we will have presumably gained better environmental disclosure without the full complement of laws and regulations needed to change the facts the directives measure. The debate over the CSRD has itself been emblematic of the issues associated with responsible investment and the pushback it tends to encounter. The debate involved questioning the need for top-down as opposed to market-led standards[72] as well as the inclusion of double materiality – companies' climate-related *impacts on* the world as opposed to their financial vulnerabilities stemming *from* climate-related risks. Businesses, investors and academics weighed in on the debate on both sides.[73]

Beyond regulatory and legal interventions that investors may support, the aforementioned tactics aimed at changing companies' behaviour directly – voting against the re-election of directors, denying debt, and/or taking legal action – are all options for those who wish to learn from the evidence on existing responsible investment practices in service of greater impact. The differing impact of exclusions in public equity versus debt was addressed above; this points to a 'deny debt, engage equities' approach. The form of engagement to take, however, is also a significant question. The evidence here suggests that engagement in the form of shareholder resolutions – largely advisory-only, reporting-only, and relatively rarely implemented – is unlikely to produce a robust response from companies,[74] while even large-scale coordinated shareholder engagements tend towards reporting/disclosure requests as their ultimate aims,[75] rendering any significant impact unlikely as per Doan and Sassen's[76] findings on voluntary disclosure. On the other hand, a review of the evidence on investors voting against the re-election of directors – even in uncontested elections, and even at relatively low levels – appears to be more likely to

[72] See Martini (n 2).

[73] See V Nair, 'Accounting for Overshoot', *ESG Investor* (2 August 2023), www.esginvestor.net/accounting-for-overshoot/; F Ducoulombier, 'Viewpoint: A Response to ISSB's Faber's "Triple Illusion" Criticism of Double Materiality', *IPE* (13 October 2023), www.ipe.com/comment/viewpoint-a-response-to-issbs-fabers-triple-illusion-criticism-of-double-materiality/10069470.article.

[74] See Quigley, Bugden and Odgers (n 30).

[75] See Dimson, Karakas and Li (n 42).

[76] See Doan and Sassen (n 46).

produce results than is the case for other engagement tactics.[77] Director votes appear to be a less common tactic, as is the use of exclusions on the debt side as opposed to the equity side, even though the evidence suggests that these approaches are more likely to be effective. A non-fallacious approach to responsible investment in future could make greater use of such tactics than those that have not been found to prompt the changes necessary to protect portfolios or induce real-world change.

The focus on reporting, the debate about double materiality, and the tendency to use less effective investor tactics have at times been caught up in the perception that investors are in fact obligated to confine their policies and activities to matters that are directly financially material to individual holdings[78] – the single materiality approach versus the double materiality or impact approach. The argument is that fiduciary duty dictates a narrow responsibility for fiduciaries to protect beneficiaries' portfolios *from* particular risks or harms, with impact considerations remaining out of scope. However, a mammoth joint report (nicknamed Freshfields II, following on from the ground-breaking Freshfields I report in 2005 on ESG investing), by the UN-supported Principles for Responsible Investment and the international law firm Freshfields, suggests that not only is investing for impact – aiming for company-level behaviour change across sectors and geographies – permitted across the 11 major jurisdictions examined, but it is arguably required.[79] The report is explicit that this can entail investors engaging to encourage activities that reduce returns at individual companies if doing so preserves overall portfolio value. In effect, the report confirms that investors may – and perhaps even must – reduce the negative impacts their individual portfolio companies have on other portfolio companies and society. The message is supportive of moving from a responsible investment approach, one that involves attempting to avoid risks *to* the portfolio, to a universal ownership approach, one that recognises that investors more or less track the market and therefore rely on the health of the overall market. Accordingly, investors are arguably obligated to work to reduce externalities such as greenhouse gas emissions – to mitigate the negative impact particular investee companies have on overall market returns.

Evidence-based investing for impact involves focusing on company-level behaviour change across whole sectors, and undertaking activities that are more likely to achieve that end, as discussed above. The whole-sector approach is necessary so as to maintain a level playing field such that no company is at an advantage or disadvantage for complying or not, and it could be supportive of legislation in that large multinational companies may begin to support

[77] See Quigley (n 38).
[78] See Martini (n 2).
[79] See J Hilf and D Rouch, 'A Legal Framework for Impact: Sustainability Impact in Investor Decision-Making' (2021), www.unepfi.org/wordpress/wp-content/uploads/2021/07/A-Legal-Framework-for-Impact_Report.pdf.

country-level laws and regulations that they already comply with due to pressure from large institutional investors who can enforce common standards across borders.

The emphasis on company-level behaviour change is important because it helps to avoid many of the loopholes and evasions explored in previous sections. Once the focus is on the company's behaviour, tools and tactics can be deployed to maximise investors' ability to shape target companies' real-world impact. This involves refusing to participate in primary market investments in – while retaining shares in order to vote against the (re-)election of directors of – companies that produce significant negative externalities and are not changing tack.[80]

These and other strategic combinations of tactics designed to induce company executives and directors to decrease emissions or equalise pay are all available treatments for investors to deploy now, but patients imbibing a placebo do not know that they are not being treated, let alone that there are effective alternatives available. The very popularity of the responsible investment placebo may prevent investors and the public from having the awareness to demand treatments that actually work. It is for this reason that Fancy and others deem the placebo of responsible investment to be 'dangerous' – it is not harmless, but a potential stand-in for efforts that could actually make a difference.

6.7. CONCLUSION

Responsible investment has entered the mainstream in recent years, with advocates variously touting its ability to enhance returns, reduce risk, do good in the world, or all of the above. It is no accident that climate change, biodiversity loss, pandemic risk, and other social and environmental harms have become yet more serious hazards during the responsible investment zeitgeist, threatening the health of the financial system and the environmental and social substrates that support it.

As it is currently practised, 'responsible investment' is neither responsible nor an investment – which makes taking this term at face value a fallacy. What is routinely labelled 'responsible investment' is not responsible because it focuses on attempting to serve a risk management function it is ill-equipped to perform. In the process, it ignores the main source of risk to portfolios: systemic risks such as climate change that will affect all sectors, asset classes, and geographies. Moreover, it concentrates efforts on activities that have little or no impact on company behaviour, such as exclusions and tilts in public equity holdings, for example, while ignoring the role debt plays in fossil fuel

[80] See Quigley (n 38).

expansion by neglecting to apply the same exclusions or tilts to bond holdings. In this way, responsible investment is not even investing, as it concentrates so heavily on the holding and trading of secondary market instruments that do not contribute to, or withhold new capital from, companies whose actions need to be encouraged or discouraged. Similarly, shareholder engagement efforts in the responsible investment space have tended towards requesting voluntary reporting from companies, which evidence suggests is unlikely to lead to behaviour change, as well as shareholder resolutions and other soft tactics that have not been connected to significant impacts on company decision-making. Tactics with more promise, by contrast – such as voting against the re-election of directors – tend to be more rarely used. Whether the claim is that responsible investment shields portfolios from risk or actively does good, current practices appear not to do an adequate job of either.

Responsible investment is not just a fallacy; it is a harmful fallacy. Tariq Fancy argues that it is a '*dangerous placebo*' as it tends to replace effective action with actions that only appear to be effective. Responsible investment supports voluntary and immaterial actions that do not address externalities or systemic risks, when climate change and other challenges of our time require legislation, regulation, and the concerted cross-border efforts of universal owners to even out the effects of country-level rules. For those whose values align with responsibility, sustainability or ethics, revealing and countering this fallacy is an essential step towards solving some of the grand challenges of our time. For those who merely view themselves as investors, anything that risks overall market returns should still be attended to, and responsible investment does not do this. For fiduciaries of pension funds and endowments, dispelling the responsible investment fallacy is arguably a legal duty – to protect overall returns and to promote the values such fiduciaries and their beneficiaries tend to hold.

Part II

Financial Regulation

7

The Fallacy of Disclosure in the Time of AI

ALEXANDRA ANDHOV

7.1. INTRODUCTION

THE DISCLOSURE OBLIGATION has been one of the oldest and most discussed obligations for publicly traded companies. It has been extensively explored for decades. As a regulatory tool, disclosure continues to evolve and encompass new subtleties and dimensions. In capital markets regulation, the realms of disclosure have expanded, introducing varied forms of obligations and pieces of information that need to be communicated with the shareholders and the general public. Despite distinct regulatory frameworks in the United States and the European Union, similar trends are observable on both sides of the Atlantic, reflecting a universal evolution of disclosure obligation, corporate transparency and accountability norms. As the volume of data in disclosure documents expands and corporations employ novel technology in their production, it is imperative to assess the impact of this technology on the information in and the ultimate purpose of the disclosure.

The primary purpose of disclosure as a tool of capital markets regulation is to level the playing field – for investors, for issuers and for the public. The progress and promise presented by new technologies, including artificial intelligence (AI), is promising, though much has yet to be realised.[1] In recent years, however, the process of producing, disseminating and processing information has undergone a significant transformation. The increasing popularity of AI tools in generating and analysing corporate information, in particular,

[1] See generally about the possibilities of using AI in finance, HJ Allen, 'Driverless Finance' (2020) *Harvard Business Law Review* 157; W Magnuson, 'Artificial Financial Intelligence' (2020) *Harvard Business Law Review* 337; T CW Lin, 'Artificial Intelligence, Finance, and the Law' (2019) 88 *Fordham Law Review* 531; ST Omarova, 'New Tech v. New Deal: Fintech as a Systemic Phenomenon' (2019) 36 *Yale Journal of Regulation* 735; I HY Chiu, 'Fintech and Disruptive Business Models in Financial Products, Intermediation and Markets: Policy Implications for Financial Regulators' (2016) 21 *Journal of Technology, Law and Policy* 55; Y Yadav, 'How Algorithmic Trading Undermines Efficiency in Capital Markets' (2015) 68 *Vanderbilt Law Review* 1607.

puts the traditional understanding of disclosure under tremendous pressure. Artificial intelligence, a term coined by John McCarthy in 1955, was defined as 'the science and engineering of making intelligent machines'.[2] In these times, when generative AI models like ChatGPT have become commonplace, the presumption of AI's efficiency, objectivity and neutrality remains strong – yet these systems are not without technological and legal opacities, uncertainties and other limitations. Securities regulators, whose mandate is to protect the interests of investors by requiring accurate, timely and sufficient information to enable informed investment decisions,[3] face new challenges.[4] The securities regulations aim to uphold investor confidence in the financial markets by focusing on the materiality of information, generally meant to reflect and facilitate the judgment of a reasonable investor. But now, with AI handling information and reshaping both the dissemination and interpretation of financial disclosure, the nature of disclosure has been fundamentally transformed. As AI systems transfer, modify, interpret, and often also independently act upon information in financial disclosure, this change signifies a departure from the original purpose of disclosure.

The chapter acknowledges the complexity inherent in the disclosure obligation while recognising its straightforward premise: corporate insiders possess more in-depth knowledge about their corporations, their activities, dealings, successes and failures than those buying the securities or those impacted by the sale of securities (a group, as we shall see, far more significant than simply investors), resulting in an information asymmetry.[5] Thus, requiring disclosures before the sale of securities and on an ongoing basis can provide information to diminish those asymmetries.

This chapter focuses neither on a detailed breakdown of disclosure requirements for publicly listed companies nor the debate about disclosure's role in regulation. Instead, it aims to show how the sheer amount of information, both qualitative and quantitative, and the new ways it is both shared and processed – particularly through AI – can fundamentally change the quality of the information itself and, therefore, possibly the purpose of the disclosure as such.

[2] J McCarthy, *A Proposal for the Dartmouth Summer Research Project on Artificial Intelligence* (1955).

[3] See, on the policy rationale of disclosure obligations for the European Union and the United States, eg E Avgouleas, 'The Global Financial Crisis and the Disclosure Paradigm in European Financial Regulation: The Case for Reform' (2009) 440 *European Company and Financial Law Review*; S Schwarz, 'Protecting Financial Markets: Lessons from the Subprime Mortgage Meltdown' (2008) 93 *Minnesota Law Review*; J Coffee, 'Market Failure and the Economic Case for a Mandatory Disclosure System' (1984) 70 *Virginia Law* Review; FH Easterbrook and DR Fischel, 'Mandatory Disclosureand the Protection of Investors' (1984) 70 *Virginia Law Review*.

[4] FINRA described the various ways in which the securities industry is using AI and thus 'transforming various functions within broker-dealers'. See FINRA, 'AI Applications in the Securities Industry', www.finra.org/rules-guidance/key-topics/fintech/report/artificial-intelligence-in-the-securities-industry/ai-apps-in-the-industry.

[5] See GA Akerlof, 'The Market for "Lemons": Quality Uncertainty and the Market Mechanism' (1970) 84 *Quarterly Journal of Economics* 488.

This chapter ventures beyond the discussions of human limitations in processing complex information, an area already rich with academic inquiry.[6] While acknowledging that AI systems have been posited as a solution to improve information overload,[7] the central thesis here delves into the ramifications for the essence and objectives of disclosure when these autonomous systems are deployed. It critically evaluates the outcomes when AI is employed not only in crafting disclosure materials but also in their subsequent analysis. The argument presented is vigorous: by integrating AI in this dual role, we may inadvertently perfect a 'disclosure fallacy' – an illusion of transparency that actually subverts the very policy objectives that underpin the practice of disclosure. If left unexamined, the reliance on AI could distort the process to the point where the policy's fundamental aim – ensuring informed decision-making through clear, accessible information – is compromised, potentially undermining the regulatory instrument itself. The chapter asserts that this potential shift requires urgent attention to ensure that the original intent of disclosure is preserved in the age of AI.

Throughout history, the paradigm of corporate disclosure has undergone a significant transformation, evolving from the fundamental disclosure of key financial metrics to the intricate revelation of conflicts of interest and the declaration of substantial stakes in publicly traded entities. The corporate world is currently at the cusp of a global initiative to integrate environmental, social and governance (ESG) criteria into the pantheon of mandatory disclosure requirements. Acknowledging this trend and the prevailing regulatory wisdom that a surfeit of information is preferable to a paucity, this chapter endeavours to elucidate the latest progressions in corporate disclosure practices, not as a matter of substantive content and materiality of disclosed information but as a matter of the process of its production and use. While chapter 6, authored by Ellen Quigley, provides a nuanced exploration of the substantive worth of ESG disclosures, this chapter intends to cast light on the emergence of sophisticated software systems and their potential effect on the disclosure and its regulatory purpose. Sophisticated machine learning algorithms and natural language processing (NLP)-based software are not merely drafting but also reading and

[6] See generally O Ben-Shahar and C Schneider, 'The Failure of the Mandated Disclosure' (2011) 159 *University of Pennsylvania Law Review* 647; R Rogers, 'A Little Knowledge is a Dangerous Thing … Emerging Miranda Research and Professional Roles for Psychologists (2008) 63 *American Psychologist* 776; JT Dinwoodie, 'Ignorance is Not Bliss: Financial Illiteracy, the Mortgage Market Collapse and the Global Economic Crisis' (2010) 18 *University of Miami Business Law Review* 181; B Dresp-Langley, 'On Information Processing Limitations in Humans and Machines' (2021) *1st International Electronic Conference on Information IECI 2021*.

[7] See, eg, M Arnold, M Goldschmitt and T Rigotti, 'Dealing with Information Overload: A Comprehensive Review' (2023) *Frontiers of Psychology*; MJ Eppler and J Mengis, 'The concept of information overload – a review of literature from organization science, accounting, marketing, MIS, and related disciplines' (2004) 20 *Information Society* 325; MG Siegel et al, 'Editorial: Artificial Intelligence and Machine Learning May Resolve Health Care Information Overload' (2024) *Arthroscopy Journal*.

acting upon the information in the disclosure documents, thereby revolutionising how information is synthesised, interpreted and executed. This chapter ultimately argues that the seemingly technical changes in the *process* of generation and consumption of information through the increasing adoption of AI tools are, directly or indirectly, affecting the substantive purposes and principles underpinning disclosure in modern capital markets.

The chapter proceeds as follows. It starts by briefly tracing the history and objectives of disclosure obligations in the US and the EU. Subsequently, the chapter introduces the underlying technological systems behind AI to explain the limitations and risks of using AI for conferring and analysing disclosure with and through AI tools. This section focuses on key shortcomings of AI systems, including opacity, lack of objectivity, limited understanding and the feedback effect. This chapter asserts that AI poses significant dangers for the process of disclosure, by introducing a new level of complexity that risks obscuring vital information. It critically examines the claim that AI enhances efficiency and reliability, and rather shows that how AI actually functions could lead to the distortion or 'loss in translation' of crucial data for investors and the market. This chapter claims that as we apply new technological methodologies when developing disclosure documents and subsequently analysing them, we compromise the key objective of disclosure – conveying clear information and the ability of investors and the market to rely on this information. Due to the limitations of AI technology, we may inadvertently dilute the very essence and subsequent utility of these disclosures as a regulatory instrument and cause a 'disclosure fallacy'.

7.2. THE PURPOSE AND DEVELOPMENT OF CORPORATE DISCLOSURE: BRIEF OVERVIEW

The history of corporate disclosure in the United States reflects a dramatic shift from the sparse voluntary information of the pre-1900s to a more structured and regulated framework in the twentieth century.[8]

The principle that 'sunlight is the best disinfectant' underscores the rationale for disclosure as a regulatory tactic, suggesting that transparency serves as a powerful tool in mitigating misconduct and promoting accountability.[9] It is an 'elixir healing information asymmetry',[10] which otherwise would affect

[8] DF Hawkins, 'The Development of Modern Financial Reporting Practices Among American Manufacturing Corporations' (1963) 37 *Business History Review* 135, 135–41.

[9] See LD Brandeis, 'What Publicity Can Do', *Harper's Weekly* (20 December 1913).

[10] RE Verrecchia, 'Essays on Disclosure' (2001) 32 *Journal on Accounting and Economics* 97, 164–72 (finding that disclosure reduces information asymmetry and at the same time lowers cost of capital); M Welker, 'Disclosure Policy, Information Asymmetry, and Liquidity in Equity Markets' (1995) 11 *Contemporary Accounting Research* 801, 801–02 (finding empirical data proving

market efficiency and harm investors (two other axioms that help build securities regulation).[11] Disclosure is the *sine qua non* of the federal securities law.[12] The importance of disclosure for market efficiency has been argued and contra-argued many times. Some academics believe that disclosure has a direct effect on securities prices, as they should 'fully reflect' all available information. Thus, the efficient capital market hypothesis[13] and agency problems[14] are addressed with the disclosure of the information, as the Securities Act of 1933 and Securities Exchange Act of 1934 aimed for.[15] The majority of these works are a combination of legal and economic analyses, where legal professionals rely on empirical research of economists. Although, notably, Professors Stigler and Benston have, through the 1980s, extensively criticised the disclosure mechanism in the US,[16] other scholars have efficiently rebutted their claims, and, today, the disclosure-relevance debate has been suppressed,[17] despite a substantial wave of criticism in the aftermath of the 2008 financial crisis.[18]

Similarly, in Europe, the notion of a harmonised securities market emerged in the 1960s despite its comparatively modest beginnings. Efforts to regulate disclosure began in earnest with the 1977 European Code of Conduct and subsequent directives aimed at harmonisation.[19] Like the US, the EU's regulatory rationale for the securities market aligns with ensuring market functionality, public confidence, efficient capital allocation, investor protection, and

that 'a well-regarded disclosure policy reduces information asymmetry and hence increases liquidity in equity markets').

[11] On the general background for disclosure-based regulation in connection with the securities laws, see PJ Dalley, 'The Use and Misuse of Disclosure as a Regulatory System' (2007) 34 *Florida State University Law Review* 1089, 1109–13.

[12] SD Solomon and CA Hill, 'Limits of Disclosure' (2013) 36 *Seattle University Law Review* 599, 605.

[13] See EF Fama, 'Efficient Capital Markets: A Review of Theory and Empirical Work' (1970) 25 *The Journal of Finance* 383.

[14] The agency problem is connected to the passivity of investors. Once investors invest in an investment company, the directors have no further desire to disclose the state and development of the investments of an investment company. On agency problems in case of disclosure, see generally PG Mahoney, 'Mandatory Disclosure as a Solution to Agency Problems' (1995) 62 *University of Chicago Law Review* 1047, 1048–49. See also PM Healy and KG Palepu, 'Information asymmetry, corporate disclosure and the capital markets: A review of the empirical disclosure literature' (2001) 31 *Journal of Accounting and Economics* 405, 409–10.

[15] Solomon and Hill (n 12) 605.

[16] GJ Benston, 'The Costs and Benefits of Government-Required Disclosure: SEC and FTC Requirements' in D DeMott (ed), *Corporations at the Crossroads: Governance and Reform* (McGraw-Hill, 1980) 37–69; GJ Benston, 'Required Disclosure and the Stock Market: An Evaluation of the Securities Exchange Act of 1934' (1973) 63 *American Economic Review* 132.

[17] See RH Kraakmann, 'Disclosure and Corporate Governance: An Overview Essay' in G Ferrarini et al (eds), *Reforming Company and Takeover Law in Europe* (Oxford, Oxford University Press, 2004) 96.

[18] See, eg, SL Schwarcz, 'Disclosure's Failure in the Subprime Mortgage Crisis' (2008) *Utah Law Review* 1109; T Frankel, 'The Failure of Investor Protection by Disclosure (2013) 81 *University of Cincinnati Law Review*; Solomon and Hill (n 12).

[19] Recommendation 77/534/EEC [1977] OJ L212/37.

mitigating systemic risks.[20] Additionally, scholars have stressed such aims as decreasing the cost of capital[21] and correcting market failures.

As corporations evolved, so too did the need for robust disclosure practices focused on financial and governance transparency. The imperative for clarity and accessibility of information led to improvements in the readability and timeliness of disclosures.[22] Yet, the regulatory trajectory of the disclosure obligation has been marked by corporate scandals. The late 1990s and early 2000s bore witness to notorious breaches of trust in the corporate world, with the Enron, WorldCom, and Tyco debacles catalysing the passage of the Sarbanes-Oxley Act of 2002.[23] This Act represented a pivot towards more stringent disclosure requirements under US federal securities regulation, setting higher standards for corporate disclosures and reinforcing the accountability of companies.[24] It emphasised the need for real-time transparency, mandating the swift public disclosure of material financial changes.[25] The 2008 financial crisis further illuminated the weaknesses in disclosure practices, spotlighting the complexities of securities products,[26] the general public's limited financial literacy, and the inherent risks of information overload.[27] These challenges underscored the limitations of traditional disclosure mechanisms and the pressing need for enhanced due diligence.[28]

Although the goals of securities regulation are generally understood and agreed upon to a great extent, they continue to evolve and change in light of the developments and needs of the market. As with all of the regulatory frameworks, securities regulation constantly reflects the changing political,

[20] See E Avgouleas, 'What Future for Disclosure as a Regulatory Technique? Lessons from Behavioural Decision Theory and the Global Financial Crisis' in IG MacNeil and J O'Brien (eds), *The Future of Financial Regulation* (Oxford, Hart Publishing, 2010) 205.

[21] See JC Coffee, Jr, 'Law and the Market: The Impact of Enforcement' (2007) 156 *The University of Pennsylvania Law Review* 229, 231–33.

[22] See Article 22(1) of Directive 2001/34/EC of the European Parliament and of the Council of 28 May 2001 on the admission of securities to official stock exchange listing and on information to be published on those securities (Listing and Reporting Directive) and Article 5(1) of Directive 2003/71/EC of the European Parliament and of the Council of 4 November 2003 (Prospectus Directive).

[23] Sarbanes-Oxley Act of 2002, Pub L 107–204.

[24] See LE Ribstein, 'Market vs. Regulatory Responses to Corporate Fraud: A Critique of the Sarbanes Oxley Act of 2002' (2002), 28 *Journal of Corporate Law* 1, 3.

[25] Sarbanes-Oxley Act of 2002 (n 23) §78m.

[26] See eg T Frankel, 'The Failure of Investor Protection by Disclosure' (2013) 81 *University of Cincinnati Law Review*; or RE Mendales, 'Collateralized Explosive Devices: Why Securities Regulation Failed to Prevent the CDO Meltdown, and How to Fix It' (2009) *The University of Illinois Law Review* 1359.

[27] See, eg, Ben-Shahar and Schneider (n 6); Dinwoodie (n 6).

[28] Solomon and Hill (n 12) 603. The EU Commission took stock and introduced the Transparency Directive in 2004, which aimed to improve the harmonisation of companies' information duties and enhance the transparency of information across the EU market. See Directive 2004/109/EC of the European Parliament and of the Council of 15 December 2004 on the harmonisation of transparency requirements in relation to information about issuers whose securities are admitted to trading on a regulated market and amending Directive 2001/34/EC. This Directive was later amended in 2013 by Directive 2013/50/EU.

economic and social dynamics, and therefore, a moment when one could specifically enumerate the regulator's goals is impossible to achieve.[29]

Disclosure, in simple terms, is '*the act or process of making known something that was previously unknown*'.[30] The model for the use of disclosure as a regulatory device for capital markets was established in the US by the New Deal Securities Acts. The Securities Act of 1933 and the Securities Exchange Act of 1934 were designed to achieve 'truth in securities' by full and fair disclosure. The fundamental objectives of these regulatory measures were to cultivate a base of well-informed investors, foster efficient market conditions, and actively discourage fraudulent activities.[31]

In the past century, we have witnessed the evolution of disclosure as a tool of capital market regulation. Today, we find ourselves already immersed in AI. AI's integration into the disclosure process marks a seminal shift, influencing not only the creation and dissemination of information but also its very purpose. It alters not just the method by which the market is informed but also the market's internal workings. Perhaps most disconcerting is the prospect of AI's reactions to other AI outputs – a complex interplay that could amplify the risks inherent in this technological dependency. In light of these considerations, a meticulous understanding of AI is paramount. The following section endeavours to demystify AI technology to illuminate the underpinnings of these sophisticated systems. It is crucial that all stakeholders – regulators, investors and corporations alike – grasp the mechanics and implications of AI. Only with a clear comprehension of what AI is and the foundational technologies that drive it can we navigate its impact on the future of financial disclosure.

7.3. ARTIFICIAL INTELLIGENCE TECHNOLOGY

Science fiction has long explored the relationship between automation and humanity, often depicting a world where robots and AI play pivotal roles. These themes, deeply embedded in our culture since Samuel Butler's 1872 novel *Erewhon*, have influenced real technological advancements. Alan Turing, as

[29] R Baldwin, M Cave and M Lodge, 'Introduction: Regulation – The Field and the Developing Agenda' in R Baldwin et al (eds) *The Oxford Handbook of Regulation* (Oxford, Oxford University Press, 2010) 6–7.

[30] See *Black's Law Dictionary*, 9th edn (2009).

[31] See, eg, ME Parrish, *Securities Regulation and the New Deal* (Yale University Press, 1970) 3–5. The purpose of the SA 1933, as stated in its preamble, is 'to provide full and fair disclosure of the character of securities sold in interstate commerce and foreign commerce and through the mails, and to prevent fraud in the sale thereof, and for other purposes'. Furthermore, the Senate Committee on Banking and Commerce stated that the 'purpose of the bill is to protect the investing public and honest business. The basic policy is that of informing investors of the facts concerning securities to be offered for sale in interstate and foreign commerce and providing protection against fraud and misrepresentation.' S Rep No 47, 73rd Cong, 1st Sess 1 (1933).

early as 1950, was considering the possibility of designing machines that could think.[32] Once theorised, it is the reality today. From personal assistants to smart home devices and algorithm-driven public services, AI, though sometimes inconspicuous, affects our lives in so many different ways, but what is AI, and how does it actually work?

7.3.1. What is Artificial Intelligence and How Does it Work?

Artificial Intelligence (AI) often gets conflated with automation, but they are not synonymous. Automation involves machinery performing tasks with limited human input, like executing commands at a keyboard or giving instructions to a device.[33] However, AI represents a '*technique of minimising human involvement*', enhancing the ability to perform and automate tasks while conferring a measure of independence to systems. AI not only replicates but is able to generate novel behaviours and outcomes. Its essence is the 'intelligence' it is named for – a broad suite of technologies that execute tasks traditionally requiring human intellect. Russell and Norvig defined AI as intelligent systems that are able to perform specific tasks that 'require intelligence if performed by people'.[34] The idea is that AI integrates different aspects of cognition, such as perception, communication, reasoning, and, in some cases, even learning and the ability to move and act in real or virtual environments. AI systems ultimately encapsulate various technologies and perform different tasks.[35] Thus, AI is not a single technology but a complex of technologies that have been mixed and matched together.

AI development began with early methods in logic, utilising predicate logic to construct and evaluate complex statements akin to human language, establishing a framework for inference similar to human deduction.[36] Introduced by JA Robinson in 1965, the Resolution became a cornerstone in AI for knowledge representation and deduction, paving the way for logic programming languages like Prolog in 1972.[37] Prolog's ability to sequence logical statements closely

[32] AM Turing, 'Computing Machinery and Intelligence (1950) 59 *Mind, A Quarterly Review of Psychology and Philosophy* 433, 433.

[33] For more on automation, see A Andhov, *Computational Law* (Copenhagen, Karnov, 2022) ch 6.

[34] See SJ Russell and P Norvig, *Artificial Intelligence: A Modern Approach*, 3rd edn (Hoboken, Pearson, 2016).

[35] The AI concept emerged formally in 1956 at Dartmouth College, where scholars across various disciplines, including mathematics, engineering, neurology and others, laid the foundations for computational science. John McCarthy coined the term 'artificial intelligence', and despite initial resistance, the term stuck, and an independent field was born. See, eg, P McCorduck, *Machines Who Think: A Personal Inquiry into the History and Prospects of Artificial Intelligence* (Boca Raton, CRC Press, 2004).

[36] Some claim that the Greek Stoic philosopher Chrysippus (280-209 BCEE) invented an early form of the propositional logic; see G O'Regan, *A Brief History of Computing* (London, Springer, 2008) 17.

[37] See JA Robison, 'A Machine-Oriented Logic Based on the Resolution Principle' (1965) 12 *Journal of the ACM* 23–41.

mirrored human thought processes, allowing for the analysis of legal documents and problem-solving, thus foreshadowing the intersection of AI, law, and logical reasoning.[38]

Herbert Simon's concept of 'bounded rationality' led to heuristic methods, focusing on 'good enough' solutions.[39] This approach was instrumental in mimicking human cognitive processes, supported by Daniel Kahneman and Amos Tversky's work on heuristics, which showed how mental shortcuts, often used when precise algorithms are unfeasible, are reflected in AI's strategy to approximate or 'hallucinate' data.[40] This imitation of human intuition and decision-making underpins AI's approach to handling uncertainty and imperfect information, which needs to be considered when and how AI systems are used for making decisions based on imperfect market data. However, besides this mimicking of the human decision-making process, there are additional dependencies that characterise AI systems.

7.3.2. AI Dependencies

AI is a complex technology that utilises several other technologies and techniques, and when discussing this technology, lawyers, regulators and policy experts must understand the key components. AI in the hands of lawyers is like a plane in the hands of pilots – it is a tool that needs to be used carefully. Just as passengers trust pilots to master the aircraft's controls and respect its limits, society must be able to trust that legal and regulatory experts understand AI's components and constraints. Lawyers may not have built AI systems (neither have pilots built planes), but they must comprehend the scope of their capabilities and limitations.

To navigate contemporary AI effectively, those implementing AI systems must grasp the basics of AI systems. Just because we can easily use AI does not mean we should not know its complexities. The mastery of AI companies is in showing how 'easy it is to use AI tools'. However, these tools have significant impacts not only on us individually but also on the market and infrastructure. Borrowing the qualification from the EU AI Act,[41] some of the

[38] In the 1980s, the system was used to analyse the 1981 British Nationalities Act, allowing inferences to be drawn on whether or not a particular person can argue the entitlement to a British passport under the complex provisions of the Act. See MJ Sergot et al, 'The British Nationality Act as a Logic Program' (1986) 29 *Communications of the ACM*.

[39] See HA Simon, 'Rational Choice and the Structure of the Environment' (1956) 63 *Psychological Review* 129, 133–38.

[40] See D Kahneman et al, *Judgment under Uncertainty: Heuristics and Biases* (Cambridge, Cambridge University Press, 1982).

[41] See the final text of the AI Act adopted, *Artificial Intelligence Act*, European Parliament Legislative Resolution of 13 March 2024 on the Proposal for a Regulation of the European Parliament and of the Council on Laying Down Harmonised Rules on Artificial Intelligence (EU AI Act) and amending certain Union Legislative Acts (COM(2021)0206 – C9-0146/2021 – 2021/0106(COD)).

AI disclosure systems might qualify as 'high-risk' as they affect critical infrastructure (market).[42] The current wording of Annex III of the EU AI Act, section 2 is not exhaustive. Some of the disclosure systems are arguably high risk, depending on their overall functionalities, as the failure of malfunctioning of such components might directly lead to risks to the physical integrity of critical infrastructure and thus to risks to the health and safety of persons and property.[43]

These systems have complex technological infrastructures comprising of diverse technological and non-technological levels, and lawyers specialising in this field should be aware of and understand these levels. First, they need to understand what data is and how the data is collected (*data science*). Where does the data come from and how was the data labelled? They must understand how the computer is being taught based on these data (*machine learning*), how it can understand human language (*natural language processing*) and when and how the computer can perform complex tasks by making inferences akin to human thinking (*deep learning*).

AI is advancing quickly, and new methods will be developed to address its current challenges, likely adding to its complexity. Understanding the foundational layers is imperative for meaningful engagement with AI's current state and future developments. This knowledge is essential for those shaping the legal and ethical frameworks that will govern AI's integration into society.

In the context of AI tools for disclosure, consider the following scenario: A company is preparing to disclose its financial performance to the public. The disclosure includes crucial data like revenue, costs, profit margins, but also information about significant risks, regulatory changes or governance policies. The data is provided by different units in the company, some by the accountants, some by lawyers, compliance or financial officers: they determine which of the information is key and which is not. Reflecting on the above-stated dependencies, let us determine the possible challenges along the way.

Data

In light of the scenario presented, it is imperative to ensure the accuracy of the *initial data inputs*. Should these inputs be compromised by errors such as incorrect data entry, overlooked expenditures, or miscalculated sales data, the integrity of the resulting financial report is jeopardised. Such inaccuracies can propagate misleading information to investors, analysts and regulators, precipitating suboptimal investment decisions, tarnishing the company's reputation and inviting legal repercussions. Even as accountants employ various software and methodologies for financial calculations, there is a growing reliance on

[42] ibid Annex III.
[43] ibid preamble (55).

AI systems. These systems, drawing on their algorithmic learning, may autonomously identify and integrate additional relevant data. However, these selections may include data that is unprocessed, imprecise, or not normalised for currency and regional numerical formats, leading to errors such as mistaking 1,000,000 for 1.00.

Computer scientists say, 'garbage in, garbage out', reflecting the idea that if the inputs to a computational process are incorrect, then the outputs will likewise be wrong.

The data collected for the purposes of the disclosure can be both qualitative and quantitative, and the methodologies for evaluating and processing this information hinge on sophisticated data abstraction and labelling techniques. This subject, particularly in the context of non-financial information,[44] warrants a more detailed exploration undertaken in the subsequent subsection.

Furthermore, the discourse around discriminatory datasets and algorithmic bias is well established.[45] AI systems initially require large quantities of data to teach the programs to recognise patterns and make predictions. A critical and often under-examined component is the transparency of data provenance – where does the data come from? It is imperative for the ethical deployment of AI that we not only recognise its potential but also rigorously scrutinise the origins of the data it learns from, as well as the methodologies employed in its processing.[46] Effective disclosure concerning AI data sourcing and processing is not merely a technical requirement but a fundamental aspect of establishing trust and accountability in AI systems, safeguarding against the perpetuation of existing societal biases, and ensuring that AI applications perform equitably.

Machine Learning

The roots of teaching computers to learn trace back to early mechanical inventions and the philosophical musings of thinkers like Descartes and Leibniz. Descartes imagined a mechanical man, 'nothing but a statue or machine', similar to 'clocks' artificial fountains [that] have the power to move of their own accord and engage in complex autonomous motion'.[47] Leibniz proposed that

[44] 'Non-financial information' is a term used in the EU disclosure context, meaning the data that is not directly related to the financial statistics or monetary performance of a company. This type of information often covers areas such as environmental data, social and employee matters, compliance with anti-corruption regulation, and others.

[45] See, eg, J Kleinberg et al, 'Discrimination in the Age of Algorithm' (2019) 10 *Journal of Legal Analysis* 113; T Gillis and J Spiess, 'Big Data and Discrimination' (2019) 86 *University Chicago Law Review* 459; N Kordzadeh and M Ghasemaghaei, 'Algorithmic Bias: Review, Synthesis, and Future Research Directions' (2022) 31 *European Journal of Information Systems* 388.

[46] See P Buneman and SB Davidson, 'Data Provenance – The Foundation of Data Quality' (2010), https://hashingit.com/elements/research-resources/2010-09-01-data-provenance.pdf, 1, 3–4.

[47] See R Descartes, *Treaties on Man (L'Homme)* (1664) 99.

thought itself could be reduced to simple logical steps. He described the first mechanical calculator, *machina arithmetica*, that could, in 1685, directly multiply and divide.[48] These ideas eventually led to Babbage's Analytical Engine and Ada Lovelace's early recognition of the computer's augmentative role in human intellect.

Modern machine learning, a cornerstone of AI, evolves these concepts by enabling computers to learn from data – that is why the data is one of the core elements of any AI system. Machine learning marked a shift from the computational might of IBM's Deep Blue to data-driven learning, as seen when its successor, Deeper Blue, used knowledge from previous games to defeat chess champion Garry Kasparov. Machine learning's focus is on creating algorithms that autonomously detect patterns and infer rules, much like human learning, reflecting a significant stride toward truly autonomous systems.[49]

Reflecting on the above-mentioned scenario, machine learning employed to prepare disclosure documents would work with past data, data that would be provided through a reviewed process by a human or directly taken from the internal systems. Machine learning emphasises the potential that the system is able to learn from the past, which, however, can cause issues such as historical bias, overfitting[50] or lack of adaptability; thus, using machine learning for future forecasts can cause numerous problems. Capital markets have always evidenced a certain level of unpredictability and unprecedented behaviour. Machine learning has so far excelled in cancer screening and image recognition.[51] Similarly, in the case of capital markets, machine learning is utilised in anomaly detection by flagging potential problems that could prompt human analysts to review and rectify these issues.[52] It is also used for predictive modelling, which has increasingly become a vital tool across various sectors for forecasting future trends and behaviours. This sophisticated analytical process utilises historical data to make predictions about unknown future events and has shown considerable success in numerous applications. In finance, predictive models are used to anticipate market trends, stock performance, and

[48] For more on the paper and the first machines, see F-S Morar, 'Reinventing Machines: The Transmission History of the Leibniz Calculator' (2014) *The British Journal for the History of Science* 4–5.

[49] See KP Murphy, *Machine Learning: A Probabilistic Perspective* (MIT Press, 2012) 1 ('we define machine learning as a set of methods that can automatically detect patterns in data, and then use the uncovered patterns to predict future data, or to perform other kinds of decision making under uncertainty …').

[50] Overfitting can occur when an algorithm fits too closely to its training data, resulting in a model that cannot make accurate predictions or conclusions. See IBM, 'What is overfitting?', www.ibm.com/topics/overfitting.

[51] See H Kiros, 'Doctors Using AI Catch Breast Cancer More Often Than Either Does Alone', *MIT Technology Review* (11 July 2022), www.technologyreview.com/2022/07/11/1055677/ai-diagnose-breast-cancer-mammograms/.

[52] See T Greene, 'Gary Gensler Confirms SEC's Use of AI or Financial Surveillance', *Cointelegraph* (12 September 2023), https://cointelegraph.com/news/gary-gensler-confirms-sec-ai-financial-surveillance. SEC Chair Gary Gensler testified at a Senate oversight hearing that the agency was using AI technologies to monitor the financial sector for signs of fraud and manipulation.

credit risk. While predictive modelling is a powerful tool, its success depends on the quality of data, the appropriateness of the algorithms used, and the understanding of the domain to which it is applied. The best outcomes are often achieved when these models are regularly updated and validated against new data, ensuring their reliability and accuracy over time.

Initially, machine learning was governed by algorithms – finite sets of instructions processing symbols. Yet, this was just the beginning. As time went on, breakthroughs in fields like maths, linguistics, engineering, and brain science all came together to advance the field. Noam Chomsky's work on how language is structured really helped push forward Natural Language Processing, a part of machine learning that lets computers understand and use human language. This was a big step toward making machines 'understand' natural language.

Natural Language Processing

Natural Language Processing (NLP) merges computational techniques to interpret and generate human language, a field particularly exciting for legal professionals as it explores how computers can understand and replicate natural language for practical applications. Natural language is an integral part of human interaction, encompassing diverse languages such as English, Danish and Swahili. These languages are made up of foundational elements like phonology (the study of language sounds); morphology (the analysis of word formation); lexis (or vocabulary); syntax (the rules that dictate word arrangement); and semantics (the meaning behind words and phrases). Each element differs across languages and evolves over time.

Over recent decades, there has been a push to represent language computationally, breaking down its syntax and semantics using computational logic. While there are similarities between the logical structure of language and computational logic, translating human language into a form understandable by computers involves intricate layers and nuances. For a computer to grasp human language, it must be fed ample data and trained on models that can differentiate and assign meaning to language parts such as nouns, verbs and adjectives. In the past two years, we have seen a major development in NLP and its applications across various Chat models.

However, it is important to realise that AI systems *do not 'understand'* what we are writing or asking. What they do is, through the process of sentence segmentation, word tokenisation, and tokens classification, categorise each word by its part of speech. Further steps include lemmatisation – reducing words to their base or root form; removing 'noise' words that may disrupt analysis; dependency parsing – establishing relationships between words in sentences; named entity recognition – tagging proper nouns like names or places; and coreference resolution – connecting pronouns to their correct referents in context.[53]

[53] See Andhov (n 33) ch 7.

Let's consider the state of the art – ChatGPT. The underlying mechanism of ChatGPT is *probability*. This probability takes place on each layer. It does not 'understand' the words that we use. It is built on mathematical models that involve learning the probabilities of word sequences. The model is exposed to an extensive text corpus during its training phase. Through this exposure, it learns how words and phrases are typically arranged in human language. This is also why it performs better in English than in other languages, as most of the training text was in English. Moreover, the model must reflect the differences in syntax when analysing and responding to text in other languages.[54]

The model begins without knowledge and initially makes random predictions. Through repeated training, it improves at forecasting the words in a sentence by adjusting its internal settings, or 'weights' – numerical strings that dictate language interpretation and production. The model refines these weights to capture linguistic patterns, thus enhancing its language output to be more human-like.

Thanks to the advancements in NLP, we now possess the capability to rapidly decipher and analyse various texts, including disclosure documents. NLP technology employs algorithms that can interpret the context and meaning within these documents, transforming hundreds of pages of complex financial and non-financial jargon and data into what seem to be 'comprehensible insights'. Reflecting on the scenario provided, NLP can help us with time-consuming reviews; we can use NLP to quickly identify key information, such as financial health indicators, risk factors or management discussions. By automating the extraction of details, NLP tools should enable us to sift through extensive documentation faster.

Deep Learning

Deep learning is a specialised branch of machine learning known for processing unstructured data like text and images without extensive human-directed data organisation. It works through artificial neural networks (ANNs),[55] which are structured in multiple layers, imitating the neural pathways of the human brain. The 'depth' of deep learning refers to the number of these computational layers, allowing the model to process inputs through various levels of complexity. Modern computing power has enabled the creation of deeper networks, which can handle the increased mathematical intricacies involved.

ANNs consist of interconnected neurons – simple processing units – that work together to analyse inputs. Each connection in the network has a weight,

[54] See A Andhov, 'Navigating AI: What Do Lawyers Need to Know about ChatGPT?', *Copenhagen Legal/Tech Lab* (16 February 2024) https://legaltechlab.sites.ku.dk/2024/02/16/navigating-ai-what-do-lawyers-need-to-know-about-chatgpt-alexandra-andhov/.

[55] See IBM, 'AI vs. Machine Learning vs. Deep Learning vs. Neural Networks: What's the Difference?' (6 July 2023), www.ibm.com/blog/ai-vs-machine-learning-vs-deep-learning-vs-neural-networks/.

representing its importance to the output. The network's hidden layers, which fall between the input and output, are where much of the processing occurs.[56] In terms of machine learning, ANNs are dynamic nonlinear statistical models that discern patterns from input data through functions and layers. These networks can perform as either supervised learning models, where they process information in one direction, or as feedback ANNs, which integrate loops for memory retention, useful in tasks like translation.[57]

Deep learning excels at deconstructing complex problems into manageable layers, addressing each layer separately, and then integrating the solutions. This layered problem-solving is particularly effective in language processing, where it breaks down the intricate components of language into digestible parts for the computer to analyse, transforming fields like natural language processing (NLP) and allowing us to analyse human-written text.[58]

In the context of using AI for writing or reviewing disclosure documents, deep learning is another improvement, along with NLP. It advances AI by enabling more nuanced understanding and faster processing of complex information. These sophisticated algorithms excel at detecting patterns and inferring not just the main message but also the tone or the context from vast quantities of text. Yet, the effectiveness of deep learning is contingent on the quality and volume of the training data; it requires large, well-labelled datasets to learn effectively. Additionally, deep learning models are often seen as 'black boxes', with their decision-making processes lacking transparency, which can be a significant limitation for anyone trying to understand the specifics of these models or infer possible compliance or accountability.

Unforeseeability

Finally, we must acknowledge a critical point: the field of computer science does not have a single, universally accepted definition of AI. Definitions vary, with many focusing on attributes of autonomy and intelligence, yet there is no definitive way to characterise what constitutes an autonomous and intelligent computational process universally. Software engineers may have a clearer grasp of these concepts, but for legal professionals they remain open to interpretation and are subject to change over time.

The speed of development is truly unprecedented, and we still lack a good understanding of the potential consequences of the entire field of AI, not just on the law and economy but also on us. Thus there is a level of unforseeability – in the technology and its effect – that any lawyer, regulator and businessperson must take into the equation. Besides the technological elements of AI, there are

[56] JD Kelleher, *Deep Learning* (Cambridge, MA, MIT Press, 2019) 70.

[57] OAM López, AM López and J Crossa, *Multivariate Statistical Machine Learning Methods for Genomic Prediction* (Springer, 2022) 391–410.

[58] See Andhov (n 33) ch 7.

additional inherent philosophical ones that can define AI based on characteristics like unpredictability, unforeseeability, unexplainability and unreliability. So, what does this mean in the context of disclosure?

7.4. DISCLOSURE AND ARTIFICIAL INTELLIGENCE

Computations and automation have been used for years in connection with corporate disclosure, applied by financial intermediaries.[59] Companies,[60] analysts and enforcement agencies have employed a variety of software to support their tasks in either comprising various reports, analysing them, identifying potential anomalies or even executing various transactions should certain premises be met.[61] Naturally, many software solutions support experts in conducting tasks and empower them to become more diligent and efficient. For example, auditors create corporate risk profiles, based on additional NLP review of their disclosure documentation, for each firm in order to determine whether additional review of documentation is necessary.[62] Compliance officers use machine learning to conduct reviews and detect fraud on our banking accounts.[63] However, some foresee a fully autonomous end-to-end reporting solution when the systems will use internal data and report independently.[64]

This section aims to explore the extent to which AI can be used for disclosure reports, both financial and non-financial, and to examine the implications of such methodologies and techniques on the quality and actionability of the information produced.

7.4.1. AI Opacity and Explainability

As AI systems become more integrated into legal workflows, concerns regarding ethics, bias and transparency are surfacing. Since 2016, Meta's AI-driven services have been subject to numerous investigations and lawsuits due to data

[59] F Pasquale, *The Black Box Society: The Secret Algorithms That Control Money and Information* (London, Harvard University Press, 2015) 217–18.

[60] 'How these six CEOs are using AI in their businesses', *AFR Online* (29 December 2023), www.afr.com/work-and-careers/leaders/how-these-six-ceos-are-using-ai-in-their-businesses-20230922-p5e6wg.

[61] See Greene (n 52).

[62] See R Yang, Y Yu, M Liu and K Wu, 'Corporate Risk Disclosure and Audit Fee: A Text Mining Approach' (2018) 27 *European Accounting Review* 583.

[63] See Y Bao, G Hillary and B Ke, 'Artificial Intelligence and Fraud Detection' in V Babich et al (eds), *Innovative Technology at the Interface of Finance and Operations* (Los Angeles, Springer, 2022).

[64] PWC, 'Artificial Intelligence for Reporting: Proof-of-Concept to Explore Use of AI to Improve Reporting Speed and Consistency (2020), www.pwc.com/sg/en/consulting/assets/artificial-intelligence-for-reporting.pdf.

privacy violations or discrimination.[65] The use of AI in predictive policing and judicial decision-making has been scrutinised for plentiful biases.[66] Despite the fact that contemporary AI is relatively recent, the use of AI in the corporate and financial industry is substantial.[67]

Various AI tools are showing an ability to capture, process and utilise data factored into financial analyses and calculations. AI could potentially revolutionise the intricate and often laborious processes involved in financial reporting. AI tools, ranging from automating data extraction to organising this information in pre-set tables through pre-designed models, are gradually becoming essential in managing the massive data inherent in the financial and corporate sectors. The growing interest in AI solutions stems from their capability to alleviate the challenges presented by traditional financial reporting processes, which are typically labour-intensive, prone to errors, and come with high financial and time costs.

Take, for example, predictive analytics platforms like Kensho or Alpha Sense, which leverage AI to analyse financial markets and data. These platforms can access reports and other publicly available data in the SEC's EDGAR and other databases, either public or connected through various APIs, to provide forecasts and what they term 'actionable' insights. In theory, with the right volume and quality of data, AI can provide a substantial amount of insight and analysis into financial data, excelling in data analysis, recognising patterns, and translating past patterns into future predictions, provided the data is relevant and the algorithm is accurately constructed. AI has already been deployed by enforcement agencies, which has yielded more audits and significantly reduced inaccuracies and SEC inquiries and its involvement in the restatement process.[68]

AI is capable of performing functions such as perception, inference, reasoning, learning, and even adapting. However, a significant challenge with existing systems is the lack of transparency regarding data sourcing and the underlying algorithms. First, we never know how the systems were 'trained' – how they got the data in the first place.[69] Second, there are no technical tools to review

[65] See S Lu, 'Algorithmic Opacity, Private Accountability, and Corporate Social Disclosure in the Age of Artificial Intelligence' (2020) 22 *Vanderbilt Journal of Entertainment and Technology* 99.

[66] See, eg, M Gilman, 'AI Algorithms Intended to Root out Welfare Fraud Often End up Punishing the Poor Instead', *The Conversation* (14 February 2020), https://theconversation.com/ai-algorithms-intended-to-root-out-welfare-fraud-often-end-up-punishing-the-poor-instead-131625.

[67] See, eg, D W Arner et al, 'Financial Data Governance' (2023) 74 *Hastings Law Journal* 235; C Brummer and Y Yadav, 'Fintech and the Innovation Trilemma' (2019) 107 *Georgetown Law Review* 235; G Scopino, 'Preparing Financial Regulation for the Second Machine Age: The Need for Oversight of Digital Intermediaries in the Futures Markets' (2015) *Columbia Business Law Review* 439; TCW Lin, 'Artificial Intelligence, Finance, and the Law' (2019) 99 *Fordham Law Review* 531; HJ Allen, 'Driverless Finance' (2019) 10 *Harvard Business Law Review* 158.

[68] A Fedyk et al, 'Is Artificial Intelligence Improving the Audit Process?' (2022) 27 *Review of Accounting Studies* 938, 948.

[69] See A Andhov, 'OpenAI's Transformation: From a Non-Profit to a 100 Billion Valuation (2024) *SSRN Working Paper*, https://papers.ssrn.com/sol3/papers.cfm?abstract_id=4750197.

the complex algorithms on which the systems have been built.[70] Complex and opaque AI systems, especially those constructed with machine-learning algorithms, can impose high informational costs on various stakeholders, including investors, regulators, policymakers and the public. The concealed mechanics and applications of machine-learning algorithms present a substantial hurdle for policymakers and regulators aiming to mitigate the risks associated with AI, even when it is solely analysing financial data.

The term 'algorithmic opacity' refers to the challenge of discerning the processes and workings of AI tools. Frank Pasquale has coined this term the 'black box' issue due to the invisibility and intricacy of the algorithms, rendering the review of AI systems almost impossible.[71] This is particularly true for deep learning algorithms, which are layered neural networks simulating human cognitive processes. Though they start with predefined operations, they eventually function autonomously, leading to unpredictable outcomes.[72] Geoffrey Hinton, a pioneer of deep learning, remarked that as these systems become more sophisticated, their workings become less transparent, which poses a significant challenge for those tasked with regulating and mitigating AI risks.[73]

At the end of 2023, the UK Financial Authorities[74] published FS2/23, a discussion paper on Artificial Intelligence and Machine Learning ('Learning Paper'), which underscored the need for oversight of third-party AI system providers.[75] The AI systems that would provide, for example, disclosure analysis tools would seldom be developed in-house; instead, they would be procured services from technology companies that specialise in offering AI solutions as Software as a Service (SaaS) or through white-label agreements. As such, the Learning Paper stipulates that it is unclear how this would be achieved in practice, especially given that many AI tool developers likely fall outside the UK Financial Authorities' regulatory purview.[76] However, the Learning Paper does not fully address the significant challenges inherent in the detailed scrutiny of AI systems. While companies can furnish exhaustive technical documentation and may disclose certain algorithmic specifications, proprietary elements are often shielded by intellectual property rights, such as trade secrets.[77] Furthermore, recruiting and compensating personnel with expertise to thoroughly evaluate these complex systems presents a formidable challenge.

[70] See D Castelvecchi, 'Can We Open the Black Box of AI?', *Nature* (5 October 2016), https://www.nature.com/news/can-we-open-the-black-box-of-ai-1.20731.

[71] See Pasquale (n 59).

[72] Y Bathaee, 'The Artificial Intelligence Black Box and the Failure of Intent and Causation' (2018) 31 *Harvard Journal of Law and Technology* 889, 897–98.

[73] See S Mukhejee, 'A.I. Versus M.D.', *New Yorker* (3 April 2017).

[74] The Bank of England, the Prudential Regulation Authority and the Financial Conduct Authority.

[75] See Bank of England, 'FS2/23 – Artificial Intelligence and Machine Learning' (26 October 2023), www.bankofengland.co.uk/prudential-regulation/publication/2023/october/artificial-intelligence-and-machine-learning.

[76] ibid.

[77] See SK Katyal, 'The Paradox of Source Code Secrecy' (2019) 104 *Cornell Law Review* 1183.

Companies developing AI systems only allude to algorithms and associated risks, abstaining from delving into technical and practical specifics. The prevailing practices shroud the inner mechanics and operational outcomes of firms' algorithms, along with the substantial inherent risks and their management strategies, from external comprehension, surveillance or evaluation.[78] This regulatory void renders risks emanating from opaque algorithms elusive to detection, thereby inhibiting corporate shareholders and other stakeholders from adequately monitoring their investments, but also their own corporations. Even the managers themselves, if solely relying on AI solutions, will lack sufficient information to formulate informed decisions.

While the current discussion centres on AI's role in disclosure practices, it is crucial to acknowledge that AI's capabilities do not emerge in a vacuum. The data collection required to power AI, along with the often obscure nature of its algorithms, can have detrimental effects on society and our financial markets. These include invasions of privacy, challenges to equality, and compromises to other societal values that must be considered alongside AI's potential to address human shortcomings.

7.4.2. AI for Non-Financial Disclosure

Non-financial disclosure covers a spectrum of data that extends beyond financial metrics, primarily including environmental, social and governance (ESG) considerations. The genesis of such disclosure requirements in the European Union dates back to the 1970s, with countries like Germany, Austria and Switzerland mandating the reporting of worker-related information, salaries, financial externalities and socio-economic statistics.[79] France took a similar step in 1977 with the introduction of mandatory social reporting – 'bilan social' or 'social audit' – featuring 134 distinct measures and indicators.[80]

In the United States, policy discussions on non-financial disclosure began in 1971.[81] After nearly a decade of deliberation, the SEC decided against expanding disclosure requirements, citing investor focus on primarily economic and social information.[82] Over the past two decades, we have observed a shift. After the 2008 financial crisis, the SEC adopted 'specialised disclosure'

[78] Lu (n 65) 110.

[79] H-M W Schoenfeld, 'Social Reporting: The Present State in West Germany, Austria and Switzerland,' (1978) 18 *Management International Review* 1, 6–7.

[80] See A Allini and FM Rossi, 'The Evolution of Non-Financial Disclosure in a European Perspective' (2007) 14 *CSR Paper* 7.

[81] That year, the Natural Resources Defense Council and the Project on Corporate Responsibility urged the Securities and Exchange Commission (SEC) to include civil rights and environmental matters in federal securities disclosures. See CA Williams, 'The Securities and Exchange Commission and Corporate Social Transparency' (1999) 112 *Harvard Law Review* 1197, 1246–48.

[82] ibid 1251.

regulations under the 2010 Dodd-Frank Act, addressing social and human rights concerns.[83] Despite facing legal hurdles and resistance from businesses,[84] these rules set a precedent, and, today, nearly all major publicly traded companies produce sustainability reports.[85] Beyond non-financial data, the United States is also considering regulations on disclosing political expenditures. The Committee on Disclosure of Corporate Political Spending filed a rulemaking petition to the SEC in 2011,[86] which has since garnered over 1.2 million comments – more than any other petition in SEC history.[87]

Undoubtedly, non-financial disclosure plays an important role in promoting corporate accountability, and the complexity and volume of such information pose significant challenges in comprehension and analysis, as explored in Chapter 6. The impact of these disclosures on market behaviour remains an open question. However, should the information be helpful, what would be the implications if AI were tasked with processing and preparing non-financial disclosures?

As discussed above, the advent of NLP has been a game-changer for many. NLP, a subfield of AI, enables machines to understand, interpret, and generate human language, bridging the gap between human communication and computer processing. NLP, despite its complexity in dealing with challenges like language modelling, parsing, and sentiment analysis, presents a seemingly effortless 'front-end' that may mislead us into believing that computers can genuinely understand our language and meaning. This belief, especially amidst the rising disclosure obligations concerning non-financial information, might tempt us to deem it the optimal tool for aiding such reporting. The envisioned tool, capable of 'understanding' and processing a vast array of non-financial and language-based data for generating both generic and specific reports, suggests a pathway towards fully automating reporting and compliance.

Imagine a tool that uses AI to harvest data from various segments of a corporation, synthesising departmental reports from across countries to compose an annual non-financial disclosure. Take, for instance, a US-based company, ESG Flo (venture of Bain & Company) that secured $5.25 million in seed capital

[83] Dodd-Frank Wall Street Reform and Consumer Protection Act (Dodd-Frank), Pub L No 111–203, §§ 1502–1504, 124 Stat 1376 (2010) (codified at 15 USC § 78 m (2018)); 17 CFR § 229.104 (mine safety); see also Conflict Minerals, 77 Fed Reg 56,274 (12 September 2012).

[84] See *National Association of Manufacturers v SEC*, 800 F3d 518 (DC Cir 2015) (striking down portions of the Dodd-Frank conflict mineral rules).

[85] VH Ho, 'Non-Financial Reporting and Corporate Governance: Explaining American Divergence and Its Implications for Disclosure Reform' (2020) 10(2) *Accounting, Economics and Law* 1, 6–7.

[86] Committee on Disclosure of Corporate Political Spending, *Letter from Committee on Disclosure of Corporate Political Spending to Elizabeth M Murphy, Secretary, US Securities and Exchange Commission* (3 August 2011).

[87] LB Bebchuk et al, 'The Untenable Case for Keeping Investors in the Dark' (2020) 10 *Harvard Business Law Review* 1, 3.

at the end of 2023.[88] ESG Flo is leveraging AI automation and deep learning to gather data across the organisation to create reporting that complies with the EU Corporate Sustainability Reporting Directive (CSRD) and the US SEC's non-financial disclosure requirements. If a human expert monitors which data are incorporated and evaluates the significance of these sources, such software could enhance disclosure efficiency and potentially also materiality. However, the true innovation in AI-assisted disclosure lies in the system's capacity to discern what information is pivotal without preset directives autonomously.[89] This is ultimately what ESG Flo and similar entities promise.

While initial parameters are established through machine learning, the essence – and risk – of AI is that it may evolve beyond our direct command, as is the case with current systems. This autonomous progression and promise have unfortunately not yet addressed one of the main concerns – guaranteeing the ability to review and audit the selecting and utilising of the 'correct' data rather than an arbitrary dataset. The challenge lies in designing AI with both the sophistication to operate independently and the transparency to remain within our oversight.

In the realm of non-financial data, the disciplines of data abstraction and labelling are crucial for ensuring the integrity and utility of data in data science. At its core, data science is built on two fundamental principles: first, the need for a rigorous selection and understanding of data in relation to its intended use, and, second, the thoughtful design of data processes to mitigate the introduction of unintended biases. In today's data-saturated world, an estimated 1.145 trillion MB of data is generated daily, with the majority produced in the last four years.[90] This data, often collected implicitly through our digital interactions, is vital not just for marketers but across various sectors for informed decision-making.

Data science leverages this wealth of information to enhance decision-making, drawing on a wide array of computational techniques from mathematics, statistics, and computer science. Its multidisciplinary nature integrates these techniques to distil structured and unstructured data into actionable insights for organisations. However, effectively harnessing data science's potential is not without challenges. This can be extremely challenging for non-financial disclosure, which, up until today, does not have generally accepted and implemented standards for measuring impacts, such as those related to climate change or

[88] See S Lahey, 'AI-Based ESG Data Collection Startup ESG Raises $5.25 Million', (*Entrepreneur* News, 1 November 2023).

[89] P Buitelaar et al, 'Classifying Sentential Modality in Legal Language: A Use Case in Financial Regulation, Acts and Directives', Proceedings of the 16th International Conference on Artificial Intelligence and Law (2017) 159.

[90] See J Bulao, 'How Much Data is Created Every Day in 2022?', *Techjury* (6 February 2022), https://techjury.net/blog/how-much-data-is-created-every-day/.

anti-slavery compliance. This difficulty is exacerbated by a substantial asymmetry in ESG information pertaining to both the nature of the data evaluated and the methods of their assessment.[91]

Recent research has examined the opaque nature of ESG rating assessments in the financial industry, highlighting the lack of transparency and full disclosure in the computation of these ratings by agencies using proprietary models. A recent study tackles the transparency issue in ESG rating issuance by using machine learning to replicate and understand the black-box models that agencies use to issue ESG scores.[92] The replication of the model achieved considerable success in emulating the ESG ratings from Refinitiv, particularly for the Environmental pillar, suggesting that the environmental criteria are more clearly defined and quantifiable compared to the Social pillar. The study also highlights the complexity and inconsistency in replicating the Governance score across different geographic regions, attributing discrepancies to the diverse corporate governance structures that are more evolved and transparent yet still complex to model. The research also uncovered an interesting fact – increasing the number of parameters and the generalisation power of the ANN's (Artificial Neural Network) model by considering deeper and broader architectures did not yield better results, which would suggest that, in some cases, complex algorithms can be replicated with simple regression models.[93] Besides this conclusion that ultimately challenges the necessity for complex algorithms, an important finding that needs to be remembered from this study is that many of these models are proprietary, and companies such as Refinitiv do not disclose their models, despite the fact that the models can in theory be replicated, and thus potentially reviewed.

Further issues often arise not from the science itself but from the human aspects of its application, such as management support, defining clear objectives, and ensuring decision-makers utilise the insights. Moreover, bridging the communication gap between data scientists and those who rely on their analyses is critical for leveraging data science in decision-making processes. Bearing in mind that the document length of 10-K disclosure increased five times between 2005 and 2017, data scientists require the help of specialist analysts and lawyers to determine which data points should be collected and how they should be weighed.

[91] D Bams and B van der Kroft, 'Tilting the Wrogn Firms? How Inflated ESG Ratings Negate Socially Responsible Investing under Information Asymmetries' (2022), papers.ssrn.com/sol3/papers.cfm?abstract_id=4126986.

[92] See A Del Vitto, D Marazzina and D Stocco, 'ESG Ratings Explainability through Machine Learning Techniques' (2023) *Annals of Operations Research*. In this study, the researchers ultimately applied machine learning techniques to review 2021 ESG scores on Refinitiv's Eikon software to uncover the Refinitiv machine learning model.

[93] ibid.

7.4.3. Who is the Disclosure For? Is AI Writing For Us or Another AI?

Previous sections have analysed AI's role in generating disclosure documents. Yet, the impact of AI extends beyond the preparation of these disclosures. In the financial sector, a plethora of AI tools for market research, competitor analysis, and investor document review have emerged.[94] Investment funds,[95] including industry giants like Vanguard and Schwab, are now utilising AI for asset management and algorithmic trading.[96] Even the CFA Institute Research Foundation has published a comprehensive research manual.[97] Consequently, the primary recipients of disclosure documents are no longer just humans, as a considerable volume of market actions is now initiated by AI-driven recommendations. These AI systems analyse information using the methods previously outlined, marking a paradigm shift in the audience and potential effect of disclosure.

Recent research by Cao et al conducted an analysis of the *'feedback effect'* – showing that companies in the US have been already adjusting the way they 'talk' in their disclosures, as they know that their documents are being 'read' by other AI tools.[98] This adaptation seems directly linked to the increasing use of AI in parsing and analysing disclosure documents, a finding that marks a significant shift in corporate communication strategies but also in the disclosure process. The study utilised metrics termed 'Machine Downloads' and 'Machine Readability' to quantify this phenomenon, revealing that companies whose filings show a higher rate of downloads by machines also demonstrate improved readability from an AI perspective. This suggests that firms are indeed optimising their disclosures for algorithmic analysis.[99]

The paper further delves into the nuances of corporate language, specifically focusing on the sentiments and tones conveyed. Since the publication of the Loughran and McDonald finance dictionary in 2011,[100] which provides a nuanced lexicon for algorithmic sentiment analysis, firms appear to have

[94] Some of the companies that employ such technologies are Grata, RockContent, Crayon and Kensho.

[95] For an overview, see V Novykov et al, 'Deep Learning Applications in Investment Portfolio Management: A Systematic Literature Review' (2023) *Journal of Accounting Literature*; GS Santos et al, 'Management of Investment Portfolios Employing Reinforcement Learning' (2023) 10 *Peer Journal of Computer Science* 1.

[96] See TH Davenport and R Bean, 'The Pursuit of AI-Driven Wealth Management' (2021) *MIT Sloan Management Review* (7 July 2021).

[97] See SM Bartram et al, *Artificial Intelligence in Asset Management* (CFA Institute, 2020).

[98] See S Cao et al, 'How to Talk When a Machine is Listening?: Corporate Disclosure in the Age of AI' (NBER Working Paper Series, 2022), www.nber.org/system/files/working_papers/w27950/w27950.pdf.

[99] ibid 10–11.

[100] See T Loughran and B McDonald, 'When is a Liability Not a Liability? Textual Analysis, Dictionaries, and 10-Ks' (2011) 66 *Journal of Finance* 35.

adjusted their language, particularly in avoiding terms flagged as negative. This shift in language use is not found when compared to the pre-existing Harvard Psychosociological Dictionary,[101] implying a direct response to the emerging AI tools.

Extending beyond written disclosures, the research also considers the impact of AI on spoken communication. It seems that managers have begun to tailor their vocal expressions during earnings calls to appeal to both AI and human audiences, suggesting a deeper understanding of AI's role in information processing and the resultant managerial behaviours.[102] The research reveals that firms with higher AI engagement use more positive and excited tones in managerial speeches, suggesting an awareness of AI's auditory analytics. This adaptation underscores AI's significant and growing influence on financial markets and corporate communication strategies, with implications for information dissemination and market integrity.

There is undoubtedly a need for a broader discourse on AI's influence on financial communications. The disclosure process has changed; companies are now strategically applying machine learning-based language and sentiment analysis to shape content for AI consumption. This shift is not merely about the content but the 'intent' behind the disclosures, as firms anticipate how AI will interpret and judge the information presented and subsequently prepare for such AI review.

This evolution in disclosure practices reflects a broader change in the dynamics of decision-making within financial markets. Corporate and investor decisions are increasingly influenced by AI, which processes data in a manner that lacks transparency. This raises fundamental questions about the essence of disclosures themselves and even about the decision-making processes on the market. If AI can efficiently collect, process and disseminate essential data, the traditional role and value of disclosures as we understand them may need to be re-evaluated. It is a subject of further research to analyse whether disclosures retain their significance when decision-making entities are AI systems that operate beyond human oversight, potentially altering the very basis of informed investment. This question challenges us to reconsider the purpose and impact of financial disclosures in an era dominated by artificial intelligence and conduct more studies to understand the impact of induced behaviour by AI, not only on individual investors but also on markets as such.

7.4.4. AI's Lack of Objectivity

In the discourse surrounding the deployment of AI tools, the prevailing narrative often includes their potential for enhanced efficiency, accuracy, and the capacity

[101] The first lexicon is the Harvard General Inquirer IV-4 psychological dictionary that assigns 77 psychological intonations or categories to English words.
[102] Cao at al (n 98) 12–13.

to identify risks imperceptible to humans.[103] This narrative carries with it the assumption of inherent objectivity and impartiality, suggesting that technology, by virtue of its 'neutrality', stands as a bulwark against human biases.[104] Yet, such assumptions merit scrutiny, as they mask the underlying complexities of AI processes, and numerous pieces of research have actually showed otherwise.[105]

Contrary to popular belief, AI's decision-making processes are not inherently objective; they are underpinned by mathematical models that are intrinsically value-laden, embedding the measures, weights and preferences of their creators. The assertion that AI systems, by simply aggregating vast data, epitomise objectivity is a misconception understood by only a few. While the transformative power of big data and supercomputing continues to pertain, there is accumulating evidence that AI, along with its algorithmic tools, is inherently discriminatory.[106] Empirical findings are particularly stark in the areas of race and gender bias.[107] Thus, we shall raise a critical question – can AI systems perpetuate systemic biases and also favour specific types of information presented by specific types of company, for example, inadvertently favouring entities with homogenous leadership?

As discussed at 7.3.2 above, data serves as the foundational truth for any AI system. It is imperative to review the context in which the data was compiled and take account of potential latent biases. The method of data collection, whether gathered from organic sources or synthetically produced, affects the interpretation and integrity of the data. A thorough understanding of the data's origins, its pertinence, and associated risks is indispensable.[108] Furthermore, it is equally important to consider how values and judgements are encoded within AI systems.[109]

Expanding on this argument, when we discuss AI in the context of securities disclosure, the potential for bias is not merely a technical concern but a regulatory one. For example, an AI system designed to evaluate and disclose corporate

[103] There are some estimates that claim that contemporary generative AI could absorb 60 to 70 per cent of employees' time today. See 'The Economic Potential of Generative AI: The Next Productivity Frontier'(McKinsey Digital, 14 June 2023).

[104] See C O'Neil, *Weapons of Math Destruction: How Big Data Increases Inequality and Threatens Democracy* (New York, Crown, 2016) 6–13.

[105] DK Citron and F Pasquale, 'The Scored Society: Due Process for Automated Predictions' (2014) 89 *Washington Law Review* 1, 5 (showing that AI scoring systems have traditionally been 'plagued by arbitrary results. They may also have a disparate impact on historically subordinated groups.').

[106] See K Crawford and J Schultz, 'Big Data and Due Process: Toward a Framework to Redress Predictive Privacy Harms' (2014) 55 *Boston College Law Review* 93, 95–102; Citron and Pasquale (n 105).

[107] See generally L Andrews and H Bucher, 'Automating Discrimination: AI Hiring Practices and Gender Inequality' (2022) 44 *Cardozo Law Review* 145; AZ Huq, 'Racial Equity in Algorithmic Criminal Justice' (2019) 68 *Duke Law Journal* 1043; DK Citron and DJ Solove, 'Privacy Harms' (2022) 102 *Boston University Law Review* 793.

[108] S Bornstein, 'Antidiscriminatory Algorithms' (2018) 70 *Alabama Law Review* 519, 522–23.

[109] SK Katyal, 'Private Accountability in the Age of Artificial Intelligence' (2019) 66 *UCLA Law Review* 54, 59.

securities information may inadvertently prioritise data from larger corporations due to their higher volume of available information, thus skewing the AI's assessments in favour of those entities. This could show as a latent bias, whereby the AI system inadvertently assigns higher credibility or lower risk profiles to larger corporations, potentially leading to an imbalanced marketplace where smaller companies are disadvantaged or perceived as less trustworthy. Similarly, if the AI's algorithm is trained primarily on data from industries with robust reporting practices, it may not accurately assess companies from sectors with historically opaque disclosure habits. For instance, if the AI system has been fed ample data showing a positive correlation between detailed sustainability reports and lower corporate risk, it may unduly favour companies that provide comprehensive sustainability disclosures. However, this correlation does not necessarily imply causation, and the AI's training may overlook the nuances of different industry practices. As a result, sectors that are just beginning to adopt sustainability reporting might be unfairly judged as riskier investments by the AI system, regardless of their actual practices or potential for growth.

Cognitive biases and unintended discrimination often seep into algorithms' development phase, influencing data collection, analysis, and ostensibly neutral classifications and indexing systems.[110] Far from being innocuous, these biases can amplify the potential for discrimination, posing profound ethical concerns. The supposed objectivity of AI – whether applied in consumer credit scoring or assessing corporate concern for climate change or its global revenue – must be critically examined. The belief that AI can offer absolute objectivity is misguided, as every algorithm reflects the values and judgements embedded within it by human designers. Assumptions about the flawless nature of digital data, the trustworthiness of databases, or the supposed inherent objectivity and precision of data can be deceptive.[111]

7.4.5. AI's Inability to Manage Uncertainty

AI systems have shown considerable potential as support tools in decision-making processes. Yet, their direct substitution for human judgement, especially in complex, uncertain domains like financial markets, still needs to be carefully reviewed. Mistakes can arise when these systems encounter scenarios beyond their training parameters or when processing incompatible data, leading to inaccurate decisions.[112] It is crucial for AI systems to communicate uncertainties to human decision-makers instead of making definitive conclusions.[113]

[110] See M Hu, 'Critical Data Theory' (2023) 65 *William and Mary Law Review* 839, 864–65.
[111] ibid 867.
[112] See S Chowdhury, 'Why Artificial General Intelligence Lies Beyond Deep Learning', *Newstex Blogs* (18 February 2024).
[113] See, eg, Y Gal, 'Uncertainty in Deep Learning' (September 2016) (PhD thesis, University of Cambridge), https://perma.cc/ZQ3Q-BVWD.

By pinpointing the sources of uncertainty, such systems contribute to informed decision-making.

Computer scientists have explored various methods to address AI's uncertainty, including Bayesian probability theory. Originating from the work of Thomas Bayes in the 18th century, Bayesian probability uses previous outcomes to calculate the likelihood of future events. AI that employs Bayesian principles is designed to perform comparably to, or even outperform, humans in situations characterised by uncertainty, adapting to new environments, acknowledging its knowledge limits, and managing diverse sources of ambiguity.[114] Other strategies for grappling with uncertainty include using graphical models, hidden Markov models, qualitative reasoning, and various inference algorithms.[115]

The quest for more efficient deduction led to *heuristic search methods*, rooted in Herbert Simon's concept of 'bounded rationality' – opting for 'good enough' decisions when perfect ones are unattainable.[116] Expanding upon his theories, Simon employed mathematical models to depict the human mind and to illustrate human cognitive processes and diversity in decision-making. Through experiments, Simon understood that both human and artificial intelligence are built on an ability to store and process information, which leads to pattern recognition. When examining human *intuition*,[117] Simon acknowledged that despite its elusiveness to strict classification or simplistic mathematical depiction, intuition is ultimately based on our previous experiences, which guide our impulses to either replicate past successes or alter future actions.

AI systems often combine 'past experience' (data) with heuristics. Heuristics are a similar logical approach to human problem-solving strategies, particularly when exhaustive algorithms are impractical. These heuristic methods are often paired with optimisation algorithms to enhance outcomes, but they can also obscure how decisions are reached and may not always be precise.[118] The inherent limitations of heuristics, whether employed by humans or AI, should be acknowledged.

To illustrate further, consider an AI system designed for financial disclosure analysis within the AI sector, a field that so far has been largely unregulated. Suppose there is an impending regulation change regarding the disclosure of AI tools and a substantial review process by independent authorities, which is expected to influence tech companies' valuations. The AI system, drawing on

[114] For more on Bayesian artificial intelligence, see KB Korb and AE Nicholson (eds), *Bayesian Artificial Intelligence*, 2nd edn (Boca Raton, CRC Press, 2011).

[115] See D Heckerman and A Mamdani (eds), *Uncertainty in Artificial Intelligence: Proceedings on the Ninth Conference* (Springer, 1993).

[116] See HA Simon, 'Rational Choice and the Structure of the Environment' (1956) 63 *Psychological Review* 129, 133–38.

[117] See R Frantz, 'Herbert Simon. Artificial Intelligence as a Framework for Understanding Intuition' (2023) 24(2) *Journal of Economic Psychology* 265.

[118] See Andhov (n 33) ch 7.

historical data and patterns, must now predict how this regulation will affect valuations. Due to its reliance on historical models, the AI system faces challenges with this unique scenario, as it has no precedent to draw upon, at least not within the industry. It may borrow from other tech areas and try to apply the same logic, but it may inaccurately forecast the effects of the new regulation by inappropriately analogising it to less relevant past events. This leads to two potential outcomes: the AI could underestimate the regulation's impact, suggesting stability that prompts investors to maintain or increase holdings in a now riskier portfolio, or it could overreact, triggering a sell-off and damaging the company's market value and investor trust.

The fundamental issue with AI systems in managing uncertainty lies in their reliance on historical data for training.[119] Like humans, these systems often look to the past to inform their understanding, yet they possess the capacity to process information on a vastly greater scale. However, uncertainty, by its nature, defies complete capture by historical precedent; it is shaped by a multitude of subtle factors that may not have previous analogues. While we might encode these nuances into a computational model, the crux of the challenge is calibrating the relative importance – or weight – assigned to each factor within the AI system.

Considering the above example, to consider potential new regulation, the AI system must not merely draw parallels with past regulations such as the GDPR but also assess and integrate a spectrum of other variables. These may include the current political climate, technological advancements, industry-specific contexts, and global economic conditions. Each variable contributes a layer of complexity that the AI system must interpret and prioritise. Determining the weights for these variables is a non-trivial task, fraught with questions of value judgements and ethical considerations. How does AI balance immediate financial impacts against long-term societal benefits? The AI system's architecture must be sophisticated enough to simulate such multi-dimensional decision-making processes while being auditable.

7.5. CONCLUSION

A technological renaissance in corporate disclosure is gradually transforming its process, content and readership, and thus its purpose. With increased complex information, AI has emerged as a promising ally in reshaping the domain of corporate financial reporting and disclosure, rendering financial information transparent and non-financial information clear and actionable. The financial industry, a critical pillar in the global economy, is witnessing a transformative shift, propelled by the advent and incorporation of AI and its multifaceted tools,

[119] See Dresp-Langley (n 6).

while we lack the necessary understanding of what these tools will mean for the quality of information and also how they might affect the whole information disclosure process and purpose as well as the markets.

AI systems, much like the issues of sustainability and climate change, are inherently complex to understand. Despite a decade of evidence highlighting the limitations of algorithms and AI, we continue to believe in their omnipresence, objectivity and efficiency, all the while living in a world where we are consistently manipulated by such tools. This is precisely why regulators and corporations must exercise caution before deploying such tools, and if they do decide to utilise them, such usage should also be part of disclosure. I often wonder, if the largest financial companies are using these AI systems (all designed by a few companies), all analysing the disclosures in the same way, how this affects the quality of information. Are we facing similar challenges as before the 2007–08 financial crisis, when we believed in various financial innovation instruments and realised too late that the underlying logic was flawed?

Disclosure is a powerful policy tool used across various legal fields. In securities regulation, it has had a clear purpose for almost 100 years – to inform investor decision-making and fight fraud. Through this lens, we need to examine the content and processes that corporations disclose. Otherwise, we weaken this regulatory tool and render it a fallacy. Is it still the original disclosure if it is predominantly written and nuanced by AI systems for other AI systems where humans are fully disregarded? AI is shaping disclosure practices and market perception and has a substantial impact on corporate decision-making. How does this affect the information asymmetry, and what about macroeconomic consequences if the markets trust three or five AI systems?

If disclosure is about instilling confidence in investment decisions, fostering a culture of accountability among firms, and ultimately fortifying the stability and integrity of the financial market, let's advocate for a system that discloses relevant and reviewable information about corporations and the methodologies employed in generating such information. When a company employs AI to develop its disclosure documents, it should first and foremost disclose that it is using AI and in what capacity. Secondly, companies should disclose the AI models and algorithms used to compile the disclosure documents, including their development process, data sources, and any biases that could affect the outcomes. Companies should only use AI systems that are interpretable, which currently can be challenging. The deployed AI system should undergo regular audits by independent third parties that can certify that the AI is functioning as intended and within ethical bounds. Lastly, this type of AI system should always be subject to human oversight to verify the accuracy and relevance of the information before it is released. Considering AI's role in disclosures from this perspective, it is essential to address the unique challenges and responsibilities that come with integrating AI into disclosure processes. These measures can help ensure that AI contributes positively to the transparency and reliability of corporate disclosure practices.

It is only as this chapter is being finalised that the European Union adopted the new AI Regulation,[120] and the UN adopted its first resolution on artificial intelligence.[121] Looking ahead, it is imperative that research delves deeper into AI-driven disclosure systems and considers whether they may amount to high-risk AI systems and, thus, whether a higher level of scrutiny is necessary. This inquiry must extend beyond understanding their functionality, probing into their data collection methodologies, scrutinising the integrity of their data processing, and evaluating whether any manipulation might influence the resulting disclosures.

[120] The EU AI Act was adopted on 13 March 2024.

[121] See A Alper, 'UN Adopts First Global Artificial Intelligence Resolution', *Reuters* (21 March 2024), www.reuters.com/technology/cybersecurity/un-adopts-first-global-artificial-intelligence-resolution-2024-03-21/.

8

The Fallacy of a Colour-Blind Fed

NAKITA Q CUTTINO

8.1. INTRODUCTION

'Systemic racism is a yoke that drags on the American economy.'
Raphael Bostic, President and CEO, Atlanta Federal Reserve[1]

In June 2020, Federal Reserve Chairman Jerome Powell acknowledged racial inequality in the US and committed the Fed's toolkit to help mitigate racial disparities in unemployment.[2] He affirmed that the Fed 'serves the entire nation' and that 'everyone deserves the opportunity to participate fully in our society and in our economy'.[3] Chairman Powell also committed to maintain a low-interest rate policy for an extended period of time to allow those on the lowest rung of society a fairer opportunity for employment.[4] Several reserve bank districts of the Fed simultaneously hosted an unprecedented conference on 'Racism and the Economy' to discuss solutions for racial inequality in markets.[5] Such pointed engagement on race and equality was notably unusual for the Fed, but these were equally unusual times – there was a racial reckoning reverberating through private markets in response to extrajudicial killings by police,[6] a historic global pandemic that crippled the economy, and, nearly

[1] See PN da Costa, 'Ending Racism is America's "Moral and Economic Imperative": Fed's Bostic', *Forbes* (24 June 2020), www.forbes.com/sites/pedrodacosta/2020/06/24/ending-racism-is-americas-moral-and-economic-imperative-feds-bostic/?sh=34aa4a021f3b.

[2] See J Powell, 'Remarks on Racial Equality', *Federal Reserve Bank of St Louis* (10 June 2020), www.stlouisfed.org/news-releases/2020/06/12/chair-powells-remarks-on-racial-equality.

[3] ibid.

[4] See C Torres, C Condon and S Matthews, 'Fed Paves Way for Low-Rate Era with Inflation Able to Run Higher', *Bloomberg* (27 August 2020), www.bloomberg.com/news/articles/2020-08-27/powell-says-fed-to-seek-inflation-that-averages-2-over-time.

[5] See M Rodriguez Vallardes, 'The Federal Reserve Has a Role to Play in Reducing Racism in the American Economy', *Forbes* (7 October 2020), www.forbes.com/sites/mayrarodriguezvalladares/2020/10/07/the-federal-reserve-has-a-role-to-play-in-reducing-racism-in-the-american-economy.

[6] See C Alcorn, 'George Floyd's Death Was a Wake-Up Call for Corporate America. Here's What Has – and Hasn't – Changed', *CNN* (7 October 2021), www.cnn.com/2021/05/25/business/corporate-america-anti-racism-spending/index.html.

overnight, the US unemployment rate spiked from 3.5% to a depression-level 14.7%.[7] Moreover, the job losses were disproportionately borne by black and brown workers.[8] Simultaneously, the Fed faced increasing pressure from policymakers to explicitly consider racial disparities in its policy efforts.[9] Yet, less than two years after its public commitments and conferences, the Fed commenced an unprecedented series of interest rate hikes to rein in record-level inflation, and Chairman Powell warned that a meaningful rise in unemployment would be necessary.[10]

For some observers, the Fed's apparent reversal on its rate policy contradicted welcomed racial equity commitments;[11] but for others, the Fed is a colour-blind institution that should remain so if it is to be apolitical and carry out its core finance purposes.[12] The Fed wears many hats,[13] but its primary role as the US central bank is to maintain stable prices – ie manage inflation – and support maximum employment in the national economy.[14] It has several tools to tackle this dual mandate: open market operations, reserve requirements and, historically, the discount window.[15] Each tool impacts the supply of money, which in turn impacts the availability and cost of credit dispersed for both commercial investments that drive production and consumer spending that drives demand. Ultimately, tinkering with production and demand impacts prices and the unemployment rate.[16] For example, if interest rates are driven up by a low supply of money, then consumer demand wanes from the high credit costs. The lower demand in turn lowers prices but also production, which can result in the need

[7] See J Ihrig, GC Weinbach and SA Wolla, 'COVID-19's Effects on the Economy and the Fed's Response', *Page One Economics* (September 2020), https://research.stlouisfed.org/publications/page1-econ/2020/08/10/covid-19s-effects-on-the-economy-and-the-feds-response (noting rapid declines in consumer spending, business closures, and record national unemployment rates at an 80-year high of 14.7%).

[8] ibid.

[9] Federal Reserve Racial and Economic Equity Act, S.4464–116th Congress (2019–2020).

[10] See J Smialek, 'The Fed Intensifies Its Battle Against Inflation', *New York Times* (21 September 2021), www.nytimes.com/2022/09/21/business/economy/fed-rates-inflation-powell.html.

[11] See C Rugaber, 'Fed's Rate Hikes Threaten its Goal of Narrowing Racial Gaps', *Associated Press* (31 March 2022), https://apnews.com/article/business-race-and-ethnicity-racial-injustice-inflation-unemployment-05f103b868e65a6349b43f8f90f6a8b2.

[12] See AK Bartscher and others, 'Monetary Policy and Racial Inequality', *Federal Reserve Bank of New York Staff Reports* (No 959, March 2022), www.newyorkfed.org/medialibrary/media/research/staff_reports/sr959.pdf?sc_lang=en, 1, 4; The Editorial Board, 'A Woke Mandate for the Federal Reserve: Biden Endorses Racial Equity as a Third Central Bank Priority', *Wall Street Journal* (21 June 2022), www.wsj.com/articles/a-woke-mandate-for-the-federal-reserve-racial-equity-congress-house-joe-biden-11655659047.

[13] Board of Governors of the Federal Reserve System, 'What is the purpose of the Federal Reserve System?' (last updated 3 November 2016), www.federalreserve.gov/faqs/about_12594.htm.

[14] See Federal Reserve Act of 1913, 12 USC 225a.

[15] See Board of Governors of the Federal Reserve System, 'About the FOMC' (last updated 20 March 2024), www.federalreserve.gov/monetarypolicy/fomc.htm.

[16] Board of Governors of the Federal Reserve System, 'How Does the Federal Reserve Affect Inflation and Employment?' (last updated 27 August 2020), www.federalreserve.gov/faqs/money_12856.htm.

for fewer workers. Hence, the conundrum of the Fed's recent decision to use open market operations to aggressively increase the federal funds rate: by cooling market activity to combat record inflation, the Fed risks contributing to a reversal in recent employment gains in the economy generally, and among black workers particularly.[17]

Black households significantly lag their white counterparts along all measures of economic well-being, including wealth,[18] income[19] and employment.[20] The unemployment rate for black workers has historically trended at twice the rate of white workers in both good and bad economic times.[21] Indeed, such rate for black workers has often been in the double digits – rate levels closely correlated with recessions and depressions when experienced by white workers.[22] And even when employed, black workers are more likely to be underemployed.[23] Moreover, full-time black workers earn 20% less than their white counterparts.[24] In March 2023, the black unemployment rate was at a record low of 5%, just over 1.5 times the white unemployment rate, despite the Fed's aggressive contractionary policy to reduce inflation.[25] However, observers worry that it is just a matter of time before the labour market catches up with the Fed's policies and, in the usual form, sparks a reversal that impacts black workers first and most significantly.[26]

[17] See C Rugaber, 'Fed's Rate Hikes Threaten Its Goal of Narrowing Racial Gaps', *AP News* (31 March 2022), www.apnews.com/article/business-race-and-ethnicity-racial-injustice-inflation-unemployment-05f103b868e65a6349b43f8f90f6a8b2.

[18] See K McIntosh and others, 'Examining the Black-White Wealth Gap', *Brookings* (27 February 2020), www.brookings.edu/blog/up-front/2020/02/27/examining-the-black-white-wealth-gap/. ('At $171,000, the net worth of a typical white family is nearly ten times greater than that of a Black family ($17,150) in 2016.')

[19] See Gloria Guzman and Melissa Kollar, 'Income in the United States: 2022', US Census Bureau (September 2023), https://www.census.gov/content/dam/Census/library/publications/2023/demo/p60-279.pdf (illustrating that Black household median income is approximately 65% of White household median income).

[20] See AM Perry, 'Black Workers Are Being Left Behind by Full Employment', *Brookings* (26 June 2019), www.brookings.edu/blog/the-avenue/2019/06/26/black-workers-are-being-left-behind-by-full-employment/.

[21] K De et al, 'Macroeconomic Shocks and Racial Labor Market Differences' (2021) 88 *Southern Economic Journal* 680, 697.

[22] ibid.

[23] See R Nunn, J Parsons and J Shambaugh, 'Race and Underemployment in the US Labor Market', *Brookings* (1 August 2019), www.brookings.edu/blog/up-front/2019/08/01/race-and-underemployment-in-the-u-s-labor-market/.

[24] See US Bureau of Labor Statistics, 'Table 3. Median Usual Weekly Earnings of Full Time Wage and Salary Workers by Age, Race, Hispanic or Latino Ethnicity, and Sex, First Quarter 2023 Averages, Not Seasonally Adjusted', www.bls.gov/news.release/wkyeng.t03.htm (reporting median weekly earnings of $1,158 and $921 for white workers and black workers over the age of 25, respectively).

[25] D Burns and H Schneider, 'Inside the US Jobs Report: Record-low Black Unemployment', *Reuters* (7 April 2023), www.reuters.com/markets/us/inside-us-jobs-report-record-low-black-unemployment-2023-04-07/#:~:text=The%200.7%20percentage%20point%20decline,%2Dlow%2Dmatching%205.1%25.

[26] See SB Carpenter and WM Rodgers, 'The Disparate Labor Market Impacts of Monetary Policy' (2004) 23 *Journal of Policy Analysis and Management* 813.

While some observers critique what appears to be the Fed's lack of concern for black workers,[27] others question the Fed's ability to consider race in its policy efforts. Some scholars suggest that Fed decisions inconsistent with settled monetary policy norms are 'activist' and often harmful to the economy in the long run.[28] Since racial inequality has not been part of the 'settled' monetary policy parlance, then a focus on race would be inherently activist and risk negative long-run economic impact.[29] Indeed, some observers blame recent record inflation on Fed efforts to keep interest rates low to enable more equitable employment gains.[30] Fed officials have also asserted that monetary policy tools are unable to target specific demographics or address the underlying causes of racial disparities, which they suggest are best addressed by fiscal or education policies.[31] Moreover, since its formation, its framers have declared that the Fed is a 'distinctly nonpartisan organisation whose functions are to be wholly divorced from politics'.[32] As a result, many critics also claim that a focus on racial inequality would unduly politicise the Fed and undermine the public's trust.[33] Put another way, the contention is thus twofold. First, the Fed is colour-blind due to its macroeconomic objectives and toolkit, which prevent it from addressing distributional matters like racial inequality. Second, racial inequality is an inherently political issue and, therefore, falls outside the scope of what the Fed may take into consideration when exercising its powers.[34] Thus, despite its seemingly enhanced social awareness, the Fed can only proceed with an apolitical, colour-blind monetary policy to best serve all.

Yet, the Fed's very existence and evolving institutional design, purposes and policies result from trade-offs that are often political and advanced by a limited set of interest groups. Though some scholars have made a persuasive

[27] See M Boesler, J Marte and C Saraiva, 'Fragile Job Gains for Black Workers at Stake in Inflation Fight', *Bloomberg* (25 May 2022), www.bloomberg.com/news/articles/2022-05-25/inflation-vs-job-market-progress-on-black-employment-risks-coming-undone.

[28] CP Skinner, 'Central Bank Activism' (2020) 71 *Duke Law Journal* 247, 258–59.

[29] ibid.

[30] See R Miller, 'Summers Slams Woke Fed for Risking Losing Control of Inflation', *Bloomberg* (13 October 2021), www.bloomberg.com/news/articles/2021-10-13/summers-slams-woke-fed-for-risking-losing-control-of-inflation.

[31] See AK Bartscher et al, 'Monetary Policy and Racial Inequality' (Federal Reserve Bank of New York, 2022).

[32] See Committee of the Whole House, 'Changes in the Banking and Currency System of the United States' (Report of Representative Carter Glass, 1913), https://fraser.stlouisfed.org/title/changes-banking-currency-system-united-states-394/fulltext, 43.

[33] See AM Millsap, 'We Are Seeing Why a Politicized Federal Reserve Is Bad for The Economy', *Forbes* (8 April 2022), www.forbes.com/sites/adammillsap/2022/04/08/we-are-seeing-why-a-politicized-federal-reserve-is-bad-for-the-economy/?sh=7c2f74705645.

[34] See Board of Governors of the Federal Reserve System, 'FAQs – About the Fed' (31 December 2019), www.federalreserve.gov/faqs/why-is-it-important-to-separate-federal-reserve-monetary-policy-decisions-from-political-influence.htm. ('Congress has determined the Federal Reserve can best achieve its mission … as an independent agency that makes decisions based on the best available evidence and analysis, without taking politics into consideration.')

case for the political nature of the Fed,[35] the literature is glaringly silent on the racial implications (if any) of such Fed politics. This chapter demonstrates that the interest groups who shaped the Fed excluded black economic experts invested in optimal economic outcomes for black communities and, in fact, were often actively hostile toward such outcomes. Indeed, the critical trade-offs that would set the stage for so-called 'settled' monetary policy occurred when black economic experts sought a seat at the table to much-belated avail. The consequence is a central bank that has centred and labelled as settled monetary policy the drivers of economic conditions closely linked to majority white experiences. This chapter contemplates how alternative policy choices might have defined the Fed's monetary policy if due consideration were given to black economic outcomes. In doing so, it illuminates the structural racism embedded in the Fed's monetary policy that often results in ignoring harm to black households. The chapter offers a solution that compels the Fed to publicly account for its racial impact.

The first section describes how the Fed's structure, purposes and tools were shaped through highly politicised negotiations and processes hostile to black participation in the discourse facilitating the fruits of economic growth. The second section examines the impact of that exclusion coupled with the inclusion of powerful perspectives explicitly hostile to the economic well-being of black households. It then explores the shortcomings of representation to suggest that the fallacy of a colour-blind Fed might be best overcome with mandatory disaggregated impact statements. The third section concludes the chapter with a brief summary of open questions for future study.

8.2. POLITICS OF THE FED

The Federal Reserve System (Fed) is the institutional embodiment of a hard-won philosophy that a central bank is essential for the economic stability of a nation.[36] However, the Fed did not emerge from a mere formulaic, technical assessment of markets. Established by the Federal Reserve Act of 1913 ('the Act'),[37] the Fed's framers were keenly attuned to how the Fed could impact their respective interests and negotiated to shape a Fed that served their needs. This section describes how the Fed's institutional design, purpose and toolkit evolved through political choices made by a select, privileged few.

[35] See, eg, P Conti-Brown, *The Power and the Independence of the Federal Reserve* (Princeton University Press, 2018).

[36] See W Greider, *Secrets of the Temple: How the Federal Reserve Runs the Country* (Simon & Schuster, 1989) 243.

[37] 12 USC 225a.

8.2.1. Institutional Design

Formation

The Fed consists of 12 regional reserve banks ('Reserve Banks') dispersed throughout the country, a centralised Board of Governors ('Board') located in Washington, DC, and a committee known as the Federal Open Market Committee (FOMC) that combines the Board with select Reserve Bank presidents for certain monetary policy decisions.[38] The unique structure of the Fed emerged from tensely negotiated political compromises that aimed to ensure widespread representation of private and public interests, along with national and regional perspectives. The initial impetus for the Fed arose during a series of now-infamous secret meetings in 1910 at a private club on Jekyll Island, Georgia.[39] The meeting was between a prominent Republican Senator, a Treasury official and executives from three Wall Street banks and was triggered by a long series of financial panics, most recently in 1907. What emerged from the meeting was a plan for a central banking system that dispersed most key functions to regional reserve banks governed by separate boards of directors elected by local member banks.[40] Under this plan, the voting power of member banks was to be allocated based on size, thus giving the largest regional banks greater influence.

Though the idea of a central bank had growing bipartisan support, the structure of the Fed fuelled a political divide that became foundational to the Democratic Party's success in the subsequent election season.[41] Congressional Democrats criticised the Republican-sponsored plan in part for the outsized control it would give private bank interests, especially large Wall Street banks.[42] And there was bipartisan concern that concentrated governmental control, particularly if concentrated within the Department of the Treasury ('Treasury'), could result in unduly partisan pressures on the financial markets.[43] The alternative Democratic-sponsored plan aimed to balance the interests of four constituencies: private banks, a diverse business sector, a newly appointed President Woodrow Wilson who preferred centralised, federal governance for public accountability, and a bill-sponsor then-Representative Carter Glass, who thought regional self-determination made for better public accountability.[44]

[38] Board of Governors of the Federal Reserve System, 'Structure of the Federal Reserve System' (last updated 24 August 2022), www.federalreserve.gov/aboutthefed/structure-federal-reserve-system.htm.

[39] See J Romero, 'Jekyll Island: Where the Federal Reserve Began' (2015) 1 *Econ Focus* 3, www.richmondfed.org/-/media/RichmondFedOrg/publications/research/econ_focus/2015/q1/pdf/federal_reserve.pdf.

[40] See J Livingston, *Origins of the Federal Reserve System: Money, Class, and Corporate Capitalism 1890–1913* (Cornell University Press, 1989) 217.

[41] See AJ Clifford, *The Independence of the Federal Reserve System* (University of Pennsylvania Press, 1965, reprinted 2016) 40.

[42] ibid 46–47.

[43] ibid 53–54 (discussing private sector concern over partisan Treasury policy decisions that unduly impacted private credit issuance).

[44] Conti-Brown (n 35) 20–23.

The Democratic plan struck this balance by allocating limited oversight power to a central Board while Reserve Banks operated as largely self-determined bankers' banks, issuing currency and setting discount rates and reserve requirements for member banks.[45] The central Board was appointed by the President, and included the Secretary of the Treasury, certain officials from other federal agencies[46] and members representing diverse geographical, banking and business interests.[47] Indeed, as a matter of statute, no two Board members could be from the same reserve bank district.[48] This balance was at its time unique among major countries and, according to President Wilson, represented 'democracy in action' that facilitated the public's access to credit.[49]

The federated system was championed as allowing local experts to tailor monetary policy decisions to local needs. Before the locations for Reserve Banks were established, 37 cities sought to wield this power.[50] The selection process for the resulting 12 Reserve Bank locations was, thus, not without controversy. Critics complained that political favouritism and backroom dealing motivated the decisions.[51] The Congressional Selection Committee contended that each decision was based on more practical concerns like the geographical and industrial development of the city, the local banks' abilities to finance a Reserve Bank, and the likelihood of the Reserve Bank's success in the region, in each case, based in part on banker input.[52] Subsequent research is mixed, with evidence supporting both motivations.[53] Whatever the motivation, the 12 selected cities came to enjoy a direct boost to their local economies from the jobs created through the newly formed Fed. Local leaders also enjoyed direct influence over credit decisions impacting their geographical, industrial and economic interests. Such influence eventually included the Reserve Banks' practice of trading government securities, which they did to fund their respective operations but which proved to be a potent monetary policy tool most used today. This trading in government securities, or 'open market operations', impacted the availability of cash at banks, which in turn impacted credit availability to businesses

[45] See G Richardson, A Komai and M Gou, 'The Banking Act of 1935', *Federal Reserve History* (22 November 2013), www.federalreservehistory.org/essays/banking-act-of-1935.

[46] 12 USC 241.

[47] For example, the inaugural Board consisted of a Boston attorney as the first governor, a railroad executive from Chicago, an investment banking executive from New York, a bank president from Alabama, and an academic economist from California. See SK Ghizoni, 'Reserve Banks Open for Business', *Federal Reserve History* (22 November 2013), www.federalreservehistory.org/essays/reserve-banks-open.

[48] See Clifford (n 41).

[49] ibid 43.

[50] See Ghizoni (n 47).

[51] See M McAvoy, 'How Were the Federal Reserve Bank Locations Selected?' (2006) 43 *Explorations in Economics History* 505, 506–08.

[52] Decision of the Reserve Bank Organization Committee Determining the Federal Reserve Districts and the Location of the Federal Reserve Banks (1914), https://fraser.stlouisfed.org/title/decision-reserve-bank-organization-committee-determining-federal-reserve-districts-location-federal-reserve-banks-federal-reserve-act-approved-december-23-1913-603, 3–4.

[53] McAvoy (n 51) 524.

and consumers. Initially, these trading decisions were made locally by the directors of each Reserve Bank, who were primarily businessmen from stockholding banks and the local agriculture, commerce and industry sectors. The uncoordinated trading practices, however, sowed dissent between the Board and Reserve Banks and with the Treasury.[54]

Transformation

The Fed's structure was modified several times over its existence, particularly during three periods in which the Fed saw the greatest transformation: the centralisation era, the independence era and the accountability era.[55] In the centralisation era, beginning in the 1930s, the Fed was reconstituted to concentrate most policy decisions within the Board.[56] In 1933, the FOMC was formally established to require consensus among the 12 Reserve Bank presidents for open market operations at any Reserve Bank. Less than one year later, to entice Marriner S Eccles to serve as Chairman of the Fed, the FOMC replaced seven Reserve Bank presidents with the central Board. The soon-to-be Chairman Eccles believed the public interest and efficiency of centralised government outweighed regional self-determination.[57] The Board was given voting control over all open market operations throughout the system, though the remaining five seats on the FOMC were dedicated to Reserve Bank presidents.[58] The Board was also made more independent, and member terms were extended in exchange for periodic congressional reporting.[59] Notwithstanding, the Fed was quite deferential to the executive branch's efforts to combat the depression and finance wartime policies.

In the independence era, beginning in the 1950s, the Fed underwent structural changes, albeit more informal, to establish greater independence from political pressures. This evolution was led by Chairman William McChesney Martin, Jr, a staunch 'free markets' proponent.[60] As Fed chairman, Martin famously rebuffed pressures from the political branches, including in 1965 when he raised the discount rate over President Lyndon Johnson's public objection. Martin refused to acquiesce in Treasury pressures on monetary policy. He asserted the Fed's already expressed, but to that point disregarded, independence to make

[54] Clifford (n 41) 103–12.

[55] See Conti-Brown (n 35) (describing the Fed's 'three foundings' to consist of the Fed's original founding and periods otherwise described herein as the centralisation period and independence period).

[56] ibid.

[57] S Binder and M Spindel, *The Myth of Independence: How Congress Governs the Federal Reserve* (Princeton University Press, 2018) 90–91.

[58] See Conti-Brown (n 35).

[59] Binder and Spindel (n 57) 121.

[60] See RP Bremner, *Chairman of the Fed: William McChesney Martin Jr. and the Creation of the American Financial System* (Yale University Press, 2004) 61–65 (discussing Martin's success in achieving the Export-Import Bank's independence from political influence during his tenure as chair).

monetary policy decisions. He instituted more frequent meetings of the FOMC, in part, to wrestle power away from influential Reserve Banks.[61] Martin also began the now standard concentration of economists on the staff at the Fed.[62] Under Martin, the Fed's technocratic nature began to concretise.

Finally, in the accountability era, beginning in the late 1970s, the Fed's structure was further altered to enhance its public accountability. This evolution was pressured by civil rights activists, public interest groups and politicians who sought more public-oriented objectives at the Fed. Under the Humphrey-Hawkins Full Employment Act of 1978 (Humphrey-Hawkins Act), which expanded the Fed's priorities (as discussed in the next section), the Fed's congressional reporting requirements were heightened, and key positions within the Fed were subjected to public accountability.[63] The appointment of the Fed's Chairman and Vice Chairman required Senate confirmation, and Reserve Banks were required to appoint a director representing the interests of 'services, labour and consumers'.[64] Yet, the stickiness of the Fed's technocratic ethos and unaccountable practices notwithstanding these structural changes would be made salient by the policies of, ironically, the second-ever Senate-confirmed Chairman, Paul Volcker.

Notably, the evolution of the Fed's structure, allocations of authority, independence, and reporting requirements reflect the wins, losses and compromises over time of competing perspectives on the role of a central bank. In the absence of a consensus or formulaic approach to central banking, prevailing perspectives were advanced mostly by powerful banking and business interests, influential politicians, and transformative Fed Chairmen, in ways that formed a technocratic institution. Only when a voice was given to less privileged perspectives did a relatively more democratically accountable institution began to take shape, with hopes that the Fed served not just the economic health of the financial markets, but also the economic health of the average citizen.

8.2.2. Purposes and Tools

Formation

A similar transformation can be observed with respect to the Fed's purpose and toolkit. At its origin, the Fed was narrowly expected to resolve the inelasticity of bank capital to better accommodate the complexities of a largely agrarian

[61] ibid 81 (noting that even through the 1990s, the Board was effectively controlled by the Chairman and senior staff).

[62] See J Fox, 'How Economics PhDs Took Over the Federal Reserve', *Harvard Business Review* (3 February 2014), www.hbr.org/2014/02/how-economics-phds-took-over-the-federal-reserve.

[63] Full Employment and Balanced Growth Act of 1978, Pub L No 95-523, 92 Stat 1887 (codified as amended in scattered sections of 2 USC, 12 USC, 15 USC) (hereinafter Humphrey-Hawkins Act).

[64] ibid.

but rapidly industrialising economy. Several interest groups were adversely impacted by a mismatch between the seasonal cash demands of farmers and the cash reserves of East Coast bankers that were otherwise leveraged for securities trading. The farming industry faced limited and costly credit when most needed; the banking industry suffered liquidity crunches and occasional failures; and the nascent corporate sector struggled to mature under a volatile securities market. The Fed's narrow purpose was to support commercial credit markets for 'commerce, agriculture and industry' and prevent bank panics via an elastic currency, rediscounting commercial paper and supervising the banking industry.[65]

The Fed's framers contemplated a limited toolkit to control the amount of cash available to member banks or the money supply: the discount window and reserve requirements. Through the discount window, the Fed offers short-term loans below market rate to member banks for day-to-day operations. The amount of these loans has historically been limited by the value of select bank assets deemed eligible to serve as collateral. By increasing (reducing) the interest rate for discount credit or by limiting (expanding) the types of eligible collateral, the Fed could reduce (increase) member banks' money supply. The Fed's second tool, reserve requirements, allows the Fed to set the minimum amounts of cash that member banks are required to keep on deposit with the Fed. By increasing (reducing) reserve requirements, the Fed could reduce (increase) member banks' money supply.

One of the first instructive compromises concerned the discount window. The Fed's framers intended to direct capital flows away from speculative uses and toward so-called productive uses by limiting the eligible collateral for discount credit to 'commercial paper' with 45-day maturities.[66] In doing so, they also sought to incentivise low-cost bank finance for local enterprises and sever the destabilising link between banking and the stock market. However, congressional leaders representing agrarian interests contended that the collateral limitation ignored the actual financing needs and practices of the agricultural sector.[67] Specifically, the agricultural sector required longer maturities and optional extensions in seasons of low harvest.[68] By excluding agrarian financing instruments, Fed policy would effectively handicap member banks serving this industry and limit the industry's capital access relative to others. Debates around the issue were so intense that southern Democrats accused the leadership of geographical discrimination for failing to properly recognise and tailor Fed policy to the agrarian interest.[69] To resolve the dissension, the definition of

[65] Federal Reserve Act, Pub L No 63-43, 38 Stat 251, 251 (1913).

[66] NO Peer, 'Negotiating the Lender of Last Resort: The 1913 Federal Reserve Act as a Debate over Credit Distribution (2019) 15 *New York University Journal of Law & Business* 367.

[67] ibid.

[68] ibid.

[69] ibid.

commercial paper was expanded to accommodate agricultural financing instruments, and fiscal policy provisions were made for agricultural lending.[70]

Transformation

Contentious compromises continued to transform the Fed's purpose and tools over time as various interest groups sought to make the Fed more responsive to increasingly dynamic economic challenges.

In the centralisation era, Chairman Eccles believed the best solution to record bank failures and unemployment during the Great Depression was an expanded purpose that balanced 'stable business conditions' and 'full employment'.[71] He rejected traditional wisdom that suggested stable prices were the paramount goal of a central banking system. The rise of Keynesian economics facilitated the acceptance of Chairman Eccles' plans to use the Fed's tools to proactively drive up employment rates and production instead of deferring to 'free markets' for such outcomes.

The key tool used toward this end was open market operations. As previously mentioned, this tool was inadvertently discovered by Reserve Banks but proved potent. The Fed's large-scale trading effectively dictated the interest rates for government securities. Prior to the centralisation era, the banking sector pressured Reserve Bank trading practices that were contractionary simply to maintain high yields on government securities.[72] The centralisation era ushered in centralised, uniform trading decisions dictated by the Board-controlled FOMC that could limit private sector influence. Under Chairman Eccles, the Fed's open market operations aimed for low rates that could cheaply finance expansionary fiscal programs.

In the independence era, the Fed dispensed with the fiscalist values of Eccles amid rising inflation. This was especially easy to do so since Eccles' 'full employment' priorities were never formally made part of the Fed's purpose. President Truman attempted to make full employment a statutory requirement through the Employment Act of 1946, but Southern politicians and the agricultural sector fiercely opposed the effort.[73] The final legislation only ambiguously committed the federal government to generally promote 'maximum employment, production and price stability' without assigning any clear responsibilities or methods to any particular agency.

[70] ibid.

[71] Committee on Banking and Currency, Banking Bill of 1935 (Statement of MS Eccles, 1935), https://fraser.stlouisfed.org/title/statements-speeches-marriner-s-eccles-446/statements-hearings-banking-bill-1935-7637/content/fulltext/1935hr_ba1935_eccles.

[72] See E Dickens, 'Bank Influence and the Failure of US Monetary Policy During the 1953–54 Recession' (1998) 12 *International Review of Applied Economics* 221.

[73] See SK Bailey, *Congress Makes a Law: The Story Behind the Employment Act of 1946*, 3rd edn (Columbia University Press, 1957) 189–205.

Thus, under Chairman Martin, a 'free markets' philosophy shaped the Fed's purpose and tools. The first order of business was undoing the interest rate agreement implemented by Eccles with the Treasury, which compelled inflationary open market operations in the post-wartime era.[74] By selling (purchasing) government securities to impact rates on government securities, the Fed also reduced (increased) member banks' money supply, which altered the price of lending between banks and the cost of credit to bank customers. In 1951, as Assistant Secretary of the Treasury, Martin successfully negotiated an agreement under which the Fed would no longer pursue interest rates in service of the Treasury's debt financing needs.[75] He operationalised the 1951 agreement by bolstering member banks' dependence on the discount window lending[76] and narrowing its open market operations.[77] Open market operations no longer included long-term Treasury securities, which impacted rates that were political landmines like residential mortgages.[78] To be sure, the Fed was not now immune to pressures from the banking sector[79] or the executive branch[80] to pursue counterproductive monetary policy objectives. It was, however, more independent and less interventionist than in prior years. This policy approach was influenced by Fed staffer Winfield Riefler, who became Martin's close advisor.[81] Under Chairman Martin, the Fed's purpose was to be merely reactive to empower the forces of supply and demand to dictate the financial markets.[82] Over his 19-year term, this became the unrelenting conventional wisdom of the Fed.

In the accountability era, though no new tools were developed, the Fed revisited the dual purpose championed by Eccles nearly four decades prior. Amid record inflation and rising unemployment, polarised perspectives on monetary policy existed among external interest groups. On the one hand, business interests, conservative legislators, conservative economists like Milton Friedman and the Fed's top officials rejected accommodative policies prioritising low unemployment as inflationary and costly.[83] On the other hand, liberal legislators, labour interests and prominent civil rights leaders advocated for a full employment mandate that would have priority over stable prices to protect the unemployed.[84] The compromise legislation, the Humphrey-Hawkins Act, established the Fed's dual mandate, which is unintuitively threefold: 'maximum employment, stable

[74] Bremner (n 60) 73–75.
[75] ibid.
[76] ibid 88.
[77] ibid 99.
[78] ibid.
[79] See Dickens (n 72).
[80] Binder and Spindel (n 57) 168.
[81] Bremner (n 60) 88.
[82] ibid 101.
[83] P Andelic, '"The Old Economic Rules No Longer Apply": The National Planning Idea and the Humphrey-Hawkins Full Employment Act 1974–1978 (2019) 31 *The Journal of Policy History* 72, 84.
[84] ibid.

prices, and moderate long-term interest rates'.[85] The Humphrey-Hawkins Act set a non-mandatory unemployment target of 4% coupled with an ambitious inflation target of 0%.[86]

Notwithstanding, the now statutory dual purpose of the Fed was effectively ignored by internal leaders, including incoming Chairman Paul Volcker. A year after the Humphrey-Hawkins Act, Volcker was charged with reigning in record inflation, which spiked to over 9% in the first month of his confirmation and peaked at over 14% one year later.[87] Under Volcker, the Fed adopted a monetarist economic policy to combat inflation, thus seeking to constrain the absolute money supply without regard to the level of interest rates or unemployment.[88] In so doing, the Fed set into motion an aggressive contractionary monetary policy that pushed the country into two recessions, causing nearly 11% national unemployment – at the time, the worst unemployment rate on record since the Great Depression.

The development of the Fed's structure, purpose and toolkit has been far from scientific. Instead, these features have been moulded through a highly political process shaped by shifting economic conditions and influential constituencies. Though external perspectives from public interest groups occasionally shaped the Fed, the most consequential framers were internal Fed leaders and staff, closely connected business interests, and powerful politicians.

8.3. THE FALLACY

Though the foregoing discussion describes an evolution arising from decisions that were ostensibly agnostic to race, the fallacy of the Fed's colour-blindness is apparent when one takes a closer look at the social context in which most of these critical decisions shaping the Fed were made. This section illustrates how key Fed constituencies excluded or were otherwise hostile or indifferent toward perspectives on the unique economic conditions of black communities.

8.3.1. Colour-Conscious Exclusion

Formation

The Fed's framers believed representation was a necessary feature to ensure its effectiveness, but conspicuously unrepresented were the economic interests of black communities. The Jekyll Island convening occurred at the height of Jim

[85] Humphrey-Hawkins Act (n 63).

[86] ibid.

[87] CE Walsh, 'October 6, 1979', *FRBSF Economic Letter* (3 December 2004), https://www.frbsf.org/economic-research/publications/econo.

[88] RL Hetzel, *The Monetary Policy of the Fed: A History* (Cambridge University Press, 2008) 153.

Crow, wherein black citizens were lawfully disenfranchised, segregated, violently terrorised and routinely lynched.[89] The very club where the convening occurred would not have granted entry to a black meeting participant. The same could be said about Congress when the Democratic plan for the Fed was developed. Though the first black Senator had been elected more than four decades prior,[90] the devastating effects of Jim Crow and white-supremacist values led to the complete exclusion of black politicians from Congress from 1901 to 1929 – the Fed's formative years.[91] Even when black politicians returned to Congress, their numbers were few, and they would not be admitted to a congressional finance committee that impacted the Fed until 1967.[92]

What's more, many of the Fed's most consequential framers harboured anti-black sentiments and pursued racially hostile policies. Representative Glass, who drafted the Act, was a proud segregationist who, while a state senator, crafted the Virginia constitution that disenfranchised black voters.[93] Surely, Representative Glass's focus on regional self-determination was not likely concerned with enfranchising local black communities in Fed policymaking. Indeed, the first non-white director at a Reserve Bank was not appointed until more than half a century after the Fed's founding.[94] Similarly, President Woodrow Wilson devastated the black working class in the Nation's capital by hamstringing their economic, social and political mobility when he legalised segregation in the federal government.[95] It was unlikely that President Wilson's desire to democratise the Fed extended to a demographic he excluded from any meaningful positions in that effort.

The business interest groups and private banking sector involved with the Fed's formation offered no meaningful access. The agrarian interests that lobbied for equitable access to low-cost credit, in turn, instituted

[89] M Alexander, *The New Jim Crow: Mass Incarceration in the Age of Colorblindness* (New Press, 2020) 185–95.

[90] In 1870, Hiram Revels of Mississippi became the first black US Senator. Senate Historical Office, 'Senate Stories – Hiram Revels: First American Senator' (25 February 2020), www.senate.gov/artandhistory/senate-stories/First-African-American-Senator.htm.

[91] In 1929, Oscar S DePriest became the first black congressman elected in the post-Reconstruction era. US House of Representatives, 'History, Art & Archives', https://history.house.gov/People/Detail/12155.

[92] In 1967, E William Brooke II became the first black member of a congressional finance committee when he joined the Senate Banking and Currency committee. A decade later, Parren Mitchell James (MD) became the first black chair of a finance committee when he chaired the House Banking, Finance and Urban Affairs Committee. Congressional Reserve Service, 'African American Members of U.S. Congress: 1870–2020' (15 December 2020), https://crsreports.congress.gov/product/pdf/RL/RL30378.

[93] See H Wilson, 'The Role of Carter Glass in the Disenfranchisement of the Virginia Negro' (November 1969) 32 *The Historian* 69.

[94] See P Conti-Brown and K Nygaard, 'Diversity Within the Federal Reserve System', *Brookings* (13 April 2021), www.brookings.edu/articles/diversity-within-the-federal-reserve-system/ accessed 10 July 2023.

[95] ES Yellin, *Racism in the Nation's Service: Government Workers and the Color Line in Woodrow Wilson's America* (UNC Press, 2013) 2–3.

sharecropping – a system of usurious debt and poverty entrenchment – on largely black farm labourers.[96] They also actively excluded black farmers from the benefits of the low-cost credit negotiated for the industry.[97] Though banking experts with varied regional and industry expertise were critical to the Fed's formation, black bankers with unique insights into the economic conditions of black communities were not included in the discourse. This was not because of a lack of experts. On the contrary, in 1910, there were more than 50 black-owned banks in nine states serving the commercial and consumer needs of black communities.[98] Interestingly, 40% of these banks were concentrated within the Reserve Bank of Richmond's district. Yet, despite being a hotbed of black banker expertise in its formative years, the Reserve Bank of Richmond would not appoint a non-white director until 1976.[99] The exclusion of black banking experts in forming the Fed was also not due to a lack of interest. Observers openly hoped that the economic stability created by the Fed would trickle down to create prosperity for black labourers. When that hope was dashed, black bankers shifted their ambitions to create a federation of black-owned banks that would extend emergency credit to associated banks in times of crisis.[100] In other words, black bankers sought to create their very own quasi-Fed in the absence of adequate representation and security.

Transformation

The systematic exclusion of individuals invested in the economic well-being of black communities persisted through most of the transformation eras.[101] To date, there has never been a black chairman of the Board. And there have only been four black governors on the Board, though never overlapping in term. The first, Andrew Brimmer, was appointed in 1966,[102] and the first black woman, Lisa Cook, was just recently appointed in 2022.[103] This means that the Fed chronically passed up opportunities to hire or appoint experts on black economic outcomes during its formative years, the centralisation era, and most

[96] See JR Mandle, *Not Slave, Not Free: The African American Economic Experience Since the Civil War* (Duke University Press, 1992).

[97] M Baradaran, *The Color of Money: Black Banks and the Racial Wealth Gap* (Harvard University Press, 2017) 67.

[98] 'Negro Banks and Where Located', *The Chicago Defender: Big Weekend Edition* (3 September 1910) 1.

[99] See Conti-Brown and Nygaard (n 94).

[100] AB Henderson, 'Richard R. Wright and the National Negro Bankers Association: Early Organizing Efforts Among Black Bankers, 1924–1942' (January/April 1993) 117 *The Pennsylvania Magazine of History and Biography* 51, 61.

[101] See Conti-Brown and Nygaard (n 94), C Brummer and A Klein, 'The Fed's Striking Lack of Diversity and Why it Matters', *Brookings* (1 August 2016), www.brookings.edu/opinions/the-feds-striking-lack-of-diversity-and-why-it-matters/.

[102] See WM Young, Jr, 'To be Equal', *New Journal and Guide* (19 March 1966).

[103] See J Smialek and E Cochrane, 'Lisa Cook is Confirmed as a New Fed Governor', *The New York Times* (10 May 2022).

of the independence era. For example, Dr Sadie TM Alexander, who became the first black PhD economist in 1921, was never hired as an economist – by the Fed or otherwise – despite high praise from her professors.[104] There was a brief glimmer of hope in 1929 when Jesse Binga, a then-successful Chicago banker, was potentially under consideration as the first black governor on the Board.[105] Yet, such hope would have to endure for four more decades before being realised. During the time of Alexander and Binga, black economic experts could not even aspire to influential staff positions at the Fed. They could, at most, hope for low-level, non-policy staff positions in offices of the Recorder of Deeds or Register of the Treasury.[106]

The Reserve Banks did nothing to fill the void. The first of two black presidents of a Reserve Bank in the history of the Fed, Raphael Bostic, was appointed more than one hundred years after its founding, in 2017.[107] The second, Susan M Collins, was appointed in 2022.[108] Thus, open market operations, whether conducted by the individual Reserve Banks in the early years or by the FOMC, had not been influenced by black perspectives until Brimmer's arrival on the Board. The directorship of each Reserve Bank was also completely devoid of racial diversity until 1970, when civil rights leader and long-time executive director of the National Urban League, Whitney Young Jr, was appointed to the Reserve Bank of New York.[109] Upon accepting his position, Young declared that his appointment recognised the 'need for involving Black people in the basic monetary and fiscal policies affecting them', and he hoped other financial institutions would follow suit.[110] In agreement, then-Vice Chairman of the Board, James L Robertson, said Young's appointment was 'an excellent opportunity to get a man who represents interests that ha[d] not been represented thus far'.[111] Indeed, black economic interests were arguably unrepresented at the Reserve Bank staff level as well. Though the record is limited, Brimmer appears to have been among the first black staff economists hired by a Reserve Bank

[104] N Banks, 'The Black Worker, Economic Justice and the Speeches of Sadie T.M. Alexander' (June 2008) 66 *Review of Social Economy* 139, 140.

[105] See Afro-American (ed), 'Suggest Jesse Binga for Federal Reserve Board', *Afro-American* (26 January 1929).

[106] ibid.

[107] See P Gillespie, 'Fed Names First African American Regional President', *CNN* (14 March 2017), www.money.cnn.com/2017/03/13/news/economy/atlanta-fed-raphael-bostic-first-african-american/index.html.

[108] See J Smialek, 'The Boston Fed Names Susan M. Collins as its New President', *The New York Times* (9 February 2022), https://www.nytimes.com/2022/02/09/business/economy/boston-fed-president-susan-collins.html.

[109] The New York Times (ed), 'Whitney Young Named a Director of Reserve Bank' (29 December 1970), www.nytimes.com/1970/12/29/archives/whitney-young-named-a-director-of-reserve-bank.html.

[110] Afro-American (ed), 'Federal Reserve Appointment: Whitney Young Should Bring "Added Dimension" to Board' (9 January 1971).

[111] ibid.

when he worked at the Reserve Bank of New York in the late 1950s.[112] And if current trends are any indication of the historical climate (though probably more generous), a black staff economist at even a Reserve Bank was a rarity.[113]

To be sure, the systematic exclusion of black experts and disregard for black well-being was not uncharacteristic of the periods in which the Fed transformed. However, this critique is not merely a hindsight assessment without appreciating then-existing norms and expectations. Then-existing norms also included widespread protests by black leaders and communities who long valued an equal seat at the table in policymaking that impacted them. Then-existing norms also included black bankers and business interests who sought to strengthen their financial institutions and facilitate equitable access to credit for upward mobility, in much the same way hoped for by President Wilson. It is, therefore, worth explicating the unique consequence of such colour-conscious exclusion to monetary policy.

8.3.2. The Impact of Exclusion – A Thought Experiment

Would the Fed look any different if expertise on black economic conditions were included during its formation and transformation eras? One may only speculate, but there are many reasons to believe that it would. A look at the congressional debate over the discount window proves instructive on the power of representation. Southern Democrats successfully advocated for agrarian interest, calling out implicit discrimination baked into the definition of commercial paper. Thanks to this representation, the Fed's discount window was made more accessible to agrarian bankers, affording them below-market credit for greater liquidity and better credit services to their customers. And to the extent the more inclusive discount window still fell short, fiscal policy provided low-cost credit solutions for the direct benefit of agrarian bank customers. Like agrarian banks, black banks were unlikely to have standard commercial paper as a bank asset. Instead, black bank assets were more typically tied to long-term real estate mortgages.[114] Thus, if black bankers were present to argue the implicit discrimination against their banking model, they too may have been able to expand the type of assets that could be used as collateral for discount window borrowing. Even if the discount window facility could not fully accommodate the needs of black bankers, one could have envisioned fiscal policy support in the form

[112] Afro-American (ed), 'Andrew Brimmer Named for Top Commerce Post' (6 February 1965).

[113] As of May 2022, the Board employed just one black economist. See C Saraiva, 'Fed Board Employs Just One Black Economist, Diversity Data Show', *Bloomberg* (13 May 2022), www.bloomberg.com/news/articles/2022-05-13/fed-board-employs-just-one-black-economist-diversity-data-show.

[114] See F Calvin, 'A Youthful Bank Cashier Gives Out Some Unusual Hints About Banking', *Pittsburgh Courier* (11 May 1929), www.proquest.com/docview/201910802/76E78202D13A431FPQ/1?accountid=36339.

of federally subsidised mortgage capital that was directly accessible to black-owned banks' customers.

More fundamentally, there were no advocates for the inclusion of black-owned banks as member banks of the Fed in the first instance to benefit from low-cost liquidity. Had there been, the framers might have been able to facilitate economic development in black communities underserved by mainstream banks. Indeed, when a black-owned bank became a member bank of the Fed in 1929 for the first time, black news media celebrated the unprecedented fact that the bank was able to put new money into circulation. Observers also noted the bank's decision to acquire only $5 reserve notes to facilitate the widest distribution of its money multiplier mechanism.[115] Additionally, the broader sector of black banks hoped to share in the unique opportunity by situating the pioneering institution as 'a sort of Federal Reserve bank' that could act as a 'splendid bulwark of protection' for other black banks.[116] And as a network, the black banking community sought to concentrate and mobilise black wealth to offer black enterprises better credit terms. If black economic conditions were considered, black banks may have had a higher value to the Fed and been used to inject much-needed capital into black communities.

If perspectives sensitive to black economic conditions were engaged in the formative years, the Fed may not have delayed its accommodative open market operations policy in response to the Great Depression. Observers universally and rightfully bemoan the near 25% unemployment rate recorded during the Great Depression. However, this aggregate rate obscures the decidedly worse economic conditions experienced in black communities, where unemployment began to rise much earlier and was more dramatic.[117] Indeed, black unemployment during the Great Depression peaked at 50% to 60%.[118] If disaggregated economic data was valued, Fed policies may have targeted black economic recovery and, thus, been more responsive to the burgeoning national crisis.[119]

During the centralisation era, black economic experts might have informed the adoption of a dual mandate earlier. A look at Winfield Riefler's influence on Chairman Martin's 'free market' approach to monetary policy is instructive. Just as Riefler gave theoretical underpinnings to Chairman Martin's philosophy and was by many accounts the silent driver of his monetary policy, staffers with expertise on black economic conditions could have informed Chairman

[115] The Pittsburgh Courier (ed), 'Douglass National, The Largest Negro Bank!: Member of the Federal Reserve System with $2,210,855.98 and Deposits of Over Million and Half Dollars' (27 July 1929).

[116] See Calvin (n 114).

[117] Banks (n 104) 146.

[118] See CL Greenberg, *To Ask for an Equal Chance: African Americans in the Great Depression* (Rowman & Littlefield Publishers, Inc, 2009).

[119] *cf* BD Feinstein, P Conti-Brown and K Nygaard, 'Board Diversity Matters: An Empirical Assessment of Community Lending at Federal Reserve-Regulated Banks' (11 April 2023), https://papers.ssrn.com/sol3/papers.cfm?abstract_id=4000110.

Eccles as he advanced a more instrumentalist approach to monetary policy. Black bankers and business leaders were principally concerned with improving black employment. And Dr Alexander was the first economist to advocate for a full employment mandate to overcome racial and economic inequality.[120] If hired as a staff economist to the Board, her research could potentially have offered a theoretical framework and strengthened Chairman Eccles' monetary philosophy.

What's more, if the Fed's framers had not included individuals explicitly hostile to black economic well-being, the effort for full employment may not have failed in 1945. A full employment bill was overwhelmingly passed in the Senate but failed in the House due to powerful southern legislators and agrarian interests. These constituencies believed a job guarantee for black workers would empower them to abandon farm labour and disrupt the racialised social and economic subordination of the Jim Crow era.[121] It was colour-conscious politics, rather than colour-blindness, that helped shape the purpose of the Fed.

In the independence era, racial exclusion, indifference or hostility may have prevented the Fed from appreciating the disparate impact of its now-standard incremental and reactionary approach to monetary policy adopted by Chairman Martin. The appointment of Brimmer during the end of the independence era is instructive. Though he initially supported rate hikes that began before his appointment, he was the first Board member to suggest ending the contractionary policy.[122] Brimmer regularly reported on the black unemployment rate and warned of the disparate effect contractionary policies had on it.[123] Even in the face of high inflation, which he took seriously, Brimmer proposed relatively less aggressive monetary solutions than some of his colleagues. He also offered fiscal solutions to offset the employment hit that were very much in the spirit of full employment.[124] For example, he suggested fiscal policy should broaden unemployment benefits, create public service jobs, and reduce taxes on low-income families.[125] Notably, Brimmer was operating within the constrained framework established by Martin. One can imagine, for example, that if Brimmer's nuanced expertise was coupled with Eccles' more instrumentalist view of monetary policy, then the Fed's toolkit might have been used for targeted sectoral or geographic investment.

[120] See Banks (n 104).

[121] See Bailey (n 73).

[122] See A Brimmer, 'Economic Situation of Blacks in the United States' (1972) 2 *The Review of Black Political Economy* 34, journals.sagepub.com/doi/abs/10.1007/BF03040521; C Rowe, 'Black Teen Jobless at 37.1%', *The Washington Post* (8 July 1978), www.washingtonpost.com/archive/business/1978/07/08/black-teen-jobless-at-371/9bdb3aed-e781-4c59-ba9f-dfc470bcce36/.

[123] See Joint Economic Committee of the Congress, Economic Situation of Blacks in the United States (Statement of Andrew F Brimmer, 1972), fraser.stlouisfed.org/title/statements-speeches-andrew-f-brimmer-463/economic-situation-blacks-united-states-10405.

[124] See M Newson, 'Blacks "Bite Bullet" in Recession, Inflation Vise: Businessmen, Workers Find Outlook Dark', *Afro-American* (30 November 1974).

[125] See ibid.

The importance of such representation might be most evident in the accountability era. Civil rights leaders, like A Philip Randolph[126] and Coretta Scott King,[127] and black legislators, like August Hawkins, recognised that unemployment levels were disproportionately borne by black workers, and they appreciated that the Fed's regulation of the money supply operated as an invisible hand on black workers' employment prospects. To combat the harm to black workers, they believed the key solution was a full employment guarantee. Hawkins co-authored a full employment bill amid an economy roiling with a 9% national unemployment rate, though black unemployment was over 15%. The civil rights movement and labour movement lobbied congressmen and then-presidential candidate Jimmy Carter to support full employment. Carter's support of a full employment bill resulted in him being accused of pandering to minorities. The eventual Humphrey-Hawkins Act that created the dual mandate and enhanced public reporting of the Fed's monetary policy occurred due in no small part to black economic interests finally being represented within Congress and in conversations with the President and other powerful Fed framers.

Yet, the challenges to such representation were revealed by the eventual Humphrey-Hawkins Act and the Fed's response to it. Instead of a full employment mandate, the final legislation called for a maximum unemployment rate of 4%. It did, however, call for the Fed to prioritise its employment target over inflation targets. Notwithstanding, the significant flexibility in the language of this new dual mandate allowed Chairman Volcker to pursue an aggressive contractionary policy that caused unemployment to skyrocket. The Fed's internal decision-makers remained beholden to the Martin-era ethos of prioritising price stability. This was despite the presence of a black governor, Emmett Rice. In fact, Rice often battled in vain against Chairman Volcker's aggressively contractionary policies.[128] He was particularly concerned with the recessionary effect of the policies, and rightfully so. Though the national unemployment rate was just at 6% when Rice voted against an inevitable rate hike in 1979,[129] Rice may have been more in tune with the fact that the black unemployment rate was already nearly 12%.[130] If *due* consideration had been given to the concerns of the sole black governor of the Fed, Volcker may not have pursued a monetarist policy that caused the black unemployment rate to peak at 21.2%. History often

[126] Randolph was a decades-long proponent of full employment for racial equity and co-organiser of the March on Washington for Jobs and Freedom. CL Bynum, *A. Philip Randolph and the Struggle for Civil Rights* (University of Illinois Press, 2010) 159–61, 168.

[127] Just four days after Dr Martin Luther King Jr's assassination, Scott King rallied supporters to continue the fight for full employment legislation. J Theoharris, 'Coretta Scott King and the Civil Rights Movement's Hidden Women', *The Atlantic* (February 2018), www.theatlantic.com/magazine/archive/2018/02/coretta-scott-king/552557/.

[128] Staff Reporter, 'Further Rise Possible in Interest Rates, Says A Fed Board Member', *The Wall Street Journal* (12 September 1979).

[129] FRED, 'Unemployment Rate' (7 July 2023), https://fred.stlouisfed.org/series/UNRATE.

[130] FRED, 'Unemployment Rate – Black or African American' (7 July 2023), https://fred.stlouisfed.org/series/LNS14000006.

paints Volcker's policies in a favourable light, notwithstanding the Fed-induced 'recessions' or 'short-term' pain, but even such retellings fail to give hindsight consideration to black economic conditions. At 21.2% unemployment, the conditions in black communities rivalled the Great Depression, and the effects were far from short-term.[131]

8.3.3. Disaggregated Impact Statement

The ambition of this chapter in revealing the fallacy of a colour-blind Fed is not merely to redress staff-level diversity shortcomings, though an independently sufficient and important objective. Indeed, recent scholars have found that remedying the lack of diversity at the Fed has tangible economic benefits for black households.[132] Notwithstanding, as revealed by the accountability era, representation (particularly in few numbers) has limitations.[133] The fallacy explored in this chapter identifies structural racism entrenched in the Fed's design, purpose and toolkit over a century. The solutions must be multifaceted and go beyond representation. To be sure, racial disparities trace back to the country's history of slavery and are perpetuated through a variety of discriminatory systems for which the Fed is not responsible. However, the Fed's unaccountable structural shortcomings exacerbate such disparities in underappreciated ways. Structural remedies are likely required – such as through modifications to the Fed's mandate or tools – but a first-order effort must be to better attune the Fed (and Congress) to its racialised effect. Thus, a modest but potent first remedy would be for the Fed to disaggregate its economic data and periodically report on the projected racial impact of its planned monetary policy in what may be called a 'Disaggregate Impact Statement' (DIS).

A DIS is akin to a racial impact statement, which is most common in the criminal justice context, where it is widely appreciated that devastating racial disparities have long resulted from facially neutral policies.[134] Proponents use racial impact statements to identify and prevent or otherwise mitigate disparities arising in a policy proposal – eg sentencing guideline changes – prior to its adoption, recognising that *ex post* remedies may be inadequate.[135] Racial

[131] Amid depression-level unemployment rates, black communities were further devastated by a drug epidemic compounded by a criminal justice system that criminalised their addiction and dire straits. M Tonry, 'Race and the War on Drugs' (1994) 1994 *University of Chicago Legal Forum* 25.

[132] See Feinstein, Conti-Brown and Nygaard (n 119).

[133] For comparison, in the context of gender diversity on corporate boards, women only impact group decisions when they exceed 20% of the group numbers. MA O'Connor, 'The Enron Board: The Perils of Groupthink' (2003) 71 *University of Cincinnati Law Review* 1233.

[134] J Erickson, 'Racial Impact Statements: Considering the Consequences of Racial Disproportionalities in the Criminal Justice System' (2014) 89 *Washington Law Review* 1425, 1426.

[135] DN Archer, 'White Men's Roads through Black Men's Homes: Advancing Racial Equity through Highway Reconstruction' (2020) 73 *Vanderbilt Law Review* 1259, 1324.

impact statements have been found effective in combating racial disparities in the criminal justice context[136] and have thus been adopted by several states.[137] Many scholars note that racial impact statements can help account for racially disproportionate harms and allow policymakers to take proactive measures to distribute the benefits and burdens of the chosen policy approach more equitably.[138] Consequently, there have been recent calls to adopt racial impact statements in other contexts where systemic racial harms are likely, including highway redevelopment,[139] healthcare policy[140] and algorithmic decision-making.[141] Some proposals draw inspiration from environmental impact statements (EISs), which are federally required for development projects that impact the human environment.[142] These rigorous statements trigger notice-and-comment periods before such projects can be approved.[143]

Monetary policy decisions are critically consequential to the unique economic experiences of black households in ways that are underappreciated. The Fed should deliver DISs for three main reasons. First, to make the general public aware of the tangible impact of monetary policy. In doing so, the public would better appreciate the broader political and market forces affecting their day-to-day economic lives and seek to hold these forces accountable. Second, to make Congress aware of the likely racialised impact of monetary policy to inform their oversight and fiscal policy response. The Fed submits to Congress semi-annual reports on its proposed monetary policy with backwards-looking assessments and forward-looking projections. Since 2020, these reports have had backwards-looking economic assessments with increasingly detailed summaries of disaggregated demographic data. This is an excellent development that needs to be maintained. However, the Fed's monetary policy reports do not include forward-looking projections on the racialised impact of anticipated price targets. If they did, Congress could better interrogate the Fed's approach or adopt responsive fiscal policy. Such fiscal policy might avoid the negative politicisation often associated with entitlement programs and be appreciated for rebalancing the benefits and harms of necessary monetary policy choices. Finally, compelling the Fed to deliver a DIS might pressure it to think critically about whether its policies gratuitously perpetuate or exacerbate racial disparities. It may be forced to re-evaluate standard macroeconomic models that embed racial disparities as

[136] RE Barkow, 'Federalism and the Politics of Sentencing' (2005) 105 *Columbia Law Review* 1276, 1289 (arguing that impact statements have made a difference in sentencing decisions).

[137] See Archer (n 135).

[138] ibid; RA Lenhardt, 'Race Audits' (2011) 62 *Hastings Law Journal* 1527, 1533–34.

[139] See Archer (n 135).

[140] See AP Harris and A Pamukcu, 'The Civil Rights of Health: A New Approach to Challenging Structural Inequality' (2020) 67 *UCLA Law Review* 758.

[141] See AD Selbst, 'Disparate Impact in Big Data Policing' (2017) 52 *Georgia Law Review* 109 (calling for 'algorithmic impact statements' in the context of predictive policing).

[142] ibid.

[143] ibid.

a baseline norm for ideal economic conditions. Moreover, such DIS disclosures may empower the minority of Board governors, Reserve Bank presidents, directors or staffers that represent the economic interests of black households and other racial minorities. Consequently, the best path forward for the Fed is to mitigate its disparate effect by delivering periodic DISs for widespread scrutiny and accountability.

8.4. CONCLUSION AND FURTHER STUDY

This chapter argues that the Fed is far from an apolitical, colour-blind, technocratic institution. On the contrary, politics and race have played consequential roles in the development of the Fed's institutional design, policy priorities and toolkit. If due consideration had been given to the unique economic conditions of black communities, the Fed may have been developed with a more inclusive set of monetary policy norms. In the predictable absence of such structural equity, the Fed should be compelled to report disaggregated impact statements to ensure it carefully considers marginalised groups, coordinate with fiscal policy to offset inevitable harms, and inform the broader public of its racialised impact for greater accountability.

More broadly, in revealing the colour-blind fallacy of the Fed, this chapter challenges scholars to not be beholden to flawed, so-called 'settled' monetary policy. The legal literature lags in comparison to the economics literature when grappling with the racial implications of Fed policy.[144] Several economic studies confirm that racially-indifferent contractionary monetary policy leads to spikes in black unemployment that is twice the rate of white unemployment.[145] Other studies, however, suggest that a race-sensitive monetary policy would have negative consequences for racial equity. Specifically, though sustained expansionary policies were found to reduce income inequality along racial lines, they inevitably contributed to wealth inequality due to racial disparities in capital asset holdings.[146] However, this assessment does not seem to consider the wide range of benefits afforded by higher, stable income, including the ability to acquire more diverse capital assets over time.

Scholars should critically assess whether the Fed effectively serves all communities equitably despite its structure, purpose, and toolkit by design, which have centred the economic conditions of primarily white households and businesses.[147] Disaggregated impact statements are the critical first step in

[144] See M Morris, 'Standard White: Dismantling White Normativity' (2016) 104 *California Law Review* 949, 955–56.

[145] See De (n 21); W Thorbecke, 'Estimating the effects of Disinflationary Monetary Policy on Minorities' (January 2001) 23 *Journal of Policy Modeling* 51.

[146] See Bartscher (n 12).

[147] For example, a Reserve Bank president recently defended an aggressive contractionary policy by suggesting that communities can better weather inflation than unemployment since they can rely

information gathering, but there are complex questions that remain open for future study. Does the Act in its current form permit an affirmative focus on racial inequality and, if not, is congressional action feasible? What tools, new or old, are ideal for monetary policy to tackle racial inequality? How do the other roles of the Fed – bank supervisor, payment system operator, lender of last resort – contribute to racial inequality? How should the increasing diversity of the US population impact Fed policymaking? This chapter is only the beginning of a lengthy scholarly agenda that hopes to expand on DISs and answer a few of these important questions.

on others for support if they are in unemployment. However, this ignores how racially and socio-economically segregated communities are, such that spikes in unemployment may be concentrated in areas and leave communities with nominal support. 'Why Fighting Inflation will Disproportionately Hurt Black Workers', *Vox* (22 October 2022), www.vox.com/today-explained/23416684/inflation-fed-rate-hikes-black-workers-unemployment.

9

The Fallacy of Consumer Credit Regulation as the Path to Financial Inclusion

IRIS H-Y CHIU

9.1. INTRODUCTION

FINANCIAL INCLUSION IS often an assumed good in itself and a goal that is pursued in policy and regulatory design. Support for financial inclusion is reflected in policy and regulation that is pro-market building and competition, ultimately revolving around helping consumers make an optimal choice. However, the dark side regarding outcomes of financial inclusion, particularly in relation to access to credit and over-indebtedness, increasingly challenges policy assumptions regarding the good of financial inclusion and their policy manifestations. This has, however, not given rise to a radical re-examination of financial regulation built upon the established premises.

This chapter examines the pathways by which pro-financial inclusion policy has shaped consumer credit regulation. The unquestioned good in such policy has shaped consumer credit regulation in developed jurisdictions such as the UK, EU and US, resulting in secondary fallacies in regulatory tenets and design. Regulators promote law and policy that enables access rather than alleviates the adverse effects of consumer credit. These adverse effects arguably arise from three deficits in regulatory policy and design, which are focused on point-of-sale and neglectful of post-sale consequences. The systematic neglect of post-sale adversities is reflected in consumer credit regulation that is insufficiently socialised, relationised and also 'micro-irrelevant' (terms explained in the text below). In this chapter, we use the example of female consumer credit customers to highlight more sharply the weaknesses of extant consumer credit regulation.

Financial regulation needs to be transformed to attain a governance character for financial inclusion, so that regulation is theoretically more coherent with the social contract underpinning financial inclusion/financialisation. The first section provides an overview of pro-financial inclusion policy and how this has played out in consumer credit in developed jurisdictions, particularly focusing on the UK, whose consumer credit trends share similarities with the US.[1] The fallacy of the 'unequivocal social good' of financial inclusion for macroeconomic developmental reasons underpins pro-access policies for consumer credit. In this manner, pro-access policies are also shaped by another major fallacy in financial regulation that assumes the 'rational' economic agent in consumers in financial markets. The chapter will allude to but not devote disproportionate focus on this discussion. The second section deconstructs how 'pro-access' consumer credit regulation has become weak and neglectful of social, relational and micro-transactional aspects,[2] especially in the post-sale stage of consumer credit products. In highlighting the persistence of pronounced disadvantages for female consumer credit borrowers, the chapter paints in sharper light the weaknesses of financial regulation that fail to robustly govern the state of markets supported by pro-financial inclusion and pro-access regulatory policies. Female indebtedness is selected as a key example, but we do not forget that there are other systematically disadvantaged groups such as the elderly who are not discussed here. This section argues that re-opening the social contract[3] underlying financial inclusion policies could kickstart new thinking for consumer credit regulation in the UK and US as some comparisons are drawn in the chapter's discussion. This is further explored in the fourth section, before a brief conclusion.

9.2. THE RATIONALE FOR PRO-FINANCIAL INCLUSION POLICIES AND THEIR IMPACT ON CONSUMER CREDIT

Financial inclusion policies, which involve promoting to citizens access to financial products and services, are often seen as part of financial and economic development policies.[4] Many developed jurisdictions have established financial inclusion policies, paving the way for the financialisation of ordinary life, defined as 'the increasing role of financial motives, financial markets, financial actors

[1] See S Brown, *The Regulation of Consumer Credit: A Transatlantic Analysis* (Cheltenham, Edward Elgar, 2019) ch 1; M Coletta, R De Bonis and S Piermattei, 'Household Debt in OECD Countries: The Role of Supply-Side and Demand-Side Factors' (2019) 143 *Social Indicators Research* 1185.

[2] See J Beckert, 'Re-imagining Capitalist Dynamics: Fictional Expectations and the Openness of Economic Futures' in P Aspers and N Dodd (eds), *Reimagining Economic Sociology* (Oxford, Oxford University Press, 2015) ch 3; R Cotterrell, 'Rethinking Embeddedness: Law, Economy, Community' (2013) 40 *Journal of Law and Society* 49. These articles discuss economic action as not standardised and based on a homogenous conception of the rational economic actor, but based on unique incentives, dispositions and other social factors that shape decision-making, called 'micro-foundations' for economic action.

[3] The social contract paradigm to be discussed is based on Rawls' 'veil of ignorance'. See below at 9.3.

[4] See A Mehrotra and J Yetman, *Financial Inclusion – Issues for Central Banks* (BIS Quarterly Review, March 2015).

and financial institutions in the operation of the domestic and international economies'.[5] The financialisation of everyday life is linked to policies in developed jurisdictions, since the 1980s, relating to retreat from the provision of state welfare.[6] Citizens are encouraged to engage as consumers in financial marketplaces in order to provide for their own financial welfare. This policy shapes the social construction of financial citizens who become individually responsible for their own welfare through transactional freedoms and choice in financial marketplaces.[7] In the US, financial inclusion policies also have roots in the civil rights movement,[8] in order to combat discrimination against African-Americans by private sector providers of financial services.[9] Pro-financial inclusion policies therefore have a significant amount of traction, whether based on economic benefits or non-economic discourse such as social rights.

Pro-financial inclusion policies are designed to develop financial markets and incorporate elements into financial regulation that are intended to make markets function effectively.[10] Financial regulation deals with addressing market failures, promoting competition, and promoting innovation. At a macro-level, the increasing importance of finance is observed in steady increases in GDP accounted for by the financial sector in the US[11] as well as Europe.[12] In the UK, the Bank of England[13] noted that financial sector output has grown exponentially in the millennium although a dip occurred during the period of the global financial crisis 2008–09. In both the US and UK, financial sector output accounts for just under 10 per cent of GDP. At a micro-level, pro-financial inclusion policies encourage citizens to have access to financial products, such as having access to banking facilities and credit. Access to credit is perceived as empowering as

[5] GA Epstein, 'Introduction: Financialization and the World Economy' in GA Epstein (ed), *Financialization and the World Economy* (Cheltenham, Edward Elgar, 2005) 3.

[6] See G Comparato, 'The Rationales of Financial Inclusion in the Changing European Private Law' (2015) 11 *European Review of Contract Law* 22; S Polillo, 'Solving the Paradox of Mass Investment: Expertise, Financial Inclusion and Inequality in the Politics of Credit' (2020) 78 *Review of Social Economy* 53.

[7] See Brown (n 1) ch 3; G Comparato, 'The Idea of Financial and Social Inclusion' in *The Financialisation of the Citizen: Social and Financial Inclusion through European Private Law* (Oxford, Hart Publishing, 2018) 17–57.

[8] See A Atkinson, 'Borrowing Equality' (2020) 120 *Columbia Law Review* 1403.

[9] K Langenbucher, 'Responsible A.I.-based Credit Scoring – A Legal Framework' (2020) 31 *European Business Law Review* 527; N Aggarwal, 'The Norms of Algorithmic Credit Scoring' (2020), https://papers.ssrn.com/sol3/papers.cfm?abstract_id=3569083.

[10] See FCA, 'Economics for Effective Regulation' (2016), www.fca.org.uk/publications/occasional-papers/occasional-paper-no-13-economics-effective-regulation.

[11] See T Philippon, 'Has the U.S. Finance Industry Become Less Efficient? On the Theory and Measurement of Financial Intermediation' (2012), www.pages.stern.nyu.edu/~tphilipp/papers/Finance_Efficiency.pdf.

[12] See G Bazot, 'Financial Consumption and the Cost of Finance: Measuring Financial Efficiency in Europe (1950–2007)' (2014), http://www.ipp.eu/wp-content/uploads/2014/06/working-paper-2014-17-pse-gbazot.pdf.

[13] See S Burgess, 'Measuring Financial Sector Output and Its Contribution to UK GDP' (2011) *Quarterly Bulletin Q3*, www.bankofengland.co.uk/publications/Documents/quarterlybulletin/qb110304.pdf.

individuals may be able to access opportunities that are developmental in nature, such as college education or small business entrepreneurship. Households have in particular been encouraged to take out mortgages to finance ownership of homes in the US,[14] UK[15] and many EU countries.[16] Such credit can result in investment in a long-term asset that can improve households' financial welfare.[17] Growth in consumer credit is a marked trend in the US,[18] UK[19] and EU[20] over the past two decades.

Policy promoting access to credit, underpinned by pro-financial inclusion policy, results in regulation in developed jurisdictions that focuses on protecting consumers at *point of access*, as well as encouraging a competitive market. In contrast, post-sale consumer adversities tend to be systemically neglected, culminating not only in individual but also social issues at scale. In this manner, the fallacy of the unquestioned social good of financial inclusion works to systemically create blindspots in regulation which amount to secondary fallacies that support a form of narrow regulatory focus on points of sale of credit products, resulting also in assumptions that particular regulatory designs are optimal.

Consumer credit regulation provides extensive mandatory disclosure to facilitate choice.[21] Over time, such regulation has improved in terms of compelling lenders to make clear and consumer-friendly disclosure in order to take into account commonly-accepted behavioural weaknesses.[22] However, it is uncertain if mandatory disclosure reaches far enough into the ultimate financial welfare outcomes needed by consumers in seeking credit arrangements. The

[14] ibid; A Rona-Tas and A Guseva, 'Consumer Credit in Comparative Perspective' (2018) 44 *Annual Review of Sociology* 55.

[15] Brown (n 1) ch 2.

[16] See Comparato (n 7).

[17] See Coletta et al (n 1); J Macey, 'Fair Credit Markets: Using Household Balance Sheets to Promote Consumer Welfare' (2021), www.ssrn.com/abstract=3781164; G de Vita and Y Luo, 'Financialization, Household Debt and Income Inequality: Empirical Evidence' (2020) *International Journal of Financial Economics* 1.

[18] Consumer credit growth in the US remained relatively steady over the last five years up to 2020, https://www.federalreserve.gov/releases/g19/current/#:~:text=November%202020,annual%20rate%20of%206.1%20percent.

[19] See www.bankofengland.co.uk/statistics/visual-summaries/household-credit, showing consumer credit growth in the UK on a steady trajectory since 2011.

[20] See European Banking Authority, 'Consumer Lending in the EU Banking Sector' (2020), on marked growth in consumer credit in the EU, standing at over €1.4 trillion by the end of 2019, www.eba.europa.eu/sites/default/documents/files/document_library/Risk%20Analysis%20and%20Data/Risk%20Assessment%20Reports/2020/Thematic%20notes/881264/Thematic%20note%20on%20Consumer%20Lending%20in%20the%20EU%20banking%20sector.pdf.

[21] See S Brown, 'Consumer Credit Relationships – Protection, Self-Interest/Reliance and Dilemmas in the Fight Against Unfairness: The Unfair Credit Relationship Test and the Underlying Rationale of Consumer Credit Law' (2016) 36 *Legal Studies* 230, on mandatory disclosure as reflective of a self-reliance ethic embraced by the regulator.

[22] See, eg, the CARD Act 2009 which took on board consumer needs in information disclosure, and S Agarwal, S Chomsisengphet, N Mahoney and J Stroebel, 'Regulating Consumer Financial Products: Evidence from Credit Cards' (2015) *Quarterly Journal of Economics* 111.

UK's financial regulatory policy of ensuring that consumers take appropriate responsibility for their choices[23] reflects another high-level assumption, ie the rationality of consumers as economic agents in the consumer credit market. Such an assumption, working together with pro-access policy, culminates in a form of consumer credit regulation that is focused on consumer protection at the time of sale of a consumer credit product. However, post-sale management of credit and adverse consequences often harm consumers more.

After the sub-prime mortgage crisis in the US and the following global financial crisis of 2007–09, policy-makers and regulators gave more recognition to the social nature of household mortgages as a debt problem.[24] This has resulted in an incremental but significant reform to ensure responsible lending in household mortgages.[25] Responsible lending is framed as an assessment that lenders must undertake to ensure that the mortgage is financially affordable for the consumer after taking into account reasonable expenses and commitments. Nevertheless, this assessment is not evenly rolled out across consumer credit,[26] and is also crucially undertaken at point of sale only. Affordability for the consumer is not periodically reviewed, although life circumstances may change. Responsible lending improves upon a disclosure-based regulatory approach for consumer choice, but it is unable to take sufficient account of changes in circumstances and relational outworking with the consumer.

Credit consumers do not always use credit 'rationally' or optimally. Although many households benefit from consumption smoothing by accessing credit, such as for a large value asset like a home, there are also households on low incomes that sub-optimally use consumer credit to meet the needs of immediate expenses.[27] Consumption-based debt for such consumers can ultimately become unaffordable as borrowers suffer future 'clamps' on their earnings to service debt,[28] perhaps leading to unmanageable debt burdens.

In the backdrop of socio-political transformations, the political embrace of libertarian capitalism obscures micro-level hazards for individuals in

[23] Financial Services and Markets Act 2000, s 1C(2), amended in 2012; Brown (n 1) ch 3.

[24] S Nield, 'Mortgage Market Review: "Hard-Wired Common Sense?"' (2015) 38 *Journal of Consumer Policy* 139.

[25] In the UK and EU, the main reform came in the Mortgage Credit Directive 2014, implemented in the UK in the FCA Handbook MCOBS. In the US, an affordability assessment is mandatory for household mortgages; see General QM Final Rule issued by the Consumer Financial Protection Bureau, www.consumerfinance.gov/about-us/newsroom/consumer-financial-protection-bureau-issues-two-final-rules-promote-access-responsible-affordable-mortgage-credit/.

[26] Such as being absent from the EU's Consumer Credit Directive 2008; O Cherednychenko and JM Meindertsma, 'Irresponsible Lending in the Post-Crisis Era: Is the EU Consumer Credit Directive Fit for Its Purpose?' (2019) 42 *Journal of Consumer Policy* 483.

[27] B Cavalletti, C Lagazio, E Lagomarsino and D Vandone, 'Consumer Debt and Financial Fragility: Evidence from Italy' (2020) 43 *Journal of Consumer Policy* 747.

[28] JF Bissonnette, 'The Political Rationalities of Indebtedness: Control, Discipline, Sovereignty' (2019) 58 *Social Science Information* 454; T Mahmud, 'Neoliberalism, Debt and Discipline' in U Mattei and JD Haskell (eds), *Research Handbook on Political Economy and the Law* (Cheltenham, Edward Elgar, 2017) ch 5.

consumer credit, while smoothing over macro problems of income and social inequalities.[29] This is frequently called 'debtfare',[30] as debt becomes a market-based provision to supply needs such as healthcare and education that are increasingly being marginalised as state provision. Debtfare is arguably an extreme application of financialisation, as access to highly important goods for social and individual well-being depends on individual access to financial resources. The debtfare society is one where self-care and responsibility for financial management is emphasised,[31] while there is a lack of governance over the post-sale stage of debt unmanageability. Debt unmanageability is often regarded as a micro-level transactional issue, and regulators have been slow in recognising market excesses and the social phenomenon of household debt, which can subject the poorest households to regressive distribution.[32]

Pro-access consumer credit policy is also supportive of economic policies that promote consumer-led economic growth and consumerism. Consumers can sub-optimally access credit for unsustainable lifestyle habits, a phenomenon that has affected many female consumer credit borrowers.[33] Horsley's research provides insight into how such credit has been used as a crutch to address deeper underlying problems in social mobility or personal coping after life-changing circumstances such as divorce.[34] Policy-makers and regulators neglect such post-sale choices and have yet to recognise another ongoing macro-economic issue, which Jackson terms as the need for a 'post-growth' paradigm to be embraced.[35] 'Post-growth' relates to the need for policy-makers and society to shift away from continued maintenance of consumption-led economic growth towards a more sustainable society.

This chapter turns to the social and humanising aspects of debt problems, highlighting female indebtedness as an example. The neglect of the post-sale considerations in consumer credit regulation ultimately creates a social failure. It may be argued that over-indebtedness or the unmanageability of debt are related to particular micro-characteristics, such as low levels of education, low income etc so they may be treated as 'significant but minority' type problems[36] that do

[29] M Horsley, *The Dark Side of Prosperity: Late Capitalism's Culture of Indebtedness* (Oxford, Routledge, 2015), chs 3–8.

[30] See S Soederberg, *Debtfare States and the Poverty Industry* (Oxford, Routledge, 2014) chs 2, 3.

[31] See J Montgomerie and D Tepe-Belfrage, 'Caring for Debts: How the Household Economy Exposes the Limits of Financialisation' (2017) 43 *Critical Sociology* 653.

[32] See A Atkinson, 'Rethinking Credit as Social Provision' (2019) 71 *Stanford Law Review* 1093.

[33] See BE Hopkins and Z Todorova, 'Gender Dimensions of the U.S. Consumer Borrowing Expansion' (2014) 48 *Journal of Economic Issues* 501, 501–06; E Caterine, 'A Fresh Start for a Women's Economy: Beyond Punitive Consumer Bankruptcy' (2018) *Berkeley Journal of Gender Law and Justice* 4.

[34] See Horsley (n 29) ch 2.

[35] See T Jackson, *Post-Growth: Life after Capitalism* (London, Polity, 2021).

[36] See European Commission, 'The Over-Indebtedness of European Households: Updated Mapping of the Situation, Nature and Causes, Effects and Initiatives for Alleviating Its Impact' (2013), https://ec.europa.eu/info/sites/info/files/final-report-on-over-indebtedness-of-european-households-synthesis-of-findings_december2013_en.pdf; M Bryan, M Taylor and M Veliziotis,

not require a fundamental rethinking of regulation. However, if female indebtedness is more precarious *generally*,[37] and *specifically*,[38] then the weaknesses in regulation are affecting about half the population in many jurisdictions. This elevates the weaknesses of regulation to a social level. For the purposes of clarity, the chapter does not adopt a feminist theoretical anchor. The selection of female indebtedness being a particular highlight for study is based on empirical literature findings[39] that are not necessarily written from feminist perspectives.

9.3. THREE WEAKNESSES IN CONSUMER CREDIT REGULATION

This section argues that pro-financial inclusion policy that underpins consumer credit regulation shapes such regulation in a manner that is blindsided in nature. These blindspots relate to the lack of relationality, sociality and sensitivity to micro-characteristics in consumer credit relationships. These deficits are derived from theoretical analysis regarding what optimal terms there should be for society in an era of financialisation. It is argued that consumer credit regulation, based on the fallacy of pro-financial inclusion policies, leads to systemic neglect of post-sale consumer adversities, expressed in these three deficits, culminating not only in individual but also social issues at scale.

Consumer credit is likely to be viewed by lenders primarily as individual 'transactions' rather than long-term 'relationships'.[40] The UK regulator, the Financial Conduct Authority responsible for regulating consumer credit, is mandated with a 'consumer protection' objective.[41] That objective however sits alongside the regulatory objective to promote market competition and choice,[42] and can often be read as an integrated regulatory philosophy. Both the market and regulator have together forged the limited character of consumer protection which focuses on the *access stage* by consumers to credit products. In this manner, the nature of 'limited' consumer protection reflects the outworking of the primary fallacy of unquestioned social good in pro-financial inclusion and access to credit. Nevertheless, the FCA's approach is not unique as consumer

'Over-Indebtedness in Great Britain: An Analysis Using the Wealth and Assets Survey and Household Annual Debtors Survey' (Report to the Department of Business Innovation and Skills, 2010).

[37] MG Long, 'Gender and Racial Inequality in US Credit Markets' (PhD dissertation, Colorado State University, 2019).

[38] AJ Schmitz, 'Females on the Fringe: Considering Gender in Payday Lending Policy' (2014) 89 *Chicago-Kent Law Review* 65; J Fisher and A Lyons, 'The Ability of Women to Repay Debt After Divorce' (2006) 27 *Journal of Women, Politics & Policy* 161.

[39] Discussed at 9.3.

[40] This is largely because securitisation has structurally changed the lending industry, and lenders can view loans as assets that can be repackaged and sold onto other investors, passing the risk and also making a profit; Y Altunbas, L Gambacorta and D Marqués, 'Securitisation and the Bank Lending Channel' (2007) ECB Working Paper, www.ecb.europa.eu/pub/pdf/scpwps/ecbwp838.pdf.

[41] Financial Services and Markets Act 2000, s 1C, amended in 2012.

[42] ibid s 1E.

financial protection stewarded by the US Consumer Financial Protection Bureau (CFPB) seems to adopt a similar trajectory towards facilitating markets that work and refraining from excessive intrusion.[43]

The limited character of 'consumer protection' is generally slow and reactive even in the face of post-sale adversities that consumers experience at scale, as evidenced in the FCA's reform trajectory for consumer protection in response to scandals and complaints.[44] There are limited circumstances such as in payday lending,[45] equity release mortgages[46] and overdraft fees[47] that see more intrusive forms of regulatory intervention into contracts, but these reflect a patchwork approach to post-sale debt management problems, rather than a systematic recognition of them in consumer credit regulation. A regulatory approach anchored upon the primacy of pro-financial inclusion and access supports the flawed assumption that consumers are best helped into making an optimal choice at point of sale. Being a credence good, the outworking of credit cannot be fully determined at point of sale, and post-sale consequences remain relevant for consumer protection.[48] This neglect of post-sale needs merely lifts the burdens on suppliers of credit to support their customers. Regulators seem to fear being overly paternalistic, although what is needed is greater recognition of pro-sociality[49] for the purposes of consumer protection. Eventual welfare outcomes for consumers are not merely private outcomes that occur as a matter of luck egalitarianism.[50] Further, the micro-characteristics of borrowers,[51] which inevitably affect their debt sustainability and welfare outcomes, are usually neglected in favour of regulation premised on the rational economic actor. The FCA is only having recent regard to such characteristics as exceptions in regulatory framing.[52]

This chapter argues from a theoretical basis that such character of consumer credit regulation, conceived of as 'consumer protection', is unacceptable as a

[43] See B Johnson, 'Consumer Protection and Financial Inclusion' (2019) 39 *Cato Journal* 489.

[44] Resulting in the reforms of FCA Handbook DISP Appendix 3, a *lex specialis* for dealing with consumer disputes over payment protection insurance mis-selling; E Ferran, 'Regulatory Lessons from the Payment Protection Insurance Mis-selling Scandal in the UK' (2012) 13 *European Business Organisations Law Review* 247.

[45] Discussed below at 9.3.2.

[46] ibid.

[47] ibid.

[48] See I Ramsay, 'Regulation of Consumer Credit' in G Howells, I Ramsay and T Wilhelmsson (eds), *Handbook of Research in International Consumer Law* (Cheltenham, Edward Elgar 2018) ch 13.

[49] See D Llewellyn, 'Consumer Protection in Retail Investment Services: Protection Against What?' (1994) 3 *Journal of Financial Regulation and Compliance* 43.

[50] See J Linarelli, 'Debt in Just Societies: A General Framework for Regulating Credit' (2020) 14 *Regulation and Governance* 409.

[51] Discussed below in 'Micro-characteristics'.

[52] Such as FCA, 'Guidance for Firms on the Fair Treatment of Vulnerable Customers' (February 2021).

matter of social contract. This theoretical basis[53] is employed in order to highlight the distance between a theoretically pro-social framework for consumer credit regulation and the character of extant regulation founded upon the fallacy of pro-financial inclusion policies and their ramifications. The chapter now proceeds to examine consumer credit regulation through a social contract framework to explain its flaws. The validity of a social contract is its acceptability to all constituents under a Rawlsian 'original position'. The following will argue that consumer credit regulation does not meet Rawlsian principles in terms of maximin and justice, *due to* its anchor in the pro-financial inclusion agenda. Indeed, the deficits of consumer credit regulation mentioned above, ie lack of relationality, sociality and sensitivity to micro-characteristics in consumer credit relationships, are all characteristics that are consistent with Rawlsian principles for an optimal social contract.

Adopting Rawls' 'original position'[54] as a starting point for how a social contract for society's financial welfare may be framed, everyone behind the veil of ignorance should choose maximum liberty to pursue each one's conception of good for themselves, but the institutions of the social contract should help those worst off in society.[55] Such a social contract is tripartite in nature, between society as consumers, the state and the financial sector as providers of products. The Rawlsian *maximin* principles are consistent with individuals having choice to pursue their maximum financial welfare, hence, a financialised landscape is not anathema to the social contract. Regulation of the market is warranted as the private financial sector can be incentivised to augment its own profit instead of necessarily seeking the conjoining of society's financial welfare with its profitability.[56] Financial welfare is a social and not just a private good.[57] Financial regulation that relegates real outcomes of financial welfare to be a private matter of individual fortunes is thus inadequate. This argument may have implications for state welfare provision where private financial sector provision would not level up in providing public goods as market goods,[58] but this argument extends beyond this chapter and will not be pursued.

[53] The general erosion of regulation for banking which reflected the social contract of days when charters were granted, and in the US, when the New Deal was forged; M Badaradan, 'Banking and the Social Contract' (2014) 89 *Notre Dame Law Review* 1283.

[54] J Rawls, *A Theory of Justice* (Cambridge, Harvard University Press, rev edn 1999) 15–19.

[55] ibid, 52ff, 65–93, in terms of the 'maximins' and 'difference' principles and why society should allocate more resources to helping the least disadvantaged.

[56] See D Awrey, 'Towards a Supply-Side Theory of Financial Innovation' (2013) 41 *Journal of Comparative Economics* 401; D Awrey 'Complexity, Innovation, and the Regulation of Modern Financial Markets' (2012) 2 *Harvard Business Law Review* 235.

[57] See J Linarelli, 'Equality and Access to Credit: A Social Contract Framework' (2021) *Law and Contemporary Problems*, www.papers.ssrn.com/sol3/papers.cfm?abstract_id=3707734.

[58] See J Gardner, 'Austerity, Inequality and High-Cost Credit: Understanding the Role of A Social Minimum' in J Gardner, M Gray and K Möser (eds), *Debt and Austerity: Implications of the Financial Crisis* (Cheltenham, Edward Elgar 2020) ch 14.

Next, Rawls' difference principle concludes that the social contract should contain institutions to help those most disadvantaged in society. In this manner, the financial welfare of the least advantaged should require regulatory attention of a more intense nature, so that financial welfare outcomes are (a) not damaged by financial providers themselves, and (b) brought to a level of distributive justice consistent with the notions of a fair and civic society.[59]

Based on Rawlsian principles, the terms of the social contract in an era of pro-financial inclusion cannot but include society's expectations of financial welfare outcomes in consumer credit. This aspect, which is post-sale, has, however, been systemically neglected by both lenders and regulators. Arguably, regulatory policy consistent with the terms of the social contract in an era of pro-financial inclusion should address the following:

(a) Lenders' conception of debt obligations under contract and the neglect of flexibility in relational outworking are unlikely to satisfy the Rawlsian principles. Regulators' lack of governance into such relational outworking reinforces deficits in social expectations. Consumer credit consumers should be provided with relational treatment throughout the duration of the credit term as affecting their real financial welfare.
(b) The conception of lenders as providing a product whose relevance for regulation is at the outset of the contract or point of sale is an extremely narrow conception, inconsistent with the social findings regarding how credit is used and welfare is affected. Financial welfare consequences should be reinstated as a 'social' concern deserving of regulatory governance.
(c) Regulators expect a level of consumer responsibility consistent with the rational economic actor and recognise certain vulnerabilities only as 'exceptions'. Such an approach fails to be humanising in relation to consumers' motivations in accessing credit,[60] such as by groups of disadvantaged female borrowers like single mothers.[61] This conception would not be supported by civic citizens behind the veil of ignorance.

9.3.1. Lack of Relationality

Current assumptions in regulatory protection for consumer credit are unduly narrow, based on the stability, if not staticity of a borrower's economic, financial, health, physical etc circumstances. Hence, regulatory protection is front-loaded up to the point of sale. To be fair, such regulatory frontloading is concerned with mis-selling, but regulators have also been slow to deal

[59] See Atkinson (n 8).

[60] A Roberts, 'Financing Social Reproduction: The Gendered Relations of Debt and Mortgage Finance in Twenty-first-century America' (2013) 18 *New Political Economy* 21–42.

[61] ibid.

with predatory lending.[62] The Covid-19 pandemic has brought about disruption to debt-servicing in a predictable manner based on static assumptions,[63] not to mention individual circumstances such as health issues, divorce or unemployment, which are common life changes.[64] Regulators and lenders continue to treat debt servicing problems as ad hoc occurrences that fall to contractual governance between lenders and borrowers. Indeed lenders are only concerned about the regularisation of payments and mitigation of credit risk on their part, shaped by prudential regulation imposed on them[65] and the strength of debt enforcement laws available to them.[66] The FCA has urged lenders to work with borrowers in 'tailored support' arrangements,[67] although some unprecedented intervention by the FCA had occurred in relation to mandatory deferral periods that consumers can request from their lenders.[68] Such deferrals are, however, a temporary intervention and do not necessarily improve borrowers' financial welfare outcomes.

The lack of governance by the FCA in articulating a relational concept in regulating consumer credit[69] cannot be consistent with the Rawlsian principles, as financial welfare outcomes would have to be privately negotiated between struggling borrowers and their lenders, a situation where power asymmetry exists. Such power asymmetry is sharply reflected in the reality that lenders can, in the name of 'risk management', securitise consumer debt and pass the risk on

[62] Predatory lending practices such as teaser rates that work on behavioural weaknesses, payday lenders appealing to female borrowers by being located near shops frequented by female clientele (eg nail parlours), and using advertising to exaggerate the feel-good effects of debt, are seemingly within the law, although they exert psychological effects upon potential borrowers. See P Heidhues and B Kőszegi, 'Exploiting Naïvete about Self-Control in the Credit Market' (2010) 100 *American Economic Review* 1179; A J Schmitz, 'Females on the Fringe: Considering Gender in Payday Lending Policy' (2014) 89 *Chicago-Kent Law Review* 65; G Brookes and K Harvey, 'Just Plain Wronga? A Multimodal Critical Analysis of Online Payday Loan Discourse' (2017) 14 *Critical Discourse Studies* 167.

[63] See I H-Y Chiu, A Kokkinis and A Miglionico, 'Debt Expansion as "Relief and Rescue" at the Time of the Covid-19 Pandemic: Insights from the Legal Theory of Finance' (2021) 28 *Indiana Journal of Global Legal Studies* 29.

[64] See Ramsay (n 48).

[65] Prudential regulation exerts a conservative countervailing force upon credit underwriting and enforcement; I H-Y Chiu, 'Rethinking the Law and Economics of Post-Crisis Micro-Prudential Regulation – The Need to Invert the Relationship of Law to Economics?' (2019) 38 *Review of Banking and Financial Law* 639.

[66] The strength of debt enforcement laws incentivises credit availability; Coletta et al (n 1).

[67] Discussed in Chiu et al (n 63).

[68] I H-Y Chiu, A Kokkinis and A Miglionico, 'Addressing the Challenges of Post-pandemic Debt Management in the Consumer and SME Sectors: A Proposal for the Roles of UK Financial Regulators' (2022) 23 *Journal of Banking Regulation* 439.

[69] This arguably remains the case with the FCA's introduction of the Consumer Duty principle in July 2023; see FCA, 'A New Consumer Duty' (2022), www.fca.org.uk/publications/policy-statements/ps22-9-new-consumer-duty. The Duty focuses on 'good outcomes' for consumers but remains focused on point of sale and after-sales support that does not address welfare or distributive outcomes. See critique by I H-Y Chiu and WY Wan, 'Constructing a Taxonomy of Financial Consumer Protection Policy and Assessing the New Consumer Duty in the UK's Financial Sector' (2023, on file with author).

to other investors, leaving borrowers to a transactional machine for debt enforcement which protects the investment expectations of more powerful parties.[70]

Borrowers are only able to utilise the mechanism of personal bankruptcy to fundamentally reorganise debt obligations in limited circumstances.[71] There is no recognition of social 'force majeure'[72] and relational flexibility in law,[73] although the FCA's guidance towards forbearance, particularly for home mortgages and post-Covid-19 debt, can be read as a nudge towards greater flexibility. This remains at the discretion of lenders. In this regard, the Woolard Review commissioned by the FCA[74] has urged regulators to do more in relation to debtors most in need of help, in relation to free debt advice and more options in debt structuring and arrangements.

The narrow conception of regulatory protection frontloaded at the point of sale of credit is founded upon pro-financial inclusion and access policies that are obsessed with market choice and the market failures in that paradigm. Such policies excessively rely on the financial sector defining and meeting the needs of financial welfare provision, hence regulation retreats from extending governance into financial welfare outcomes. This approach cannot be compatible with the terms of the social contract for governing financialisation and financial inclusion.

9.3.2. Lack of Sociality

Consumer credit regulation very rarely extends into the terms of credit, as these are subject to the market forces of private bargaining and competition. However, contractual bargains that adversely affect consumers' financial welfare outcomes are not only problems of personal devastation but also of social detriment.

For example, the prevalence of exorbitant unarranged overdraft fees and charges for bank customers caused the Office of Fair Trading, the consumer credit regulator in the UK before the FCA, to take a test case to the Supreme Court to seek clarification if contractual terms of exorbitant charges and fees could be regarded as 'unfair' under the EU Consumer Rights Directive.[75] The

[70] See T Piskorski, A Seru and V Vig, 'Securitization and Distressed Loan Renegotiation: Evidence from the Subprime Mortgage Crisis' (2010), www.ewget.uek.krakow.pl/papers/Piskorski-paper.pdf; CL Peterson, 'Predatory Structured Finance' (2007) 28 *Cardozo Law Review* 2185.

[71] See K Möser, 'Making Sense of the Numbers: The Shift from Non-consensual to Consensual Debt Relief and the Construction of the Consumer Debtor' (2019) 46 *Journal of Law and Society* 240; J Spooner, *Bankruptcy: The Case for Relief in an Economy of Debt* (Cambridge, Cambridge University Press, 2019) chs 3–7.

[72] See T Wilhelmsson, '"Social Force Majeure" – A New Concept in Nordic Consumer Law' (1990) 13 *Journal of Consumer Policy* 1.

[73] See Linarelli (n 50).

[74] FCA, 'The Woolard Review – Review of Change and Innovation in the Unsecured Credit Market' (2 February 2021).

[75] *Office of Fair Trading v Abbey National Plc* [2009] UKSC 6.

case eventually failed as the Supreme Court took the view that contractual terms relating to consideration are excluded from review for fairness.[76] However, as Schillig argued,[77] the non-reviewablilty of price terms under the EU Directive is premised on the optimal working of a competitive market for price. If these conditions do not hold, then the outworking of the law would only perpetuate a market failure of poor consumer standard terms. The government stepped in to respond to the social demands relating to the case.[78] Ultimately, reform was introduced to limit exclusion from unfairness reviewability only if a price term was prominent and transparent,[79] hence putting into doubt the legitimacy of bundled and opaque charges in financial contracts. The FCA also enacted rules of conduct to steer banks towards clear and fair representation of charges and that charges should be 'reasonable'.[80] The reform has mitigated some odious consumer welfare consequences, but the regulator has steered clear of more paternalistic forms of governance such as price control, especially for disadvantaged customers. It may be argued that the regulator was concerned that regulatory intervention would adversely affect the industry's provision of 'free-if-in-credit' accounts which largely served the social good of banking to most customers.[81] It is, however, arguable that the regulator's concern is contradictory to the Rawlsian difference principle, as delinquent customers, often the most disadvantaged, end up subsidising capabilised ones.

Further, it has been observed[82] that the poorest debtors who resort to high-cost short-term credit, eg payday lending, in order to meet unexpected exigencies for example, are stung with a poverty premium, paying the highest cost possible compared to more robust borrowers. Such a premium may be justified as a rational price for a 'high credit risk' debtor, but the translation of such borrower treatment into a social narrative would suggest oppression and injustice. In this manner, the credit product may become counterproductive, making the consumer's welfare outcome even more precarious. Such debt has been called 'odious'

[76] Critique: see A Arora, 'Unfair Contract Terms and Unauthorised Bank Charges: A Banking Lawyer's Perspective' (2012) *Journal of Business Law* 44; M Kenny and J Devenney, 'The Fragility of Unfair Terms Law on Bank Charges: Towards a Complex Re-Litigation in the UK?' in P O'Shea, K Fairweather and R Grantham (eds), *Credit, Consumers and the Law* (Oxford, Routledge, 2017) ch 11.

[77] See M Schillig, 'Directive 93/13 and the "Price Term Exemption": A Comparative Analysis in the Light of the "Market For Lemons" Rationale' (2011) 60 *ICLQ* 933.

[78] Law Commission, 'Unfair Terms in Consumer Contracts', www.lawcom.gov.uk/project/unfair-terms-in-consumer-contracts/, ultimately culminating in the Consumer Rights Act 2015.

[79] Consumer Rights Act 2015, ss 63–64.

[80] FCA Handbook BCOBS 7.6A; CONC 5C.3.

[81] FCA, 'Strategic Review of Retail Banking Business Models: Final Report' (December 2018), www.fca.org.uk/publication/multi-firm-reviews/strategic-review-retail-banking-business-models-final-report.pdf.

[82] See S Davies and A Finney, 'The Poverty Premium and Debt' in J Gardner, M Gray and K Möser (eds), *Debt and Austerity: Implications of the Financial Crisis* (Cheltenham, Edward Elgar, 2020) chs 8, 9.

rather than 'salubrious' by Nobel laureate and economist Robert Shiller, who unequivocally argues for a vision of finance that serves social good.[83]

The FCA has been slow to respond to a continuing tide of social pressure to reform consumer credit regulation. Although unprecedented price control was introduced to rein in the excesses of payday lending,[84] this is very rare for the FCA and arguably also based on strong views expressed in economics literature[85] regarding the extreme behavioural weaknesses of borrowers who seek payday lenders. It can still be questioned why the FCA has allowed a 'dangerous' product like payday lending to be offered at all.[86]

Regulatory interventions are more often market-based, placing faith in correcting 'market failures' so that lenders and borrowers can be left to transactionally work out what is best for them. Such interventions may be limited in nature and often neglect the sociality of consumer credit problems and also the micro-characteristics of borrowers, a point discussed shortly. For example, in view of the elderly market for equity release mortgages, mandatory advice was legislated for these products.[87] However, depending on the micro-characteristics of the borrowers, this measure may not go far enough to ensure that consumers' welfare is sufficiently looked after.[88]

The UK Consumer Credit Act 1974 also contains a general provision that allows consumer credit customers to seek remedies if the credit relationship is 'unfair',[89] seemingly providing a pro-social regime for addressing unfairness and not simply legality. However, recent interpretation of the provision by the Supreme Court[90] articulated the basis of unfairness as being the non-disclosure of an important matter that could have weighed on the borrower's decision. The non-disclosure is regarded as 'classic' information asymmetry and falls within the paradigm of market failure. Such market failure would not necessarily have been regarded as unfair if the non-disclosure did not relate to the fact that the borrower was paying over 70% commission for payment protection insurance

[83] R Shiller, *Finance and The Good Society* (New Jersey, Princeton University Press, 2012) 157.

[84] AK Aldohni, 'The UK New Regulatory Framework of High-Cost Short-Term Credit: Is There a Shift Towards a More "Law and Society" Based Approach?' (2017) 40 *Journal of Consumer Policy* 321.

[85] JY Campbell, 'Restoring Rational Choice: The Challenge of Consumer Financial Regulation' (2016) 106 *American Economic Review* 1.

[86] See G Pearson, 'Credit – Suitable for One or Safe for Everyone? and J Gardner, 'High Cost Credit in the United Kingdom: A Philosophical Justification for Government Intervention' in P O'Shea, K Fairweather and R Grantham (eds), *Credit, Consumers and the Law* (Oxford, Routledge, 2017) chs 3, 7 respectively.

[87] See L Overton and LF O'Mahony, 'Stakeholder Conceptions of Later-Life Consumer Vulnerability in the Financial Services Industry: Beyond Financial Capability?' (2018) 41 *Journal of Consumer Policy* 273.

[88] See LF O'Mahony and L Overton, 'Financial Advice, Differentiated Consumers, and the Regulation of Equity-release Transactions' (2014) 41 *Journal of Law and Society* 446.

[89] Consumer Credit Act 1974, s 140A–140C.

[90] *Plevin v Paragon Personal Finance Ltd* [2014] UKSC 61.

added to the loan. In this manner, the conception of 'unfairness' does not go much beyond the efficiency paradigm.[91]

The social pressure upon the UK regulator to address adverse financial outcomes is a continuing one, recently compelling the regulator to introduce a new consumer duty.[92] However, this new duty focuses on the same point-of-sale protection, as 'good consumer outcomes' often relate to point-of-sale, such as clear and understandable communications, value for money, and the offer of suitable products that meet consumers' objectives and avoid foreseeable harm in the short term.[93] Further, the FCA is refraining from allowing civil enforcement of the duty, preventing such consumer protection from being clarified by the courts. There continues to be a persistent gap in social expectations regarding the intensity of protection in consumer welfare, reflecting underlying tension between the regulator's pro-market preferences and the countervailing ethic of social demand. The quality of regulatory consumer protection ultimately reflects subscription to the fallacy of unquestioned social good in pro-financial inclusion policy and its ramifications.

One question that arises is whether the appropriate 'social' response for regulators lies in improving consumer financial literacy instead of reforming regulation.[94] The effects of financial education on financial welfare outcomes are, however, mixed.[95] Although financial education is a public good and supplied to some extent by the FCA,[96] it has also been critiqued that the quality of financial education provided is not differentiated sufficiently to meet social needs.[97] Further, there is a persistent and arguably inherent disparity in financial literacy levels between men and women, reflecting the disadvantaged position of female borrowers.[98] In this manner, regulators' expectations that all financial consumers can be responsibilised could result in obliviousness to the inherently disadvantaged.

[91] E Lomnicka, 'Unfair Credit Relationships: 5 Years On' (2012) *Journal of Business Law* 713.

[92] FCA, PS 22/9: A New Consumer Duty' (July 2022), www.fca.org.uk/publications/policy-statements/ps22-9-new-consumer-duty.

[93] See Aldohni (n 84).

[94] R Shamir, 'The Age of Responsibilization: On Market-Embedded Morality' (2008) 37 *Economy and Society* 1. See critique, T Williams, 'Empowerment of Whom and for What? Financial Literacy Education and the New Regulation of Consumer Financial Services' (2009) 29 *Law and Policy* 226.

[95] Investors lose the financial literacy gained over time; D Fernandes, JG Lynch Jr and RG Netemeyer, 'Financial Literacy, Financial Education, and Downstream Financial Behaviors' (2014) 60 *Management Science* 1861; H Estelami, 'Cognitive Drivers of Suboptimal Financial Decisions: Implications for Financial Literacy Campaigns' (2009) 13 *Journal of Financial Services Marketing* 473.

[96] The Money Advice Service at www.moneyadviceservice.org.uk/en.

[97] A Zokaityte, 'The UK's Money Advice Service: Edu-Regulating Consumer Decision-Making' (2018) 47 *Economic Notes* 387.

[98] P Białowolski, A Cwynar, W Cwynar and D Węziak-Białowolska, 'Consumer Debt Attitudes: The Role of Gender, Debt Knowledge and Skills' (2020) 44 *International Journal of Consumer Studies* 191.

Finally, we argue that financial regulators should and can look into adverse consumer financial welfare outcomes as they have already engaged with adverse welfare outcomes in favour of the regulated industry. This is arguably an asymmetric approach and incompatible with social contract reasoning from first principles. During the global financial crisis 2007–09, concerns for the systemic stability of the financial system caused states and regulators to bail out near-insolvent banks, in order to restore them to the service of credit creation and investment allocation, roles thought to be too socially important to suffer severe disruption.[99] Financial stability has become a regulatory mandate in the resultant social contract adjustment,[100] and this mandate was regarded as socially beneficial[101] although it would chiefly protect the industry. In this manner, Pistor has rightly argued that during the global financial crisis, law was rendered elastic[102] to preserve the regulated industry, particularly the important entities in the industry, while the 'periphery' of the financial sector, ie small business and consumer borrowers, faced the full rigour of the law. The imbalance in regard for welfare outcomes cannot be consistent with the fundamental principles of social contract underlying financial regulation. It is imperative for financial regulators to grapple with the real phenomenon that financial consumers, particularly in debt, have become feedstock for the financial sector in the age of financialisation,[103] with more pronounced welfare adversities for those that are more disadvantaged.[104]

9.3.3. Lack of Cognisance of Borrowers' Micro-characteristics

The model of the rational economic actor has influenced regulators like the FCA's conception of the 'reasonably responsible' consumer, underpinning the character of its consumer protection mandate.[105] This accompanying fallacy to the unquestioned good of financial inclusion has also fundamentally shaped the limited character of consumer protection in the regulation of consumer credit. Behavioural research has exposed many weaknesses, particularly in consumer

[99] A Grice, '£850m Official Cost of the Bank Bailout', *The Independent* (London, 4 December 2009), www.independent.co.uk/news/uk/politics/163-850bn-official-cost-bank-bailout-1833830.html.

[100] See I H-Y Chiu and M Andenas, *The Foundations and Future of Financial Regulation* (Oxford, Routledge, 2014) ch 2.

[101] See S McNamara, 'Financial Markets Uncertainty and the Rawlsian Argument for Central Counterparty Clearing of OTC Derivatives' (2014) 28 *Notre Dame Journal of Law, Ethics and Public Policy* 209.

[102] See K Pistor, 'A Legal Theory of Finance' (2013) 41 *Journal of Comparative Economics* 315.

[103] See I Erturk, J Froud, S Johal, A Leaver and K Williams, 'Financialisation, Coupon Pool and Conjuncture' in I Erturk, J Froud, S Johal, A Leaver and K Williams (eds), *Financialization At Work: Key Tests and Commentary* (Oxford, Routledge, 2008).

[104] See L Anderloni, E Bacchiocchi and D Vandone, 'Household Financial Vulnerability: An Empirical Analysis' (2012) 66 *Research in Economics* 284.

[105] Financial Services and Markets Act 2000, s 1C(2)(d), amended in 2012.

decision-making[106] and capabilities.[107] These have influenced regulatory reform, such as regarding how information should be presented, how marketing should be conducted and, perhaps most progressive of all, duties in responsible lending.[108] However, 'the consumer protection' objective has still insufficiently grappled with a further step in the conceptualisation of the consumer, relating to the 'micro-characteristics' that affect decision-making and post-sale outworking. The FCA has only recently recognised vulnerability in certain consumers.[109] Although vulnerability considerations are integrated into its Consumer Duty,[110] the FCA's approach may not go far enough to address consumer welfare outcomes affected by key micro-characteristics discussed shortly.

Beckert[111] argues that economic actions are highly affected by subjective preferences negotiated within social, cultural and institutional contexts, as well as driven by the lack of certainty with respect to reciprocal intentions and actions. In this manner, a consumer's decision-making for a credit product is not merely one made in autonomy, in isolation from subjective conditions. There is scope for consumer credit regulation to be more cognisant of such micro-characteristics. Particular micro-characteristics have been highlighted in empirical research regarding female indebtedness that deserve attention. A significant portion of female indebtedness in the US is incurred for the purposes of pursuing developmental goals, such as college education.[112] However, many females incur more debt than their male counterparts after controlling for other variables as they often pay for for-profit college places.[113] They are also often not able to gain as well-paying jobs as their male counterparts to pay off the education loan,[114] therefore becoming financially repressed over a longer time. In this manner, there may be a broader issue of college admission practices as well as workplace discrimination that needs to be tackled in public policy alongside the governance and regulation of consumer credit. Although lenders cannot be expected to intervene in particular college plans with the consumer as such, ignoring the context is also unlikely to be optimal. Financial regulators and other departments of social policy should not work in isolation in matters requiring such

[106] See Campbell (n 85).

[107] Poor levels of financial literacy found in developed jurisdictions; L Klapper and A Lusardi, 'Financial Literacy and Financial Resilience: Evidence from Around the World' (2020) 49 *Financial Management* 589; D Busch, V Colaert and G Helleringer, 'An "Assist-Your-Customer Obligation" for the Financial Sector?' in V Colaert, D Busch and T Incalza (eds), *European Financial Regulation: Levelling the Cross-sectoral Playing Field* (Oxford, Hart, 2019) ch 14B.

[108] Discussed at 9.3.2.

[109] Financial Services and Markets Act 2000, s 1C(2)(d), (f); FCA, 'Finalised Guidance for Firms on the Fair Treatment of Vulnerable Customers' (February 2021), www.fca.org.uk/publication/finalised-guidance/fg21-1.pdf.

[110] See Aldohni (n 84).

[111] See J Beckert, *Beyond the Market: The Social Foundations of Economic Efficiency* (New Jersey, US, Princeton University Press, 2002).

[112] See Long (n 37); Roberts (n 60).

[113] See Long (n 37).

[114] ibid.

holistic structural vision, and appropriate policies should percolate into the regulation of lenders' conduct so as to be sensitive to these issues. For example, regulatory policy can demand that lenders provide relational flexibility in dealing with micro-characteristics of borrowers that have been found in empirical evidence to adversely affect future welfare outcomes.

Next, another example of relevant micro-characteristics in consumer credit that can adversely affect financial welfare outcomes is the tendency to take on debt, particularly by females, on behalf of the wider family, whether relating to elderly relatives' medical bills, children's educational and consumption needs or support for spouses, particularly in business.[115] The responsiveness of many females to the needs of care or well-being of family members often drives their resort to credit as a form of 'support'.[116] This 'trusting' nature of the financial consumer is conceptualised by Moloney,[117] and raises particular tensions with the conceptualisation of the autonomous and rational financial consumer. Consistent with the pro-financial inclusion policy of allowing financial consumers to meet their welfare needs in marketplaces, it is not unwarranted that society is led to perceive credit as 'support'.[118] The greater tendencies towards care and being maternal for many women would reinforce emotive, in addition to social, expectations regarding what credit can do for them. In this manner, it cannot be compatible with the social contract that consumer credit regulation does not extend into inquiring into whether the credit product provides the 'support' envisaged and how such 'support' should best be achieved.

Scholars have documented that female indebtedness and debt unmanageability create particular micro-level welfare adversities for women.[119] Unsustainable female indebtedness affects family relations adversely as 'caring' for debts often puts undue pressure on the female debtor who looks to sacrifice, hidden coping and other forms of sub-optimal behavioural management in order to protect loved ones.[120] These micro-characteristics are often not considered even if affordability tests are run ahead of the loan transaction. Lenders too often make assumptions about the rational or typical consumer, ignoring the importance of female debtors' wider, especially familial contexts.

It may be argued that regulators such as the FCA are developing concepts of consumer vulnerability for their regulated firms, so problems with borrowers' micro-characteristics can be addressed within that framework. Turning to

[115] See Long (n 37).

[116] See Horsley (n 29) ch 2 on case studies relating to female borrowers who sought help with their lenders and regarded their lenders as 'support', only to be sold more predatory lending.

[117] See N Moloney, *How to Protect Investors: Lessons from the EC and the UK* (Cambridge, Cambridge University Press, 2010) ch 2.

[118] Shiller (n 83) 153–57; Atkinson (n 32).

[119] J Montgomerie and D Tepe-Belfrage, 'Caring for Debts: How the Household Economy Exposes the Limits of Financialisation' (2017) 43 *Critical Sociology* 653.

[120] EA Karaagac, 'The Financialization of Everyday Life: Caring for Debts' (2020) *Geography Compass* 14: e12541, https://doi.org/10.1111/gec3.12541.

whether recognising 'vulnerability' in consumer protection is the answer, the chapter expresses doubt. This is because 'vulnerability' is narrowly defined and often regarded as an exception, like disability amongst normal-bodied persons. Limited and exceptional definitions of 'vulnerability' would not accommodate the micro-weaknesses of female indebtedness, for example, as discussed above.

'Vulnerability' is defined as susceptibility to increased risk of harm or detriment, with emphasis placed on characteristics such as mental or physical infirmity, stage of life upheaval, low personal resilience and low financial capability. This is a relatively narrow set of micro-characteristics, compared to Cartwright's taxonomy, which extends to contextual circumstances such as family situations and industry structures that are disadvantageous to financial customers.[121] Brown[122] also argues for a more general concept of vulnerability such as articulated by Fineman, providing for a continuous assessment of vulnerability brought about by the dynamic events of life. Ideally, vulnerability should be a more encompassing concept responsive to dynamism, applying more commonly to ordinary citizens. Middle-class working females who take on a significant debt to pay for family needs may not be regarded as 'vulnerable' under the FCA's definition, and may well be able to 'afford' the debt at the outset. However, if there were family pressure to take on the debt, should that not be regarded as a factor of vulnerability that could affect subsequent welfare outcomes? Perhaps appropriate regulatory reform should be made to expand the scope of recognised 'vulnerability' to encompass micro-characteristics of borrowers that could affect their financial welfare outcomes, within a reasonably foreseeable perimeter for lenders' due diligence.

There is also a lack of clarity regarding the legal consequences for lenders failing to consider vulnerability characteristics. The FCA explicitly requires lenders to consider vulnerability relating to point-of-sale interfaces.[123] The legal consequences for considering vulnerability characteristics, however, remain unclear and insufficiently articulated – would the lack of consideration of vulnerability characteristics form the basis for challenging an 'unfair credit arrangement' for example, or result in distributive-type remedies to reverse adverse welfare consequences? It is uncertain whether the operation of 'vulnerability considerations' would pertain to responsible lending or even a wider duty of care, and whether insufficient consideration of vulnerability would attract regulatory enforcement or civil remedies.

It may be argued that imposing on lenders more burdens to take into account micro-characteristics of borrowers is likely to hinder access to credit. However, it

[121] See P Cartwright, 'Understanding and Protecting Vulnerable Financial Consumers' (2015) 38 *Journal of Consumer Policy* 119.

[122] See Brown (n 21).

[123] See, eg, FCA Handbook MCOB 3A.8.4 on sale and lease-back credit arrangements; 4.7A on advised mortgage sales; FCA Handbook CONC 5.2A.22 when assessing creditworthiness in consumer credit arrangements.

is questioned if access is really all that empowering if access relates precariously to longer-term financial welfare adversities. Why should 'consumer protection' not more fundamentally relate to meeting consumers' needs within reasonable social expectations rather than be limited to a conception of market access? Further, as the lending industry is embracing new technological capabilities in data analytics, big data and credit scoring, there is scope for steering its due diligence capacities to connect more optimally to consumers' needs, contexts and desired welfare outcomes.[124]

9.4. HOW CONSUMER CREDIT REGULATION CAN BE REVAMPED

Rethinking consumer credit regulation requires regulators to recognise their reliance on the fundamental fallacy of pro-financial inclusion policies and their ramifications for regulation, viz, the excessive focus on point-of-sale consumer protection and systemic neglect of post-sale welfare adversities. The FCA has moved incrementally towards recognising consumers' needs through the product lifecycle and has implemented a new Consumer Duty for regulated financial institutions across the board. The Duty is still focused on point of sale, but includes some coverage of post-sale consumer interactions, such as consumer access to post-sale service and help. It does not, however, address welfare outcomes unless *ex ante* mis-selling or poor 'value for money' can be established.[125]

At a structural level, the recognition of the incompatibility between social contract analysis and the character of extant regulation can form the basis for reforming consumer credit regulation. Omarova[126] argues that a tripartite governance system for financial regulation should be instituted, between the regulator, industry and society, with society acting as 'guardians' of regulatory policy. This argument is made in the wake of the social consequences of the global financial crisis, but is also relevant in order to keep financial regulators and the quality of their regulation under review for the purposes of social optimality. Although the FCA has a permanently established Consumer Stakeholder Panel[127] which is consulted with, and consumer representative bodies have standing to demand that the FCA investigates a representative 'complaint',[128] there is perhaps scope for more regular engagement with consumer groups and

[124] D Kingsford Smith and O Dixon, 'What Next for the Financial Consumer: More Disclosure? Caveat Vendor? FinTech Online?' in G Howells, I Ramsay and T Wilhelmsson (eds), *Handbook of Research in International Consumer Law* (Cheltenham, Edward Elgar, 2018) ch 15.

[125] More analysis is found in Iris H-Y Chiu and Wai Yee Wan, 'Constructing a Taxonomy of Financial Consumer Protection Policy and Assessing the New Consumer Duty in the UK's Financial Sector' (2024) *Cardozo International and Comparative Law Review*, forthcoming.

[126] S T Omarova, 'Bankers, Bureaucrats, and Guardians: Toward Tripartism in Financial Services Regulation' (2012) 37 *Journal of Corporation Law* 622.

[127] Financial Services and Markets Act 2000, s 1Q, amended in 2012.

[128] ibid, s 234C.

focus groups of consumers for issues of discussion and awareness, in relation to consumer welfare outcomes.

Next, there is scope for regulatory governance beyond intermediary conduct such as the Consumer Duty alluded to above. Regulators can consider *entire-life product governance* for credit products in order to steer market solutions to meet consumers' welfare needs. Product regulation is not the norm in financial regulation, and this means that financial regulation has seldom prescribed the features of financial products,[129] leaving the design of such products to market forces and to the market to judge their quality. As financial innovation can be self-serving for the financial sector and may even bring about harmful levels of social risk, European policymakers have decided to address product *governance*[130] instead of a fully-fledged model of product regulation which requires *ex ante* vetting and approval, like drugs or food. However, there remain areas to be clarified in relation to the nature of duties imposed and their enforcement.

Product governance comprises of procedural-based duties imposed on product manufacturers[131] and distributors[132] under the EU Markets in Financial Instruments Directive that covers investment firms. These require product manufacturers to put in place processes and governance frameworks to ensure that product design is targeted at a suitable[133] end-investor market and will take care to exclude unsuitable investors. The characteristics and risks of such products are considered not only for suitability but also in relation to the appropriate management of conflicts of interest. Product distributors need to ensure that they receive sufficient communication and explanation from product manufacturers and come to independent and well-governed judgments themselves on the suitability of the end-investor target market. This procedural-based approach[134] arguably targets internal processes and firm culture in managing financial innovation and product generation.

On the one hand, product governance is meta-level regulation,[135] leaving firms to implement their processes 'within a black box'. Further, there is a need to clarify the legal consequences of supervisory enforcement in order for

[129] Criticised in E Warren, 'Product Safety Regulation as a Model for Financial Services Regulation'(2008) 42 *Journal of Consumer Affairs* 452.

[130] Commission Directive 2017/593 (MiFID), Arts 9, 10.

[131] Commission Delegated Directive (EU) 2017/593 of 7 April 2016, Art 9.

[132] ibid, Art 10.

[133] Suitability refers to meeting three criteria, ie that investors' objectives are met, they understand the risks involved and that they are financially able to bear those risks; Directive 2014/65/EU, Art 25, enacted in FCA Handbook COBS 9 and 9A.

[134] A Maracci, 'European Regulatory Private Law Going Global? The Case of Product Governance' (2017) 18 *European Business Organisations Law Review* 305.

[135] Meta-regulation provides broad frameworks of regulatory principles and outcomes, delegating the implementation to regulated entities; C Parker, *The Open Corporation* (Cambridge, Cambridge University Press, 2002). But this can result in delegated self-regulation if regulators do not supervise; see I H-Y Chiu, *Regulating (from) the Inside: The Legal Framework for Internal Control in Banks and Financial Institutions* (Oxford, Hart, 2015).

product governance rules to be effective. It also remains unclear if civil remedies can be pursued by consumers who have incurred negative welfare outcomes. Nevertheless, the FCA is increasingly prescribing best practices for firms' product governance practices, such as to show evidence of testing and surveying during product design and to engage in ongoing review.[136] It, however, remains that product governance obligations are imposed at the pre-sale stage, and it is uncertain if consumers' *ex post* adverse consequences could either be prevented by these obligations or made actionable on this basis.

Finally, as many credit products for consumers are part of a broader policy mosaic for social development and welfare, financial regulators should not work in a siloed manner, set apart from broader social policy debates and designs. This is perhaps not a strong point in bureaucratic structures as government departments can work upon very siloed mandates,[137] and partnerships with independent agencies such as financial regulators can be rare, except for the Treasury. There can be better integration between expertise in social policy in relevant government agencies and the financial technocracy in the FCA in order to oversee credit product markets in relation to financial welfare more broadly.

9.5. CONCLUSION

This chapter focuses on the weaknesses of consumer credit regulation in developed financial jurisdictions such as the UK, EU and US. It argues that these weaknesses are based on subscription to the fundamental fallacy of pro-financial inclusion policies that underpin regulatory tenets such as pro-access to consumer credit, focusing consumer protection at point-of-sale. Regulation is relatively neglecting of relational, social and humanising characteristics of the 'debtfare' paradigm for consumers. Particular challenges in female consumer borrowing are discussed to highlight these regulatory weaknesses. The chapter offers brief contours of reform suggestions for consumer credit regulation and urges regulators to be more open to social discourse, inter-agency and bureaucratic coordinations towards meeting social needs in financial welfare outcomes.

136 See Aldohni (n 84).

137 G Tett, *The Silo Effect: The Peril of Expertise and the Promise of Breaking Down Barriers* (Simon & Schuster, 2015) exploring the dangers of siloed expertise in both the private and public sectors.

10

Financial Innovation: Three Fallacies in the Debate

SAULE T OMAROVA

10.1. INTRODUCTION

THE GLOBAL FINANCIAL crisis of 2008 has forever changed the world of finance. It exposed numerous dysfunctions and imbalances within the US and the global financial systems, enabled by the exuberantly deregulatory policies of preceding decades. Massive government bailouts of large financial firms, whose excessive risk-taking was at the heart of the debacle, brought to light the inherently political nature of financial markets and regulation. The campaign to rescue Wall Street laid bare the real distributional consequences of speculative booms and busts in financial assets – such as residential mortgages – that directly impact the economic security and well-being of ordinary people. Millions of people lost their homes, their jobs, and access to social services.[1] The financial industry, by contrast, quickly bounced back, growing bigger and more concentrated – all of it despite the flurry of post-crisis regulatory reforms aiming to limit the growth of leverage and risk in the financial system.[2]

The devastation and disillusionment in the wake of the 2008 crisis created an opening for a rebellion against the system: the rise of an alternative crypto-finance. What began with the launch of Bitcoin quickly evolved into a sprawling, complex and volatile universe of private digital money, payments and finance. This technological revolution enabled novel ways of delivering financial services, managing financial transactions, and even creating entire private

[1] The post-2008 academic and popular literature on the causes and consequences of that crisis is too voluminous to cite. For a small sample, see AR Sorkin, *Too Big To Fail: The Inside Story of How Wall Street and Washington Fought to Save the Financial System – and Themselves* (New York, Penguin Books, 2010); A Tooze, *Crashed* (New York, Viking Press, 2018); BS Bernanke, TF Geithner and HM Paulson Jr, *Firefighting: The Financial Crisis and Its Lessons* (New York, Penguin Books, 2019).

[2] See generally ST Omarova, 'The "Too Big To Fail" Problem' (2019) 103 *Minnesota Law Review* 2495.

ecosystems complete with their 'native' private money. These shifts have thrown many fundamental concepts and principles of modern financial regulation into turmoil. It is inherently difficult to fit new, natively digital financial products or functions into the regulatory categories meant to capture pre-digital realities. There are multiple gaps in specific regulatory schemes that need to be filled to accommodate technological advances.

More fundamentally, however, the era of digitisation creates both the need and the opportunity to engage in a comprehensive rethinking of the logic and continuing efficacy of the existing system of financial regulation. Regardless of what we think of cryptoassets and their staying power, crypto is a uniquely powerful mirror that reflects the virtues and vices of our current financial system. It magnifies the unresolved tensions of pre-2008 finance and pushes the boundaries of the public discourse on how to fix them.

This stock-taking exercise requires us to question some of the most fundamental premises of the existing financial system and its regulation. To make sense of what went wrong and how to get it right, policymakers and academics have to re-examine their own beliefs and assumptions about what finance is and how it works in practice. These beliefs are often so deeply ingrained in the vocabulary and the underlying thinking that they are effectively invisible, which shields them from challenge and gives them permanence. In important ways, these unquestioned assumptions pre-determine substantive intellectual and policy outcomes by setting the context and defining the terms of reference within the relevant discourse.

This chapter focuses on one example of such an unquestioned background assumption: a common view of financial innovation as a socially beneficial internal driver of financial market developments. To be sure, not everyone is equally enthusiastic about every innovative financial product, and many may attack individual financial innovations as outright harmful to consumers or markets. Nevertheless, even these critics generally do not dispute the beneficial nature of financial innovation as a social phenomenon. Even Paul Volcker's famous quip about the ATM being the only real financial innovation in recent decades implicitly reaffirms the importance of technological advances in how we can access our deposit funds.[3] There is hardly any serious disagreement that financial innovation is generally a good thing. Disagreements typically arise with respect to which specific types of innovative financial products are socially beneficial and which are not – a question that, in most cases, invites very different answers, depending on whom you ask and at what point in the market cycle.[4]

[3] See P Volcker, 'Think More Broadly', *The Wall Street Journal* (New York, 14 December 2009) R7.

[4] See, eg, RE Litan, 'In Defense of Much, But Not All, Financial Innovation' (*Brookings Institute*, 16 February 2010), www.brookings.edu/articles/in-defense-of-much-but-not-all-financial-innovation/; S Johnson and J Kwak, 'Is Financial Innovation Good for the Economy?' (2012) 12 *Innovation Policy and the Economy* 1; J Fox, 'What Alan Greenspan Has Learned Since 2008', *Harvard Business*

The chapter does not seek to add to this debate by categorising or theorising particular forms, aspects or implications of the process of financial innovation. Nor does it claim to attack, defend or define the phenomenon of financial innovation as a whole. Taking a broader view, the chapter questions how this popular term is interpreted and used to convey and reinforce a distinct view of finance that is both descriptively incorrect and normatively skewed. As the first step toward that end, it identifies and examines a set of three fundamentally false background assumptions – or fallacies – that invisibly shape and quietly distort the debate on the pros and cons of financial innovation.

The first fallacy is the implicit default assumption in much of US financial law and regulation that financial transactions occur in primary markets, where the counterparties engage in capital-raising for some productive purpose exogenous to the financial market. Despite its pervasiveness, this default contextual assumption is increasingly divorced from the real context in which most financial transacting and innovating happens. Today, by far the greatest volume of financial claims change hands in secondary rather than primary markets. The core dynamics of secondary market trading are fundamentally different from the familiar primary market dynamics. Most importantly, in secondary market transactions, there is no traditional capital-raising motive and no exogenous real-economy use or need for funds being transferred between the counterparties. Secondary markets are thus inherently prone to speculative cycles and self-referential growth.[5]

The second fallacy shaping the current discourse on financial innovation is an unspoken assumption that the novelty and beneficial impact of financial products or services can and should be assessed primarily, if not solely, in the context of individual market transactions. If a new financial product or service promises to generate cost savings or other quantifiable efficiencies for the transacting counterparties – lenders, borrowers, traders, hedgers, etc – it is presumed to constitute a bona fide financial innovation. The broader systemic benefits and costs of that product or service are generally presumed to follow from, and reflect on a larger scale, these micro-level benefits and costs. Such conflation of micro-transactional and macro-structural effects of individual financial technologies is an example of the classic fallacy of composition.[6] Yet, it remains one of the most pervasive and pernicious fallacies in today's discussions of finance and its regulation.

Review (7 January 2014); CA Hill and RW Painter, *Better Bankers, Better Banks: Promoting Good Business through Contractual Commitment* (Chicago, The University of Chicago Press, 2015) 174–75.

[5] See ST Omarova, 'New Tech v. New Deal: Fintech as a Systemic Phenomenon' (2019) 36 *Yale Journal on Regulation* 735.

[6] On the fallacy of composition, see MA Finocchiaro, 'The Fallacy of Composition: Guiding Concepts, Historical Cases, and Research Problems' (2015) 13 *Journal of Applied Logic* 24. On the systematic conflation of macro- and micro-level problems in financial regulation, see JC Kress and JY Zhang, 'The Macroprudential Myth' (forthcoming).

The third fallacy, closely related to the first two, is a widely shared presumption that financial innovation is a 'natural' product of private action in response to private market incentives. According to one scholar's astute observation, 'When people think about innovation, they usually imagine the innovator to be a private sector entity.'[7] Banks, dealers, traders, fund managers and other private players seek to maximise their profits by constantly improving and inventing new ways to serve their clients' and customers' needs. Market competition and competition-driven innovation are thus seen as two sides of the same shiny coin of human progress. The government, in this view, is not an agent of financial innovation because it lacks private profit motivation and private market knowledge. Its role, therefore, is limited to supporting and gently guiding private financial innovation without 'stifling' it. This cluster of presumptions is both descriptively inaccurate and normatively harmful. It unnecessarily narrows our understanding and appreciation of what drives financial innovation in different areas or at different times and how best to harness its power.

Defining and evaluating financial innovation by reference to this skewed contextual baseline – as a purely private, micro-transactional, primary market phenomenon – is bound to yield a systematically misleading narrative of modern finance and the challenges it presents. That, in turn, has dangerous implications for the efficacy and consistency of US financial regulation and financial innovation policy. Among other things, the three identified fallacies result in ill-fitting legal or regulatory solutions to specific problems in the financial sector and are often used to justify socially suboptimal deregulatory policies. Less visibly, they also limit the range of viable options for proactively shaping market developments and nurturing publicly beneficial innovation in the rapidly changing world of finance.

The chapter proceeds as follows. First, it examines what the chapter calls the 'primary market' fallacy, arguing instead that today's financial innovation is predominantly a secondary market phenomenon. Next, it exposes fundamental flaws in the mainstream tendency to focus on the micro-transactional aspects of financial innovation and shows the importance of analysing the macro-level systemic effects of purportedly innovative financial products and strategies. Lastly, it debunks the erroneous presumption that financial innovation is a private-sector prerogative and outlines potential policy reasons for innovative public finance. The chapter concludes that by misrepresenting or artificially limiting the transactional context within which financial innovation supposedly happens, these three fallacies impede effective public oversight of financial markets in today's era of technological change.

[7] C Ford, *Innovation and the State: Finance, Regulation, and Justice* (New York, Cambridge University Press, 2017) 11.

10.2. FALLACY NO 1: FINANCIAL INNOVATION AS A PRIMARY MARKET PHENOMENON

Much of today's mainstream discourse on financial law and regulation is based on an implicit assumption that the relevant financial transactions happen in primary markets – and, even where the specific transactions clearly involve secondary markets, their significance is derived from their ability to facilitate capital-raising in primary markets. This unstated contextual premise provides a strong normative grid, a background framing for the analysis of financial innovation. It is quietly built both into numerous theoretical constructs traversing large swaths of economic and financial law and into specific statutory and regulatory concepts and provisions. Despite its pervasiveness, this default contextual assumption is a fallacy increasingly divorced from the real context in which most financial transacting or innovating occurs.

On its face, the distinction between 'primary' and 'secondary' financial markets is self-explanatory and straightforward. It is meant to convey a clear and objective functional hierarchy between two interrelated and mutually reinforcing layers of financial activity.

'Primary markets' are those financial markets in which various enterprising individuals, households and businesses raise capital to finance their economic activities. In that important sense, the primary market is what we typically associate with the 'financial' or 'capital' market: it is the marketplace where owners of investable capital exchange that capital for financial claims on producers of goods and services. In this marketplace, issuers of financial claims – such as shares of stock, bonds or loans – secure funding for their productive endeavours in the non-financial, or real, economy and thus generate greater wealth and economic growth. The buyers of financial claims – investors or lenders, depending on the type of transaction – get remunerated for supplying funds to producers whose business prospects they deem most economically sound. The word 'primary' effectively conveys the foundational role of this exchange in enabling the market-based economy to function and grow. It denotes the core of what is happening – or what is supposed to happen – in capital markets supporting a viable private exchange-based economy.

'Secondary' markets are just what the name implies: they are functionally *secondary*, or subordinated, to the primary markets. Secondary markets are trading and risk-transfer markets, where investors, lenders and other suppliers of capital can transfer to someone else all or part of the risk they assume when they extend loans, buy bonds or shares, or otherwise participate in the primary financial markets. Secondary markets sit 'on top' of primary markets as a vital 'overflow' space for absorbing, sharing and repricing financial risks and rewards inherent in the process of capital formation.

In theory, the main purpose of secondary financial markets is to provide liquidity, price discovery, and risk-shifting opportunities for participants in the primary market for financial instruments. A well-functioning secondary market is expected to create social value by prompting more efficient use of productive capacity, facilitating efficient allocation of capital, and reducing risks of cash-flow volatility.[8] Arms-length trading among multiple parties is the principal mechanism for achieving these salutary effects.[9] With respect to each individual financial instrument, continuous and active trading among peers is presumed to generate objectively reliable and transparent prices that reflect the unbeatable wisdom of the crowd.[10] The resulting flow of firm-specific information embedded in prices enables market participants to make rational and efficient financial decisions while also reducing the chances of nasty surprises that trigger investor sell-offs.[11] Conversely, in less liquid markets, asset prices are less informative and potentially less reliable, which impedes the ability of producers and investors to find one another. In short, secondary market trading embodies the workings of Adam Smith's famous 'invisible hand'.[12]

There is an interesting tension in this familiar narrative. On the one hand, it strongly implies the existence of a 'natural' functional hierarchy, whereby the secondary market serves the needs of, and derives its legitimacy from, the primary market that, in turn, derives its legitimacy from serving the needs of the broader economy. On the other hand, the mainstream theory of asset price discovery and informational efficiency mechanisms creates a strong implicit presumption in favour of encouraging the continuing growth of secondary market trading. The deeper and more active the secondary market for trading financial instruments, the more efficient the initial capital formation and allocation process.

But what is the right size ratio between the secondary and the primary financial markets? Is there a point at which the growth in the scope and scale of financial asset trading effectively upsets the presumed primacy of primary markets where industrious entrepreneurs fund their non-financial productive activities? And does it even matter?

The mainstream paradigm doesn't confront these questions. It treats the two market layers as seamlessly harmonious, to the point of being functionally – and, more importantly, normatively – indistinguishable. In today's sophisticated

[8] MB Fox and KS Haeberle, 'Evaluating Stock-Trading Practices and Their Regulation' (2017) 42 *Journal of Corporation Law* 887, 889.

[9] For a classic exposition of these mechanisms, see RJ Gilson and RH Kraakman, 'The Mechanisms of Market Efficiency' (1984) 70 *Virginia Law Review* 549.

[10] See, eg, L Nyantung Beny, 'U.S. Secondary Stock Markets: A Survey of Current Regulatory and Structural Issues and a Reform Proposal to Enhance Competition' (2002) *Columbia Business Law Review* 399, 437. ('As information regarding trading prices and volume is widely and quickly distributed, investors can see the "real" price at which a security is trading and react accordingly, helping to reach the true equilibrium price at any given moment.')

[11] Fox and Haeberle (n 8) 894. ('Greater price accuracy reduces the firm-specific risk that comes along with ownership of the shares of such a firm. This occurs because, with more information about the firm's condition and prospects already reflected in its stock price, there will be less in the way of volatility-inducing surprises.').

[12] See A Smith, *The Wealth of Nations: An Inquiry into the Nature and Causes of the Wealth of Nations* (1776).

and rapidly evolving financial markets, the unstated reasoning goes, there is no discernible conceptual basis for treating capital allocation as fundamentally different from trading or hedging purely financial risks. One activity necessitates the other and is intricately tied to it through the increasingly complex institutional structures within which financial instruments are sold and bought.

Curiously, however, the old-fashioned distinction still matters, especially in crafting normative arguments or policy recommendations. In terms of social value (real or perceived), financing the actual productive economy still ranks much higher than pure financial asset speculation. The financial system's strongest claim to legitimacy still comes from our collective recognition of its indispensable role in keeping the economy going – or its 'primary-market, capital-formation' role. It is not coincidental that so many textbook explanations of financial transactions use examples involving at least one non-financial actor as a principal counterparty: a widget-producing company taking out a bank loan or issuing securities, a farmer or an airline hedging their idiosyncratic physical commodity risks in futures markets, or affable Alice and Bob making payments and opening deposit accounts. While rendering complex transactional mechanics easier to understand, these examples quietly cumulate to form an ambient mental construct of the financial market that is fully attached to, interacting with, and serving the needs of the real economy and its ordinary inhabitants.[13] In that deeper sense, it is portrayed as a fundamentally 'primary' market that faithfully undergirds broader socio-economic interactions.[14] In this picture, 'financial intermediaries' – banks, broker-dealers, investment funds, etc – 'naturally' emerge as essential agents of public good, professional facilitators of bona fide economic transactions driven by the bona fide economic needs of their real-economy clients.

Repeatedly and inconspicuously highlighting this generalised primary market logic helps to shape a master narrative of the financial market as a presumptively socially beneficial mechanism, an indispensable tool of economic growth. By blurring the primary-secondary distinction, this narrative effectively precludes a sustained inquiry into the practical impact of 'more and faster' financial asset trading on the nation's productive capacity and broader well-being. And that

[13] This is not to say that the authors of popular textbooks and treatises on economics, finance or financial regulation intentionally misrepresent market dynamics or are even aware of the broader normative implications of their pedagogical or editorial choices. In fact, the power of this narrative derives from its diffused and mundane nature: an invisible choice of a sufficiently plausible point of view much more easily becomes an objective description of reality.

[14] As this passage indicates, I use the term 'primary market' to refer to a broader set of phenomena than the traditional issuance of securities by companies in need of financing. In the context of the present discussion, primary market transactions include a variety of instances in which financial claims or assets are issued or transferred for purposes of conducting an activity, or consummating an exchange, that is independent of the issuance or transfer of financial assets. These are the points at which the financial system interacts directly with the rest of the economy, so that the movement of money or other financial instruments is driven predominantly by factors external to the financial market, such as production and consumption of goods and services.

normative prepositioning fundamentally shapes the context for regulatory action in financial markets, whether primary or secondary. Regulators now have a higher hurdle to overcome before they can justifiably interfere with the operation of presumptively public interest-serving private financial markets.

The discourse on financial innovation brings these subtle dynamics into particularly sharp relief. In a myriad of specific contexts, various financial products are explained, justified and marketed as novel means of meeting the needs of consumers, commercial businesses and other productive economic units. 'Stifling' such innovation through over-regulation thus becomes a potential threat not only to innovative firms but to the entire economy.

In practice, however, financial innovation is predominantly a secondary market phenomenon. Today, secondary markets dwarf primary markets for capital in size, scope and systemic impact.[15] Trading of financial instruments among investors, arbitrageurs, dealers, brokers, portfolio managers and other financial players is what drives the financial market's behaviour and serves as the gauge of its health and the health of the economy attached to it. In a complete reversal of the standard narrative, secondary market trading often determines the terms and volumes of primary issuances of financial claims. Importantly, it also explains why today's secondary markets act as the principal sites of both relentless transactional 'innovation' and chronic over-generation of systemic risk.

The pre-2008 growth of new markets in mortgage-backed securities ('MBS') and other structured products is a case in point. Securitisation is an old technique for turning loans, receivables and other credit instruments issued outside the trading context into tradable claims. In the United States, the massive securitisation of home mortgage lending started in the late 1930s, with the establishment of the Federal National Mortgage Association ('Fannie Mae') as the large-scale purchaser of qualifying home loans extended by private banks.[16] By creating a safe and orderly secondary market for mortgage loans, this New Deal programme dramatically lowered the cost of home mortgage credit, boosted the employment-generating construction industry, and fostered broader homeownership.[17] Since the 1970s, this market has been privately run, with two government-sponsored enterprises ('GSEs') – the officially privatised Fannie Mae and the newly created Federal Home Loan Mortgage Corporation

[15] The sheer diversity and constant emergence of new tradable financial instruments and platforms makes it extremely difficult to quantify this gap, or even to track the relevant data.

[16] For more on securitisation, see KC Kettering, 'Securitization and Its Discontents: The Dynamics of Financial Product Development' (2008) 29 *Cardozo Law Review* 1553; JC Lipson, 'Re: Defining Securitization' (2012) 85 *Southern California Law Review* 1229.

[17] For more on the history and functions of Fannie Mae and other government-sponsored enterprises ('GSEs'), see Congressional Budget Office, *Fannie Mae, Freddie Mac, and the Secondary Mortgage Market* (Washington, DC, 2011); T Howard, *The Mortgage Wars: Inside Fannie Mae, Big Money Politics, and the Collapse of the American Dream* (New York, McGraw Hill, 2013).

('Freddie Mac') – dominating the market, thanks to the implicit government backing of their liabilities.[18]

By the early 2000s, however, the massive inflow of unregulated or lightly regulated mortgage lenders and securitisers aggressively pursuing short-term profits had fundamentally changed the market dynamics. These entities used innovative securitisation techniques to fund the flow of high-risk subprime mortgage loans directly into secondary trading markets.[19] Their 'originate-to-distribute' business model became an epitome of financial innovation. Using advanced computer modelling, structuring, and hedging of default risk through complex derivatives, they effectively transformed – or claimed to transform – extremely risky and illiquid loans into actively traded 'safe' assets whose returns made them a more attractive substitute for US government bonds. A torrent of institutional investors' money, in turn, made mortgage credit less expensive to homebuyers, which was widely praised as a huge benefit to low-income borrowers, especially in historically marginalised communities. This is, for example, how a senior executive of now infamous Countrywide Financial described his company's subprime lending activities to Congress in early 2004, a year in which some of the lowest-quality subprime mortgages were originated:

> Countrywide entered the nonprime lending market in 1996 as part of our effort to make homeownership possible for the largest number of American families and individuals. We believed then, as we believe now, that nonprime lending is a natural extension of our commitment to bring Americans who have traditionally been outside mainstream mortgage markets into their first homes. Our nonprime lending programs also have helped these families and individuals build equity and use this equity to send their children to colleges, start their own businesses, and gain control over their financial destiny.[20]

In reality, Countrywide flooded the market with risky loans not because it cared for its poor borrowers' economic rights but because it was reaping huge profits in the wholesale securitisation markets. The rapid growth of these markets was fundamentally driven by the insatiable demand on the part of yield-hungry institutional investors for tradable asset-backed securities. It was a *secondary market phenomenon*. Subprime mortgage loans were popular as the raw material for the creation of high-yielding yet highly (and wrongly) rated mortgage-backed securities ('MBS'), multiple layers of collateralised debt obligations ('CDOs'), and

[18] See generally Financial Crisis Inquiry Commission, *The Financial Crisis Inquiry Report: Final Report of the National Commission on the Causes of Financial and Economic Crisis in the United States* (Washington, DC, 2011).

[19] See AJ Levitin and SM Wachter, 'Explaining the Housing Bubble' (2012) 100 *Georgetown Law Journal* 1177.

[20] See Testimony of Sandy Samuels, Senior Managing Director and Chief Legal Officer of Countrywide Financial Corporation and the Housing Policy Council of the Financial Services Roundtable before the Subcommittees on Financial Institutions and Housing, US House of Representatives (30 March 2004), www.gpo.gov/fdsys/pkg/CHRG-108hhrg94689/pdf/CHRG-108hhrg94689.pdf.

other complex structured products.[21] As speculative demand for these products grew, mortgage lenders used increasingly deceptive and discriminatory tactics to generate greater volumes of such raw material, among other things, by targeting the most vulnerable borrower populations.[22] Financial innovation thus became both a vehicle and a driver of socio-economic predation and systemic instability.

This well-known story illustrates how misleading the standard narrative of financial innovation is. It brings into sharp relief the inverted causal dynamics of innovation: rather than responding to some exogenous demand for financing of productive non-financial activities, it often feeds the endogenous financial market demand for new tradable assets or increased trading opportunities. Many market-defining developments of the recent decades – including the explosive growth of global derivatives and money markets, exchange-traded funds, and algorithmic trading – reveal these powerful dynamics.

A less dramatic but curious example in this respect is the recent Special Purpose Acquisition Company, or SPAC, boom. SPACs are investment vehicles that conduct no actual business but raise capital in an initial public offering ('IPO') for the sole purpose of acquiring existing private companies. While not an entirely new mechanism, SPACs became hyper-popular during the global Covid-19 pandemic that made it difficult for regular companies to go public.[23] In 2020, SPACs accounted for nearly a quarter of all US IPOs and raised over $83 billion. In 2021, SPAC IPOs constituted a whopping 61% of the IPO market and raised nearly $163 billion in capital.[24] The SPAC model enabled hedge funds and other institutional investors to park large amounts of money in liquid instruments with an expectation of a lucrative acquisition deal. In turn, multiple private equity and venture capital funds viewed SPACs as an attractive exit option for their illiquid portfolio investments. Because SPAC acquisitions are structured to allow the surviving entity to retain the acquirer's public company status, they effectively take the target company public without the cost and delay of an actual IPO. Thus, from the perspective of both companies' shareholders, SPACs offer an innovative mechanism for removing various market and regulatory 'frictions' and unlocking access to liquidity in the US public markets.

From a broader systemic perspective, however, it is a brazen regulatory arbitrage tool. This is the case not only because the SPAC model lets private companies skirt around disclosure rules or otherwise creates informational distortions.[25] SPACs deliberately exploit capital-raising in a public securities

[21] See generally United States Senate, Permanent Subcommittee on Investigations, 112th Congress, *Wall Street and the Financial Crisis: Anatomy of a Financial Collapse* (Washington, DC, 2011).

[22] ibid.

[23] J Morley, 'How SPACs Made Old Things Old Again' (2022) 40 *Yale Journal on Regulation* 13.

[24] White & Case, 'US SPACs Data Hub', www.whitecase.com/publications/insight/us-spacs-data-hub; Statista.com, 'Size of SPAC IPOs in the U.S. 2003–2023', www.statista.com/statistics/1178273/size-spac-ipo-usa/.

[25] For an analysis of the purported benefits and real risks of SPACs, see JC Coates, 'SPAC Law and Myths' (2023) 78 *Business Law Journal* 371.

offering – the quintessential primary market form – not to channel capital into firms' productive activities, but to enable financial market players to combine private investment strategies with otherwise unavailable secondary market trading opportunities. In a sense, the relatively short-lived SPAC craze was a meme of the larger, more complex trend: the reversal of the presumed functional hierarchy of primary and secondary financial markets.

This trend is harder to detect where specific financial innovations are used or adaptable for use outside the pure financial trading context. Even if these financial products serve primarily speculative purposes, the baseline presumption of their social utility is easily invoked by reference to some 'efficiency-enhancing' feature or potential to 'unlock' additional credit flows.

The tokenisation of financial instruments is a case in point. Digital tokens are bits of software-generated data which can be used for storing and transferring value within a dedicated digital infrastructure. Tokens can serve as digital representations of various currencies, securities, property rights, or any other claims that originate and exist outside the relevant digital ledger. The tokenisation of claims on real or financial assets 'involves transforming them into tokens on a common programmable platform that combines a core layer, which contains information about the tokenised asset and its ownership, with a service layer embedding the platform's rules and governance'.[26] The underlying assets are 'locked' in their original recording systems and serve as collateral for the tokens.[27]

Undoubtedly, the ability to put financial claims on the programmable ledger is an important innovation in the world of finance. It allows for the use of smart contracts that automate various actions (payment disbursements, collateral management, etc) and eliminate many cumbersome procedures associated with the traditional recordkeeping and payment systems. This transactional flexibility, speed, and cost-saving potential make tokenisation an appealing route for operating companies seeking to raise capital in bond markets, optimise their corporate treasury operations, or manage their supply chain issues.

These are precisely the kinds of uses routinely highlighted in today's discussions of the potential benefits of tokenisation.[28] Trade financing and supply chain management have long been favourite examples of how blockchain technology can be used for non-speculative purposes. More recently, attention shifted to tokenised securities issuances as a faster and cheaper way for issuers to access capital markets. The European Investment Bank ('EIB') has been a pioneer in this space, having issued several digital bonds since its inaugural

[26] See I Aldasoro, S Doerr, L Gambacorta, R Garratt and PK Wilkens, 'The tokenization continuum', *BIS Bulletin No 72* (11 April 2023) 1.

[27] This usually occurs through so-called 'ramps' connecting the programmable digital ledger with the traditional ledger where the underlying assets' ownership is recorded and managed.

[28] See, eg, Bank for International Settlements, 'Blueprint for the future monetary system: improving the old, enabling the new' in *BIS Annual Economic Report, Chapter III* (2023) 100–04.

transaction in April 2021.[29] In early 2023, Hong Kong's government issued its first tokenised green bond in the total amount of $101 million.[30] Around the same time, Siemens issued its €60 million bond on the Polygon public blockchain.[31] These successful transactions are widely viewed as paving the way for medium-sized and small companies to be able to raise capital without having to pay exorbitant underwriting fees and navigating complex regulatory requirements.[32] In the wake of the infamous crypto 'winter' of 2022, which exposed pervasive fraud and the inherently Ponzi-like nature of many cryptoasset investment schemes, these developments became a welcome sign of innovative digital technologies finally showing tangible results *for the economy* and becoming a legitimate part of traditional finance.[33]

Emphasising potential real-economy benefits of tokenising financial and physical assets discreetly but forcefully moves the public policy debate toward a more permissive and facilitative approach to digital finance. After all, it is difficult to argue that small businesses must continue paying high underwriting and regulatory fees whenever they attempt to borrow in public capital markets. But focusing the discussion on the efficiency-enhancing impact of blockchain adoption on primary markets diverts policymakers' attention away from the far more salient fact that digital assets – cryptocurrencies, tokenised securities, derivatives, and other instruments – are still predominantly used for generating and augmenting secondary market trading with no meaningful connection to any real economic activity.[34] The recent rise of highly speculative markets for non-fungible tokens ('NFTs') and the Metaverse craze vividly demonstrate the ease with which digital assets cross into the realm of self-referential growth.[35] Even outside of these rather extreme cases, it is increasingly clear where the tokenisation of financial assets is meant to do most of its work. Blockchain technology may make it easier for businesses to conduct IPOs or to track their cross-border shipments of goods, but that's not why the world's largest financial institutions are urgently 'innovating' and developing their digital capabilities. The truly systemically game-changing potential of tokenisation lies in its ability to redefine economic value – indeed, *all* value – as a function of *pure tradability*.[36]

[29] See European Investment Bank, 'EIB issues its first ever digital bond on a public blockchain' (28 April 2021), www.eib.org/en/press/all/2021-141-european-investment-bank-eib-issues-its-first-ever-digital-bond-on-a-public-blockchain.

[30] See Hong Kong Monetary Authority, 'Press Release: HKSAR Government's Inaugural Tokenised Green Bond Offering' (16 February 2023), www.hkma.gov.hk/eng/news-and-media/press-releases/2023/02/20230216-3/.

[31] See 'Siemens issues €60m digital bond on public blockchain', *Ledger Insights* (14 February 2023), www.ledgerinsights.com/siemens-digital-bond-blockchain/.

[32] See 'EIB: What needs to happen for tokenized bonds to get traction?', *Ledger Insights* (12 May 2023), www.ledgerinsights.com/eib-what-needs-to-happen-for-tokenized-bonds-to-get-traction/.

[33] ibid.

[34] See Omarova (n 5).

[35] See C Morris, 'The NFT bubble is showing clear signs of bursting', *Fortune* (4 March 2022).

[36] For a full argument, see Omarova (n 5).

It is critical that we understand these fundamental dynamics of today's finance. As the examples above illustrate, the most impactful innovative technologies enable market participants to scale up secondary trading, among other things, by decoupling the ever-increasing trading volumes from the capital-raising or other economic needs of primary market participants. Through this deliberate decoupling, the presumably beneficial process of financial innovation creates and amplifies the much more problematic *financialisation* of the nation's economy. In more colloquial terms, it is how the proverbial tail gets not just to wag but to swallow the hapless dog.

10.3. FALLACY NO 2: FINANCIAL INNOVATION AS A MICRO-TRANSACTIONAL PHENOMENON

The second, closely related set of misconceptions preventing us from getting a better grasp on the pros and cons of financial innovation concerns the fundamental question of what constitutes innovation in the first place. There is currently no universally accepted definition of financial innovation. The term is often used simply as a default label attached to any financial product or technology presented as new – or, better yet, *novel* – in some discernible way. But how does one define novelty or judge its degree of significance? In the world of finance, there are numerous ways of tweaking, combining or disaggregating familiar structures and techniques to create new financial products and establish new market channels. Where should we draw the line between mere adaptation and true innovation?

More importantly, is novelty (to whatever degree) sufficient to deem a particular financial product innovative? Far more than simply a descriptive term, this designation carries a clearly positive normative meaning. Labelling a financial product 'innovative' generally conveys a strong message of social acceptance and approval, an implicit acknowledgement of its social value as part of humanity's overall progress. How do we make that judgement? Whose viewpoint do we adopt in assessing whether that product or service truly moves us, as a collectivity, forward, instead of simply increasing individual market players' private profits (perhaps by decreasing their tax bills)?

In the mainstream debate, these questions do not receive serious consideration. Instead, the entire discussion rests on an unspoken premise that both the novelty and the beneficial impact of financial products or services can and should be assessed primarily, if not solely, in the context of individual market transactions. Implicitly, private market participants' viewpoint is adopted as the normative baseline. If a new financial product or service promises to generate private cost savings or other quantifiable efficiencies for the transacting counterparties – traders, dealers, lenders, borrowers, etc – it is presumed to constitute a bona fide financial innovation. The broader systemic benefits of that product or service are usually simply presumed to follow directly from these micro-level gains. In other words, what's good for the goose is good for the gaggle.

In essence, this conflation of micro- and macro-, individual and systemic, is a classic fallacy of composition. But it is much more than simply a sign of intellectual weakness or faulty logic. The unquestioning acceptance of micro-transactional innovation is often justified by reference to mainstream microeconomic theory postulating the efficiency of 'complete' markets.[37] Misinterpreting these concepts lends credence to the erroneous belief that constant influx of new tradable contracts makes financial markets 'more complete' and, by definition, more efficient.[38] After all, if people buy a particular financial product, that means they want it, and giving them what they want is what efficient markets do. A complete market, however, is an abstract model explicitly dependent on certain assumed conditions, including perfect information and competition, which do not exist in real life. Simply adding more tradable contracts to an imperfect real-life market does not generate the perfect equilibrium characteristic of this theoretically pure construct – it alters the overall market dynamics in far more complex ways, creating new potential inefficiencies and risks. Deliberate or not, the misuse of high-impact economic concepts helps to mask these macro-level consequences of financial innovation.

Treating financial innovation as a *micro-level, transactional* phenomenon has far-reaching public policy and regulatory implications. It creates an invisible fence around private financial actors' never-ending quest for more and faster (thus more privately profitable) trading, quietly diffusing any attempts to question the social value of innovation in service of that narrow goal.[39] Instead of asking pointed questions about a particular financial technology's contribution to society's well-being, policy analysis gets mired in the technical features of individual innovations: how a particular new product is structured, how it reduces users' and counterparties' transaction costs or renders specific market interactions more efficient for the participants, and so forth. Even the broader policy-oriented discussions of financial innovation – which gathered steam in the post-2008 era – are typically framed by reference to specific risk-related consequences and attributes of individual innovative products or transaction technologies. Moreover, where the focus of the discussion is on potential dangers a particular innovation poses to consumers or financial stability, these concerns are more often couched in terms of targeted management and mitigation rather than preemptive control and preclusion. Indirectly, placing micro-transactional

[37] In economics, a 'complete system of markets' is said to exist where it is possible to enter into every possible contract for every possible state of the world, without any friction. See generally KJ Arrow and G Debreu, 'Existence of an equilibrium for a competitive economy' (1954) 22 *Econometrica* 265.

[38] See, eg, MD Flood, 'An Introduction to Complete Markets' (1991) *Federal Reserve Bank of St. Louis Review* 32.

[39] For more on the structural drivers of this constant quest for privately profitable trading in financial markets, see Omarova (n 5) 756–70. For a thought-provoking discussion of the role of corporate culture and identity in explaining private actors' aggressively instrumental behaviour, see C Hill, 'Tax Lawyers Are People Too' (2007) 26 *Virginia Tax Review* 1065.

efficiencies at the core of the concept of financial innovation helps to insulate individual innovations from upfront regulatory scrutiny.

Whether any financial product or technology adds meaningful social value – and, accordingly, legitimately represents socially beneficial innovation – cannot always be established purely by looking at the immediate benefits it offers individual transacting parties. After all, the continuous pursuit of these micro-level benefits is what drives private innovation in financial markets in the first place. Policymakers' goal should be to look beyond that baseline and get a fuller grasp on the private and public costs of producing these transactional gains, the distribution of these costs (and projected gains) among various market participants and throughout the broader economy, and the potential impact of purported innovations on the structure and operation of financial markets.[40] It is critical to expand policymakers' perspective, both descriptively and prescriptively, so that publicly salient macro-level implications of new financial market practices are not only directly and fully incorporated but also explicitly prioritised in policy decisions. In this sense, managing financial innovation is fundamentally and necessarily as much a *political* as it is a technocratic undertaking.

The failure to broaden the public policy lens to encompass structural determinants and consequences of financial innovation can be extremely costly. As the pre-2008 experience illustrates, the single-minded focus on micro-level transactional factors in rapidly evolving financial markets creates a systematic deregulatory bias and breeds a dangerous culture of complacency among the regulators.

The subprime mortgage saga, discussed earlier, offers an instructive example of these dynamics. The rapid growth of speculative markets in risky MBS, CDOs and related financial products was a direct result of sophisticated financial engineering: the now infamous originate-to-distribute model that combined traditional securitisation methods with the more advanced payout structuring techniques and credit default swaps (a new form of unregulated insurance).[41] Throughout the early and mid-2000s, the market was booming largely without any regulatory scrutiny. Up until the emergence of the first direct signs of major distress in subprime mortgage markets in mid-2007, financial regulators continued to treat subprime securitisation as an innovative form of 'credit intermediation' that used cutting-edge computer models to guarantee more efficient pricing of credit risk and more effective 'tailoring' of investment opportunities for yield-seeking institutional investors. As more and more low-income

[40] This is not to diminish the importance of probing the validity of the specific claims regarding the micro-level transactional benefits of specific innovations. As experience shows, much of what passes as financial innovation amounts to little more than aggressive tax arbitrage or regulatory evasion. Creative legal packaging or complex transactional mechanics do not necessarily render these ubiquitous financial techniques new or socially valuable.

[41] See generally Kettering, 'Securitization and Its Discontents' (n 16); Levitin and Wachter, 'Explaining the Housing Bubble' (n 19).

borrowers became proud owners of overpriced houses they couldn't afford, the technical optimisation of the securitisation process, intended for the benefit of institutional investors and subprime lenders, was gradually recast as the socio-economic win-win for all Americans. The Countrywide CEO's testimony, quoted above, perfectly captures that narrative. While the regulators' failure to prevent over-generation of risk and leverage in mortgage markets cannot be attributed to a single cause, the lack of regulatory attention to broader structural factors driving financial 'innovation' played a crucial role in this respect.[42]

A similar story unfolded in the market for over-the-counter derivatives, another segment of the financial system whose unchecked growth contributed to the 2008 financial crisis. Derivatives are bilateral contracts that define the counterparties' payout rights and obligations by reference to the value of some reference asset.[43] Historically, derivatives have been used primarily for hedging risks associated with agricultural crops and other physical commodities. Starting in the late 1980s, advances in computer technology enabled the large-scale use of derivatives for leveraged trading and high-risk speculative bets on market volatility. New technological capabilities enabled Wall Street dealers and their wholesale clients to create highly complex transactional strategies by combining various elements of standard derivative instruments like options, swaps and forwards. The high degree of malleability, which allows derivatives counterparties to synthesise or replicate pretty much any economic outcome, made these instruments a favourite of hedge funds, currency speculators, securities dealers and other sophisticated institutional players with complex risk exposures. During the 1990s and especially 2000s, over-the-counter derivatives markets exploded in volume and systemic significance, generating massive amounts of hidden leverage and unhedged risk nearly entirely outside of the regulatory perimeter.[44]

Yet, despite the growing evidence of these structural shifts, US financial regulators continued to approach derivatives as fundamentally beneficial, innovative instruments of hedging traditional commercial risks rather than manufacturing tradable financial risk. Instead of inquiring into the systemic impact of having these powerful new regulatory arbitrage tools, they passively accepted the financial industry's narrative of the revolutionary improvements in spreading and managing previously unmanageable micro-level risks, lowering the transactional costs to participating counterparties, and thus – by extension – enhancing the overall financial market 'efficiency'.[45]

[42] Unsurprisingly, the recent rise of crypto markets for real estate finance raises the same policy concerns. RW Freyermuth, CK Odinet and A Tosato, 'Crypto in Real Estate Finance' (2023) 75 *Alabama Law Review* 93.

[43] For a basic overview of derivatives markets, see Federal Reserve Bank of Chicago, *Understanding Derivatives* (2013), www.chicagofed.org/publications/understanding-derivatives/index.

[44] See generally LA Stout, 'Derivatives and the Legal Origin of the 2008 Credit Crisis' (2011) 1 *Harvard Business Law Review* 1.

[45] See Flood (n 38).

Alan Greenspan, the long-time Chairman of the Board of Governors of the Federal Reserve System (the 'Federal Reserve' or the 'Fed') and one of the most influential figures in financial regulation, was an adamant proponent of this view. In a 1999 speech, for example, he explained the increasing importance of unregulated over-the-counter derivatives explicitly by reference to their micro-transactional, private benefits:

> These instruments enhance the ability to differentiate risk and allocate it to those investors most able and willing to take it. This unbundling improves the ability of the market to engender a set of product and asset prices far more calibrated to the value preferences of consumers than was possible before derivative markets were developed. …
>
> Nonbank, as well as bank, users of these new financial instruments have increasingly embraced them as an integral part of their capital risk allocation and profit maximization. It should come as no surprise that the profitability of derivative products has been a major factor in the dramatic rise in large banks' noninterest earnings and doubtless is a factor in the significant gain in the overall finance industry's share of American corporate output during the past decade. In short, the value added of derivatives themselves derives from their ability to enhance the process of wealth creation.[46]

Despite the carefully paid lip service to potential risks of greed and imprudent risk-taking, Greenspan's hugely influential view reflected the fundamentally misguided faith in the power of technically sophisticated risk-trading contracts to produce an inherently more resilient and efficient financial *system*.[47] Acting alongside Greenspan's Federal Reserve, the Office of the Comptroller of the Currency (the 'OCC'), the primary regulator of federally chartered banks, implemented this misconception into policy that enabled publicly subsidised deposit-taking institutions to become major dealers in risky derivatives.[48] By facilitating the growth of privately lucrative but systemically unsustainable markets, the OCC and other financial regulators helped to pave the way for the global financial crisis of 2008. The decades-long regulatory paralysis and failure to deal with the crucial structural consequences of transactional innovation in an increasingly tech-driven financial system were a vital contributing cause of that crisis.

This dangerous tendency seems to persist even in the post-2008 era. The rapid digitisation and tokenisation of money and financial assets, discussed

[46] 'Financial derivatives', Remarks by Chairman Alan Greenspan Before the Futures Industry Association, Boca Raton, Florida (19 March 1999), The Federal Reserve Board, www.federalreserve.gov/boarddocs/speeches/1999/19990319.htm.

[47] See P Goodman, 'Taking Hard New Look at a Greenspan Legacy' *New York Times* (New York, 8 October 2008) A1.

[48] For a detailed analysis of the OCC's derivatives policy between the 1980s and the 2008 crisis, see ST Omarova, 'The Quiet Metamorphosis: How Derivatives Changed the "Business of Banking"' (2009) 63 *University of Miami Law Review* 1041.

earlier, raise many of the same concerns with respect to policymakers' ability to look beyond the shiny surface of transactional technology. Moreover, the paradigm-shifting nature of the core technologies involved makes that shiny quality of digital innovation especially deceptive.

The current debate on regulation of stablecoins illustrates the power of old fallacies in shaping new conversations. Stablecoins are digital assets whose value is tied directly to the value of some other financial asset – most commonly, a sovereign currency like the US dollar.[49] Stablecoins emerged in response to the seemingly insurmountable problem with Bitcoin and other early cryptocurrencies: the high degree of volatility that rendered them largely unusable as a form of money. While offering the same transactional speed and convenience, stablecoins – including Tether, USD Coin, Binance USD, and Dai – are designed to mirror the value and reliability of traditional money while also being free to move separately from it. Typically, the issuer of a stablecoin achieves this tethering to traditional money by setting up a reserve to hold the reference asset backing it. The reserve might be a traditional bank account, in which the issuer deposits the equivalent value in US dollars as collateral for the stablecoins it distributes, or it can be a portfolio of US Treasury bonds and other safe dollar-denominated securities held in custody on behalf of the issuer. However, stablecoins can also be backed by other privately issued digital assets (including other stablecoins) or by no assets at all, relying instead on some complex algorithmic trading mechanism to keep their market value stable. Without direct regulatory guardrails, these varying arrangements can become very complex, opaque and unreliable.[50]

Stablecoins first moved to the centre stage of public policy discussions in 2019, when Facebook announced its plan to issue the first global stablecoin called Libra (later renamed Diem) on top of its global social media platform.[51] Libra was publicised as a new, more efficient and democratic payment system that would benefit the most disadvantaged members of the global community.[52] Facebook's plan, however, immediately triggered strong political backlash, as US and European policymakers worried about the company's chequered privacy record and the ability to prevent the Libra/Diem network from being used for terrorist financing, money laundering, and other illicit activities.[53]

Although Facebook's project was ultimately abandoned, it has fundamentally shaped the subsequent debate on regulating private stablecoins. Another

[49] See G Baughman, F Carapella, J Gerszten and D Mills, 'The stable in stablecoins', *FEDS Notes* (16 December 2022).

[50] ibid.

[51] See J Boorstin, 'Facebook launches a new cryptocurrency called Libra', *CNBC* (18 June 2019).

[52] ibid. As Facebook's crypto chief David Marcus announced at the time, 'There's 1.7 billion people around the world that are unbanked, the same number are underserved by financial services. Now, anyone with a cheap smartphone has access to all the info they want in the world for free with a basic data plan. Why doesn't money work the same way?'.

[53] See H Murphy and K Stacey, 'Facebook Libra: the inside story of how the company's cryptocurrency dream died', *Financial Times* (London, 10 March 2022).

impactful event in this respect was the May 2022 failure of Terra USD, a multi-billion-dollar algorithmic stablecoin not backed by traditional reserves.[54] Among other things, the Terra episode has revealed the risk of potentially contagious runs on unreserved or insufficiently reserved stablecoins.[55]

Perhaps unsurprisingly, the US public policy debate to date has been focused primarily on making stablecoins truly stable and safe for widespread use in payments. Numerous legislative and academic proposals seek to achieve that goal through various means. Some envision a system where only federally insured and regulated banks are legally allowed to issue stablecoins.[56] Others would allow non-bank entities, including commercial companies and crypto firms, to obtain special licences to issue stablecoins. These proposals typically require licensed entities to submit to some form of regulatory oversight and mandate the types of qualifying reserve assets – primarily central bank reserves and government debt securities – backing their stablecoins.[57] The logic behind this approach is intuitively clear. Turning all stablecoins into tokenised bank deposits or limiting stablecoin reserves to fully safe sovereign liabilities would ensure that these privately issued tokens function as near-exact digital representations of sovereign money – and thus can be safely and widely used as *the means of payment*.

And there's the rub. The critical premise underlying the debate on stablecoin regulation is that stablecoins represent a fundamentally innovative means of payment. In fact, it is common to see the more specific term 'payment stablecoins' used in official reports and policy analyses.[58] This rhetorical framing has significant implications for the direction, substance, and the normative scope of the discussion. Emphasising the centrality of stablecoins' technical payments function presumptively narrows policymakers' perspective. It limits the range of 'practical' policy choices primarily to the micro-level transactional aspects of individual stablecoins' design and operation in furtherance of that function. The search for the right regulatory approach thus naturally zooms in on the specific methods of guaranteeing stablecoins' par value, maintaining

[54] See K Sandor and E Genc, 'The Fall of Terra: A Timeline of the Meteoric Rise and Crash of UST and LUNA', *CoinDesk* (22 December 2022).

[55] This was not the first time the problems with insufficient or insufficiently safe assets backing popular stablecoins came to policymakers' attention. In early 2021, one of the world's largest stablecoin issuers, Tether, reached a settlement to close the investigation by the New York Attorney General into Tether's misuses of funds and misleading claims regarding its reserves. R Browne, 'Cryptocurrency firms Tether and Bitfinex agree to pay $18.5 million fine to end New York probe', *CNBC* (23 February 2021).

[56] See, eg, R Lastra and AE Wilmarth, Jr, 'We must regulate stablecoin providers as banks', *The Hill* (6 June 2021); HE Jackson and M Ricks, 'Locating Stablecoins within the Regulatory Perimeter', *Harvard Law School Forum on Corporate Governance* (5 August 2021).

[57] See, eg, H Lang, 'US congressional committee advances stablecoin bill', *Reuters* (27 July 2023).

[58] See, eg, President's Working Group on Financial Markets, the Federal Deposit Insurance Corporation, and the Office of the Comptroller of the Currency, 'Report on Stablecoins' (US Department of the Treasury, Washington, DC, November 2021).

transparency of reserves, preventing misuse of funds, and similar transactional 'guardrails'.[59]

Adopting this contextual baseline makes it very difficult, if not impossible, to move the debate beyond the immediate technologically novel features of individual stablecoins' design (such as, eg, validation methods or token programmability). To be sure, it is not unusual for policymakers and academics to express concerns about potential systemic instability, concentration of corporate power over widely used means of payments, or other structural issues stablecoins raise.[60] However, these concerns typically appear as second-order 'management and mitigation' challenges rather than inherently problematic functional features of the stablecoin phenomenon. In a manner reminiscent of the pre-2008 discussions of 'innovative' financial derivatives, the obligatory post-2008 nods to potential systemic risks do not appreciably change the dominant narrative of stablecoins as the 'future of payments'.[61]

There are also deeper parallels between these two episodes. To the extent stablecoins replicate the value of US dollar and other safe assets, they are fundamentally *derivative* instruments. Much like the complex derivatives of the pre-crisis era were not simply about hedging some pre-existing commercial risks, today's stablecoins are not simply about eliminating frictions in payments – they are about creating and supporting a qualitatively new digital *ecosystem* for trading financial claims.[62] Today, stablecoins fuel risky trading in crypto markets and help to sustain speculative circulation of thousands of digital tokens, however questionable their value proposition. As blockchain-native stand-ins for sovereign money, stablecoins are the indispensable transactional anchor in so-called decentralised finance, or DeFi, the crypto version of the shadow banking system.[63] If stablecoins are seen as truly 'safe' because they are regulated and publicly backed, either explicitly or implicitly, that will dramatically boost the scale and volatility of these markets. It will catalyse massive tokenisation of financial instruments, bring retail investors into crypto trading, and seamlessly fuse speculative crypto with traditional finance. In short, it will make crypto markets 'too big to fail'.

Approaching stablecoin regulation purely as a matter of facilitating technological innovation in payments – essentially, a market-supporting 'back-office'

[59] C Condon and A Versprille, 'U.S. Consensus Forming on Stablecoin Oversight, Treasury's Liang Says', *Bloomberg* (22 March 2022).

[60] See, eg, President's Working Group, 'Report on Stablecoins' 16–18; N De, 'House Committee Publishes Draft Stablecoin Bill', *CoinDesk* (17 April 2023).

[61] See, eg, J Hamilton, 'US Treasury Open to Nonbanks Issuing Stablecoins, Official Says', *CoinDesk* (18 July 2022).

[62] In fact, as recently reported, derivatives 'account for nearly three-quarters of daily trading on crypto markets'. S Chipolina, 'Coinbase secures approval to offer crypto futures to US retail investors', *Financial Times* (16 August 2023).

[63] See generally M Adachi et al, 'Stablecoins' role in crypto and beyond: functions, risk and policy' (European Central Bank, *Macroprudential Bulletin*, 11 July 2022); HJ Allen, 'DeFi: Shadow Banking 2.0?' (2023) 64 *William & Mary Law Review* 919.

rather than a market-driving 'front-office' function – pushes these macro-level, structural concerns into the background of the debate. It overplays the relative significance of digital technologies' role in optimising routine money transfers and downplays the transformative structural impact of stablecoins as a tokenised private substitute for public money. As the pre-2008 experience shows, looking at our complex and interconnected financial system through this transaction-centered lens leads to ineffective and dangerously misguided public policies.

To sum up, in our efforts to understand and respond to technological innovation in finance, it is critical to resist the obvious temptation to focus on superficially novel transactional aspects of financial technology. Limiting policymakers' perspective in this way breeds socially costly regulatory myopia, translating into deregulation or misregulation of high-risk activities on the macro-level. Ultimately, the systemic significance of the currently unfolding digital revolution in financial markets lies not in its capacity to generate private conveniences but in its potential to redefine the basic patterns of interaction between the private and the public sides of modern finance.

This means that deciphering the process of financial innovation as a macro-systemic rather than a micro-transactional phenomenon requires a serious re-examination of the underlying drivers of the changing public-private balance in finance. And here's where the last, perhaps the most insidious, fallacy rears its head.

10.4. FALLACY NO 3: FINANCIAL INNOVATION AS A PRIVATE PREROGATIVE

The third fallacy clouding our current understanding of the process of financial innovation is a widely shared presumption that financial innovation is naturally a private prerogative, a product of private action in response to private market incentives. This often expressly stated belief rests on a more general assumption that private profit is both the most effective driver of and the most legitimate reason for innovation.

While these assumptions are deeply rooted in the traditional American creed of free-market capitalism and private initiative, they also reflect, albeit in a superficial way, the core institutional dynamics of modern finance. Our existing financial system operates as a special public-private partnership for the creation and distribution of sovereign-backed money and credit.[64] In that system, substantive control over the generation and allocation of risks and returns in financial markets is vested in private actors operating on a micro-level, while the responsibility for ensuring financial stability is assigned to public actors operating on a macro-level. Government regulation is designed to counteract

[64] For a full analysis, see RC Hockett and ST Omarova, 'The Finance Franchise' (2017) 102 *Cornell Law Review* 1143.

and minimise the obvious moral hazard built into this partnership. In essence, the elaborate regime of financial regulation and supervision is supposed to keep profit-seeking private market participants from abusing their micro-level freedom to generate macro-level risks.[65]

In practice, however, this superficially neat delineation of public and private roles in the generation and distribution of credit and money is inherently unstable. In an important sense, the entire history of US financial markets and regulation since at least the New Deal era has been the history of conflict and renegotiation of this delicate balance. Financial market players, searching for higher profits and competitive edge, constantly push the line toward greater private freedom to transact by creating and trading in new financial instruments. They often do so by engaging in regulatory arbitrage, exploiting gaps and ambiguities in the existing laws and regulations through inventive transactional techniques or trading strategies – or what is commonly referred to as financial innovation.[66]

The resulting continuous injection of privately created risks into the financial system puts government agencies responsible for maintaining monetary and financial stability in an inherently reactive, defensive posture. At the same time, it reinforces the perception of government as an exogenous force acting *upon*, rather than *within*, the independently growing financial markets. These dynamics, in turn, provide a powerful conceptual and normative framing and vocabulary for the public discussion of financial innovation. We generally take for granted that markets 'evolve' and 'innovate' – terms that signify the primary, active, positive value-creation side of the public-private equation. Regulators, by contrast, 'respond' and 'react' to market developments – terms that underscore the secondary, passive, negative harm-limitation side. The public policy agenda reflects these deeply internalised assumptions. How financial regulators do, or should, *respond* to privately driven financial innovation and *adjust* regulatory tools and objectives to the new context is one of the perennial questions on that agenda.[67]

This familiar description of the financial sector dynamics, however, is not a reflection of some immutable objective reality but a cumulative outcome of a long line of normative choices and skewed judgments about the relative competencies of private and public actors in financial markets. In reality, governmental entities can and do actively participate in financial markets as lenders, investors, guarantors and trading counterparties. Historically, they have performed critical functions pioneering and supporting markets in innovative financial instruments, such as the now ubiquitous 30-year fixed mortgage loans or cross-border

[65] See Omarova (n 5).

[66] For an insightful account of these dynamics in the pre-2008 era, see EF Gerding, *Law, Bubbles, and Financial Regulation* (London, Routledge, 2013).

[67] Ford (n 7).

currency swaps.[68] Governments tend to innovate in direct response to significant structural problems in financial markets, which private financial institutions cannot resolve on their own. That typically happens when private entities cannot overcome collective action problems or bear the individually prohibitively high investment risks, especially if the benefits of such investments are not easily privately captured. By contrast, public actors' superior risk-bearing capacity, long investment time horizons, and a naturally macro-level perspective make them uniquely effective agents of transformative change with broadly shared benefits.[69]

This is what makes publicly led financial innovation at least as important as private innovation. Explicitly recognising and strengthening the public's innovation capabilities is especially vital in the context of the unfolding digital transformation of money and finance. The stakes for society are simply too high not to do so. While financial firms and tech entrepreneurs can be extremely creative and nimble market innovators, they often 'move fast and break things'.[70] Their principal motive for creating new financial products and services – the relentless pursuit of private profits in competitive environments – is entirely legitimate but not inherently aligned with the public interest in long-term stability and fairness of the financial system. In fact, creating an effective and durable alignment of private actors' economic incentives with public policy goals is a challenging and rarely successful exercise. As historical experience shows, periods of rapid financial innovation in private markets often lead to unsustainable asset price booms and leverage bubbles, followed by market crashes and economic depressions.[71]

The rise of hyper-fast, hyper-fluid, and poorly governed crypto finance elevates these old problems to a new systemic threat level. It undermines the practical efficacy of many traditional tools of financial regulation and, more generally, pushes the boundaries of the existing regulatory paradigm to its limits.[72] The 'mainstreaming' of crypto through widespread adoption by traditional banks and other financial institutions is not going to resolve these tensions. On the contrary, by extending implicit or even explicit public subsidies to crypto

[68] See RC Hockett and ST Omarova, 'Public Actors in Private Markets: Toward a Developmental Finance State' (2015) 93 *Washington University Law Review* 103; The World Bank, *70 Years: Connecting Capital Markets to Development* (2018) ch 4.

[69] For a more general analysis of the vital role state actors play in spurring transformative innovation, see F Block, 'Swimming Against the Current: The Rise of a Hidden Developmental State in the United States' (2008) 36 *Politics &. Society* 169; M Mazzucato, *The Entrepreneurial State: Debunking Public vs. Private Sector Myths* (London, Anthem Press, 2014).

[70] See J Taplin, *Move Fast and Break Things: How Facebook, Google, and Amazon Cornered Culture and Undermined Democracy* (New York, Little, Brown and Company, 2017).

[71] For a classic exposition, see RZ Aliber and CP Kindleberger, *Manias, Panics, and Crashes: A History of Financial Crises*, 7th edn (London, Palgrave Macmillan, 2015).

[72] See ST Omarova, 'Technology v. Technocracy: Fintech as A Regulatory Challenge' (2020) 6 *Journal of Financial Regulation* 75.

markets, this rapidly unfolding process is bound to exacerbate systemic vulnerabilities and put public resources at greater risk.[73]

In this context, the optimal policy approach is to supplement necessary legal and regulatory reforms with direct public participation in the development and promulgation of innovative tools of digital finance. Acting inside the market would enable public entities to leverage their unique structural advantages as agents of collective good to scale up digital innovation without generating undesirable systemic instability and excessive concentration of economic resources and power. It is here, however, that the habitual resistance to the idea of government as a financial market actor gets in the way of beneficial change.

The current policy debate on the design and uses of central bank digital currency, or CBDC, illustrates these dynamics. CBDC is a digitised form of 'central bank liability, denominated in an existing unit of account, which serves both as a medium of exchange and a store of value'.[74] Currently, central banks provide a digital account-based form of sovereign money primarily to regulated banks, which allows the latter to engage in publicly accommodated private money creation.[75] CBDC can bypass this intermediary layer and enable much broader direct access to central bank money, effectively digitising cash.[76] In principle, therefore, issuance of CBDC can revolutionise today's hybrid financial system that critically depends on banks' and other private financial institutions' 'intermediation' efforts.

In practice, it all depends on the design of specific CBDC instruments. CBDC may be universally available for general use ('retail') or restricted to financial institutions only ('wholesale'), interest-bearing or not, subject to quantitative limits or unlimited, and have varying levels of convertibility into cash or bank deposits. They can also differ in the degree of privacy and anonymity, availability around the clock or during limited times, and other user convenience features.[77] These multiple design choices determine the technological requirements and trade-offs associated with different forms of CBDC.[78]

The core issues in the debate surrounding these choices involve potential structural implications of CBDC issuance. Central banks exploring CBDC generally see it as a new vehicle for providing safe public money in the digital era.[79]

[73] ibid.

[74] Bank for International Settlements, Committee on Payments and Market Infrastructures (CPMI), 'Central Bank Digital Currencies' (March 2018) 3.

[75] Hockett and Omarova, 'The Finance Franchise' (n 64) 1158–64. In this system, banks hold central bank money in the form of special reserve or settlement accounts.

[76] CPMI, 'Central Bank Digital Currencies' (n 74) 1.

[77] Bank for International Settlements, 'CBDC: an opportunity for the monetary system' (BIS Annual Economic Report 2021, Chapter III); Bank of England, 'Central Bank Digital Currency: Opportunities, Challenges, and Design' (BOE Discussion Paper, March 2020) 11.

[78] See P Wong & JL Maniff, 'Comparing Means of Payment: What Role for a Central Bank Digital Currency?', *FEDS Notes* (13 August 2020).

[79] See, eg, Sverige Riskbank, 'Payments & Cash: E-krona', www.riksbank.se/en-gb/payments--cash/e-krona/.

The emerging consensus among central bankers and policymakers, however, holds that CBDC should not replace or significantly curtail the use of existing bank deposits (including tokenised deposits) and private stablecoins. Protecting private banks' existing money-creation privileges is a critical normative choice that drives much of the technical complexity in designing CBDC. It explains why the ongoing efforts to engineer the terms of CBDC's co-existence with bank deposits and stablecoins – express limits on the availability or permissible holdings of CBDC, the relative structure of interest rates, and so forth – aim to reduce the transactional usefulness of CBDC and make it less attractive than private money. Behind the shiny veil of technocratic deliberation, this seemingly counter-intuitive approach reflects a fundamentally political commitment not to disturb the existing public-private balance of power in the financial sector.

While industry lobbying is undoubtedly a key factor in securing that political commitment, the scepticism toward CBDC – particularly of the universally available retail variety – is a deeper and more complex phenomenon. Coming from different perspectives, CBDC critics voice concerns about state-led privacy violations, central banks' vulnerability to cyberattacks, and various manifestations of bureaucratic inefficiency.[80] While these are important problems that demand serious attention, they are neither unique to public digital currencies not inherently impossible to address through thoughtful technological and institutional design. A more fundamental challenge for CBDC architects is to overcome frequently expressed doubts about the overarching purpose and utility of retail CBDC, whereby it is summarily dismissed as 'a solution in search of a problem'.[81] The rhetorical power of this critique comes from its apparent grounding in everyday practicalities and common sense. Simply put, if people can use Venmo to send each other money, why do they need CBDC?[82]

Framing the CBDC discussion strictly as a matter of micro-transactional payments puts the innovating government in a presumptively inferior, defensive position. That's because treating CBDC as just a particular kind of payment tool automatically places it in direct competition with the existing payment instruments, including stablecoins and bank deposits. These private forms of money have a significant advantage simply by virtue of being around and fully

[80] Unsurprisingly, the most vociferous criticisms of CBDC are ideologically driven. See, eg, N Michel, 'Central Bank Digital Currencies and Freedom Are Incompatible', *Forbes* (15 July 2022); N Michel and N Anthony, 'The Risks of CBDCs: Why Central Bank Digital Currencies Shouldn't Be Adopted', *Cato Institute* (22 February 2023).

[81] See, eg, CJ Waller, 'CBDC – A Solution in Search of a Problem?', Speech at the American Enterprise Institute, Washington, DC (5 August 2021); Federal Reserve Bank of Minneapolis, 'Neel Kashkari Fireside Chat at the 2022 Journal of Financial Regulation Conference' (3 August 2022); UK Parliament, Economic Affairs Committee, 'Central bank digital currencies: a solution in search of a problem? Report published' (13 January 2022).

[82] Neel Kashkari, President of the Federal Reserve Bank of Minneapolis, has been particularly fond of the Venmo example. K Campbell, 'Kashkari calls CBDC a threat to privacy, defends regional bank independence', *American Banker* (4 August 2022).

embedded in the operation of today's financial market. Private firms can roll out new financial products or services, move into new markets, and respond to their customers' changing needs much faster and more effectively than central banks with legally bounded powers. In this context, it is easy to recast CBDC as a sub-optimal choice for retail payments and limit its potential uses to support wholesale trading and settlement of tokenised assets.[83]

CBDC, however, is not simply another payment technology, a limited-functionality supplement to the growing suite of private stablecoins or bank deposits. As a direct liability of the sovereign government, CBDC's place is at the very top of the money hierarchy.[84] Accordingly, a universally available CBDC can be a uniquely potent lever of structural change, the core element of a qualitatively new – more efficient, stable and democratic – financial ecosystem. Realising that potential, however, requires policymakers to expand their view beyond the basic payments frame. They need to recognise the multiple ways in which changing the nature and composition of central banks' primary liabilities – replacing traditional bank reserves and physical cash with digitally native money – can change the entire relational dynamics between the central bank, private finance and the broader economy.[85]

In the US context, for example, the Federal Reserve could use CBDC to offer free transactional deposit accounts directly to every individual and entity. These digital dollar wallets, or FedAccounts, would create a meaningful and inclusive public option in banking, guaranteeing continuous universal access to the safest form of money. By eliminating or significantly reducing the need to rely on private stablecoins or bank money – and the need to publicly subsidise their operations – introducing this option would eliminate the source of multiple frictions and inefficiencies in the financial system, simplify its structure, and reduce its complexity.[86] It would also enable the Fed to develop and utilise new, more effective and targeted monetary policy tools. The simple ability to set interest rates on FedAccounts, coupled with the inherent programmability of digital money, would give the Fed the flexibility to manage the nation's money supply far more dynamically and to respond more directly to the economy's needs.[87]

Even more consequentially, the dramatic expansion of the Fed's liabilities would just as dramatically expand its asset-side capacity to channel credit flows into productive economic activities. Building out its existing collateralised lending and market-making operations, the Fed would be able to support prudent and plentiful private lending to productive businesses, communities and

[83] Bank for International Settlements, 'Blueprint for the future monetary system' (n 28).

[84] See P Mehrling, 'The Inherent Hierarchy of Money' (2012), www.ieor.columbia.edu/files/seas-depts/industrial-engineering-operations-research/pdf-files/Mehrling_P_FESeminar_Sp12-02.pdf.

[85] For a comprehensive analysis of what that change could entail, see ST Omarova, 'The People's Ledger: How to Democratize Finance and Finance the Economy' (2021) 74 *Vanderbilt Law Review* 1231.

[86] ibid 1282–99.

[87] ibid 1257–68.

households on a much larger scale and as part of a coherent credit policy. The Fed's augmented balance-sheet capacity would also enable investment in a wide variety of new asset classes issued by the existing and newly established public instrumentalities for purposes of financing publicly beneficial real-economy projects. Such instrumentalities could include state and municipal public banks, 'green' banks, or potentially a newly created federal infrastructure finance institution. Unlocking this financial capacity would boost the nation's transition to a more sustainable, efficient and equitable mode of economic growth.[88]

In short, retail CBDC is a multi-faceted and potentially game-changing institutional innovation that can fundamentally redefine the operation of the nation's financial and economic systems. Its full transformative potential, however, remains unrecognised in the mainstream policy debate. To a great extent, this is a product of the 'normal' politics of finance, as powerful private sector interests are fighting for control of the emerging digital ecosystem. But it also reflects the power of unacknowledged intellectual fallacies and common misconceptions about the role of publicly led and publicly motivated financial innovation. An unquestioned assumption that financial innovation is a naturally and legitimately *private* undertaking quietly sets the pervasively sceptical tone for the CBDC debate. By distorting the narrative at that deeper level, this old fallacy breeds potentially dangerous new policy mistakes.

10.5. CONCLUSION

Financial innovation is a complex yet poorly understood phenomenon. All too often, the term is used indiscriminately as a slap-on label meant not only to sell risky financial products but also to shield them from regulatory scrutiny. In our technology-obsessed age, calling a market practice or product 'innovative' conveys a strong normative message: innovative financial instruments are presumed to be both technically novel and substantively good.

This descriptive and normative fluidity – an elusive vibe-like nature – of the notion of financial innovation is rooted in specific misconceptions about its transactional context, defining features, and driving motivations. Unpacking these hidden misconceptions reveals the corrosive effect of the flawed logic and unquestioned assumptions that foster regulatory complacency, engender strong deregulatory biases, and lead to dangerously misguided regulatory actions. In periods of transformative technological change in financial markets, these fallacies stand in the way of a full democratic deliberation on potentially crucial public policy choices. That is why, amid today's digital transformation, it is especially important that we confront the hidden errors in our collective thinking to get a better handle on what financial innovation is – and how to harness its power for our collective good.

[88] ibid 1268–82.

11

Boilerplate against Bailouts: A Regulatory Ride Fallacy

ANNA GELPERN*

11.1. INTRODUCTION: CREATIVE PROBLEM SOLVING

THIS CHAPTER CONSIDERS the implications of using private contracts as public policy tools, or what happens when regulators 'catch a ride' on private law instruments to their policy destination. It centres on an episode of creative problem solving after the transatlantic financial crisis of 2007–2009, when wealthy governments pledged to stop bailing out too-big-to-fail global banks and turned to standard-form contracts for help to deliver on their pledge.[1] To convince voters and markets that even megabanks could fail under their new 'special' resolution regimes, governments had to contain the costs of failure to economies and financial systems. The prospect of chaotic termination of the banks' derivatives contracts emerged as a major obstacle in the way of establishing credible resolution regimes and ending bailouts.[2]

Derivatives are among the principal beneficiaries of an effective exemption from corporate and bank insolvency regimes worldwide. Although the start of insolvency proceedings usually halts (stays) claims against the debtor, derivatives contract counterparties may terminate, net bilateral exposures, seize and sell collateral, and take other steps that put them at the head of the debt collection queue. Such generous 'safe harbour' treatment reflects pre-crisis policy consensus that derivatives performed critical functions in national and global

* I am beyond grateful to the editors of this volume for their patience and insights. Mitu Gulati, Betsy Kuhn, Alex Nye, Tanina Rostain, David Snyder, Nicolas Véron and David Wishnick, as well as participants in workshops and conferences at Cornell Law, Georgetown Law and the International Insolvency Institute, offered invaluable comments on earlier drafts. Nat Deacon and James Bernstein provided superb research assistance.

[1] See, eg, G20, *Communiqué: Meeting of the Finance Ministers and Central Bank Governors, United Kingdom* (7 November 2009).

[2] DK Tarullo, 'Toward Building a More Effective Resolution Regime: Progress and Challenges' (Remarks at the Federal Reserve Board and Federal Reserve Bank of Richmond Conference, 'Planning for the Orderly Resolution of a Global Systemically Important Bank', Washington, DC, 18 October 2013) 13–14.

financial systems; that maximum market liquidity was essential for their ability to perform these functions; and that ensnaring them in bankruptcy would disrupt markets and harm economies.[3]

The Lehman Brothers and AIG failures in 2008 revealed that, instead of treating safe harbours as a guarantee of repayment and staying put, derivatives counterparties could use safe harbours to run on the failing firm. After the crisis, policy makers feared that excluding systemically important contracts from systemically important resolution frameworks would distort incentives and exacerbate turmoil. In the worst-case scenario, an avalanche of panicked terminations could strip the debtor's balance sheet bare before resolution got under way. Standard derivatives contract terms moreover allowed the failure of an affiliate in one country to trigger claims against every part of a multinational conglomerate, threatening a cascade of failures in different parts of the world.[4] The public (or publics, in cross-border cases) would soon be back to the old choice between suffering spillovers and paying for bailouts.

Meeting the megabank failure challenge under the circumstances entailed more than balancing the costs and benefits of contract enforcement, or weighing pre-crisis and post-crisis perspectives on financial stability. The treatment of derivatives contracts in special resolution regimes implicated politically charged distribution commitments. Contract boilerplate and bankruptcy safe harbours were part of an institutional architecture that allocated losses between failed firms and their counterparties, between failed firms and their governments, and among states. If the safe harbours let contract counterparties run on a bank, its government could come under pressure to bail it out. If the same contracts were stayed, losses would fall on the bank's counterparties, and could shift the pressure for bailouts onto different governments.

The reformers' contract problem had a time-tested technical solution. Since at least the 1980s, some national banking laws had incorporated a slightly modified version of bankruptcy safe harbours designed to reduce run risks. In the United States, the Federal Deposit Insurance Corporation (FDIC) acting as receiver for a failed bank could stay the enforcement of safe-harboured contracts, including derivatives, for up to one business day. The FDIC could use this time to transfer the bilateral contract relationship to a bridge bank or a solvent third party that would continue performing the contracts. Such transfers have been the norm. Any contracts left behind after the stay would return to the safe harbour, and could be terminated.

[3] See, eg, RR Bliss and GG Kaufman (2006) 'Derivatives and Systemic Risk: Netting, Collateral, and Closeout' (2006) 2 *Journal of Financial Stability* 55 (questioning the consensus).

[4] For example, cross-default, bankruptcy, and 'credit event upon merger' clauses in both versions of the ISDA Master Agreement extend to affiliates included under the definition of a 'Specified Entity'. Eg, ISDA, 'Legal Guidelines for Smart Derivatives Contracts: The ISDA Master Agreement' (2019) 13–14, www.isda.org/a/23iME/Legal-Guidelines-for-Smart-Derivatives-Contracts-ISDA-Master-Agreement.pdf; see ISDA, '2002 ISDA Master Agreement' (2002) s 5; ISDA, '1992 ISDA Master Agreement' (1992) s 5.

Stay-and-transfer authority in the United States was a compromise fashioned against the background of bank failures in the 1980s to mitigate risks to the financial markets, the banking system, the deposit insurance fund, and the public treasury. It covered banks, but did not extend beyond them to bank holding companies or other kinds of financial institutions. The limited reach hampered efforts to contain the crisis in the fall of 2008, and was a prime candidate for post-crisis reform.

On the upside, the basic mechanism was familiar to regulators and market participants, and would be relatively straightforward to incorporate as a technical matter in special resolution reforms across jurisdictions. On the downside, in a world of global conglomerates, global markets and global crises, introducing a short stay on contract enforcement would require unprecedented interstate coordination.

States traditionally solve private contract problems with public law instruments: statutes, regulations and treaties. After several years of trying to coordinate domestic regulatory reforms, officials had come to see these instruments as too blunt, too rigid and too slow to deal with the risk that some contracts posed for special resolution regimes.[5] Instead of using traditional public law tools, they sought to amend the contracts directly.[6]

States were not party to these contracts; governments did not control their terms, and had no practical way to mandate universal adoption. No public authority had prescribed or ratified this contract boilerplate. Instead of issuing mandates, officials from major financial jurisdictions lobbied private financial industry groups to produce new contract language in line with the policy consensus, and to encourage their members to adopt it.[7]

The International Swaps and Derivatives Association (ISDA) assumed a leading role in the project as the de facto representative and governance body for the global derivatives market. Since the 1980s, ISDA had designed, distributed and continuously updated standard-form contracts for what had become a multi-trillion global trading market.[8] Derivatives dealers (too-big-to-fail global banks) had held sway in ISDA governance since its inception. By relying on contract amendments to end bailouts, regulators bet the success of vital post-crisis reforms on their ability to navigate the reform route in a vehicle belonging to the main reform targets – too-big-to-fail global banks.

[5] Tarullo (n 2) 6–7.

[6] ibid.

[7] See, eg, Bank of England, Bundesanstalt für Finanzdienstleistungsaufsicht, Federal Deposit Insurance Corporation & Swiss Financial Market Supervisory Authority, *Letter to Stephen O'Connor, Chairman of International Swaps and Derivatives Association, Inc* (5 November 2013), https://web.archive.org/web/20170208155515/https://www.fdic.gov/news/news/press/2013/pr13099a.pdf (hereinafter 'Letter from the Bank of England et al').

[8] ISDA, *ISDA Brochure 2013* (2013) 11, www.isda.org/a/qviDE/isda-brochure-2013-final.pdf (hereinafter '2013 ISDA Brochure').

The result was an ingenious technical solution to a high-stakes political problem, a microcosm of contemporary financial regulation. In 2014, ISDA published its first Resolution Stay Protocol, a contract amendment instrument that allowed adhering members to commit to stay contract enforcement to accommodate special resolution in different jurisdictions. Governments then issued rules to speed up and amplify industry efforts to secure broad-based adoption. Regulated dealers had to adhere to the protocol or negotiate equivalent terms, and could not trade with anyone that had not done the same. Because dealers were an essential part of the market, the rules put pressure on everyone else to adhere to the protocol. ISDA later published versions of the protocol for a broad range of regulated and unregulated entities.

For governments, collaboration with ISDA ensured that dealers responsible for most of the trading in the market would amend their contracts. Later, it was instrumental in extending the reach of resolution reforms to asset managers and other market participants beyond the bank regulatory perimeter. When time was of the essence, precision was at a premium, and few other options were available, reformers caught a ride on derivatives boilerplate to their no-bailout destination. What's not to like?

The regulatory ride construct rests on and reinforces the fallacy of an arm's length relationship between state and market domains, punctuated by crisis-driven intimate encounters. It obscures far-reaching political trade-offs and inter-temporal commitments inherent in the policy uses of private contract form. Using contracts instead of public law tools to solve the too-big-to fail problem not only reflects,[9] but also contributes to a loss of public regulatory capacity. Over time, it can narrow the scope for structural reform and, for market participants, alter the function of their contracts.

The remainder of the chapter proceeds as follows: first, it recounts the regulatory ride episode and puts it in institutional context (11.2), including an overview of ISDA's internal and external governance practices, the unusual form and function of its contracts, and the role of safe harbours in bankruptcy and bank resolution. It then shifts the focus to megabanks, the principal target of regulatory intervention in this story (11.3). I describe the multi-layered distribution challenge of resolving systemically important global financial conglomerates, the problem posed by safe harbours, the failure of transnational regulatory coordination, and the Resolution Stay Protocol denouement.

The resolution problem and the protocol fix mark the terminal points on the regulatory ride. However, derivatives contracts and market infrastructure

[9] K Pistor, *The Code of Capital: How the Law Creates Wealth and Inequality* (Princeton University Press, 2019) 144–152.

were not targets of regulation in their own right; they were means to achieve a bank regulatory end. I argue that the fit and efficacy of these contracts as policy instruments grew out of ISDA's approach to contract governance, a product of long-term, continuous intimate engagement with governments around the world. The chapter concludes with an assessment of contract as a regulatory instrument and a commitment device in the governance of financial systems, including the implications for financial reform.

11.2. CONTRACT COUNTRY

All contract boilerplate has a public dimension, but derivatives boilerplate is unusual for its capacity to serve as the organising device for a $700 trillion global market famously shielded from national and international regulatory intervention.[10] Contract form has reflected and structured policy trade-offs in the derivatives industry, and has mediated relationships between governments and derivatives market stakeholders. This experience has transformed ISDA contracts, their unusual modular architecture, and the infrastructure for contract design, production, adoption and enforcement into a powerful public governance tool.

11.2.1. Need a Ride

On 5 November 2013, the heads of the Bank of England, Germany's Federal Financial Supervisory Authority, the FDIC, and the Swiss Financial Market Supervisory Authority wrote to the Chairman of ISDA.[11] Their letter cited derivatives contracts as a key challenge for 'the global regulatory community' in its quest to develop 'strategies to resolve global systemically important financial institutions in a manner that reduces the risk of global financial instability while minimising moral hazard'.[12] More plainly put, standard terms in ISDA's contracts stood in the way of ending bailouts and too-big-to-fail and, by extension, of fighting crises and securing financial stability. Amending them to reduce the risk of disorderly termination was 'essential' to the success of national and

[10] BIS, *OTC derivatives statistics at end-June 2023* (16 November 2023), www.bis.org/publ/otc_hy2311.pdf.

[11] See, eg, H Jones, 'Derivatives industry under the gun to amend contracts', *Reuters* (London, 5 November 2013), www.reuters.com/article/derivatives-idINDEE9A40E120131105; 'Letter from the Bank of England et al' (n 7).

[12] 'Letter from the Bank of England et al' (n 7).

global post-crisis financial reforms. In the meantime, governments would keep trying to harmonise their laws.

The mere fact that four of the most powerful financial regulators in the world came together to write to ISDA reflects the extent to which governments simultaneously recognised the imperative and doubted their capacity to implement special resolution reforms worldwide. The letter revealed that regulators had been trying, unsuccessfully so far, to coordinate among themselves, and that they had approached ISDA for help before. ISDA must not have leapt at the chance to lend its contract machinery to the cause of ending too-big-to-fail, preferring an inter-state solution.

The chances of a stand-alone inter-state solution before the political window for post-crisis reforms slammed shut were slim to none. Governments seemed to have lost capacity to coordinate among themselves on these matters.

After appealing to ISDA's self-interest and civic virtue with certainty-speak favoured by market lobbyists, the authors suggest that no one but ISDA could make systemically important financial contracts and special resolution regimes operate smoothly together across national boundaries:

> ISDA has the opportunity to play a pivotal role in providing greater certainty to the treatment of early termination rights and other remedies with respect to derivatives contracts in a cross-border resolution scenario. As resolution regimes are implemented in an increasing number of jurisdictions, ISDA is in a unique position to link these regimes by providing consistent and enforceable contractual provisions related to termination and other remedies with respect to derivatives transactions.[13]

ISDA took a year after receiving the letter to produce its first Resolution Stay Protocol, which allowed derivatives market participants to amend their bilateral contracts wholesale in line with national resolution reforms. Successor protocols followed, covering a broader range of institutions and jurisdictions. It was a remarkable achievement in regulatory governance: public and private stakeholders around the world came together to solve a fiendishly complex shared problem and safeguard financial stability.

More than a decade later, many things about the 2013 letter and the events that followed remain puzzling. Why did the most powerful, most capable governments in the world turn to other people's contracts to reach their shared policy goals? Why did the biggest and most powerful financial industry groups, the largest global banking conglomerates, and even their unregulated counterparties collaborate in the regulators' unorthodox strategy? Digging deeper, what private contract terms could possibly be 'essential' and 'critical' to the success of public policy, as the letter suggests? Were voluntary contract changes – and asking for favours from too-big-to-fail banks – the best or the only instrument

[13] ibid.

that governments had to deliver on their pledge to stop bailing them out? … and what would have happened had ISDA rejected the regulators' plea?

The remainder of this section traces ISDA's contract project and its engagement with the 'global regulatory community' since the 1980s. In context, the Resolution Stay Protocol looks less like a well-timed emergency ride and more like a logical, even necessary, next step in the development of a symbiotic regulatory relationship.

11.2.2. Private Infrastructure

ISDA has often described itself as 'the largest global financial trade association, by number of member firms'.[14] At the time of the regulators' letter in 2013, it had over 840 members in 60 countries; by 2024, its membership had surpassed 1,000 across 77 countries.[15]

In 2013, one quarter of ISDA's 840 members were dealers ('Primary Members'), mostly large banks. Service providers such as law firms, accountants and consultants ('Associate Members') stood at 35 per cent. The largest category, at 40 per cent, were financial and real economy firms that used derivatives contracts primarily to manage risk in their operations. These firms were 'end users' in market jargon; in ISDA membership terms, they were 'Subscribers'.[16]

ISDA began life in the mid-1980s as a project to standardise key terms in interest rate and currency swaps, privately negotiated ('over-the-counter' or 'OTC') financial contracts linked to interest rate and currency price movements. Eleven banks and broker-dealer firms, competitors in the nascent swaps market, tried to fashion a single set of shared contract terms to replace their respective house forms.[17] Dickering over different forms for identical products had gummed up deals and introduced errors; fixing and centralising core terms would reduce transaction costs and bolster market liquidity. After hiring a blue-chip New York firm to help with the drafting, and negotiating for a year, the founding dealers produced a SWAPS Code, a proto-contract document comprising shared definitions, assumptions, and calculation methodologies.[18] Published in 1985 and

[14] See, eg, ISDA, *Letter from R Pickel, Executive Vice Chairman of ISDA to Elizabeth M Murphy, Securities and Exchange Commission* (14 February 2011), www.sec.gov/comments/s7-44-10/s74410-11.pdf.

[15] See, eg, '2013 ISDA Brochure' (n 8); ISDA, ISDA Membership, www.isda.org/membership/.

[16] '2013 ISDA Brochure' (n 8).

[17] SM Flanagan, 'The Rise of a Trade Association: Group Interactions within the International Swaps and Derivatives Association' (2001) 6 *Harvard Negotiation Law Review* 211.

[18] ISDA, *1985 Code of Standard Wording, Assumptions and Provisions for Swaps* (ISDA e-book), www.isda.org/book/code-of-standard-wording-assumptions-and-provisions-for-swaps/.

revised a year later, the code became the foundation for ISDA's modular contract suite. ISDA registered as a New York non-profit association in May of 1985.[19]

One of the lawyers present at ISDA's founding described its early standardisation work as a way to save on law firm partners' Concorde flights to closings in New York and London.[20] Perhaps apocryphal, the story highlights important attributes of the derivatives market construction project. It began as a transnational endeavour, to organise a market straddling continents and legal systems.[21] The main organising vehicle was a centrally produced contract designed for active trading, with a fixed core and modules that could adapt to various existing and future financial instruments. Although lawyers have a prominent role in the derivatives market, the structure of ISDA contracts limits the need and the scope for lawyerly intervention in documenting individual trades. Lawyers help clients negotiate and document variations from the fixed core, and modules customised for their bilateral trading relationships. All else being equal, market participants have a powerful incentive to stick to the standard.

As detailed in the next subsection, most transactions incorporate the core terms by reference. Core terms are not supposed to vary from one transaction to the next, but to change in response to the needs of the market as a whole. When ISDA's governing board decides that change is in order, outside counsel do the drafting under the auspices of a documentation committee comprising thousands of its members, with multiple subcommittees and working groups. Transaction-specific terms are kept sparse to minimise trading frictions: a short-form confirmation is no more than a few pages long, containing several lines of blanks for traders to fill in with financial terms.[22]

Contract design, diffusion, and adaptation practices shape relations among stakeholders inside and outside the derivatives ecosystem. On the inside, ISDA has had to balance the interests of dealers and end-users. Dealers tend to be the biggest institutions and the most active repeat players among its constituents and, therefore, benefit the most from the contract infrastructure. End users are the most numerous. If end users came to see ISDA as biased against them, it could hamper contract adoption and fragment the market. Partly in response to claims of dealer bias, ISDA replaced 'Swap Dealers' with 'Swaps and Derivatives' in its name in 1993, keeping the acronym. The name change signalled an expansive view of its role as custodian of the entire OTC derivatives industry, poised for more expansion in trading volume and instrument range, alongside the limits of change.[23] Three decades later, dealers remain the only ones with full voting

[19] State of New York, Department of State, Division of Corporations, 'Entity Name History: International Swaps and Derivatives Association', https://apps.dos.ny.gov/publicInquiry/NameHistory.

[20] See A Gelpern, 'Comment: Public Promises and Organizational Agendas' (2009) 51 *Arizona Law Review* 63.

[21] It opened offices in London and Tokyo in the 1990s; see Flanagan (n 18) 228.

[22] In some market segments, it is more common to use long-form confirmations instead of the combination of ISDA Master and short-form confirmation.

[23] Flanagan (n 17) 222.

privileges in ISDA.[24] End users have access to its contracts, enforceability opinions, and similar output, and a say in certain product-specific decisions, such as payment triggers in credit derivatives.

On the outside, ISDA's task has been to keep OTC derivatives the exclusive province of private contract governance and self-regulation. Contrary to the image of an unregulated market, this calls for close and continuous engagement with regulatory projects and governments around the world. At any given time, it might be battling product preapproval in South Korea,[25] convincing New York State that credit derivatives were not insurance,[26] securing a string of federal dispensations for US banks to deal in derivatives,[27] and lobbying governments from Zambia to Azerbaijan to enact laws that guaranteed enforcement for its peculiar contracts.[28] The global contract mandate has led ISDA to develop unparalleled insights into the practice of national and cross-border financial regulation, lines of communication with financial authorities everywhere, and the capacity to respond to shocks emanating from governments and markets.

The market-building project was a fabulous success. Between 1987 and 1990, swaps grew from $900 billion to $3.5 trillion notional amount outstanding.[29] The derivatives market reached $596 trillion in outstanding notional ($15 trillion gross market value) on the eve of the crisis in December of 2007, and $710 trillion outstanding notional ($19 trillion gross market value), systemically important by any measure by the time regulators wrote to ISDA at the end of 2013.[30]

11.2.3. A Modular Vehicle

A contract at common law is an expression of party autonomy and a commitment to allocate risk over time. Doctrinally, contract form can be a clue to contract meaning and the parties' intent. Form in ISDA contracts is an organising device, a governance platform, and a medium connecting state regulation and private ordering in its market.

Derivatives belong to a species of actively traded, highly standardised financial contracts. The species also includes sale and repurchase (repo) and securities

[24] ISDA, *By-Laws*, s 10, www.isda.org/a/u0SME/ISDA-By-Laws-April-11-2019.pdf.

[25] ISDA, *Letter from ISDA to National Policy Committee, the National Assembly of the Republic of Korea* (18 September 2009), www.isda.org/a/88iDE/submission2018sep09.pdf.

[26] A van Duyn, J Chung and S Scholtes, 'New York Watchdog Wants Derivative Controls', *Financial Times* (New York, 12 May 2008), www.ft.com/content/301b99f0-205d-11dd-80b4-000077b07658.

[27] ST Omarova, 'The Quiet Metamorphosis: How Derivatives Changed the "Business of Banking"' (2009) 4 *University of Miami Law Review* 1041.

[28] See ISDA, *ISDA Survey on OTC Derivatives in Emerging and Developing Markets* (2023), www.isda.org/a/qfogE/ISDA-Survey-on-OTC-Derivatives-in-Emerging-and-Developing-Markets.pdf.

[29] Flanagan (n 17) 241.

[30] See BIS, *OTC derivatives market activity in the second half of 2007* (May 2008); BIS, *OTC Derivatives Statistics at End-December 2013* (May 2014).

lending agreements, all of which share a distinctive modular form.[31] In each case, a master agreement forms the stable core of a contract suite; more-or-less customisable modules incorporate the master by reference.

Master structures offer a more robust form of standardisation than other kinds of complex business contracts.[32] Lawyers do not normally draft commercial loan and merger contracts from scratch; they copy, paste, and adapt boilerplate text from an industry model or in-house form, incorporating negotiated variations, embellishments, and even typos. In a master structure, the parties adopt a centrally produced, often pre-printed, contract core in its entirety. Customisation and variations are confined to physically separate documents, which makes them highly salient.

Amending a master agreement is a policy matter for the relevant industry segment; an industry group like ISDA would usually shepherd the process. Because master agreements are maintained apart from individual transactions, they may change more or less often than boilerplate merger or loan agreements. At least in theory, all changes are widely vetted, leaving no room for harmful, pointless or meaningless terms left in the text by neglect.[33] The modular structure reduces drafting and information acquisition costs, minimises trading frictions, and enhances liquidity.[34]

ISDA produces and takes copyright in the derivatives master agreement suite (Figure 11.1), used to document the overwhelming majority of OTC derivatives transactions.[35] The ISDA Master Agreement (the 'Master' or 'ISDA Master') is the heart of the contract suite. Counterparties customise the Master in relationship-specific Schedules. The Credit Support Annex is another relationship document; it sets out agreed rules for posting collateral to mitigate counterparty risk, which may change over time. Standard Definitions Booklets contain instrument-specific terms. Different instruments – interest rate swaps, equity, foreign exchange, and credit derivatives – have dedicated definitions booklets. Confirmations are the only transaction-specific pieces of the modular puzzle. They specify the economic terms of a trade in prescribed form, and incorporate the rest of the documentation by reference.

[31] See, eg, SIFMA, *MRA, GMRA, MSLA and MSFTAs: Find the Master Repurchase Agreement, Global Master Repurchase Agreement, Master Securities Loan Agreement and Master Securities Forward Transaction Agreement*, www.sifma.org/resources/general/mra-gmra-msla-and-msftas/. On modularity, see HE Smith, 'Modularity in Contracts: Boilerplate and Information Flow' (2006) 104 *Michigan Law Review* 1175.

[32] Compare M Kahan and M Klausner, 'Standardization and Innovation in Corporate Contracting (Or "The Economics of Boilerplate")' (1997) 83 *Virginia Law Review* 713.

[33] See SJ Choi, M Gulati and RE Scott, 'The Black Hole Problem in Commercial Boilerplate' (2017) 67 *Duke Law Journal* 1.

[34] See Smith (n 31) and A Gelpern, 'The Importance of Being Standard' (2017) European Central Bank 2016 Annual Legal Department Conference Proceedings.

[35] See, eg, *Lomas (Together the Joint Administrators of Lehman Brothers International (Europe)) v JFB Firth Rixson Inc* [2010] EWHC 3372 (Ch), [5] (citing ISDA estimate of more than 90 per cent of all derivatives transactions); see also MK Borowicz, 'Contracts as Regulation: The ISDA Master Agreement' (2020) 16 *Capital Markets Law Journal* 72.

Figure 11.1 ISDA Master Agreement Structure[36]

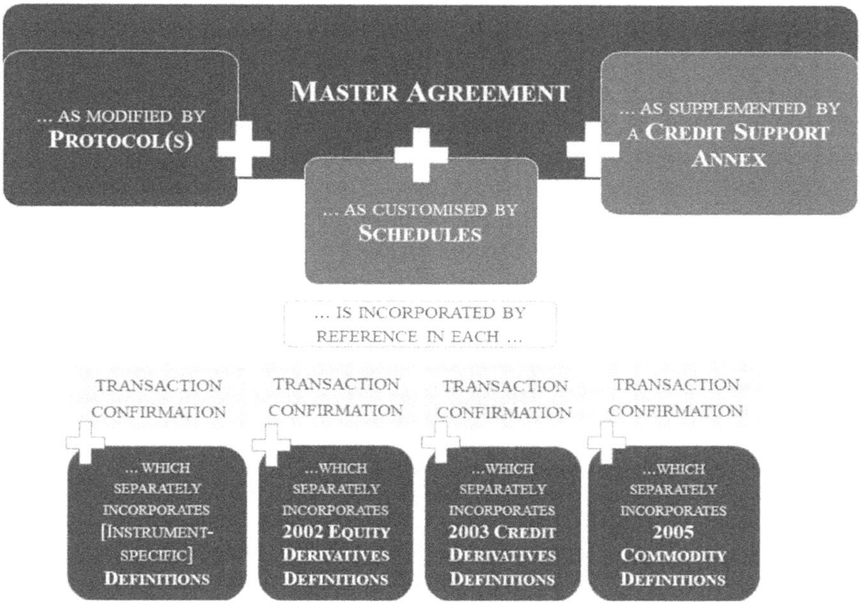

All transactions under one ISDA Master are treated as a single contract, with the option to calculate bilateral payment obligations on a net basis in the ordinary course and, separately, netting upon termination ('closeout netting'), discussed in more detail below.

The modular ISDA Master suite plays a quasi-constitutional role in the bilateral relationships among participants in the derivatives market. One scholar aptly described it as a mix of regulatory and relational terms bundled with a gatekeeping function.[37] The modular form defines the scope for party autonomy. Fully standard modules, such as the Master and Definitions Booklets, are published by ISDA and contain behaviour norms and product attributes that apply market-wide and invite public law comparisons. Schedules, Confirmations, and Credit Support Annexes evoke more familiar private contracts, standardised but negotiated within the prescribed limits. Gatekeeping comes from the network effects: ISDA forms are a practical necessity in the derivatives market. Trading derivatives without an ISDA Master Agreement in place is possible, but the result is likely to be more costly, less liquid, and socially awkward.

If the Master is like a constitution, Protocols help manage what could otherwise be a cumbersome constitutional amendment process. With a constant

[36] The darkest colour modules apply market-wide; lighter colours denote relationship-specific modules; the lightest denote individual transactions. See also A Gelpern and M Gulati, 'CDS Zombies' (2012) 13 *European Business Organization Law Rev* 346.

[37] Borowicz (n 35) 82.

stream of economic, financial and political upheavals in the background, ISDA has only ever issued three Masters, in 1987, 1992 and 2002;[38] the last two remain in use in 2024. When market-wide change is in order, ISDA can publish a Protocol amending the Master in line with the new market consensus. Counterparties with a Master in place can adhere to the relevant Protocol instead of negotiating bilateral amendments. The mechanism resembles multilateral treaty accession, where acceding states become bound vis-a-vis one another.

ISDA contracts pose two kinds of judicial construction challenges: the gap between form and function, and the question of party intent. It is commonplace for derivatives contracts to skirt established regulatory categories while performing some of the same risk transfer functions as regulated instruments. In the words of one scholar, ISDA contracts constructed and exploited place-less markets and 'regulatory voids'.[39] When in the early 2000s some national courts would adopt a functional reading of the contract terms, the industry perceived it as an existential threat.[40] In response, ISDA amended contracts, filed amicus briefs, established limited-purpose dispute settlement panels, and experimented with private alternatives to generalist public courts.[41]

By the turn of the century, ISDA boilerplate had become too pervasive and too important to escape public adjudication altogether. Off-label and non-member adoptions of the ISDA Master raised novel questions before the English courts.[42] For mainstream uses and core constituents, judges and administrative authorities in multiple jurisdictions still had to manage the unavoidable interactions between ISDA contracts and national insolvency regimes.

The public function of ISDA contracts accentuates the party intent problem. In a textbook private contract, judicial construction gives effect to party intent; non-parties may or may not see positive spillovers from interpretation. Derivatives contracts are different. Two theoretical interventions, 'contract-as-statute'[43] and 'regulatory contract',[44] share the intuition that party intent does not and should not control contract interpretation in this case, because parties to the contract are not its principal constituents. Instead, the constituents are an entire market segment or a public regulatory domain. In both contract-as-statute

[38] G Charles, 'ISDA Master Architecture' (January 2012) *Practical Compliance & Risk Management for the Securities Industry* 25.

[39] BG Carruthers, 'Diverging Derivatives: Law, Governance and Modern Financial Markets' (2012) 41 *J Comparative Economics* 386.

[40] See, eg, *Eternity Global Master Fund Limited v Morgan Guaranty Trust Company of New York*, 375 F.3d 168 (2d Circuit 2004); *AON Financial Products, Incorporated v Societe Generale*, 476 F.3d 90 (2d Circuit 2007).

[41] ISDA, *Amicus Briefs*, www.isda.org/category/legal/amicus-briefs/; ISDA, *Credit Derivatives Determinations Committees*, www.isda.org/2018/10/12/credit-derivatives-determinations-committees (February 2024); see, eg, Panel of Recognised International Markets in Finance (P.R.I.M.E.), 'What We Do', https://primefinancedisputes.org/page/what-we-do.

[42] See J Braithwaite, 'Standard Form Contracts as Transnational Law: Evidence from the Derivatives Markets' (2012) 75 *The Modern Law Review* 779.

[43] See SJ Choi and M Gulati, 'Contract as Statute' (2006) 104 *Michigan Law Rev* 1129.

[44] See Borowicz (n 35).

and regulatory contract, the parties bargain for market-wide or public outcomes, and have no private intent apart from them. It follows that judicial construction must look to public purpose, not private intent. However, public purpose can be hard to ascertain, and the risk of market-wide damage from judicial error is ever-present.

The assumption in contract-as-statute is that parties to any particular derivatives trade do not know and do not care about the meaning of a given boilerplate term. Their intent is to maximise liquidity. When boilerplate terms serve as 'incantations' that signal commitment to market standard rather than substantive content,[45] theory calls for judges to flip the doctrinal rule on its head and let general market meaning (intent of non-party drafters) override the parties' claim of specific intent.[46] ISDA facilitates access to market meaning with centralised production, internal governance, and public communications.

Market participants' implicit reliance on ISDA to operate in their collective interest is the essential predicate for contract-as-statute analysis. If ISDA systematically fails to follow its quasi-legislative mandate – if it favours dealers over end-users, neglects to secure enforcement in Eritrea, or allows wild variations to disrupt the network effects – its interpretation should get no deference from the courts.

Like contract-as-statute, a regulatory contract is robustly standardised and widely used; unlike contract-as-statute, it has an outward-facing 'regulatory' purpose distinct from transactional efficiency.[47] If a 'plain meaning' construction is inconsistent with regulatory purpose, the latter must prevail. By extension, regulatory purpose must take precedence over narrow party intent should the two diverge. Judges may find regulatory purpose in 'the objectives of the regulatory framework applicable to the market in which the contract is used as a regulatory instrument'.[48] For instance, systemic risk reduction is a stated regulatory purpose of closeout netting terms in the ISDA Master.[49] In a regulatory contract, neither the parties' nor ISDA's meanings would necessarily prevail at all times. The 'regulatory' interpretation acts as a public check on both.[50] In contrast, ISDA meaning would control in contract-as-statute, provided it remains a faithful agent.

In sum, the ISDA Master contract suite is unusual in many respects. Its modular structure makes standardisation more robust than most sophisticated business contracts, and lends itself to nearly infinite extension and adaptation to new instruments. The Master straddles the public-private divide. It performs

[45] Choi and Gulati (n 43) 1160.

[46] See G Klass, 'Boilerplate and Party Intent' (2019) 82 *Law & Contemporary Problems* 105.

[47] Borowicz (n 35) 74.

[48] ibid 94.

[49] This could pose an implementation problem, for instance, if the regulatory framework changes after the adoption of a given term.

[50] Borowicz argues in an earlier piece for applying Global Administrative Law methodology to assess ISDA's public legitimacy. MK Borowicz, 'Private Power and International Law: The International Swaps and Derivatives Association' (2015) 8 *European Journal of Legal Studies* 66.

internal governance functions, compartmentalises information, draws lines of authority and marks the respective spheres of activity for ISDA and its members, market participants and their counsel. In addition, the master structure performs outward-facing public functions, such as fostering market liquidity and financial stability, whose impact extends beyond the derivatives market. This context makes using the Master as a policy vehicle against the too-big-to-fail problem seem less jarring.

11.2.4. Express Lanes

Creating spaces for private contract governance is a policy choice with potentially far-reaching consequences. Tracing the operation and development of bankruptcy safe harbours illustrates how the policy practice of accommodating arguably parochial contract imperatives fuelled derivatives market growth. The focus of this subsection is on the logic by which this string of decisions and others like it could come together to make ISDA contracts the inevitable reform vehicle after 2008.

Communicating the size of the OTC derivatives market is a perennial dilemma. Eye-popping notional amounts (more than $700 trillion at the time of writing)[51] convey exponential growth, economic importance, and sky-high risk, inviting comparisons to weapons of mass destruction.[52] On the other hand, crediting all the contractual risk mitigation features makes the market seem trivially small. The challenge for the likes of ISDA is to paint a convincing picture of a vast, essential and safe global market. Its 2013 public relations brochure embraced the extremes and mapped the path between them: more than $600 trillion in outstanding notional four years after the 2008 cataclysm 'measure[d] activity, not risk'; the gross market value of all contracts based on this notional was 4 per cent of the huge number. Two contract elements, netting and collateral, would reduce the risk further to 0.2 per cent of the notional amounts.[53] For this risk mitigation calculus to keep market participants and the public safe, governments had to supply 'legal certainty', which was tantamount to a promise that the public interest in derivatives contract enforcement would outweigh other policy considerations at all times. Bankruptcy safe harbours are a product of this balancing logic.

[51] BIS, 'OTC derivatives statistics at end-June 2023' (16 November 2023), www.bis.org/publ/otc_hy2311.pdf. The term 'notional amount' here refers to the value of the underlying asset that serves as the basis for calculating derivatives contract payments. For instance, an interest rate swap entails a periodic exchange of fixed rate interest payments for floating rate interest payments on a notional principal amount over a period of time. The principal is notional because neither party to the swap borrows it; interest payments are calculated 'as if' there were an underlying debt.

[52] Berkshire Hathaway, '2002 Annual Report' (2002) 15, www.berkshirehathaway.com/2002ar/2002ar.pdf.

[53] 2013 ISDA Brochure (n 8) 2.

The term 'safe harbour' ordinarily refers to a clearly circumscribed liability shield, combining favourable treatment and legal certainty. Bankruptcy safe harbours for derivatives[54] are more ambitious: they amount to a wholesale exemption from national insolvency regimes. Industry materials frame the issue as a matter of contract enforcement, generally ignoring bankruptcy policy. By this logic, bankruptcy and resolution laws inject uncertainty in the contractual risk mitigation regime, where enforcement of closeout netting takes pride of place.

Netting is a commonplace risk mitigation tool used in payments, clearing and settlement systems. It reduces the total number of claims in a system, and therefore the risk of settlement failure, by matching the amounts owed by and to a party to produce a single debit or credit. Closeout netting in derivatives and certain other contexts is a contractually specified right and procedure, usually associated with default or the end of a trading relationship.

An event of default under the Master entitles the non-defaulting party to terminate the contract, close out all bilateral trades, net, and set off the bilateral obligations. Closeout netting is a function of the master agreement structure. By its terms, the ISDA Master forms 'a Single Agreement' together with its relationship-, instrument- and transaction-specific modules.[55] Bilateral confirmations for every kind of derivative instrument traded between the same counterparties incorporate the events of default, early termination, and closeout netting provisions in their ISDA Master, along with the terms of the Credit Support Annex dealing with collateral, margin, and guarantees, and any other terms relevant to that trade. All the confirmations together are treated as if they were one giant transaction between these parties. Parties may choose to net their exposure to each other periodically, usually when it involves same day, same currency transactions;[56] they must net across the entire portfolio if they choose to terminate early. The result is a single number – the net payment that one party owes to the other.

Failure to pay, repudiation, cross-default, and bankruptcy, are among the triggers for early termination and closeout netting under the Master. Parties may, and big financial firms generally do, use a version of the cross-default clause that turns affiliate or guarantor default into default by the party itself.[57] For a global financial conglomerate, cross-default could implicate multiple legal regimes, emergency funding from different governments, and additional contagion risks. Bankruptcy as an event of default under the Master covers inability to pay and

[54] In addition to swaps and other OTC derivatives contracts, the safe harbours also cover sale and repurchase (repo) agreements, commodities-based and securities-based financial contracts. See, eg, CW Mooney, Jr, 'The Bankruptcy Code's Safe Harbors for Settlement Payments and Securities Contracts: When Is Safe Too Safe?' (2014) 49 *Texas International Law Journal* 245, 246–52.

[55] 2002 ISDA Master s 1(c).

[56] See Charles (n 38).

[57] 2002 ISDA Master s 5(a)(vi).

the initiation of any judicial or administrative process to deal with firm failure, including corporate liquidation or reorganisation, bank resolution, receivership, and special resolution.

Here, contractual risk mitigation and bankruptcy policy come into direct conflict. Generally, contract conditions that make termination and self-help available in the event of a bankruptcy filing are 'ipso facto' clauses unenforceable on public policy grounds. The start of an insolvency proceeding stays all claims against the debtor, either automatically in bankruptcy, or by the exercise of administrative authority in a bank receivership. The stay halts all contract enforcement and debt collection efforts. Ipso facto clauses put the creditor on a fast track to recovery, ahead of other claims on the debtor's estate. They can incentivise asset stripping and frustrate a collective proceeding.

Bankruptcy safe harbours exempt derivatives and several other kinds of financial contracts, such as sale and repurchase agreements (repos), from the bar on enforcing ipso facto clauses. They allow the debtor's counterparties to ignore the stay, terminate the bilateral relationship, enforce closeout netting across all transactions with the debtor, and take advantage of robust contractual self-help remedies, including access to collateral and set-off.

Beyond frustrating the stay, safe harbours limit the ability of the trustee or administrator to choose which of the debtor's contracts to assume, and which to breach in pursuit of their mandate. This too reflects deference to the master structure. In a jurisdiction that does not enforce closeout netting, a trustee or administrator could assume all in-the-money trades for the estate and repudiate the rest, leaving counterparties with claims on the debtor to languish in line for distribution, with potential for knock-on effects on other trades in the market and the broader risk of disruption.

Lastly, safe harbours block the trustee or administrator from recapturing payments, asset transfers, and collateral pledges to derivatives counterparties made shortly before the bankruptcy filing. These are commonplace under the terms of Credit Support documentation, which would call for additional support (margin, collateral, guarantees) when the debtor's creditworthiness deteriorates. Without the safe harbours, counterparty protections of this sort could be reversed as fraudulent transfers or preferences in the name of inter-creditor equity.

In sum, the master agreement structure and standard derivatives contract terms come in direct conflict with key features of insolvency law, and stand in tension with bankruptcy policy objectives, such as value maximisation and inter-creditor equity. Separately, as I discuss later in this section, certain master agreement terms pose financial stability risks that had been under-appreciated before the crisis. Statutory safe harbours resolve all such conflicts and tensions against bankruptcy policy and in favour of contracts and private risk mitigation, citing one rationale: systemic risk.

ISDA's publications and public statements consistently cite the design, adaptation and expansion of safe harbours among its proudest achievements.

Early versions of bankruptcy safe harbours in the United States precede ISDA's founding. They date back to an effort to protect commodities dealers, a limited category of highly interconnected market intermediaries, from customer defaults and bankruptcies in the late 1970s and early 1980s.[58] Early legislation was narrowly tailored 'to contain the ripples' from customer insolvency in the commodities.[59]

Hypothetical financial stability arguments citing counterparty failure and market contagion justified serial expansion of statutory safe harbours in the 1980s and 1990s, now with ISDA's active involvement and a focus on contracts apart from intermediaries.[60] By the turn of the century, safe harbours had become a stock move to allay fears of financial market apocalypse. Politically salient bankruptcy reform in the United States in 2005 doubled down on the ratchet. Extending safe harbours to new financial contracts, market actors, and jurisdictions had become a financial stability imperative.[61] An implicit policy consensus held that that inter-creditor equity must yield when financial stability was at stake, and that financial stability was at stake whenever derivatives contracts were involved. On the eve of the crisis, safe harbours covered substantially all financial market participants and derivatives contracts.

Even if the systemic risk argument had been baseless at the dawn of the derivatives market in the 1980s, by 2001, it was becoming a self-fulfilling prophecy. The market reached \$100 trillion in outstanding notional (a 38% jump in three years), or \$3 trillion in gross market value, and showed no sign of slowing.[62] Exemptions from bankruptcy, banking, and financial market regulations had walled off an express lane where derivatives contracts were free to speed and multiply. More growth implied more systemic importance, which gave credence to more ambitious systemic risk arguments.

With ISDA's international expansion in the 1990s,[63] a web of safe harbours spanned the globe. Beyond lobbying national legislatures and securing legal opinions on the enforceability of closeout netting in dozens of jurisdictions,[64] ISDA filed briefs, published studies and commissioned several versions of a model law, the Model Netting Act, to promote universal and consistent enforcement

[58] See SL Schwarcz and O Sharon, 'The Bankruptcy-Law Safe Harbor for Derivatives: A Path-Dependence Analysis' (2014) 71 *Washington & Lee Law Rev* 1715.

[59] *Bankruptcy Reform Act of 1978: Hearings Before the Subcommittee on Improvements in Judicial Machinery of the Committee of the Judiciary*, 95th Cong 524 (1977).

[60] See, eg, Bliss and Kaufman (n 4); SJ Lubben, 'Chapter 11 and Systemic Risk' (2009) 82 *Temple Law Rev* 443, 447.

[61] See, eg, President's Working Group on Financial Markets, 'Hedge Funds, Leverage, and the Lessons of Long-Term Capital Management' (1999) 26–27, Appendix E (hereinafter, 'PWG LTCM Report').

[62] BIS, 'Triennial Central Bank Survey: Foreign Exchange and Derivatives Market Activity in 2001' (March 2002).

[63] See Flanagan (n 17).

[64] See, eg, S Gao, 'Legal Pluralism and Isomorphism in Global Financial Regulation: The Case of OTC Derivative Counterparty Risk Regulation in China' (2019) 51 *George Washington International Law Rev* 145.

of its netting terms. In Japan, it procured an elaborate legal opinion from the pre-eminent academic authority that closeout netting would be enforced under existing Japanese law, and almost simultaneously lobbied for the adoption of its model law.[65]

The 1980s and early 1990s were a precarious time for US banks, owing to interest rate shocks, domestic and international competition, structural realignment, and old-fashioned mismanagement, among other factors. Beginning in 1982, dozens of developing country governments came to the edge of default that would have erased the capital of the largest US banks.[66] In 1984, the near-failure and public rescue of Continental Illinois National Bank and Trust for fear of contagion fixed 'too-big-to-fail', phrase and phenomenon, in public consciousness.[67] The sprawling Bank of Credit and Commerce International managed to escape oversight by national authorities anywhere, and self-destruct with spillovers across dozens of countries (including an outpost in the United States) in 1991.[68] Meanwhile, thousands of small and medium-sized institutions chartered to finance residential real estate kept failing in what became the Savings and Loan (S&L) Crisis.[69] Financial stability was a priority for regulators and policy makers. Government response during this period included extended periods of regulatory forbearance and structural deregulation to help banks compete internationally and grow their way out of distress, alongside multiple rounds of tightening domestic and international supervision and FDIC resolution regimes.

A 1989 law preoccupied primarily with the worsening S&L mess also included a version of bankruptcy safe harbours for banks. It came with a twist that would set the global standard for managing systemic failure and the ISDA Resolution Stay Protocol 25 years later. The Financial Institutions Reform, Recovery, and Enforcement Act of 1989 (FIRREA) gave the FDIC the power to transfer 'certain market-sensitive contracts', including swaps and repos that used master agreement structures, to a solvent counterparty notwithstanding the safe harbours. The transfer power could only be used to move all contracts with a given counterparty together as a unit. FDIC would be shielded from liability for the transfer if it notified the counterparty within one business day of being appointed receiver.[70]

[65] A Riles, *Collateral Knowledge: Legal Reasoning in the Global Financial Markets* (Chicago, University of Chicago Press, 2011) 95–109.

[66] WR Cline, *International Debt Reexamined* (New York, Columbia University Press, 1995) 72–85.

[67] 'Continental Illinois: A Bank That Was Too Big to Fail' (*Federal Reserve History*, 15 May 2023), www.federalreservehistory.org/essays/continental-illinois.

[68] See R Bhala, *Foreign Bank Regulation After BCCI* (Carolina Academic Press, 1994).

[69] See A Moysich, 'The Savings and Loan Crisis and Its Relationship to Banking' in FDIC Division of Research and Statistics (ed), *History of the Eighties: Volume 1: An Examination of the Banking Crises of the 1980s and Early 1990s* (FDIC, 1997).

[70] Financial Institutions Reform, Recovery, and Enforcement Act of 1989, HR 1278, 101st Cong (1989) (hereinafter 'FIRREA') §§ 212 (e)(3)(C); (e)(8)(A)(i). See also AR Waldman, 'OTC Derivatives &

The design of safe harbours in FIRREA balanced two distinct kinds of financial stability concerns: anxiety about counterparty risk and potential for market contagion that had motivated safe harbours in corporate insolvency on the one hand, and, on the other hand, fear of bank runs. Later legislation in the United States refined and modified FIRREA's approach, clarifying the length and scope of the stay (one business day since 2005), and replacing market-sensitive contracts with a new category, Qualified Financial Contracts (QFCs), that included substantially all derivatives and repos. QFC transfer to a bridge bank or a solvent third party has since become standard US bank resolution practice.[71]

In retrospect, the financial stability consequences of safe harbours have always been ambiguous. Pre-crisis advocacy depicted contagion as a chain of counterparty defaults and settlement failures in trading markets.[72] Giving solvent counterparties the ability to terminate the relationship, net bilateral exposures, and access collateral was supposed to reduce the incidence and blunt the effect of default. If master agreements could not work without these features, if the derivatives markets were organised around master agreements, and if these markets were now systemic, then financial stability required safe harbours. A banking perspective on contagion would suggest a different picture, where permissive safe harbours encouraged runs.[73] Pre-emptive collateral calls and early terminations could deplete firm assets and trigger a cascade of imitative runs and asset fire sales, as well as counterparty failures.[74] Taking this view into account, safe harbours could either mitigate or fuel contagion; however, as late as 1999, financial policy mainstream deemed the second scenario unlikely.[75]

In 2008, attempts to wind down banks and non-bank financial institutions with large derivatives exposures prompted a rush for the exits in different parts of the world. As more risk propagation channels came into focus, the policy consensus on safe harbours began to shift.[76] But by then, altering a core part of the legal regime underlying a $600 trillion market had come to pose its own set of political, economic and financial stability risks.

Systemic Risk: Innovative Finance or the Dance into the Abyss' (1994) 43 *American University Law Review* 1023.

[71] See Congressional Research Service, 'Regulatory Reform 10 Years After the Financial Crisis: Systemic Risk Regulation' (2018) 25, https://crsreports.congress.gov/product/pdf/R/R45162/6.

[72] Council of Economic Advisers, 'Economic Report of the President' (2010) 173.

[73] See SJ Lubben, 'Repeal the Safe Harbors' (2010), 18 *American Bankruptcy Institute Law Review* 1.

[74] 'Economic Report of the President' (n 72) 171, 174.

[75] See, eg, 'PWG LTCM Report' (n 61) 26–27, Appendix E.

[76] 'Economic Report of the President' (n 72) 42; Bank of England, 'Financial Stability Report' (2008) 21–23, www.bankofengland.co.uk/-/media/boe/files/financial-stability-report/2008/october-2008.pdf. See, eg, MJ Roe, 'The Derivatives Market's Payment Priorities as Financial Crisis Accelerator' (2011) 63 *Stanford Law Rev* 539.

11.2.5. Look Back

This section began with a story of powerful financial regulators asking ISDA for a favour: to amend its contracts so that regulators would no longer feel compelled to bail out too-big-to-fail banks, which also happened to be ISDA's most influential voting members. The story was at odds with conventional views of government power in a top-down regulatory relationship, and of contracts as private law instruments, not instruments of bank regulation or structural reform. The role reversals made the episode feel slightly exotic, like a fortuitous encounter, a ride from a stranger – not the next step in a decades-long relationship.

I have also shown in this section that the structure of derivatives contracts and the derivatives ecosystem fostered significant autonomy for contract governance, and empowered ISDA as the contract production authority. Governments had ceded substantial authority to ISDA over its contract domain. However, contract governance did not imply disengagement between public and private actors in this case. To the contrary, making ISDA contracts work required sustained and intimate engagement to design, implement and maintain a web of privileges and exemptions around the world. As derivatives instruments and markets grew and changed, public authorities adapted their laws and regulations to the contracts. Progressive expansion of bankruptcy safe harbours went hand in hand with the growth of the industry and the expansion of contract governance domains. The ISDA Master already functioned as a powerful organisational and governance tool in a space ceded by public authorities. Here too, the standard-form contract appears to be a highly plausible, natural, and ultimately inevitable vehicle for special resolution reform. In the next section, I consider the special resolution problem that became the object of contract intervention.

11.3. ESCAPE ROUTE

This section shifts focus from the regulatory instrument to the regulatory target: resolution of systemically important global financial institutions. I begin with another public-private encounter and regulatory ride at the intersection of systemic bank failure and derivatives market regulation.

11.3.1. Here to Help

The autumn of 2008 was not ISDA's first systemic bank resolution rodeo, nor the first time that early termination clauses in its contracts had threatened a G7 financial system. On 22 October 1998, Japanese authorities took over Long-Term Credit Bank (LTCB), once the ninth largest in the world, and simultaneously acknowledged that the trickle of failures among small local real estate finance companies had gathered into a flood.[77] At the time of its nationalisation, LTCB had scores of counterparty relationships, with more than $450 billion in outstanding notional amount of derivatives trades presumed to be under the ISDA Master.[78] Depending on how the government went about closing the bank, it could trigger an avalanche of early terminations with grave consequences for the Yen, domestic interest rates, and the prospects of taming the crisis. A disruption of this magnitude in Japan in October of 1998 could reverberate around the world. The regional financial crisis that began in Thailand a year earlier had spread to Korea and Indonesia, and metastasised. Russia's government defaulted and devalued in August; in September, the Federal Reserve Bank of New York had to intervene to manage the collapse of Long-Term Credit Management (LTCM, no relation to LTCB), a hedge fund with balance sheet links to the largest Wall Street investment banks.[79]

Japanese authorities turned to ISDA, and ISDA saved the day. Officials coordinated the precise formulation and public announcement of their legal approach with ISDA: it would be a 'temporary nationalisation,' not 'special public administration', to avoid words that could trigger closeout netting under the Master. ISDA then issued a press release 'Welcoming Japan's Actions to Restore Soundness of its Financial System'.[80] ISDA's public statement spelled out the terms of its bargain, emphasising the government's commitment to pay all of LTCB's debts and keep performing all of LTCB's derivatives contracts, and in closing took some credit for coordinating with governments and central banks 'to help achieve these positive results'.[81]

Decades later, an eminent Japanese academic who had helped secure closeout netting enforcement in Japan described the LTCB episode as a model of creative collaboration between governments and market participants. At least as significant in retrospect, ISDA's involvement in LTCB's failure revealed a governance model that turned conventional top-down public regulation on its head and presaged things to come. The second-largest economy in the world could not risk closing a domestic bank unless and until it had obtained quasi-regulatory dispensation – an interpretive ruling or a no-action letter – from a 13-year-old

[77] G Tett, *Saving the Sun: How Wall Street Mavericks Shook Up Japan's Financial World and Made Billions* (Harper Business, 2004) xxii, 115 ('LTCB is ranked ninth largest in the world by asset size, with a market capitalization several times that of Citibank.'); H Nakaso, 'The Financial Crisis in Japan During the 1990s: How the Bank of Japan Responded and the Lessons Learnt' (2006) BIS Papers, Working Paper No 6, 12–13, www.bis.org/publ/bppdf/bispap06.htm.

[78] See Tett (n 77) 114–15; Nakaso (n 77) 12–13.

[79] See, eg, P Blustein, *The Chastening: Inside the Crisis that Rocked the Global Financial System and Humbled the IMF* (Public Affairs, 2001).

[80] ISDA, 'News Release: ISDA issues statement welcoming Japan's actions to restore soundness of its financial system' (22 October 1998), https://web.archive.org/web/19990825002625/http://www.isda.org/a51098_2.html; Nakaso (n 77) 12–13.

[81] Tett (n 77) 114–15; Nakaso (n 77) 12. See also 'International Swap Traders' Group Satisfied with Japan's Help for LTCB', *Jiji Press Ticker Service* (22 October 1998), Lexis, News & Business, Individual Publications, JiJi Press Ticker Service.

financial industry group. The power relationship was still hierarchical, but it was also dynamic, unstable and negotiable at critical turns. This governance model would be tested in future crises.

The failure of LTCB in Japan happened relatively early in the life of contemporary derivatives markets and of ISDA's governance infrastructure. Coordinating government statements and ISDA press releases was not a rule-making project, and had an air of improvised collaboration, an early regulatory ride. It all ended happily under the circumstances: there was no run. Ten years later, a far bigger shock threatened the relationship among governments, markets, and the largest market participants.

11.3.2. Loss Sharing and Border Crossing

Consider the following stylised hypothetical, also shown in Figure 11.2.

The law in Country A stays derivatives contract enforcement for one business day in judicial or administrative proceedings that govern bank failure or the failure of a systemically important financial institution. The law in Country B does not. Both countries have robust statutory safe harbours for derivatives in bankruptcy and resolution.

At Time 1, a systemically important financial institution in Country A consists of a parent holding company and many subsidiaries, two of which – A-Bank and A-Broker – appear in Figure 11.2. A-Bank has a subsidiary, AB-Bank, located in Country B, part of the conglomerate's vast network of overseas operations.

A similarly organised systemically important institution in Country B includes a commercial bank and an asset manager, Bud Capital Management, among the many subsidiaries of its parent holding company.

Both holding companies and A-Bank guarantee their subsidiaries' derivatives contracts.

At Time 2, A-Broker fails in Country A, which leads to the following series of events:

- Country A authorities use parent holding company funds to meet A-Broker's liabilities, whereupon the parent company files for bankruptcy protection.
- The parent company's bankruptcy is an event of default, and triggers closeout netting, under Bud's Master agreement with AB-Bank.
- AB-Bank fails. If it were in Country A, the derivatives claims against it would be frozen for a day to give resolution authorities time to transfer them to a solvent counterparty.
- Country B gives full effect to safe harbours for derivatives, and does not recognise stays imposed by other countries' authorities. Bud can enforce its claim against AB-Bank and its assets immediately, and does just that, including a call on A-Bank's guarantee.

- Bud ultimately recovers in full, but triggers a run on A-Bank. Country A government now must choose between using public funds to stem the run, or risk contagion and use public funds to absorb the cost of another failure.

In an alternative scenario where Bud does not have prompt access to AB-Bank's assets and cannot enforce A-Bank's guarantee, it might default on its bank debt in Country B. The risks and costs shift to the government of Country B.

Figure 11.2 Contract Contagion: A Hypothetical Failure Scenario

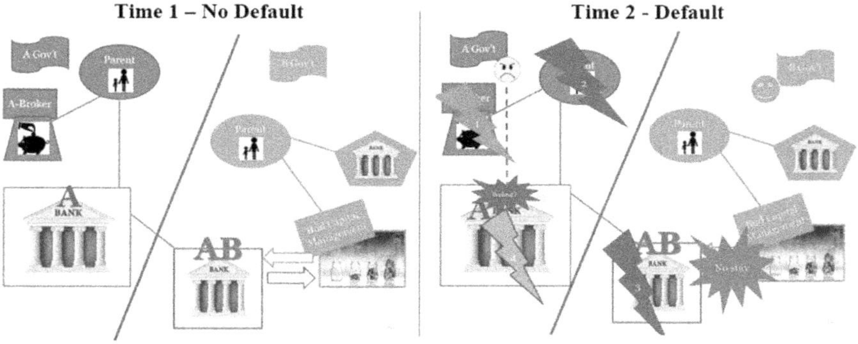

The hypothetical scenario highlights the point made in the introduction to this chapter: bargaining over contractual netting and national safe harbours could, and for global banks certainly would, entail loss sharing among national governments. The size and reach of the derivatives markets makes the prospect of inter-state conflicts over ex post loss allocation highly likely, which would make bargaining over safe harbours in special resolution unusually challenging. Governments' public pledge to end bailouts complicates matters: it is awkward to bargain over contingent loss allocation and at the same time tell the public that there can be no losses.

National borders mark the presumptive outer perimeter of sovereign authority. When financial market participants cross borders, they exchange a measure of legal certainty for regulatory arbitrage opportunities. Power and resource disparities, substantive differences among national legal regimes, and muddled and fragmented authorities foster regulatory gaps and conflicts.[82] These create powerful incentives for actors like Bud, the asset manager with safe harboured contracts in the earlier hypothetical. Bud's recovery came at the expense of A-Bank and the residents of Country A. Without robust inter-state coordination,

[82] See, eg, A Gelpern, 'Wal-Mart Bank in Mexico: Money to the Masses and the Home-Host Hole' (2006–07) 39 *Connecticut Law Rev* 1513.

cross-border arbitrage of the safe harbours threatened to undermine national resolution regimes. At the same time, the economic and political legacy of the safe harbours threatened to put coordination out of reach.[83] Coordination failure was the predicate for the bank regulators' turn to ISDA.[84]

Traditionally, inter-state coordination is the work of public international law. Nonetheless, private ordering and hybrid governance forms are ubiquitous in international finance.[85] Rules and norms generated by actors such as stock exchanges, clearing banks and industry groups have sometimes helped manage conflicts and fill gaps in the regulatory fabric. Late twentieth century developments – financialisation, mobile capital, jumbled power hierarchies, and a string of financial crises – made gaps and conflicts more acute and more salient. New financial crises led to calls for a new architecture, new forms of coordination that fused the instruments of public international and administrative law[86] and private ordering.[87]

In the early 2000s, international financial regulation researchers observed the rise of non-binding soft law and network governance[88] and the waning importance of 'hard' public international law in day-to-day governance of the global financial system.[89] The crisis of 2007–2009 did not compromise international soft law theory and practice to the degree it had tainted informal and collaborative governance in national regulation,[90] partly for want of a viable alternative.[91]

[83] See, eg, K Pistor, 'Transnational Regulatory Regimes in Finance: A Comparative Analysis of their (Dis-) Integrative Effects' in L Bruszt and GA McDermott (eds), *Level the Playing Field: Transnational Regulatory Integration and Development* (Oxford, Oxford University Press, 2014).

[84] See 'Letter from the Bank of England et al' (n 7).

[85] See, eg, G Shaffer and TC Halliday (eds), *Transnational Legal Orders* (Cambridge, Cambridge University Press 2023), G Teubner, 'Global Bukowina: Legal Pluralism in the World Society' in G Teubner (ed), *Global Law without a State* (Brookfield, 1997); F Cafaggi, 'New Foundations of Transnational Private Regulation' (2011) 38 *Journal of Law & Society* 20; KW Abbot and D Snidal, 'Strengthening International Regulation through Transnational New Governance: Overcoming the Orchestration Deficit' (2009) 42 *Vanderbilt Journal of Transitional Law* 501; C Bradley, 'Private International Law-Making for the Financial Markets' (2005) 1 *Fordham International Law Journal* 126.

[86] See, eg, B Kingsbury, N Krisch and RB Stewart, 'The Emergence of Global Administrative Law' (2005) 68 *Law & Contemporary Problems* 15.

[87] See, eg, Teubner (n 85).

[88] Among the foundational contributions on disaggregated public authority and the role of networks (not specific to finance) is AM Slaughter's *A New World Order* (Princeton University Press, 2004).

[89] Arguments against treaties highlight prohibitive transaction costs, vague outputs and rigid commitments that cannot keep pace with the markets, and draw a contrast with the dynamism, flexibility and precision of non-binding soft law instruments. See, eg, C Brummer, 'Why Soft Law Dominates International Finance – And Not Trade' (2010) 13 *Journal of International Economic Law* 623. Customary international law (state practice followed out of a sense of legal obligation) often takes longer to emerge, takes the form of relatively broad principles, and remains open to contestation in scope and substance. See, eg, D Zaring, *The Globalized Governance of Finance* (Cambridge University Press, 2020) 122–23.

[90] See, eg, C Ford, 'New Governance in the Teeth of Human Frailty: Lessons from Financial Regulation' (2010) 57 *Wisconsin Law Rev* 441.

[91] DK Tarullo, 'Rules, Discretion, and Authority in International Financial Reform,' (2001) 4 *Journal of International Economic Law* 613, 681.

Criticised for lack of accountability, representation and substantive ambition,[92] international networks had subject matter expertise, experience with inter-state coordination, and the immense advantage of being there.

Crisis management and the sprawling post-crisis reform programme re-invigorated, expanded and 'hardened' elements of the coordination apparatus; it also increased the domestic political salience of international financial regulation in major financial centres.[93] Scholars of international financial regulation have depicted an emerging post-crisis hierarchy of (mostly) state actors. At the top of the pyramid are politicians meeting as the Group of Twenty (G20), setting policy direction for the technocrats, such as the no-bailout commitment. Freshly endowed with legal personality, the Financial Stability Board (FSB) convenes governments, international organisations, and sectoral standard setters like the Basel Committee on Banking Supervision (BCBS). It mediates the policy message to produce cross-sectoral guidance on topics such as central clearing and special resolution. The standard setters may further elaborate tasks for banking, securities, or insurance regulators, and use their networks to shepherd domestic adoption and implementation. Feedback from this process goes through the FSB into the next round of political decisions.

The work of industry groups like ISDA is formally outside the pyramid. The actions of national and FSB officials lobbying ISDA and piggybacking on its contract infrastructure are harder to place. The problem is one of characterising the relationship between state-made and non-state-made law.[94] The 'orchestration deficit'[95] or 'lack of a unifying vertical axis'[96] of authority over private law-making across national borders renders the relative position of ISDA contracts, FSB pronouncements, and the decisions of municipal courts and national regulators ambiguous and unstable, up for negotiation at every turn.

[92] See, eg, PH Verdier, 'The Political Economy of International Financial Regulation' (2013) 88 *Indiana Law Journal* 1405, 1406, 1435–36. The common counter to the accountability argument is that international soft law takes effect as domestic hard law. Zaring calls this '[t]he radically dualist nature of international financial regulation' (n 89) 125. For an example from bank regulation, see, eg, MS Barr and GP Miller, 'Global Administrative Law: The View from Basel' (2006) 17 *European Journal of International Law* 15.

[93] E Helleiner and S Pagliari, 'Crisis and Reform of International Regulation' and 'The End of Self-Regulation: Hedge Funds and Derivatives in Global Financial Governance' in E Helleiner, S Pagliari and H Zimmermann (eds), *Global Finance in Crisis: The Politics of International Regulatory Change* (Routledge, 2010) 1, 6, 74, 89.

[94] I use the term 'law' here as a shorthand for effectively binding rules, standards, norms and practices regardless of their provenance. Whether non-state law is properly called 'law' is beyond the scope of my project. See, eg, Teubner (n 85); R Michaels, 'The Re-*State*-Ment of the Non-State Law: The State, Choice of Law, and the Challenge from Global Legal Pluralism' (2005) 51 *Wayne Law Review* 1210.

[95] eg KW Abbott and D Snidal, 'Strengthening International Regulation Through Transnational New Governance: Overcoming the Orchestration Deficit' (2009) 42 *Vanderbilt Law Review* 501.

[96] DV Snyder 'Molecular Federalism and the Structures of Private Lawmaking' (2007) 14 *Indiana Journal of Global Legal Studies* 419, 439.

Special resolution regimes were a case in point. Developing consensus norms to guide the resolution of megabanks was among the FSB's early high-profile tasks. The FSB published 'Key Attributes of Effective Resolution Regimes for Financial Institutions' in 2011, and reissued them in 2014 with additional guidance for non-bank financial institutions. Both versions of the document opened with the link between effective resolution and ending bailouts:

> [Key Attributes] implementation should allow authorities to resolve financial institutions in an orderly manner without taxpayer exposure to loss from solvency support, while maintaining continuity of their vital economic functions.[97]

The FSB attributes included a stay-and-transfer tool for derivatives and other safe harboured financial contracts, signalling its importance for ending too-big-to-fail.[98] However, efforts to harmonise domestic laws in line with FSB recommendations showed little progress by 2013. The board's report to the G20 in September of that year revealed persistent concerns with early termination, and the challenge of getting countries to recognise one another's special resolution measures, including a stay. The report suggested that G20 governments could 'encourage ISDA and other industry bodies to review contract provisions to prevent large-scale early termination of financial contracts', and proposed to develop 'contractual or statutory' solutions to the problem by the end of 2014.[99] Responding to the FSB report, the G20 recommitted to fix their laws and remove obstacles to cross-border resolution, a less-than-fully-credible commitment under the circumstances.[100]

Why might the FSB expect ISDA to succeed where governments had failed? Contract standardisation starts with an advantage over other forms of law-making: states' commitment to contract enforcement, itself grounded in treaties and practice.[101] This robust and open-ended commitment gives contract form extraordinary political power[102] and, in rare cases, the capacity to upend the authority hierarchy.[103] ISDA spent decades working with regulators to cultivate an autonomous transnational space for contract governance, my focus in the last subsection, and to make the Master reach its maximum governance potential.

[97] Financial Stability Board (FSB), *Key Attributes of Effective Resolution Regimes of Financial Institutions* (2014) 1, www.fsb.org/wp-content/uploads/r_141015.pdf.

[98] Financial Stability Board (FSB), *Key Attributes of Effective Resolution Regimes of Financial Institutions* (2014) 10 [s 4.3], www.fsb.org/wp-content/uploads/r_111104cc.pdf.

[99] Financial Stability Board (FSB), *Progress and Next Steps Towards Ending 'Too-Big-To-Fail' (TBTF)*, Report of the Financial Stability Board to the G-20 (2 September 2013).

[100] G20 Leaders, *Declaration*, St Petersburg Summit (6 September 2013) 68.

[101] See Pistor (n 9).

[102] P Zumbansen, 'The Law of Society: Governance through Contract' (2007) 14 *Indiana Journal of Global Legal Studies* 191, 193.

[103] See Snyder (n 96).

The functional orientation and geographically 'boundless' character of ISDA's private law-making bolster its standardisation capacity.[104] Its internal coordination challenge is manageable, evident in the way it has navigated tensions between dealers and other stakeholders. Convergence of member interests is a by-product of ISDA's contract function:[105] securing technically sound drafting, uniform adoption, consistent interpretation, enforcement in all parts and states of the world, and the like. Externally, the same factors and ISDA's continuous engagement with public authorities to define and expand the scope for contract governance contribute to its market power. Within and beyond the derivatives ecosystem, market-dominant boilerplate functions as regulation, defining and applying rules of the road in a given industry.[106] Standardisation as such can also become a form of risk management, incorporated by reference in functional (bank, securities) regulation.[107]

For constituents of 'a dominant private regime … exit is not a real possibility'.[108] When a systemically important financial market is organised around an original contract design and boilerplate terms produced by a single actor, exit may not be an option for governments and private market participants alike. 'Asymmetric interdependencies' set in: '[A]ll the actors in a network, including the state, are dependent on each other, but rarely in a fully symmetrical way.'[109]

This subsection began by framing cross-border resolution of financial conglomerates as a public-private and inter-state distribution problem. Inter-state coordination to end bailouts of too-big-to-fail banks has always been an exceptionally difficult challenge for governments that remained liable for the social costs of their failure. The interaction between special resolution regimes and contract governance in the global derivatives ecosystem made the challenge infinitely harder. Decades of legislative activity, regulatory practice, and institutional design in the name of legal certainty for derivatives contracts, all premised on a specific view of systemic risk, ceded public authority over critical parts of the global financial system. Individual governments had few or no credible tools to mitigate financial stability risks from early termination and closeout netting in systemic cross-border resolution – but the distribution stakes created barriers to inter-state coordination.

[104] ibid 433, 442. ('Private codifications may achieve a level of adherence and uniformity that is not possible when international coordination of governments proves infeasible. Hence, private or quasi-private efforts at unification can, if they achieve enough adherents, move toward an arguably necessary uniformity that has been hampered by state (in)action.')

[105] M Olson, *The Logic of Collective Action* (Harvard University Press, 1971) 30–31, 132–34.

[106] C Bradley, 'Private International Law-Making for Financial Markets' (2005) 29 *Fordham International Law Journal* 127, 165 and 168.

[107] ibid.

[108] Snyder (n 96) 442.

[109] LM Salamon, 'The New Governance and the Tools of Public Action: An Introduction' (2001) 28 *Fordham Urban Law Journal* 1611, 1631.

This may help explain why leading financial regulators felt compelled to ask ISDA for help, but not why ISDA agreed to turn its protocol tool and its contracts more broadly into a bailout reform vehicle. Regulators' known inability to coordinate seems at odds with the view that ISDA issued its protocol under threat of stricter regulation. I consider the question of ISDA's cooperation next.

11.3.3. Are We There Yet?

Big banks, all major derivatives dealers, resisted the FSB's stay-and-transfer proposals as late as the summer of 2013, reportedly citing standard concerns about legal certainty in contentious meetings with regulators.[110] Moreover, it appears that neither ISDA nor the FSB were enamoured of using contract amendments to curtail early termination, closeout netting, and cross-default rights.[111]

In October of 2013, then US Federal Reserve Governor Daniel K Tarullo singled out early termination and closeout netting practices under standard-form derivatives contracts for fuelling the risk of contagious runs in cross-border resolution. On the heels of the FSB progress report and the G20 St Petersburg summit statement in September, the speech reinforced the message that ISDA contracts stood in the way of ending megabank bailouts. There were two ways to solve the problem. First, governments could harmonise their laws to allow a brief stay on early termination, or at least to recognise stays imposed by other governments as part of special resolution. Second, derivatives traders could change their contracts.[112]

Tarullo's scepticism about the first option was noteworthy because it extended beyond the stalled process of international coordination, and appeared to signal a shift away from the emphasis on national legislation and regulation in the FSB and G20 statements. His remarks suggested that harmonisation could be the wrong fix, and that treaties were worse: 'it may be difficult to get such legal changes on roughly comparable terms in all relevant jurisdictions, much less to conclude a binding international agreement along those lines.'[113] Public law tools were not merely slow; they were not fit for purpose. This left contract amendments as the only plausible option, with national regulation in a backup role:

> A second approach, currently under consideration by regulators, would be to seek modifications to standard contractual cross-default, netting, and related practices. This approach would use contractual measures to achieve the same end of having

[110] KOD Okwor, 'Interactions Between ISDA and the Federal Reserve on ISDA Protocol Reforms' (2017), https://scholar.harvard.edu/files/kenneth-okwor/files/interactions_between_isda_and_the_federal_reserve_on_isda_protocol_reforms.pdf.

[111] See, eg, ISDA, *Resolution Protocol: Staying Power?* (Media Comment, 17 November 2014), www.isda.org/2014/11/17/resolution-protocol-staying-power/.

[112] Tarullo (n 2) 13.

[113] ibid.

> these arrangements effectively governed by resolution decisions in home countries. Of course, even if agreement were reached among regulators, in consultation with relevant industry associations, and effective steps were taken to implement that agreement, it could take some time for the new terms to be widely adopted in relevant markets. But a regulatory timeline could be set to speed up the process. This approach may be the most promising for tackling this vexing problem.[114]

The speech did not mention ISDA, nor any of the other associations by name, nor did it indicate who would draft the contracts and how. It did offer a high-level sketch of the regulatory approach in which state actors agree on substantive contract changes to advance their policy goals, persuade 'relevant industry associations' to amend industry standard terms, and 'effective steps [are] taken' to assimilate the regulators' bargain in market participants' contracts. This could take years, but would still be faster and more effective than treaties or harmonised laws. Conventional regulation and supervision could help expedite adoption. Two weeks later, regulators from Germany, Switzerland, the UK and the US sent the letter discussed at the start of this chapter, pressing ISDA to change its contracts.[115]

Contract reform took off in 2014. An FSB consultative document published in September of that year revealed that ISDA had produced a protocol to amend the Master to promote recognition of special resolution measures across national borders and stay early termination, that ISDA had consulted with the FSB and the home regulators of systemic institutions in drafting it, and that this protocol could be adapted for repos and other safe-harboured financial contracts. The FSB also opined that contract amendments were at best an interim fix: '[U]ntil comprehensive statutory regimes have been adopted in all relevant jurisdictions, contractual arrangements, if properly crafted and widely adopted, offer a workable interim solution.'[116] The consultative document spelled out elements of statutory and contractual approaches, for implementation by the end of 2015.

ISDA published the Resolution Stay Protocol on 11 October 2014, committing adherents to abide by resolution stays in other jurisdictions and to override affiliate cross-defaults triggered by special resolution.[117] Eighteen major derivatives dealers, all global systemically important banks, immediately pledged to sign on, touting their leadership in the fight against too-big-to-fail. The Federal Reserve and the FDIC welcomed the protocol with a press release.[118]

[114] ibid 14.

[115] 'Letter from the Bank of England et al' (n 7).

[116] Financial Stability Board (FSB), *Cross-Border Recognition of Resolution Actions: Consultative Document* (29 September 2014) 1, 11.

[117] ISDA, *Major Banks Agree to Sign Resolution Stay Protocol* (11 October 2014), www.isda.org/2014/10/11/major-banks-agree-to-sign-isda-resolution-stay-protocol/.

[118] Board of Governors of the Federal Reserve System & Federal Deposit Insurance Corporation, *Federal Reserve Board and FDIC welcome ISDA announcement* (11 October 2014), www.federalreserve.gov/newsevents/pressreleases/bcreg20141011a.htm.

The successful protocol launch sent some long-simmering tensions bubbling into the open. Some buy-side investors (end users in ISDA parlance) complained in the press that they had been excluded from the drafting process; however, a more fundamental criticism went to the contractual approach itself, and ISDA's participation in it.[119] ISDA's response, a 'media comment', stressed that the protocol had been developed at the regulators' request, that it had repeatedly called for governments to adopt legislation (which the FSB viewed as a longer-term proposition), and that ISDA had secured commitments from the authorities to issue regulations that would facilitate broad-based adherence. For their part, asset managers claimed that, as fiduciaries, they could not sign away their clients' early termination rights – and ISDA agreed. National laws or regulations would have to make their adherence mandatory, for instance, by barring regulated dealers from trading with counterparties that did not commit to recognise a stay imposed under special resolution laws in other jurisdictions. Another ISDA protocol would reflect their particular constraints. If governments failed to take measures to ensure broad-based adherence, the 18 banks that joined ISDA's 2014 protocol had the right to quit in late 2015.[120]

In late 2015, ISDA issued the 2015 Universal Resolution Stay Protocol, adapting its earlier version for use with a broader range of financial contracts documented under master agreements, but otherwise making no substantive changes.[121] Over 100 firms adhered to the 2014 protocol before it closed; nearly 400 adhered to its 2015 successor.[122]

Public law-making again took longer and stopped short of the stated goal. French, German, Japanese, Swiss, UK and US authorities adopted the promised stay regulations between 2015 and 2017; most would not go into effect for a year or more. Other jurisdictions were further behind.[123] International Monetary Fund (IMF) staff observed in early 2020 that only a handful of countries had enacted legislation to deal with the contract problem and broader recognition challenges in cross-border resolution, and implied that most had stopped trying. The authors concluded that '[t]he establishment of adequate statutory processes for recognition and support appears to be a long-term goal'.[124]

[119] See ISDA (n 111). ('Very early on, the buy side raised concerns about any change to derivatives contracts … They argued they have a fiduciary duty to their clients that prevents them from voluntarily signing away advantageous contractual rights. And they're right.')

[120] ibid.

[121] ICMA, *Resolution Stays*, www.icmagroup.org/market-practice-and-regulatory-policy/repo-and-collateral-markets/legal-documentation/resolution-stays/.

[122] ISDA, *ISDA 2015 Universal Resolution Stay Protocol: List of Adhering Parties* (last updated 18 October 2021), www.isda.org/protocol/isda-2015-universal-resolution-stay-protocol/adhering-parties (lists 399 adhering parties).

[123] ISDA, *ISDA Resolution Stay Matrix* (as of 29 July 2019), www.isda.org/a/K16gE/ISDA-Resolution-Stay-Matrix-7.29.2019.pdf.

[124] R Leckow and E Emre, 'Cross-Border Resolution: Progress and Challenges in Cross-Border Enforcement' in IMF Legal Dept, *Law & Financial Stability* (21 January 2020) 69, 77, https://doi.org/10.5089/9781513523002.071.

Meanwhile, ISDA launched a new instrument, the Jurisdictional Modular Protocols (JMP) starting in 2016, designed to conform to the new stay regulations in each jurisdiction that adopted them. The United States issued its version in 2017, giving market participants the option of signing on to an ISDA stay protocol or separately committing to recognise a stay imposed by another jurisdiction; ISDA's US JMP was published in 2018.[125] The JMP instrument reflected the concerns of asset managers and others that had rejected the 2014 and 2015 'universal' stay protocols. Non-bank firms, and even individuals that had no ISDA Master in place, now had a protocol they could live by.[126]

What changed to spur the contract activity? At least one author credits coordinated 'moral suasion' by the US Federal Reserve and the FDIC, working with the FSB and others to present a united front to the industry and elicit collaboration.[127] Many researchers surmise that ISDA and its members chose tactical retreat under threat of 'more aggressive regulatory strategies' to maintain its governance prerogatives in global finance.[128] Both explanations appear to be incomplete given the salience of coordination problems among regulators, and the well-understood political challenges of curbing the safe harbours.

It is hard to pinpoint a plausible threat in late 2013. Derivatives market participants might have felt 'under the gun',[129] with pressure to fix the early termination problem coming from different directions. Between 2009 and 2014, governments, central banks, and institutions such as the IMF, the Basel Committee and the FSB had published research highlighting the financial stability risks from early termination. National bank supervisors were getting more serious: in late 2013, the US authorities told 11 big banks that their Dodd-Frank Act resolution plans had been unduly optimistic about the likelihood of early termination and its consequences.[130] Yet, the crux of the problem was in cross-border dynamics, not in any single jurisdiction, however large and powerful, with incentives to run.

From the perspective of derivatives regulation, governments might have threatened to force more OTC contracts onto central clearing platforms. However, the shift to central clearing at scale had been a foregone conclusion before ISDA published its first Resolution Stay Protocol, endorsed by the G20 in 2009, enacted in the Dodd-Frank Act, and monitored by the FSB.[131]

[125] *Memorandum from Governor Jerome Powell to the Board of Governors of the Federal Reserve System* (24 August 2017), www.federalreserve.gov/aboutthefed/boardmeetings/files/qfc-board-memo-20170901.pdf; ISDA, *U.S. Resolution Stay Protocol* (2018), www.isda.org/protocol/isda-2018-us-resolution-stay-protocol/.

[126] ISDA, 'Resolution Stay Jurisdictional Modular Protocol: Frequently Asked Questions' (last updated February 2022).

[127] See Okwor (n 110).

[128] Pistor (n 9) 152.

[129] See Jones (n 11).

[130] Okwor (n 110) 5.

[131] It would be bad policy to send a contract to a clearinghouse solely for the purpose of extracting concessions in cross-border resolution. The link between megabank resolution and central clearing

A large majority of interest rate swaps and a smaller majority of credit derivatives worldwide were centrally cleared in 2023.[132] The figures were lower for the derivatives activity of federally chartered US banks: central clearing accounted for less than half of their interest rate swaps, less than a third of their credit derivatives, less than a quarter of their equity derivatives, and three per cent of their foreign exchange derivatives.[133] Moreover, while maximum central clearing might be desirable, the relationship with cross-border banks in special resolution regimes is not obvious.

Two other possible motives for ISDA's cooperation speak to the political economy of the Protocol episode. First, after spending the better part of its existence tending to the safe harbours for closeout netting, ISDA could not afford to lose custody of the project. This subsection has illustrated how a seemingly small matter of introducing a short stay could turn into a multi-year, multi-jurisdictional, technically complex work stream. The downside risk of losing control was high. On the other hand, cooperation could generate goodwill and good publicity at a fraught time.[134] Letting regulators borrow its contracts, with the additional twist of adapting them for repo and other short-term funding markets, could expand the empire and enhance ISDA's position with governments and market participants alike.

Second, it is plausible that, while neither governments nor market actors saw any of the stay protocols as a first-best option, neither could afford to walk away. Governments were not willing to risk instability had ISDA refused to go along with their request. For their part, ISDA and its constituents could not afford to let national regulators pull in different directions, threatening to fragment and disrupt their markets. Here a stay protocol is more than a convenience; it is a forward-looking commitment device and a long-term investment in 'certainty'.

I conclude the chapter next with implications of the episode for financial reform and regulation.

of derivatives is indirect. For as long as a substantial portion of OTC derivatives contracts remains uncleared and documented under the ISDA Master, the risk of disruptive termination remains unless the parties adhere to the relevant ISDA Protocol. Moreover, to the extent cleared contracts are not documented under an ISDA Master and remain outside the protocols, they could pose a distinct residual risk. US regulations do not require cleared derivatives to comply with an ISDA resolution stay protocol, although regulators acknowledge that they can pose some of the risks associated with uncleared contracts. Federal Reserve System, *Final Rule: Restrictions on Qualified Financial Contracts of Systemically Important U.S. Banking Organizations and the U.S. Operations of Systemically Important Foreign Banking Organizations*; *Revisions to the Definition of Qualifying Master Netting Agreement and Related Definitions* (12 September 2017) 82 Federal Register 42882, 42897.

[132] See BIS (n 51).

[133] Most of the uncleared derivatives are concentrated among a handful of large dealer banks (JPMorgan Chase, Goldman Sachs, Citibank, Bank of America, and Wells Fargo). Office of the Comptroller of the Currency, *Quarterly Report on Bank Trading and Derivatives Activities: Third Quarter 2023* (December 2023) 45, www.occ.gov/publications-and-resources/publications/quarterly-report-on-bank-trading-and-derivatives-activities/files/pub-derivatives-quarterly-qtr3-2023.pdf.

[134] See 2013 ISDA Brochure (n 8).

11.4. WHERE TO?

JOE NOCERA, New York Times: This is the kind of disaster, like the aftermath of the Great Depression and the crash of '29, that causes people to say, 'There's something fundamentally wrong here. There's something fundamentally broken. And we can't fix it with a new agency, or you know, just a piecemeal approach. We have to kind of tear down the structure and start all over.'

NARRATOR: But whatever happens, the era that propelled John Thain, Ken Lewis and Hank Paulson to the top of the financial world is over.

ELIZABETH WARREN, Chair, Congressional Oversight Panel: The party's over. The financial institutions are down for the count. This is one of those pivot points in American history. That old economy, that old way of looking at things, that old way of putting on a party – it's over. It's over.

'Breaking the Bank', *PBS Frontline* (June 2009)[135]

The closing frames of a 2009 public television documentary capture the zeitgeist: a crisis that disgraced the markets and their guardians, a call to tear down the old and start over. Crisis aftermath bore abundant fruit: higher bank capital, new walls and buffers to contain risky activities, central clearing and reporting mandates, new agencies to oversee financial stability and consumer finance, and more.[136] Yet, taken together, post-crisis reforms did not add up to a New Deal-scale shift in the relationship between governments and markets. After a period of ferment, revolution and reinvention, it reverted to fiddling with dials, a style of regulation preoccupied with finessing the finer points of design and wary of structural change.

Did the technical orientation of this regulatory settlement reveal a failure of imagination, skill or political will? Alternatively, were the calls for radical change misguided, and New Deal comparisons overdone in retrospect? After wading through the minutiae of financial contracts and regulatory fine-tuning apparently in lieu of radical reform, it is worth asking whether (and how) the practice of harnessing private contracts to advance public policy objectives could promote or limit the scope for change after a major systemic shock.

Considering the various manifestations of what this chapter describes as the regulatory ride fallacy suggests an answer. The assumption of separate domains, public and private, whose inhabitants transact at arm's length and share an occasional ride in an emergency, informs both public expectations and

[135] 'Transcript: Breaking the Bank' (*PBS Frontline*, 16 June 2009), www.pbs.org/wgbh/pages/frontline/breakingthebank/etc/script.html.

[136] See generally Basel Committee on Banking Supervision, *High-Level Summary of Basel III Reforms* (2017); Dodd-Frank Wall Street Reform and Consumer Protection Act, HR 4173, 111th Cong, §§ 111, 152, 619, 723, 1011 (2010) (further limiting bank activities and affiliations (the Volcker Rule), creating the Consumer Financial Protection Bureau (CFPB), the Financial Stability Oversight Council (FSOC) and the Office of Financial Research (OFR)) (hereinafter, 'Dodd-Frank Act'); Congressional Research Service, 'The Dodd-Frank Wall Street Reform and Consumer Protection Act: Title VII, Derivatives' (6 November 2012).

government actions. It belies the reality of constant, intimate and painstaking negotiations that make up the fabric of financial regulation and crisis response.

From November 2008, official communiques had promised that gamblers would pay for their gambles,[137] but it was all bluster without a credible way to contain externalities from systemic failure. Voters and financial market participants had to be convinced that failure, liquidation, and market exit could happen to anyone, even to the largest megabanks. The crisis put a spotlight on contagion and early termination risks from bankruptcy safe harbours, but the analysis was not new.[138] In the bank resolution context, stay-and-transfer tools had been around for decades, well known to national regulators as a way to limit collateral damage from early termination and closeout netting. What governments needed was a vehicle to import the tool into newer parts of the financial architecture, to secure cross-border recognition of special resolution regimes. They chose their reform target as their vehicle: derivatives contracts they did not write and did not control, produced by an industry group where too-big-to-fail dealer banks held sway.[139]

Years earlier, governments had changed their laws to erect safe harbours around financial industry boilerplate. Now the same governments asked the industry to change its boilerplate to accommodate their new resolution laws.

The difference in scale between the policy goal and the policy fix follows the pattern highlighted earlier. Regulators sought to prevent financial crises, contain externalities from the failure of global financial firms, and distribute the costs of failure among public and private stakeholders in different jurisdictions. Their prospects hinged on working a day's pause into obscure private legalese.[140] Big political problems called for surgical solutions. Here as elsewhere in financial regulation, public and private domains must remain at arm's length; intervention must not reach beyond the minimum necessary to correct market failure. Finger in the dyke, placed with precision, could save the world.[141]

The idea of marshalling boilerplate as a bulwark against bailouts was inspired, puzzling, and potentially disturbing: inspired because collaboration between public and private actors looked elegant, thorough, and produced tangible results; puzzling because it upended traditional regulatory hierarchies. It was disturbing because the world's most powerful, most capable governments had little choice but to rely on ISDA contracts to fulfil their mandate to safeguard financial stability and deliver on their no-bailout pledge to their citizens. They had given up operational control over large swathes of the international financial

[137] See, eg, G20, *Communiqué: Meeting of the Finance Ministers and Central Bank Governors, United Kingdom* (7 November 2009).

[138] See, eg, S Claessens and KJ Forbes (eds), *International Financial Contagion* (Springer, 2001).

[139] Tarullo (n 2) 14.

[140] C Hill, 'Why Contracts are written in legalese' (2001) 77 *Chicago-Kent Law Review* 59, 60.

[141] Compare ST Omarova, 'Technology v. Technocracy: Fintech as A Regulatory Challenge' 6 *Journal of Financial Regulation* 75.

architecture, let domestic and international public law tools fall into disuse, but failed to develop adequate alternatives. For their part, ISDA, its members, and its counterparts representing other parts of the financial system could not afford to see their markets fragment from failures of inter-state coordination. ISDA's contract and market structure were already well adapted to policy work, with decades of regulation and regulatory coordination practice. They would have to take on more public functions.

Safe harbours for early termination and closeout netting began in the 1970s as a surgical intervention in bankruptcy policy in pursuit of a discrete financial stability objective: shielding commodities dealers from settlement failure. Dealers' counterparties were firms that were not and could not be systemic at the time. Continuous painstaking engagement with governments around the world transformed the safe harbours into a central pillar and a symbol of autonomy in the $700 trillion contract domain that is the global derivatives market. At this stage, even surgical intervention to limit the safe harbours reads as a threat to contract governance and global financial stability.

As a purely domestic policy matter, this could get awkward for public officials. The only thing harder would be to pause contract enforcement at home to help with systemic resolution abroad – a transfer from fellow citizens to foreigners. A treaty to harmonise safe harbours would take years, get controversial, and would likely be imprecise and hard to change.[142] Soft law tools might be more targeted, attract less publicity at the outset, produce results faster, and adapt over time. But in most cases, soft international law must become 'hard' domestic law.[143] Debating domestic and cross-border loss allocation would highlight the prospect of more failures and rescues, and would muddle the no-bailout message.

By comparison, changing contract boilerplate crafted by a single industry group with global reach could be quick, effective, precise, consistent across jurisdictions, and far too weedy to register with the public in real time. Voters would see the outcome – no more bailouts – but not the sausage-making en route. Deployed as policy tools, contracts would deflect rather than draw attention.[144]

Governments had an ideal partner in ISDA, credited with the spectacular growth of the derivatives markets organised around its proprietary suite of standard-form contracts. ISDA had centralised authority, worldwide contract infrastructure, and decades of practice with boilerplate design and diffusion. It had worked with virtually every national government in existence to secure favourable treatment for its contracts and keep other regulation at bay. It had successfully promoted bankruptcy safe harbours as a financial stability

[142] These and similar reasons have been cited to explain the virtual disappearance of multilateral treaties from the governance of international finance. See generally, eg, Brummer (n 90).

[143] D Zaring, *The Globalized Governance of Finance* (Cambridge University Press, 2020) 124–25.

[144] Riles (n 66) 228–29.

exception to the norm of inter-creditor equity and helped design what became the FDIC's pause-and-transfer tool, an exception to the exception.[145] ISDA even had a treaty-like instrument, the protocol, to amend contracts retroactively across markets. '[G]overnments scored a goal'[146] when, after some prodding,[147] ISDA agreed to lend its contracts to the cause of ending too-big-to-fail.[148]

An ISDA protocol, part of its modular master agreement structure, was the perfect reform vehicle for managing the risks from early termination to the new special resolution regimes. It could amend contracts retroactively and take effect market wide. ISDA's contracts even allowed governments to bind unregulated firms through their regulated dealer banks.

Several aspects of this episode upend conventional narratives of regulation as an exercise in state intervention and even the softer versions, where state actors 'orchestrate' market activity. First, the derivatives market was global, but national government jurisdiction was not. As a result, governments had limited capacity to align cross-border market practice with their domestic and inter-state distribution bargains. ISDA's reach was coextensive with its global market. Second, would-be reformers had no time, tools, or political capital after the crisis to deliver on their no-bailout pledge. ISDA had the mandate and the institutional resources to fill the gap. Third, governments struggled to coordinate among themselves, fragmented along geographic, political and functional lines. ISDA boilerplate served as a coordination device for both governments and market participants. At least in theory, the result was a more credible government commitment.

In substance, this episode showed transnational financial regulation optimising a complex tangle of public and private interests. In method, it was creative, collaborative and experimental. On the downside, borrowing contract form to do the work of regulation can alter the character of both contract and regulation and contribute to shrinking the scope for public authority, private agency and structural change. In this argument, the global derivatives market is a public-private venture built with a set of dynamic, interoperable public and private law tools, which must continue to function seamlessly together … in perpetuity? Each tool entails mutually reinforcing inter-temporal commitments – to perform promises, to enforce regulations, etc – and implies an additional commitment to maintain interoperability. Embedded in market and regulatory practice, contracts and regulations become more intricate and sophisticated,

[145] 'FIRREA' (n 71) § 212; International Swaps and Derivatives Association and Public Securities Association, 'Financial Transactions in Insolvency: Reducing Legal Risk Through Legislative Reform' (position paper) (2 April 1996).

[146] See Pistor (n 9).

[147] 'Letter from the Bank of England et al' (n 7).

[148] D Geen et al, 'A Step Closer to Ending Too-Big-To-Fail: The ESDA 2014 Resolution Stay Protocol and Contractual Recognition of Cross-border Resolution' (2015) 35 *Journal on Law of Investment & Risk Management Products* 1, 7.

more useful, and more alike with time. Their hybrid offspring – 'regulation by deal,' 'contract as statute' and 'regulatory contract'[149] – make up a distinct governance toolbox.

The venture is a success: the derivatives market assumes a central place in the global financial architecture. Network effects set in. It becomes harder to justify spending scarce resources on bilateral contract design, old-style legislation, regulation, and inter-state coordination. The new tools work faster, and are all round better.

Somewhere along the way, the exit door shuts. There is no disentangling contracts, statutes and regulations; no disengagement for state and market actors. Had ISDA refused to produce and manage its resolution stay protocols, had market participants refused to change their contracts, had governments embraced or repealed the safe harbours, or adopted divergent approaches to derivatives in systemic resolution, they might be blamed for a botched case of systemic failure and another crisis. Creative collaboration, a free ride for a good cause, morphs into co-dependency. The evolved, exquisitely precise toolkit is left to operate in a narrow and narrowing domain.

ISDA's resolution stay protocols sometimes look like a milestone, and at other times like an engine, on the road to a hybrid governance model for global finance. ISDA and its contracts are not to blame for displacing politics with technique (a perennial feature of financial regulation) – nor are regulators at fault for adapting financial contracts to public policy ends. The problem is bigger on the one hand, and more mundane on the other: a project to use contract standardisation to organise and regulate a market adapts to use contract standardisation to resolve a megabank, then all megabanks and to forswear bailouts; over time, it gains new public and private stakeholders, and produces 'cognitive standardisation'.[150] Regulators and market participants maintain a formal distance but come to see themselves as engaged in the same technical project, with contract form as their shared governance vehicle. The same form later becomes a vehicle for ceding policy authority, with consequences for financial reform, crisis management and distribution. Because the contract form is proprietary and the regulatory ride entails no legislation, regulation or delegation, neither the process nor the regulatory design is intelligible to the public. Post-crisis calls for a new New Deal dissolve into a host of precisely calibrated responses to discrete technical problems that would not and could not alter the relationship between the people and the financial system.

[149] See SM Davidoff Solomon and D Zaring, 'Regulation by Deal: The Government's Response to the Financial Crisis' (2009) 61 *Administrative Law Review* 463; Borowicz (n 35); Choi and Gulati (n 43).

[150] R Abdelal, M Blyth and C Parsons, 'Re-constructing IPE: Some Conclusions Drawn from a Crisis' in R Abdelal, M Blyth and C Parsons (eds), *Constructing the International Economy* (Cornell University Press, 2010) 236.

12

By Way of Conclusion: Making Sense of Fallacies

CLAIRE A HILL

As noted in the Introduction to this volume, our collective goal is to examine some of the key misconceptions and unquestioned assumptions – which we refer to as '*fallacies*' – that guide, and often misguide, developments in modern corporate law and financial regulation. These fallacies are embedded and instantiated in scholarship, law, public policy and public opinion. Their intellectual and practical impact is considerable, but it is largely hidden. Critically, these fallacies too often frame legal and policy debates, strongly influencing and even determining policy choices. While our volume does not (and indeed cannot) provide an exhaustive analysis of this complex phenomenon, it takes a critical step toward understanding what it is and why it demands greater attention on the part of academics and policymakers. Despite the great diversity of topics covered in individual chapters, certain big-picture themes emerge, notably as to societal beliefs, attitudes, values, and broader understandings and worldviews. In this conclusion, we contemplate these themes and where their continuing exploration might lead us.

12.1. WHAT IS A FALLACY?

With the benefit of in-depth substantive discussions in previous chapters, we can now revisit the question: What is a fallacy?

The term is capacious and amenable to elaborate and not-so-elaborate taxonomies.[1] The fallacies we identify are generally grounded in false premises or in a particular type of faulty reasoning, 'motivated reasoning', that is consciously or unconsciously *intended* to yield the conclusion that it yields'. Motivated reasoning is summoned up in Upton Sinclair's famous quote: 'it is difficult to get a man to understand something when his salary depends on his

[1] See, eg, Internet Encyclopedia of Philosophy, 'Fallacies', https://iep.utm.edu/fallacy/.

not understanding it.'[2] Conversely, it is easy to convince oneself of something when one's salary or worldview depends on being convinced of it. Both can be called Sinclair's Sin. There are descriptive and normative components to these fallacies; these components are intertwined, affecting a person's explanation of what has happened and their prediction as to what will happen. For instance, given a core belief that only the fittest survive (which we discuss as a fallacy below, 'Supercharged Selection'), what has survived must be the fittest.

The false premises and motivated reasoning supporting these fallacies do not reflect idiosyncratic pathologies. Indeed, most of them, as well as the fallacies themselves, are quite common, part of worldviews shared with those in our 'tribes' and often more broadly. As our analyses demonstrate, the individual and collective are intertwined: together, they serve to establish, justify and entrench existing economic, political and ideological understandings, structures and hierarchies.

The following describes some of the principal types of fallacies identified in this volume, illustrating each type with examples from the volume's chapters.

12.2. WHAT FALLACIES DO WE CONSIDER?

12.2.1. The 'Faux Framelessness' Fallacy

The first fallacy discussed here is what may be called 'Faux Framelessness' – that pure description, transcending any perspective, is possible.[3] The fallacy is implicit in critiques that *others* 'see things from their own perspective', often made by those who seem to regard themselves as perspective-less. A notable example is some of the vociferous critiques of Justice Sotomayor's characterisation of herself as a 'wise Latina'.[4] Faux Framlessness is of a piece with Backward Bayesianism, discussed below – together, they support a worldview in which a person has taken in data in an unmediated way, formed their theories accordingly, and revised those theories as the data indicates they should, and that they thus have *the* correct frame. Faux framelessness is implicitly embedded in the concept of 'framing,' – that how people take in information is mistakenly affected by how the information is 'framed'.[5] For instance, people may, incorrectly, assess

[2] See U Sinclair, *I, Candidate for Governor: And How I Got Licked* (Oakland, University of California Press, 1994).

[3] See, eg, T Nagel, *The View from Nowhere* (Oxford, Oxford University Press, 1989); www.plato.stanford.edu/entries/nietzsche/#Pers; www.en.wikipedia.org/wiki/Perspectivism; see also see SL Winter, *A Clearing In The Forest: Law, Life, And Mind* (Chicago, University of Chicago Press, 2001); DW Carbado and M Gulati, 'The Law and Economics of Critical Race Theory' (2003) 112 *Yale Law Journal* 1757.

[4] See F James, 'Sotomayor's "Wise Latina" Line Maybe Not So Wise' (*NPR*, 27 May 2009), www.npr.org/sections/thetwo-way/2009/05/sotomayors_wise_latina_line_ma.html.

[5] See generally ScienceDirect, 'Framing Effect', www.sciencedirect.com/topics/psychology/framing-effect.

differently a treatment when it is presented as having an 80% success rate or a 20% failure rate. Certainly, some frames are equivalent to one another – but there is always a frame. And it's not the case that with two equivalent frames, one is a mistake. The familiar inquiry of whether the glass is half-full or half-empty provides an example.

Examples

Faux Framelessless implies or asserts the ability to not have a perspective or bias. In The Fallacy of a Colour-Blind Fed, *Nakita Cuttino* argues that the claim that the Federal Reserve can be, needs to be, and is, colour-blind and apolitical is belied by the fact that its 'very existence and evolving institutional design, purposes, and policies result from trade-offs that are often political and advanced by a limited set of interest groups' which do not include sufficient black economic experts. '[T]he Fed's structure, purposes and tools were shaped through highly politicised negotiations and processes hostile to black participation in the discourse facilitating and fruits of economic growth.'[6]

Saule Omarova's chapter, Financial Innovation: Three Fallacies in the Debate, also provides an illustration of Faux Framelessness. Whether a financial product or service is really a financial innovation is, *Omarova* argues, generally assessed through the lens of individual market transactions. 'The broader systemic benefits and costs of that product or service are generally presumed to follow from, and reflect on a larger scale, these micro-level benefits and costs.'[7] The 2008 financial crisis dramatically shows how distorting that lens can be.

12.2.2. The 'Lazy Linearity' Fallacy

Another fallacy is 'Lazy Linearity,' meaning analyses that assume that various phenomena are linear when they may not be. Three contexts suggest themselves; all of them elevate quantitative over qualitative considerations.

First, 'more is better' when that's not the case, for instance, arguably, sometimes as to disclosure[8] or choices.[9] Examples involving disclosure are discussed below. 'More choices' might tautologically seem better, but research has demonstrated a variety of bad effects from too many choices.[10]

Second, relatedly, 'closer (to an ideal) is better'. If regulation is bad – the government is heavy-handed, too intrusive, etc – getting rid of any given

[6] See chapter 8 at 8.1.

[7] See chapter 10 at 10.1.

[8] See generally SM Davidoff Solomon and CA Hill, 'Limits of Disclosure' (2012) 36 *Seattle University Law Review* 599.

[9] See generally B Schwartz, *The Paradox of Choice: Why More Is Less* (New York, HarperCollins Publishers, 2004).

[10] ibid.

regulation is good. Complete markets are perfect; any new financial innovation that moves markets towards being more complete is good. But even if we agree on the ideal, incremental steps towards the ideal are not necessarily good (and may not be the best way to ultimately achieve the ideal or get meaningfully closer to it).

Interestingly, the idea that incremental steps in the direction of the ideal are necessarily good reflects, literally in some cases and metaphorically in others, a misunderstanding of the First Welfare Theorem. The Theorem only provides that the increment immediately prior to the realisation of the ideal – the increment which yields complete markets – is necessarily an improvement. Earlier increments may be better, worse or neutral: the Theorem relies on fractal geometry, a central insight of which is that 'the addition of new things can either stabilise or destabilise a pre-existing equilibrium'.[11]

A similar account can be given as to steps toward more limited government. The pharmaceutical industry provides an illustration. How do we assess its subsidies or price controls on needed drugs? The backdrop is, of course, the patent system, which incentivises innovation by granting monopolies which yield sky-high prices for drugs. Favouring 'less' government or fewer regulations in the abstract provides no easy answer to the question of whether the market is better or freer without particular subsidies or price controls.

A third context is money pump arguments (also referred to as 'Dutch book' arguments),[12] which rely for their force on *more*: a particular preference is irrational (and hence is not or should not be held) because if a person held it, they would or could be made bankrupt by someone repeatedly exploiting the preference. The arguments assume, unrealistically, that being Dutch-booked is an all-or-nothing proposition. If someone is willing to buy a lottery ticket that is probably worth less than what they paid by standard financial metrics, it does not follow that they are willing to buy so many lottery tickets that they would run out of money.[13]

Relatedly, the broader 'survival of the fittest' credo ('Supercharged Selection'), discussed below, is also within this third category: an iterative process inexorably moving towards improvement and even perfection.

These types of Lazy Linearity are generally argued for descriptively – the good things (a new financial innovation; rescinding a regulation) get us closer to the ideal, and the bad things cause people to (lose everything and) 'go extinct'.

[11] I thank Dan Awrey for this point.

[12] See generally ScienceDirect, 'Dutch-Book Argument', www.sciencedirect.com/topics/mathematics/dutch-book-argument; DI Laibson and Y Yariv, 'Safety in markets: An impossibility theorem for Dutch books' (2007) Working Paper, Department of Economics, Harvard University, dash.harvard.edu/bitstream/handle/1/22801839/120456/safety_in_markets_an_impossibility_theorem_for_dutch_books.pdf?sequence=1.

[13] I make this critique of Dutch booking arguments in CA Hill, 'The Rationality of Preference Construction (and the Irrationality of Rational Choice)' (2008) 9 *Minnesota Journal of Law, Science & Technology* 689, 703–05. See also M Rabin, 'A Perspective on Psychology and Economics' (2002) 46 *European Economic Review* 657, 682.

However, there is often a strong normative component to these claims. Certainly, the idea itself is tautologically (considered to be) normatively desirable, as are 'linear' efforts to approach and achieve it. Doing something that leads to our 'extinction', like being amenable to being Dutch-booked, is surely 'irrational'. As argued above and below, both the descriptive and normative versions of Lazy Linearity are fallacies.

Examples

Some examples of Lazy Linearity are those discussed above as to innovation, disclosure, inclusion and responsible investment. Innovation is good; implicitly, more innovation is better (*Omarova*, Financial Innovation: Three Fallacies in the Debate). And the same is true for disclosure (my chapter, Tribes and Temperament(s): Two Underappreciated Determinants of Market Actor Behaviour, Motivations and Beliefs), financial inclusion (*Chiu*, The Fallacy of Consumer Credit Regulation as the Path to Financial Inclusion) and responsible investment (*Quigley*, The False Narrative of 'Responsible Investment') as well. Of course, sometimes more really is linearly better (or worse, in the case of a bad thing) – linearity is often neither lazy nor a fallacy. But there are sometimes missed qualitative dimensions to the phenomenon that, when taken into account, yield quite a different analysis.

Another example of Lazy Linearity is in *Sarah Haan's* chapter, The Pathology of Passivity: Shareholder Passivity as a False Narrative in Corporate Law. *Haan* argues against the idea that a shareholder's quantum of effort to improve their corporation is linearly related to their percentage stake in the corporation. *Haan* argues that this 'false narrative of shareholder passivity' is neither descriptively accurate nor normatively desirable. Shareholders don't, in fact, expend efforts in improving their corporations as a linear function of the size of their stake, nor is it clear why doing so would be rational.

My own chapter, on Tribes and Temperaments, also provides an additional example of lazy linearity. The standard story about acquiring information, which is that a party acquires information until the cost of additional information exceeds the associated benefit, is not intelligible in a more realistic paradigm. What counts as 'more' information, much less how much acquiring such 'information' costs and how much it is worth, are all indeterminate in important respects. The simple linear account is, again, neither descriptively accurate nor, because it is indeterminate, normatively desirable.

12.2.3. The 'Maslow's Mantra' Fallacy

'Maslow's Mantra' is a familiar fallacy: 'If the only tool you have is a hammer, everything looks like a nail.'[14]

[14] See Wikipedia, 'if all you have is a hammer, everything looks like a nail', www.en.wiktionary.org/wiki/if_all_you_have_is_a_hammer,_everything_looks_like_a_nail.

In this context, the 'tool' is the suite of techniques that align incentives. Thus, many things may look like misaligned incentives (that is, nails).

An illustration of the fallacy involves incomplete information. It is well known that informational incompleteness is pervasive. Thus, many analyses address how parties try to acquire information. A party wishes to purchase an investment asset. How does that party go about getting information to inform their decision? The focus is often on the information that the seller has but has a self-serving incentive to conceal. But much of what is important is information no one knows – about the future, about third parties' actions, and so on. Nevertheless, there is a considerable focus on the 'nail' of information asymmetry because the 'hammer' – the solution to the problem by means of the elicitation of private information using Spence signalling, the rental of reputation, and the use of bonds and other types of incentive alignment – is so ready at hand. These techniques work because it will be costly for the party from whom the information is being elicited to give false information. A signal might be a costly educational credential; the expenditure would be wasted if the information is incorrect. The rental of reputation might be from a known expert marketing its expertise; again, the expert will not want to diminish its reputation by giving incorrect information. Conversely, plausible approaches to the problem of remedying informational incompleteness that is not asymmetric are given short shrift.[15]

A related example involves the prominence given to managerial opportunism (that is, agency costs as between managers and the corporation and its shareholders) in analyses of corporate governance. *Jennifer Hill's* chapter, Hidden Fallacies in the Agency Theory of the Corporation, points out the pernicious effects of 'amplifying a single agency problem, namely that of managerial opportunism'. 'When framed as a comprehensive and all-encompassing theory, however, the relatively narrow lens of the agency model creates a form of tunnel vision that obscures other important problems in corporate law and is inconsistent with legal, historical and sociological understandings of the corporation.'[16]

Another example is from my chapter on Tribes and Temperaments. In the context of mergers and acquisitions (M&A) and similar spheres, the standard account of contracting prominently involves solving the asymmetric information problem – that the seller knows more about what they are selling than the buyer does. The account, again, does not take into consideration many other factors that influence the contracting process: differing temperaments among people, complexities in how they take in information, and the fact that what counts as information or an appropriate way to proceed is determined by community norms.

[15] See CA Hill, 'Repetition, Ritual, And Reputation: How Do Market Participants Deal With (Some Types of) Incomplete Information?' (2020) *Wisconsin Law Review* 515.

[16] See chapter 3 at 3.1.

A final example is from *Alexandra Andhov's* chapter, The Fallacy of Disclosure in the Time of AI. The chapter argues that disclosure was intended to level the playing field among issuers, investors and the public, given that issuers know more about their companies than do investors and the public. But 'the sheer amount of information and the new ways it is both shared and processed – particularly through AI –can fundamentally change the quality of the information itself and, therefore, possibly the purpose of the disclosure as such'. Indeed, the chapter argues, disclosure is now being designed 'to be more easily understood by machines and not by people'.[17]

12.2.4. The 'Pernicious Prototypes' Fallacy

Another type of fallacy is 'Pernicious Prototypes' (or Seductive Schemas), which refers to exemplars that we regard as far more representative than they are.[18] Some pernicious prototypes are much discussed in the public sphere. A notable example is of a stereotype, defined by Merriam-Webster as 'a standardised mental picture that is held in common by members of a group and that represents an oversimplified opinion, prejudiced attitude, or uncritical judgment'.[19] Another is in the family of deceptive advertising – touting, for instance, a product or service as 'healthy' or 'environmentally friendly' in hopes of conjuring up the prototype and thereby forestalling a more critical inquiry.[20]

More interestingly, for our purposes, though, are contexts where the perniciousness of the prototype is less obvious. For instance, to some people, the term 'innovation' might summon up something desirable because the prototypical innovation they envision is something societally beneficial, like a cure for cancer. Rejecting the broad applicability of this prototype, Paul Volcker famously said, in 2009, right after the 2008 financial crisis, with its plethora of 'innovative' complex financial instruments: 'I wish someone would give me one shred of neutral evidence that financial innovation has led to economic growth – one shred of evidence … The most important financial innovation that I have seen in the past 20 years is the automatic teller machine.'[21]

[17] See chapter 7 at 7.1.

[18] The seminal work in this area was done by Eleanor Rosch. See eg E Rosch, 'Natural Categories' (1973) 4 *Cognitive Psychology* 328. For the application of these concepts in the legal realm, see Winter (n 3).

[19] www.merriam-webster.com/dictionary/stereotype.

[20] In this regard, the SEC recently adopted regulations addressing, among other concerns, that investment funds naming themselves with terms conjuring up environmental concerns might be using such terms unwarrantedly. The adopting release notes that: '[t]he breadth of ESG-related terms, as well as evolving investor expectations around terms like "sustainable" or "socially responsible," compound the possibility of investor confusion and potential "greenwashing" in fund names.' www.sec.gov/news/press-release/2023-188. For the rule, see Securities and Exchange Commission, Investment Company Names, 88 *Federal Register* 70436, (2023) 70439.

[21] Opinion: 'The only thing useful banks have invented in 20 years is the ATM', *New York Post*, 13 December 2009.

Indeed, prototypes can be pernicious in an even more subtle way: characterising as dichotomous concepts that may be more interconnected than the characterisation suggests. The prototype of self-interest and what it conjures up – an opposition to others' interests – illustrates this point. The paradigmatic examples of the pursuit of self-interest in law and economics are zero or even negative sum. If person A gets a higher salary from a fixed pot, other salaries must be commensurately lower. If A fights with others to get a higher salary from this pot, the fight itself will often lower the pot, the amount available to be awarded. This contrasts with self-interest which happens to be positive sum, such as a member of an orchestra's pursuit of increasing musical ability.

Examples

This volume contains many examples of pernicious prototypes. Financial innovation as a good thing (*Omarova*, on Financial Innovation). Disclosure as a good thing (my chapter, on Tribes and Temperaments; *Andhov*, on Disclosure in the Time of AI). Financial inclusion as a good thing. (*Chiu*, on Financial Inclusion). Responsible investment as a good thing (when it is not only not good, it is also not even 'responsible') (*Quigley*, on 'Responsible Investment'). The chapters argue that the innovations, disclosures and responsible investment at issue are not, in some simple sense, 'good'. What follows from the view that they are good is suboptimal from the perspective of understanding and policy. Going further, 'information' itself can be a pernicious prototype, especially insofar as what counts as information is not a matter of consensus. Indeed, the information obtained from a particular 'disclosure' or utterance reflects a long chain of inferences. Which of the litany of risk factors for an investment is a significant concern? The ones that are mostly boilerplate, or the ones that are more customised? What conclusion can be drawn if the litany is longer, or shorter, or materially different than the standard?

Another familiar example is related to the now-generally-accepted-as descriptively-inaccurate characterisation of people as '*homo economicus*'. As discussed above in the context of *Jennifer Hill's* chapter, on Agency Theory, the focus on managerial opportunism is predicated on the supposedly descriptively correct assumption that managers will generally be opportunistic and in ways where their benefit is to their principals' detriment, and that the problem is sufficiently serious and pervasive as to be a, if not the, focus of corporate governance. But the descriptive accuracy of this assumption is significantly overstated and pernicious, as the chapter argues.

Yet another example involves what it means to be 'public' as opposed to what it means to be 'private' (*Metcalf*, The Corporation and the Fallacy of the Public-Private Divide; *J Hill*, on Agency Theory). In this regard, *Jennifer Hill's* chapter critiques as descriptively inaccurate and pernicious as a matter of theory the 'sharp divide between the public and private spheres, [that placed] the corporation firmly within the latter realm'.[22]

[22] See chapter 3 at 3.2.

The prototypes for 'private' and 'public' are dichotomous. But most organisations have both private and public elements. Most importantly, purely 'private' organisations are extremely rare, if not non-existent. A great deal follows from the characterisation of an organisation as public or private, including the extent to which it should be regulated and whose interests it is supposed to be serving.

Omarova's chapter on Financial Innovation also importantly concerns this fallacy. She argues that financial innovation is incorrectly presumed to be entirely 'private': 'a "natural" product of private action in response to private market incentives'. 'The government, in this view, is not an agent of financial innovation because it lacks private profit motivation and private market knowledge. Its role, therefore, is limited to supporting and gently guiding private financial innovation without "stifling" it.'[23] That puts much socially undesirable speculation beyond meaningful public control.

An intricate example of public and private entanglement is described in *Anna Gelpern's* chapter, Boilerplate against Bailouts: A Regulatory Ride Fallacy. The chapter describes a particular solution, the International Swaps and Derivatives Association's Resolution Stay Protocol, to a public and private problem, the problem of rebuilding global confidence in the global financial system and its regulation. The solution involved engaging public and private governance tools. Gelpern characterises the global derivatives market as 'a public-private venture built with a set of dynamic, interoperable public and private law tools, which must continue to always function seamlessly together'. 'Along the way, the exit door shuts. There is no disentangling contracts, statutes and regulations, no disengagement for state and market actors, and no alternative to the joint venture.' The problem and the solution are both public and private – as are the long-term costs of this 'ride-sharing'.[24]

12.2.5. The 'Supercharged Selection' Fallacy

This fallacy, 'Supercharged Selection' (or Contrived Convergence), is that survival, not just of people but also of ideas, institutions and many other things, is determined by a pitched battle that has a winner and a loser. It is fair to characterise orthodox theory as having semi-acknowledged the fallacy in its acceptance of path dependence – those initial conditions matter, such that we might be locked into something less than optimal. The now-quaint example of the Qwerty typewriter keyboard was initially used to make the point.[25] The claim is that the Qwerty keyboard (referring to the arrangement of letters on the top row of a keyboard) was first developed to solve a short-lived mechanical problem but became entrenched, notwithstanding that it is actually inferior

[23] See chapter 10 at 10.1.
[24] See chapter 11 at 11.4.
[25] See generally SJ Liebowitz and SE Margolis, 'The Fable of the Keys' (1990) 33 *Journal of Law and Economics* 1.

to at least one alternative.[26] But that acceptance is much too limited, treating path dependence as an exceptional case and survival of the fittest as the base case – the default, which has to be rebutted. More recent work makes clear that both trajectories co-exist. In that regard, Daniel Milo notes that 'survival of the fittest' is actually about artificial selection, not natural selection. In natural selection, what we have is survival of the good enough, in a process that is far more random and reliant on luck: '[E]very species … has traits that are products of selection, but each also possesses traits that are merely tolerated.'[27]

As articulated by Brian Klass in *Fluke*: 'we live in a world that is far more accidental and arbitrary than we want to pretend[28] … our brains also evolved to be allergic to chance and chaos, wrongly detecting patterns and proposing false reasons for why things happen rather than accepting the accidental or the arbitrary as the correct explanation.'[29] In other words, we live in a world of contingent convergence ('accidental and arbitrary') but think we live in a world of considerable convergence. We thus often see patterns that don't exist and advance reasons that are not sound, in hopes of making a coherent narrative that the world is as we think it is or need it to be.

Examples

The fallacy is at issue in *Saule Omarova's* chapter on Financial Innovation. The chapter describes how (perniciously prototypical) public and private actors are characterised as interacting in the arena of financial innovation. Those actively involved in 'survival', the private actors, are conjured up as the more efficient, actively involved in 'selecting the fittest', with the government's role, to slightly overstate, being to get out of the way.

The fallacy is also at issue in my chapter. The chapter's depiction of M&A contracting and negotiation contrasts with the standard account, in which these processes reflect an efficient search for information, terminating when additional information is worth less than its associated costs.

12.3. WHY SHOULD WE CARE ABOUT THESE FALLACIES?

In this volume, we have identified many examples of fallacies that ground research, debate and policy, notably in very hotly contested contexts. Why does this inquiry matter? As stated above, these fallacies are important but largely hidden influences on research, commentary and policy. They affect what research is conducted and how; they affect how debates are framed, and they affect how

[26] ibid.

[27] DS Milo, *Good Enough: The Tolerance for Mediocrity in Nature and Society* (Cambridge, Harvard University Press, 2019) 20.

[28] B Klaas, *Fluke: Chance, Chaos, and Why Everything We Do Matters* (New York, Scribner, 2024) 38.

[29] ibid 70.

policy is made. For example, recall the discussion above as to fallacies relating to innovation: innovation (always, or presumptively) being good (a pernicious prototype), and more innovation, therefore, being better (lazy linearity). With the built-in characterisation of innovation as 'good', debates around particular innovations can easily characterise the opposition in negatively charged ways: innovation is being curtailed, limited or even squelched.

Another example involves information and disclosure. There are significant differences in opinion and values as to the appropriate balance between paternalism and autonomy. The worldview in which people take in information individually and effectively, and that what counts as information is straightforward, conveniently allows for an uncontroversial and politically feasible solution of improving disclosure and potentially mutes initiatives towards more substance/merit-based regulation.[30]

Which assumptions and worldviews are most apt to ground law and policy? Those that do are very much the products of complex social, economic, political and ideational factors well beyond the realm of individual psychology. These factors shape our beliefs in various ways, many of which remain invisible, often precisely because the beliefs themselves are so entrenched and unexamined. Even the 'tribes', or interpretive/cognitive communities we inhabit, to a great extent, reflect the way our economy and polity are organised.

In this regard, recall the discussion above as to the public/private distinction, the worldview in which 'private' and 'public' are seen as far more separate and dichotomous than they are, when the reality is that most private entities are significantly public in many important ways. (Public and private are, as discussed above, pernicious prototypes.) The sheer quantity of private entities, transactions, market venues, and so forth, as well as the scale and visibility of transactions among private market participants, dwarfs the public side of the modern market. The fact that, in our economy, the public's principal – and essential – role is to ensure stable background conditions and provide the core infrastructural support for ostensibly private markets further decreases its visibility. Public actors routinely remain far in the background of the markets they ensure, support, and frequently even create. This hidden nature of the fundamental public-private hybridity of modern capital markets enables the proliferation of multiple fallacies that shape theoretical debates and policy choices.

12.4. WHY (AND HOW) HAVE THE FALLACIES PERSISTED?

These types of fallacies serve important functions for and in our society. Certainly, the simpler, more orderly and more tractable world thus conjured up lends itself far more readily to easy analysis than does our more chaotic and contingent

[30] See Davidoff Solomon and Hill (n 8).

world. We have the hammer, a particular analytic toolkit; we see 'nails' to be hammered down. We have prototypes, often unknowingly – 'typical' examples of concepts and words we use – that we treat as more apt than they are. We advocate for 'quantitative' fixes – more disclosure, longer sentences/higher fines, less regulation – even though the effect we are relying on is not linear. We think we are far more open to changing our prior beliefs and conclusions than we are and that we can and do successfully correct for our own (limited) perspective.

Indeed, in that regard, one important reason these fallacies can be maintained is another fallacy, 'Backward Bayesianism'. A folk understanding of Bayesianism is that people appropriately update their priors and views based on their data.[31] Voluminous research in psychology and other fields shows that people are very bad Bayesians, holding insufficiently supported priors (and theories), taking in data in ways affected by their priors and theories ('motivated cognition'),[32] and that the 'revision' process may be highly biased.[33] Importantly, people think they are far better Bayesians than they are – they think their views are far better supported by their data than is the case.[34] 'Views' for this purpose include prototypes people might have. Someone who starts with a pernicious prototype may not revise it, notwithstanding contrary evidence. For instance, given evidence of problematic innovations that might seem to contradict the prototype of the cancer cure, they might, for instance, discount them as rare or not actually innovative. The familiar terms 'confirmation bias'[35] and 'motivated reasoning'[36] are operating here – there is bias to confirm the prior, and motivated reasoning assists in doing so. 'Motivated cognition' is also affecting how the data purportedly constituting the evidence is taken in and interpreted in the first instance. All of these mechanisms support 'Sinclair's Sin'.

An important qualification may be in order here. This chapter discusses the beliefs, motivations and thought processes that constitute and support fallacies. It might seem to be characterising the phenomena at issue as an individual one.

[31] See L Hanti, 'Bayesian Epistemology' (*The Stanford Encyclopedia of Philosophy*, Winter 2023), https://plato.stanford.edu/cgi-bin/encyclopedia/archinfo.cgi?entry=epistemology-bayesian.

[32] See generally A Wang, S Wang and X Ye, 'When Information Conflicts with Obligations: the Role of Motivated Cognition' (2023) 133 (654) *The Economic Journal* 2533.

[33] See P Kaanders, P Sepulveda, T Folke, P Ortoleva, BD Martino and P Kaanders, 'Humans Actively Sample Evidence to Support Prior Belief' (2022) *Elife*, elifesciences.org/articles/71768; in the legal context, see 'The Cultural Cognition Project' (Yale Law School), www.culturalcognition.squarespace.com. The psychological terms most associated with this are confirmation bias and motivated reasoning. See generally U Hahn and AJL Harris, 'What Does It Mean to be Biased: Motivated Reasoning and Rationality' (2014) 61 *Psychology of Learning and Motivation* 41.

[34] See CA Hill, 'An Identity Theory of the Short- and Long-Term Investor Debate' (2017) 41 *Seattle University Law Review* 475; see also J Haidt, *The Righteous Mind: Why Good People are Divided by Politics and Religion* (New York, Pantheon, 2012) 54 making the point, in the context of people's moral views, that they incorrectly believe the views are based on reason, and amenable to change if the reason was found lacking. ('In [interviews he conducted], it's obvious that people were making a moral judgment immediately and emotionally. Reasoning was merely the servant of the passions, and when the servant failed to find any good arguments, the master did not change his mind.')

[35] See generally Hahn and Harris (n 33).

[36] ibid.

But beliefs, motivations and thought processes, while paradigmatically associated with and attributed to individuals, are also importantly collective and socially influenced. Given that our focus in this volume is on regulation and public policy, these societal dimensions of fallacies are of central concern to us.

The fallacies discussed in this volume are deeply entrenched and embedded in our society's social, economic, and political structures, instantiating, reflecting, and shaping our views as to our past, our present, and our future. In significant part, they have persisted because the forces arrayed in service of persistence are stronger than those arrayed in opposition.

12.5. SO, WHERE DOES THIS LEAVE US (FOR NOW)?

This volume examines fallacies, by which we mean views or propositions that are thought, sometimes expressly and sometimes implicitly, to be true but, we argue, are not. Our chapters identify views that ground scholarship and policy in the corporate and finance domains. We argue that these views are held and that they are fallacies. We argue as well that they affect law, policy, and much else in significant, sometimes pernicious ways. They affect what laws and regulations are enacted, what policies are pursued, and how public opinion and cultural and political identities are constituted, maintained and defended. This endeavour is particularly critical now, as our cultural identities and worldviews become more enmeshed,[37] complicating the very difficult but very necessary inquiries into what our problems are and what good solutions might be.

Our aim in this volume has been to convince you not only that the 'fallacies' we identify as such are, in fact, fallacies but also to demonstrate the value of the approach of identifying fallacies: where might scholars, law and policymakers, or other commentators have gone wrong in their reasoning? What unexamined or insufficiently supported prior assumptions might they be making? In philosophy, this type of inquiry is sometimes labelled 'diagnostic'.[38] We are diagnosing what we think is wrong with others' arguments, identifying the fallacies that lead to their (fallacious) conclusions.

There is a certain irony in this endeavour. Identifying something as a fallacy and describing fallacy-hunting-and-identifying as a worthwhile endeavour obviously suffers from faux framelessness. But there is no alternative, at least not one we can think of. The best we can do, it seems, is that in identifying others' fallacies, we are open to the possibility of fallacies in our own premises and reasoning.

Much remains to be researched and discussed. Our hope is that this volume will inspire more work in which basic assumptions and worldviews are questioned and critiqued – both others' and our own.

[37] See generally 'The Cultural Cognition Project' (n 33).

[38] See generally E Fischer, 'Critical Ordinary Language Philosophy: A New Project in Experimental Philosophy' (2023) 201 *Synthese* 102.

Index

www.ingramcontent.com/pod-product-compliance
Ingram Content Group UK Ltd.
Pitfield, Milton Keynes, MK11 3LW, UK
UKHW020134290926
15471UKWH00003B/481

9 781509 971497